THE *Mexican National Army, 1822–1852*

WILLIAM A. DEPALO, JR.

TEXAS A&M UNIVERSITY PRESS
College Station

Manufactured in the United States of America

First edition
04 03 02 01 00 99 98 97 5 4 3 2 1

The paper used in this book meets the minimum requirements
of the American National Standard for Permanence
of Paper for Printed Library Materials, Z39.48-1984.
Binding materials have been chosen for durability.

Library of Congress Cataloging-in-Publication Data

DePalo, William A. (William Anthony), 1941–
The Mexican National Army, 1822–1852 / William A. DePalo, Jr.
p. cm. — (Texas A&M University military history series ; 52)
Includes bibliographical references (p.) and index.
ISBN 0-89096-744-X
1. Mexico. Ejército—History—19th century. 2. Mexico. Ejército—History—Chronology. 3. Mexico—Politics and government—1821–1861. 4. Mexico—History, Military. I. Title. II. Series.
UA603.D47 1997
355′.00972′09034—dc21 96-51447
CIP

CONTENTS

MAPS

PREFACE

Some years ago, when I was a master's student at the University of Oklahoma, the late Professor Max L. Moorhead ignited my interest in Latin American history with his supremely interesting and provocative lectures and seminars. That fire continued to smolder until the conclusion of my lengthy army career afforded me an opportunity to resume formal study at the next higher level. Although quite challenging, the period of intensive study and research that ensued was exceptionally rewarding. Changing careers after nearly three decades in a single profession is no mean feat, and I owe a special measure of gratitude to the University of New Mexico Latin American Institute, whose renowned doctoral program greatly facilitated my transition.

The study emanating from that enterprise is a manifestation of my longstanding fascination with military history in general. The dearth of English-language studies addressing the nineteenth-century Mexican army made Mexico a good regional choice. Originally I set out to investigate the Mexican national army from independence to the Revolution; very quickly, however, I found that time-frame too extensive to accommodate any worthwhile, in-depth analysis. Cutting off the study at 1852 made it much more manageable, because it included the postwar reform period without venturing into the myriad events that began with Santa Anna's eleventh and final presidency. At about this time, moreover, the last of the independence-era warriors faded from national prominence. From 1855 on, a new generation of military leaders began to emerge from the shadow of the independence-era protagonists to assume political and military prominence in their own right. Gone were the ambitious but politically inexperienced royalist and insurgent chieftains who engineered Mexican independence and orchestrated the country's political evolution for the succeeding three decades.

The enormous territorial losses Mexico sustained following its defeat in the war with the United States irretrievably discredited the army's senior leadership. In the postwar epoch a new group of military leaders gradually superseded those who had guided Mexico through the preceding decades of unabated political instability and economic stagnation. Although the new generation of officers had been exposed to greater professional socialization than their predecessors, they had neither acquired a firm code of ethical conduct nor accepted the principle of civilian primacy. As a result, Mexico continued to experience the debilitating effects of predatory militarism that had vexed the nation since independence. Civil war, foreign intervention, and ideological factionalism continued to retard economic development, inhibit social cohesion, and promote political instability. Not until the 1880s, when Porfirio Díaz finally crushed the regional warlords, who for so long had influenced the removal of ideologically incompatible governments, did Mexico achieve the political equilibrium necessary for economic growth. Such progress, however, came at the expense of liberty and would not endure.

This study examines the institutional development of the Mexican army during its first thirty years as a national force. By looking at the role and performance of the army amid the profusion of internal and external conflicts tormenting the nation throughout this period, it is possible to evaluate the effects of separate military reform initiatives upon modernization and professionalization. Such an approach mandates analysis of ideological factionalism, regional insecurity, social upheaval, fiscal instability, and economic stagnation. To enhance continuity and place military issues and events in context, I have treated political, social, and economic factors affecting the army and the nation, but I make no pretense of comprehensiveness in other than the military domain. The need still remains for a thorough examination of the social aspects of the Mexican army.

The body of published historical literature examining nineteenth-century Mexico is growing, but none as yet presents, in English, a comprehensive and cohesive analysis of the Mexican army in the immediate post-independence era. This study aspires to fill that void with an analytical, interpretive, and chronological portrait of the army's institutional development from independence to midcentury. To help the reader understand issues and events that follow, I have begun with a rather lengthy discussion of colonial antecedents to post-independence military development. I have elected to focus on the officer-corps senior leadership, because they were directly responsible for the army's institutional progress or lack thereof throughout the interval under consideration. In researching this study I relied heavily on archival records, manuscript collections, newspapers, and printed primary source documents. I also referred extensively to relevant English- and Spanish-language secondary sources. Any errors of fact or interpretation are my responsibility, exclusively.

Many people contributed to the preparation of this work. I am particularly indebted to Professor Linda Hall, who suggested the topic and graciously guided its development throughout the entire dissertation process. I wish also to acknowledge the various readers of the manuscript, whose incisive commentary greatly improved its content, accuracy, and clarity. Especially helpful were Gilbert Merkx, Director of the Latin American Institute, and Professors Donald Coes, Robert Himmerich y Valencia, and Enrique Semo, who provided insightful assistance and suggestions at the outset and along the way. Finally I would be remiss in neglecting to thank my wife, Deborah, and my children, Katie, Brian, Chris, and Lee, for their patience, understanding, and indulgence throughout my lengthy doctoral program and the refinement of this manuscript.

The Mexican National Army, 1822–1852

CHAPTER 1

Colonial Antecedents and the Independence War, 1764–1821

For nearly three centuries the defense of Spain's American possessions entailed little more than deterring aspiring freebooters, curbing Indian raiders, and parrying the intermittent and irresolute encroachment of European rivals. Spain's humiliating defeat in the Seven Years' War (1756–63), however, prompted an urgent quest for resourceful and prudent means to redress territorial vulnerabilities. This strategic reassessment engendered a sweeping military reorganization of the Viceroyalty of New Spain that for the first time sanctioned provincial militias and bestowed officer commissions and military privileges upon creoles. This momentous decision afforded creoles an opportunity to extend their political activities beyond the municipal council *(cabildo)* and had long-term ramifications for the army that emerged in republican Mexico.[1]

The task of revamping New Spain's 2,600-man army and creating a viable militia was entrusted to Lieutenant General Juan de Villalba y Angulo, a highly regarded veteran. As Inspector General of all Regular and Militia Troops of the Kingdom, the former captain-general of Andalusia was empowered to offer, for the first time, senior officer commissions to members of upper-echelon creole families. By appealing to the vanity of this societal element, the Crown aspired to build a loyal, spirited officer corps with a vested interest in the success of the militia program. But difficulty in acquiring the materiel necessary to arm and support the proposed formations, together with lack of enthusiasm among eligible Mexican males for service in the ranks, undermined the general's best efforts.[2]

Villalba's mandate specifically subordinated him to Viceroy Marqués de Cruillas (1760–66), but from the moment he arrived in Veracruz he began making policy decisions without consulting his superior. The escalating animosity between these two royal officials obstructed militia reform and ultimately precipitated the recall of both.[3] The procession of inspectors-general who followed in Villalba's stead persevered in the colonial army project. But the best efforts of the regular army cadre assigned to train the provincial militia regiments failed to inculcate the requisite discipline and martial values in their recalcitrant charges. Instead the officer and enlisted cadres succumbed to the same "slovenliness, drunkenness, thievery and other vices" frequently ascribed to Mexican militiamen. Moreover, even regular army units on rotation in the viceroyalty soon became ineffectual; in as little as seven years, desertion, death, and retirement rendered these formations almost entirely colonial in composition.[4]

Spain's impending involvement in the War of American Independence, coupled with Portuguese encroachment in the Banda Oriental (present-day Uruguay), refocused imperial attention on the colonial army enterprise. To help Viceroy Antonio María Bucareli y Ursúa (1771–79) strengthen the colony's defenses, the Crown appointed Pascual de Cisneros Inspector of Troops for New Spain in 1772. After a lengthy inspection of existing units, the field marshal devised a comprehensive reorganizational plan the recommendations of which Charles III ultimately endorsed. At the end of his tenure, in 1779, Bucareli claimed to have raised militia units comprising 14,000 men.[5] But his successor reported the following year that both the regular army and the militia were in a state of general disarray and that the population at large was vehemently opposed to military service. Those units that could be mobilized, Viceroy Martín Díaz de Mayorga (1779–84) placed on as much of a war footing as the viceroyalty could reasonably afford, and for the first time ever, he deployed Mexican soldiers beyond the confines of the realm.[6]

The Peace of 1783, the death of José de Gálvez in 1787, and the truncated tenures of the next three viceroys removed the imperatives propelling military reform, leaving the colony without definitive strategic direction for the next decade. The prevailing disarray was aggravated by the introduction of intendants into the upper echelons of the colonial political hierarchy.[7] After sorting through the confusion and reestablishing his authority within the revamped administrative structure, Viceroy Manuel Antonio Flórez (1787–89) found the army in deplorable condition and directed his sub-inspector general, Pedro de Mendinueta, to conduct a thorough examination of the militia's manifest weaknesses and reassess the feasibility of implementing the proposals rendered three years earlier by Colonel Francisco Crespo.

A career officer who spent thirteen of his forty years of service in various assignments in New Spain, including governor of Sonora during a period of fierce Indian hostilities, Crespo understood the political, economic, and social obstacles to raising credible armed forces in the viceroyalty.[8] Acknowledging the impracticability of attempting to garrison the colony with regular formations that, because they were prohibitively expensive, would be reduced to near uselessness within two years, Crespo advocated a modest regular army garrison of 5,807 men organized into four infantry regiments, two dragoon regiments, and one infantry battalion.[9] Additionally he suggested fundamental changes to the organization and recruitment of provincial, urban, and sundry other militias, which, at the time of his report, showed a paper strength of 39,106 men and an annual cost to the royal treasury of 449,420 pesos for the provincials alone. He recommended reducing the peacetime provincial establishment from 16,755 to 11,075 men and restructuring the force to enable its expansion to 25,000 men in the event of open hostilities. He also proposed extending service-eligibility criteria to encompass more of the colony's available population. Crespo's innovative study would remain the general model for all subsequent reorganizational initiatives.

Both Flórez and Mendinueta endorsed the main proposals of Crespo's plan and received unusually quick approval from the Crown to begin implementation. The following year, the king also sanctioned that segment of the plan dealing with the militia, retaining all its essential recommendations save those pertaining to the manning levels of selected formations, for which a reduction in size was directed.[10] Since no additional European troops were envisioned for the near term, the stipulated regular army regiments would have to be formed from local resources. A serious illness, however, prompted Flórez's premature resignation in 1788, postponing the entire army project.

Revived the following year by the Conde de Revillagigedo (1789–94), Crespo's plan was adjusted to accommodate the new viceroy's concept of colonial armed forces organization.[11] Despite explicit instructions to complete formation of the new regular regiments and establish the various categories of militia, he ordered the militia disbanded and attempted to create a larger, more proficient regular army. To replace the provincial militia regiments, the viceroy embraced the notion of standby reserve companies that would impose minimal cost, hold no privileges, and serve only in time of emergency.[12] Revillagigedo's reorganizational proposals were stifled by the French Revolution and the ensuing European wars, which diverted Spain's attention, sapped its energy and treasure, and caused the redeployment of several battalions of regular troops from New Spain to parts of the empire considered more vulnerable.

The new viceroy, Marqués de Branciforte (1794–98), did not share his predecessor's aversion to establishing militia units composed primarily of creoles. Suspending the formation of Revillagigedo's reserve companies, the marqués concentrated his attention on reestablishing the provincial cavalry, dragoon, and infantry militia units espoused in the Crespo plan.[13] His initiatives largely resolved the debate over military organization, and the much-argued composition of the colonial army ceased to be an issue of major contention among Spain's military and political authorities.

Settling organizational questions, however, did not alleviate the problem of manning units with quality soldiers. Because exemptions and proscriptions removed a sizable portion of the viceroyalty's population from militia eligibility, recruiters resorted to forced levies, which routinely brought in vagabonds, criminals, and other riffraff generally unemployable elsewhere. Low wages, poor equipment, and the risk of active duty with a regular regiment inspired prospective inductees to evade the lottery *(sorteo)* and, if conscripted, to desert at the first opportunity. The mere hint of a census in a town, usually the prelude to a local recruiting initiative, precipitated wholesale evacuation of the affected community's eligible male population.[14] Even the extension of military privileges *(fueros)* and immunities *(preeminencias)* to all militia categories was insufficient to stimulate any significant increase in volunteers.

The intractability of this problem obliged Viceroy José de Iturrigaray (1803–1808) to relax eligibility criteria. Under his amended enlistment policy of July 8, 1807, all nontributary castes, including Indians, were eligible for military service if other manpower sources had been exhausted. Had the army paid decent and reliable wages and made accommodations to support a soldier's family, young Mexican males might not have been so resistant to military service. Under the prevailing system, however, a soldier had everything to lose and virtually nothing to gain; therefore, potential recruits sought to avoid martial duty at all costs.[15]

Militia-officer recruitment encountered little of the resistance encumbering efforts to fill the ranks. In addition to affording social recognition, officer status constituted one of the few avenues by which prosperous creoles could extend their political activities beyond the municipal council *(cabildo)* and satisfy ambitions to hold local office. In exchange for recognition, social status, and a modicum of power, these patricians and property owners *(vecinos)* were expected to donate generously to the royal treasury. A second, though less-compelling, incentive was the benefits conferred upon officers by the *fuero militar.*[16] Besides granting military jurisdiction in both civil and criminal cases, the *fuero militar* entitled its holder to such privileges as relief from various taxes and municipal responsibilities and exemption from the obligation to furnish lodging, transportation, and subsistence to the regular army.[17] While the *fuero militar* may have encouraged irresponsible behavior among a small segment of officers disposed to invoke its special allowances as a general license for evading the law, the majority did not abuse these privileges. In fact, men to whom the *fuero* was extended were under more obligations than ordinary citizens to obey and uphold the law. Spanish military authorities were adamant that "privileges encompassed in the *fuero militar* were to honor and not to grant special exemptions of any kind from existing laws." Transgressors faced tough sanctions.[18]

Despite their apparent ardor for the status and martial trappings bestowed by a commission, most creole militia officers harbored little enthusiasm for the rigors of real military duty. Motivated primarily by self-interest, many provincial militia officers were unwilling to invest the energy required to produce a proficient, cohesive, and spirited unit. In an environment of such uninspired leadership, and with little prospect of social advancement, negative regard for service in the ranks persisted into the republican era, contributing fundamentally to the inability of the institution to modernize and professionalize. Not only did this perpetual dearth of patriotic volunteers inhibit the development of a competent professional army; it also promoted praetorianism among the officer corps by fostering a callous disregard for the welfare of subordinates.[19]

Spain's security concerns were not restricted to the viceroyalty's core districts. Royal officials harbored an almost pathological suspicion regarding the intentions of antagonists toward the silver mines dotting the colony's northern periphery. As an adjunct to his principal duties elsewhere in the viceroyalty, Visitador General José de Gálvez was instructed to inspect the frontier military posts *(presidios)* from Sonora to Texas and submit recommendations for their realignment. To carry out this arduous task, Gálvez selected the Marqués de Rubí, an impressively credentialed veteran officer who first reached the colony in Villalba's retinue. Rubí's two-year odyssey produced a lengthy report that offered three principal recommendations:

(1) establishment of a single cordon of presidios extending from Altar, in the province of Sonora, to San Antonio de Béjar, in Texas; (2) formation of alliances with non-Apache Indians; and (3) initiation of a war of total extermination or exile against the Apaches.[20] The preponderance of his proposals were accepted by the king and promulgated in the Royal Regulations of 1772. The new document, which superseded the ineffectual Reglamento of 1729, established a uniform and pragmatic Indian policy that called for an active and incessant war against declared Indian enemies, more humane treatment of prisoners, the maintenance of peace with friendly or neutral nations, and the realignment of frontier presidios.[21] The Reglamento of 1772 also called for the immediate appointment of a commandant inspector to centralize command of the frontier army. The first to occupy this position was Lieutenant Colonel Hugo O'Conor, one of the many Irish Catholic "Wild Geese" who emigrated to the Americas in search of military service with the enemies of England. Having found a home in the Spanish army, O'Conor came to New Spain in 1765 to join Villalba's military mission and subsequently held a number of posts on the northern frontier, including governor of Texas from 1767 to 1770. Among the Indians of the region, his distinctive red hair earned him the sobriquet *capitán colorado*.[22]

The remoteness of the northern provinces from viceregal supervision led José de Gálvez to advocate their amputation and reorganization into a separate politico-military jurisdiction. Despite Viceroy Bucareli's vehement opposition, the precarious condition of frontier security, the acquisition of Louisiana, and growing Russian encroachment along the northern fringes of Alta California persuaded the king that the visitador's proposal had significant merit.[23] Accordingly, in May, 1776, he authorized establishment of the autonomous Comandancia General de las Provincias Internas del Norte, comprising the provinces of Alta and Baja California, Sonora, New Mexico, Nueva Vizcaya, Coahuila, and Texas, with the capital initially in Arispe, Sonora. Aside from retention of limited control over finances and the development of Alta California, the new administrative unit was entirely independent of viceregal authority.[24]

The king appointed Don Teodoro de Croix, Caballero of the Teutonic Order and nephew of the former viceroy Marqués de Croix, to command the new territorial unit. Royal instructions directed the commandant-general to begin forming provincial militia corps in Nueva Vizcaya and Coahuila capable of operating with existing presidial forces to strengthen the region's defensive posture. Croix also was ordered to establish, through territorial consolidation, well-organized frontier settlements capable of self-defense against Indian attacks.[25] To assess the condition of his new command firsthand, Croix conducted an extensive inspection, during which he convened several councils of war *(juntas de guerra)* to solicit the opinions of subordinates. Based on his own observations and the recommendations emanating from the juntas, Don Teodoro concluded that the presidial line established by Brigadier Hugo O'Conor was "a lamentable error" that left the interior settlements exposed to a well-armed and elusive enemy.[26]

The commandant-general's pacification strategy envisioned two separate but mutually supporting lines of defense: an outer perimeter of presidios and an interior cordon of military settlements garrisoned by the provincial militia corps.[27] First priority was given to adjusting the presidial line to offer better protection to the most-exposed civilian communities, which gradually were being abandoned. Relocating the presidial line entailed mostly the redistribution of extant forces, whereas completing the secondary cordon required both the establishment of additional settlements and the formation of separate militia garrisons. Finding only 1,997 troops on the frontier in 1776, Croix asked Viceroy Bucareli for an immediate increase of 2,000 men. But standing military forces already were burdening the royal treasury with an annual requirement of 800,000 pesos, and the looming threat of international war precluded allocation of additional funds for this purpose.[28] Despite such impediments, Croix confidently told Gálvez that the proposed reorganization would decrease the cost of frontier defense and end the need for subsequent expansion of militia units.[29]

Those attempting to create a frontier militia encountered many of the same obstacles that impeded its formation in the core districts of the viceroyalty. The North, however, possessed a distinct advantage over the interior: its inhabitants faced an implacable foe who daily threatened their very survival. Armed with this singular circumstance and firsthand knowledge of local conditions, by mid-1779 Croix succeeded in establishing militia units in all the principal settlements along the 250-league stretch of frontier between the Sierra Madre Occidental and Coahuila for which he was responsible. Realizing that local variations precluded numerical uniformity in the structure of the seven militia corps, Croix apportioned the 1,852 Spaniards he had recruited to accommodate the uniqueness of each specific district.[30] Only in the municipalities *(villas)* of Parras and Saltillo did he encounter difficulty in completing the formation of prescribed units. There his initiatives were vigorously resisted by the Marqués de San Miguel de Aguayo and Don Lucas de Lasaga, two prosperous creole landowners whose relentless recriminations caused no end of irritation.[31]

To "carry the war to the huts *[rancherías]* of the hostile Indians, dislodge those who may penetrate between the lines and punish those who attempt to introduce hostilities into the province," Croix formed a special unit of 300 dragoons to be retained on active duty at all times.[32] Soldiers were enlisted for a term of six years, following which they were to receive a certificate awarding permanent exemption from further frontier military service. Additionally, upon completing their prescribed enlistments, these militiamen were eligible for grants of land *(solares)* within the military settlement line.[33] For particularly arduous missions, Croix organized a contingent of 176 grenadiers *(granaderos)* composed of the four tallest, strongest, and most robust men in each of the forty-four militia companies. The members of this elite formation were to remain with their respective militia companies until assembled in part or intact at the direction of the commandant-general. Although the dragoon and grenadier units reduced to 1,376 the number of uncommitted Spanish militiamen available to garrison the military settlement line, Croix believed that this disposition of forces facilitated offensive operations, strengthened the defense of frontier communities, and relieved the royal treasury of expenditures it otherwise would have been obliged to make.[34]

The Spanish militiamen were augmented by 1,331 Indian auxiliaries, who served without pay even when engaged in offensive campaigns, the provision of rations being their sole remuneration. Although the auxiliaries' principal function was to defend their respective villages, the commandant-general often employed them to interdict hostile infiltrators and apprehend intransigent residents of nearby Tarahumara and Tepehuana villages.[35] During offensive campaigns, Croix permitted the auxiliaries to wear their native clothing, use their own weapons (mainly bows and arrows), and conduct their marches on foot. However, they were placed under the command of the captain of the militia unit to which they were assigned, and they were subject to the supervision of the commandant of militias and the inspector of militias. The Indians were permitted to reside within their own villages but required the written permission of their local Spanish commander for even brief absences.[36]

The employment of unpaid Indian auxiliaries is one salient feature that distinguished the frontier militia from its counterparts in the interior of the realm. In an area of unremitting danger, the threshold of racial accommodation was higher than elsewhere in the viceroyalty. Spaniards residing on the periphery were grateful for military assistance in any form, ethnicity notwithstanding. Such distinctions, which engendered social values and political beliefs markedly different from those prevailing in more pacific districts of the colony, helped perpetuate regionalism in post-independence Mexico.

Unlike the core regions of the viceroyalty, where males of eligible military age bolted at the slightest hint of an impending recruiting drive, in sparsely populated areas of relentless hostilities, primitive economies, and scant occupational differentiation, service in the ranks provided one of the only means of social mobility. Despite the arduousness of army life, the salary, benefits, and spoils furnished a reliable income enjoyed by few other frontiersmen.[37] Such tangible and dependable assets helped overcome humble family origins and gave frontier soldiers a singular advantage to which few in central Mexico could aspire. In an area where shared danger and dissociation from authority encouraged egalitarianism and solidarity, competence counted more than social standing in advancing a soldier's military aspirations. A handful of recalcitrants notwithstanding, the perilous nature of frontier life left little doubt in the minds of most settlers that an organized system of defense was more than a luxury.

The need for sustainable revenues was the most vexing obstacle to the establishment and maintenance of a viable militia. The Royal Order of 1779, promulgated to conserve government funds for Spain's impending intervention in the War of American Independence, obliged the commandant-general to rely exclusively upon local sources to finance his militia project.[38] Funds were acquired by imposing a form of excise tax *(arbitrios)* on selected products and soliciting contributions *(donativos)* from prosperous landowners. At first, because most of the region's settlers acknowledged the merit of contributing to their own security, Croix's revenue-raising initiatives encountered negligible opposition. Levies on such products as livestock, wine, *aguardiente*, flour, wool, tobacco, wheat, wood, salt, cheese, fruit, and mescal yielded 80,400 pesos in 1780, an amount Croix deemed sufficient to sustain the militia.[39] Despite growing resistance to such revenue-generating measures, *donativos* and *arbitrios* appear to have yielded enough monies to defray the cost of both the military settlement line and the seven militia corps through the end of Croix's tenure.

On August 15, 1783, Croix relinquished command to Felipe de Neve, an experienced frontiersman whose previous assignments included governor of Alta California and Commandant Inspector of the Internal Provinces. Commenting to the king on the unprecedented era of peace and stability enjoyed on the frontier during his predecessor's administration, Neve observed "that hostilities had decreased, the proficiency of troops and officers had increased, and active offensive campaigns had become a common occurrence."[40] Neve's premature death the following year shattered administrative continuity and set in motion a series of jurisdictional redefinitions that wreaked havoc upon frontier militia organization. Growing public apathy and escalating opposition to unremitting taxation prompted Viceroy Bernardo de Gálvez to order Commandant-General Jacobo Ugarte y Loyola to prepare recommendations for restructuring the force.[41] Unfortunately for denizens of the northern frontier, realization of even these modest reorganizational initiatives perished with the viceroy's untimely demise in 1786. The contradictory military policies enacted by his successors crippled the militia even further by enervating its already limited tactical capability and subjecting the force to the vicissitudes of partisan political interests. Bishop Estéban Lorenzo de Tristán noted in 1788 that lack of pay, low morale, and inactivity had reduced the frontier militia to a point of ineffectuality.[42]

The deterioration of the militia probably was inevitable under any circumstances. Besides the reorganizations and policy changes disturbing the commandancy-general, internal and external events were reshaping the destiny of the entire colony. The European wars spawned by Napoleon's imperialism had interrupted Spain's political and economic links to the viceroyalty at a time when many prominent colonial citizens were debating the merits of continuing that relationship. More ominous, the animosity between native-born creoles and peninsular-born Spaniards was inching inexorably toward violent confrontation.

Of all the political occurrences agitating the *peninsulares* at this time, none elicited more concern than Viceroy Iturrigaray's enactment of the infamous Royal Law of Consolidation. First promulgated in Spain in 1798, and extended to the empire six years later, the law directed colonial authorities to seize and auction all real estate belonging to the Church's chantries *(capellanías)* and pious works *(obras pías)*. The Crown intended to use the proceeds of these forced loans to redeem outstanding bonds *(vales reales)* and liquidate other war debts. Because the Church functioned as the viceroyalty's principal banker, however, and because nearly all colonial Mexican entrepreneurs were deeply indebted to that institution, the royal decree imposed severe economic hardship upon the entire population by undermining the credit system upon which the colony was utterly dependent.[43] Despite howls of protest from residents representing all walks of life, Viceroy Iturrigaray implemented the law in July, 1805, precipitating a financial crisis of such magnitude that the common interests of the landowning aristocracy converged with those of the lower clergy. In an unavailing effort to mobilize colonial fealty in the wake of Napoleon's occupation of Madrid, Iturrigaray suspended the law on July 22, 1808. But the economic havoc it had caused was irreparable, and the viceroy's belated rescission placated neither faction.[44]

The fragile coalition formed in opposition to the Law of Consolidation quickly unraveled with Ferdinand VII's coerced renunciation of the Spanish Crown in 1808. This latest political crisis persuaded most peninsular Spaniards to await clarification of events in Spain before embracing a specific course of action. The creole elite, on the other hand, advocated some immediate form of home rule in which the viceroy would assume complete governmental authority within the colony.[45] In a desperate attempt to retain his office and protect the fortune he allegedly had amassed through graft and corruption, Iturrigaray agreed to the novel concept of a governing council *(junta de gobierno)* wherein issues germane to the administration and defense of the colony could be deliberated by a body that, for the first time, included prominent creoles.

Alarmed that the perception of weakened royalist authority would fuel creole ambitions, the peninsular leadership plotted to depose the viceroy, who, they believed, was becoming dangerously acquiescent to creole interests.[46] Shortly after midnight on September 16, 1808, Gabriel de Yermo, a wealthy Basque merchant and urban militia officer, led a 232-man volunteer force, recruited from among the mostly immigrant employees of the Spanish merchant guild *(consulado)*, that summarily deposed and expatriated Iturrigaray back to Spain. Marshal Pedro Garibay (1808–1809), an eighty-year-old army veteran who succeeded Iturrigaray as viceroy, wasted little time in implementing policies more favorable to peninsular fiscal and commercial interests.[47]

Official recognition of the new government by the Junta Suprema de Sevilla convinced the disgruntled creole elite to seek, through coercive means if necessary, a restoration of political legitimacy and a redefinition of socioeconomic priorities.[48] Such discontent engendered a plethora of conspiracies, the most serious of which originated in the city of Valladolid in the fall of 1809. The perpetrators, Lieutenant José Mariano Michelena, a member of the royal infantry, and Captain José García Obeso, a provincial militiaman, expected their respective military affiliations would rally nearby army and militia units, while the *castas* could be mobilized with promises of tribute abolition and tax relief. The Michelena-Obeso conspiracy, however, unraveled prior to the anticipated implementation date, and its leaders were arrested and charged with treason. Significantly, neither the army nor the militia took part in either the viceroy's ouster or the Valladolid conspiracy. These events were perpetrated by individuals acting on their own volition and not as representatives of the royalist military establishment.[49] The army's senior leadership evidently sympathized with the conspirators' apprehension over the looming prospect of autonomy and, with it, creole majority rule. With no tradition of political interference and because they were reluctant to oppose one of their highest ranking commanders, however, the royalist army chose not to contest the forcible removal of a legally constituted colonial government.[50]

The Valladolid affair inspired a similar conspiracy in Querétaro, where militia captains Ignacio Allende, Juan Aldama, and Mariano Abasolo and parish curate Miguel Hidalgo y Costilla schemed to replace the viceregal government with a creole junta that would rule New Spain in the name of Ferdinand VII.[51] Premature disclosure of the plot and the subsequent arrest of several principal conspirators obliged Hidalgo and Allende to launch their uprising from Dolores on September 16, 1810, where it was anticipated Abasolo's militia company would join the insurgents.[52] The rebel leaders, believing that "if the movement was openly revolutionary it would not be seconded by the general mass of people," were careful to portray the uprising as a struggle to preserve New Spain for the legitimate king.[53]

The Bajío in 1810 was a peculiar region, where all the factors necessary to produce rebellion on a massive scale were present.[54] For some time this district had been in the throes of an agrarian transformation in which the financial incentives presented by commercial agriculture were inexorably altering the traditional relationship between landlord and peasant. At one time the Bajío suffered from a labor scarcity that attracted substantial Indian migration from other districts of the viceroyalty, especially the Valley of Mexico. However, as the population increased and the nature of agriculture changed, many previously secure peasants found themselves in an environment of surplus labor that shoved them onto marginal lands and concomitant insecurity.[55] This situation was exacerbated by the great famine of 1795–96, during which thousands perished from the failure of two consecutive maize crops and the greed of many estate owners *(hacendados)*, who withheld stored grain in order to drive up its market value. Such avarice ultimately provided the peasants with social grievances acute enough to convert their rage into armed insurrection. Thus, when a second famine ravaged the region in 1809 and 1810, the Bajío's rural inhabitants were more than primed to respond to Hidalgo's call to arms.[56]

The perceived weakness of the colonial state engendered by Iturrigaray's ouster produced debates over imperial legitimacy, which Hidalgo's followers discerned as deep divisions among the landed aristocracy. The *cura* and his principal allies, however, were marginal elites who represented only a small fraction of the Bajío's elite community.[57] The majority of patrician landowners, initially sympathetic to what appeared to be a creole-inspired movement for autonomy, swiftly withdrew their tenuous backing when the slaughter of European-born Spaniards *(gachupines)* at the Guanajuato public granary *(alhóndiga)* clearly demonstrated the inability of rebel leaders to control the aroused masses.[58] The authentic landed aristocracy might grouse among themselves over matters affecting the colony, but they were loath to jeopardize their wealth and power by subscribing to an uprising that surely would unleash a social revolution. Placing the movement for colonial autonomy in abeyance until the political situation permitted achievement of that goal without upsetting the status quo, most estate owners sided with royalist military efforts to crush the rebellion.[59]

The task of restoring order and preserving viceregal authority was entrusted by Spain's Council of Regency to Lieutenant General Francisco Javier de Venégas (1810–13), a career officer whose distinguished role in the Spanish victory at Bailén during the Peninsular War earned him promotion to Spain's highest military rank. Honest and hard-working, he was endowed with the ability to make rapid decisions and grasp the nuances of complicated tactical operations.[60] The new viceroy, however, was not afforded an opportunity to implement the measures necessary to revive confidence in colonial government. He took the oath of office just two days before Hidalgo's call to arms, when the nascent regime was assailed by massive social upheaval that seriously challenged imperial authority in several core districts of the viceroyalty. The alarming spread of the rebellion prompted Venégas to order Brigadier Félix María Calleja del Rey, Colonel Diego Conde García, and the volatile José de la Cruz to launch a coordinated counter-offensive to destroy the insurgents. The army, however, was poorly disposed for rapid response. Fearful of another coup, Garibay had relocated regiment-sized formations to remove those garrisons from striking distance of the capital.

The October 30 encounter at Monte de las Cruces revealed fatal weaknesses in the tenacity and discipline of the rebel army, which outnumbered the defenders at least twenty to one. Despite inadequate numbers and equipment, resolute royalist resistance daunted insurgent ardor, likely preserving the viceregal capital from capture and pillage. Though badly mauled, Colonel Torcuato Trujillo's 2,500-man brigade demonstrated that a well-trained royalist unit employing massed small-arms and artillery fires from fortified positions could check an unregimented mob several times its size.[61] Among royalist forces the confidence inspired by that achievement carried over to subsequent engagements. Eight days later, 7,000 green militiamen from Calleja's recently formed Army of the Center intercepted the decrepitly armed, disorganized, and demoralized rebels at Aculco and obliterated any prospect of success the insurrectionists might still have harbored.

Neither the royalist army nor the provincial militia wavered in its loyalty to the Crown. Despite intensive efforts the rebels never were able to recruit more than one hundred creole militiamen and a handful of their officers. Even susceptible militia units in rebel-infested areas were rendered virtually ineffectual by the dearth of competent officers.[62] Unlike the peasants of the Bajío, who had suffered worsening poverty as a result of the agrarian transformation affecting that region, Calleja's San Luís Potosí militiamen, most of whom were estate residents, benefited from a pervasive labor shortage in the northern reaches of the viceroyalty. Given this level of security, these rural laborers not only opposed the insurrection but also remained with their militia units to defend the colonial regime and the agrarian society from which they originated.[63] The steadfast loyalty of the royalist military establishment was instrumental in preserving viceregal authority against a serious challenge, but in the final analysis the rebellion failed because it could not mobilize support beyond the confines of the Bajío and limited portions of Jalisco. Additionally the violence and bedlam unleashed by this army of rural proletarians menaced almost every class of Mexicans, most of whom opted for passive resistance over active participation. Creole desire for liberty was not so strong that its advocates could contemplate the loss of their own social and material superiority.[64]

The capture and execution of Hidalgo and his principal subordinates following a catastrophic defeat at Puente de Calderón on January 17, 1811, permanently scattered the rebel army. But simply decapitating the insurrection did not eradicate anti-government sentiment. More than an ephemeral peasant uprising, the Hidalgo phenomenon aroused latent discontent among significant segments of the non-Spanish population, discontent that burgeoned in the prevailing disorder.[65] Organized resistance to Spanish colonial authority was quickly resuscitated by parish curate José María Morelos y Pavón, who assumed the tenuous mantle of rebel leadership in October, 1811, and gave coherence to the vestiges of Hidalgo's social movement.

Unlike the marginal elite leaders of the Hidalgo revolt, Morelos was the mestizo son of a Valladolid carpenter whose poverty and limited schooling relegated him to the impecunious parish of Carácuaro in the tropical lowlands *(tierra caliente)* of Michoacán. There he exploited the pervasive social inequities to foster resentment against the province's canons and bishop.[66] With the help of talented field commanders such as Leonardo and Miguel Bravo, Hermenegildo Galeana, Miguel Fernández y Félix (Guadalupe Victoria), and Vicente Guerrero, Morelos formed a small but effective guerrilla force that at first enjoyed considerable tactical success. But the absence of creole support, the royalist army's continued loyalty to the Spanish Crown, and Calleja's ruthless counter-terror campaign eventually quelled this rebellion, too. Following devastating defeats at Valladolid and Puruarán, Morelos was captured, convicted of treason, and executed on December 22, 1815.[67]

With the extirpation of Morelos, a jubilant Calleja proclaimed, "We have cut off the head of the insurrection, now we will bury its remains or disperse its ashes."[68] The general's sanguine assessment, however, seriously misjudged the depth and tenacity of anti-Spanish sentiment infecting much of the Mexican countryside. The Morelos rebellion had indeed been suppressed, but large rural tracts remained under the control of disparate guerrilla bands that emerged periodically from their sanctuaries to torment nearby haciendas or small villages. Over the next five years these resilient insurgents subjected the royalist army to an exhausting war of attrition in which government dominion was limited to districts physically occupied by viceregal forces.

A remarkably talented commander who had acquired much of his military experience in the African campaigns of Charles III, Félix María Calleja reached New Spain in 1789 with the retinue of Viceroy Conde de Revillagigedo. Subsequently he played a key role in implementing Viceroy Marqués Branciforte's militia reforms, for which he was rewarded with command of the 10th Militia Brigade in San Luís Potosí. Described as "arrogant, suspicious, vain, ruthless, cruel, but easily the most competent and effective of the viceroy's generals," and as being "of sagacious and somber spirit, taciturn and determined, politically and militarily accomplished," Calleja was respected by his troops despite a propensity for strict discipline.[69] With his appointment by the Spanish Cortes as Viceroy of New Spain on March 4, 1813, Calleja reached the pinnacle of his extraordinary career.

Buttressed by the restoration of the monarchy in 1814, which removed the encumbering restraints of constitutionalism, and by the arrival of 15,000 Spanish expeditionary soldiers, Calleja launched a series of coordinated and relentless campaigns aimed at exterminating lingering guerrilla activity. Rather than crushing the insurgency, however, the intensified offensive merely fragmented the guerrillas into regional bands that required an even wider dispersal of royalist forces.[70] The viceroy's response to this latest challenge was to introduce an innovative counterinsurgency strategy entailing the formation of local self-defense units in every hacienda, rancho, and pueblo and the fortification of each community. His intent was to employ these popular forces to secure their respective settlements, freeing up newly organized flying detachments *(destacamentos volantes)* to run down insurgents and punish their civilian supporters.[71] Village "organization" was complemented by rigid measures to control both the population and resources of insurgent-infested territory, including the resettlement of inhabitants from outlying areas too exposed for effective protection by government forces. Relocation was intended to deprive the guerrillas of food, shelter, and intelligence and to create a discernible demarcation zone beyond which anyone encountered would be considered hostile and disposed of accordingly.[72]

Royalist offensives aimed at expanding pacified areas were impeded by the presence of sanctuaries formed where provincial borders created zones of overlapping responsibility. The insurgents capitalized on the reluctance of regional military commanders to impinge upon the territorial prerogatives of their counterparts in contiguous administrative jurisdictions. The intendancies of Michoacán and Veracruz were especially troublesome. There the customary lack of royalist operational coordination was exacerbated by the unabated hostility of the local population and an enervating tropical climate that exacted a severe toll upon European soldiers who possessed no natural immunity to yellow fever *(vómito negro)*.[73]

The inability to pacify Michoacán obstructed Calleja's efforts to dislodge the guerrillas from their strongholds in Guanajuato and restore economic viability to that highly productive region. Moreover, royalist pacification strategy unintentionally regionalized political authority, creating military satrapies that by 1820 had become the seats of effective power throughout most of the viceroyalty. Civilian leaders who abandoned the war-torn provinces for the refuge of Mexico City and Havana were replaced by army officers who attempted to control the population and restore social stability through arbitrary military rule.[74] The brutality of the insurgents had hardened the soldiers' attitudes to the extent that most viewed Mexicans in general, but particularly the dark-skinned and poor, as the enemy. Their malevolent and repressive policies not only promoted local support for the insurgents but also provided them a nearly limitless source of new recruits.

Despite Calleja's ostensible success in curbing rebel activity, lingering suspicion about his loyalty rendered the king susceptible to the furtive machinations of the viceroy's enemies, particularly Antonio Joaquín Pérez, the newly installed bishop of Puebla. After numerous petitions to the Crown, the bishop's sentiments prevailed and on September 20, 1816, Calleja was replaced by Juan Ruíz de Apodaca, Conde de Venadito (1816–21).[75] Soon after taking office, the new viceroy recast his predecessor's counterinsurgency strategy with amnesty as its linchpin. By creating attractive conditions for a cessation of hostilities, Venadito believed he could exploit the divisiveness that continued to vex the rebel ranks.[76] Despite his granting 29,818 amnesties by December 31, 1818, multiple defections by the same insurgents and the return of others to their guerrilla bands subverted the amnesty program as a means of bringing the insurgency to an acceptable conclusion. Factionalism and war weariness notwithstanding, a core of intractable dissidents remained in their sanctuaries, their audacious raids discrediting local government and frustrating royalist efforts to pacify the countryside.[77]

Enervated by a decade of brutalizing guerrilla warfare, the counterinsurgency army was demoralized further by the political discontinuities ravaging Spain. On January 1, 1820, Colonel Rafael Riego, commander of the batallón de Asturias, led a revolt that restored the liberal Constitution of 1812 and triggered a political struggle between constitutionalists and absolutists that was pursued with single-minded determination, to the detriment of colonial military campaigns. The war-weary creole officers were especially agitated when, on September 29, 1820, the reconvened Cortes enacted legislation subjecting provincial militiamen on active duty to civil jurisdiction in all offenses save those of a direct military nature, and when, seven months later, the law was extended to deprive the regular army of its military *fueros*.[78] As the undisputed agents of victory in the Hidalgo and Morelos rebellions, this new generation of creole military leaders, most of whom had spent the majority of their adult lives as royalist officers, was understandably protective of the social status and judicial immunities acquired through lengthy and dangerous military service. Convinced that their institutional prerogatives were under systematic attack by "revolutionary sympathizers in the halls of the Spanish Cortes," growing numbers of disenchanted royalist officers came to regard self-determination as preferable to continued Spanish rule.[79]

The Cortes followed up its assault on military privilege with legislation abolishing ecclesiastical *fueros*, an edict that propelled the Church into an alliance with disgruntled army officers. Believing separation from Spain to be the only realistic means of restoring the status quo, the ecclesiastical hierarchy co-opted the recently appointed commander of southern Mexico, Colonel Agustín de Iturbide, whom they considered the most qualified royalist officer available, to treat with insurgents active in that jurisdiction.

A thirty-seven-year-old creole from Valladolid, Iturbide had been obliged to resign his commission in 1816 amid allegations of financial impropriety. Restored to active duty in the wake of Spain's 1820 revolution, he was appointed to this important regional command when incompetence and poor health finally precipitated Colonel José Gabriel Armijo's removal.[80] Persuaded that a union of insurgents with the seven regular and seventeen provincial militia regiments could shatter the eleven peninsular expeditionary regiments *(regimientos expedicionarios)* sustaining Spanish colonial rule, Iturbide set about courting Nicolás Bravo, Vicente Guerrero, and other prominent guerrilla leaders. Predictably, these chieftains greeted his overtures with extreme skepticism, but, once convinced that total independence was the foremost objective, they embraced the proposed collaboration.[81] By openly committing himself to a treasonable act, Iturbide persuaded all but the most cynical guerrilla leaders of his genuine dedication to Mexican independence.

Proclaimed on February 24, 1821, Iturbide's Iguala manifesto urged all Americans to join in a common effort to achieve Mexican independence and declared all inhabitants equal regardless of racial origin or place of birth. While the plan sought to attract Europeans by guaranteeing their personal and property rights, its success was largely contingent upon the royalist army's reaction to Iturbide's revolutionary entreaties. To this point, the colonial military establishment had steadfastly upheld the interests of its imperial benefactor.[82] But after a decade of debilitating guerrilla warfare, most of the royalist counterinsurgency army had deteriorated into mutinous bands of threadbare and hungry soldiers whose pay was months in arrears, led by officers increasingly antagonistic toward viceregal authority. The dreadful economic toll exacted upon the colony's most commercially productive districts and popular exasperation with suffocating *arbitrios* and coerced contributions caused a precipitous decline in tax revenues and, with that, the ability of the government to sustain the army.[83]

Rampant corruption and deteriorating discipline induced an accelerating number of senior commanders to regard Iturbide's autonomy proposal as the most expedient means of preserving institutional integrity. Responding to the cascading mutiny, Conde de Venadito declared a state of emergency and reintroduced Calleja's ruthless counterinsurgency policies. But the insurrection's accrued momentum quickly exceeded the level at which it could be checked even by such extreme measures. As regiment after regiment flocked to Iturbide's Army of the Three Guarantees *(Ejército Trigarante)*, prospects for government survival waned proportionately.[84] In a desperate attempt to salvage Spanish colonial rule, several expeditionary regiments in Mexico City mutinied on July 5, 1821, ousting Venadito and proclaiming Field Marshal Francisco Novella interim military governor. Assuming direct control of colonial government, the mutineers *(golpistas)* believed, would mobilize uncommitted elements to resist the autonomists. But coercing the resignation of a moderate and popular political leader simply drove fence-sitters into the rebel camp.[85] By mid-August, the collapse of Veracruz province left Mexico City as the lone bulwark of royalist authority.

The loss of Veracruz coincided with the arrival from Spain of General Juan O'Donojú, the recently appointed captain-general of New Spain and a close friend of independence activist Miguel Ramos Arispe. Empowered with a royal mandate to restore order in the colony, O'Donojú quickly appraised the situation as hopeless and opted instead to arrange a peaceful accommodation with the rebels.[86] The Treaty of Córdoba, signed on August 24, 1821, declared the independence of Mexico and called for the establishment of a Mexican empire under Ferdinand VII or another suitable prince. The treaty left unresolved the festering issue of royalist troops in the capital, but O'Donojú agreed to use his authority as captain-general to convince Novella to stand down the Mexico City garrison.[87] The Novella clique, meanwhile, had determined to carry on, and the field marshal ordered the municipal council *(ayuntamiento)* to exact yet another forced levy from the population. The municipal leaders, however, balked at the demand, retorting, "[Y]ou cannot realize as you wish the contribution of 100,000 pesos a month, because of the wretched misery to which the capital has been reduced as a consequence of war."[88]

The *ayuntamiento*'s defection removed what little political legitimacy the Novella regime possessed, leaving it reliant upon armed force exclusively for survival. Faced with overwhelming odds and a loyalist army that was rapidly losing its will to fight, Novella informally capitulated to O'Donojú on September 13, ending the standoff and signaling the de facto achievement of Mexican autonomy. Various face-saving devices written into the Treaty of Córdoba enabled Novella to accept its provisions and relinquish command of the garrison without ceremonial degradation of the imperial standard. Refusing remunerative offers of integration into the Ejército

Trigarante, most loyalist expeditionary troops opted to return to Spain.[89] Despite the death of O'Donojú at the end of September and the Cortes's repudiation of the Córdoba agreement, the independence movement had progressed too far to be truncated by toothless pronouncements from a distant assembly lacking the capability to enforce its will.

Spanish imperial rule collapsed because the mother country was unable to perpetuate the legitimate right to sovereignty that had sustained it for the preceding three centuries. Political legitimacy actually began to decay in 1816 but was not completely expunged for another five years. The royalist army had been too powerful, and there was no one in whom the colony could vest authority until Iturbide managed to assemble the requisite corporate coalition. A decade of brutalizing civil war had enervated the royalist army to the point at which it lost all incentive to preserve the interests of the Crown. Many previously loyal creole and peninsular officers chose to break ranks with the monarchy in a common effort to safeguard the institutional prerogatives being assailed by a vehemently antimilitary Cortes. Pressed by the lingering economic repercussions of the consolidation law, the Church and landed aristocracy followed suit by severing their traditional imperial ties and entering into a conspiratorial alliance with dissident military elements.[90] In a desperate bid to preserve Spanish authority, loyalist army officers seized political power in Mexico City. But once established, the expedient regime was repudiated by the civilian populace and eventually foundered for lack of political consensus. Resolutely led, the undermanned Spanish expeditionary regiments might have mustered the strength to delay Iturbide's army, at least for a while. But the demoralized and despondent peninsular soldiers had come to regard service in the colonies with particular disdain, an insidious attitude increasingly shared by their superiors, who were eager to return to the patronage of the Spanish metropolitan army.[91]

Extirpation of absolutist opposition cleared the way for Iturbide's forces to supplant the delegitimized imperial regime. However, the delicate political alliance that he negotiated proved exceedingly ephemeral. New patterns of factionalism pitting the colony's conservative *fuero*-endowed institutions against noncorporate liberal reformists quickly shattered Iturbide's fragile coalition. The traditionalists (upper clergy, senior army officers, and landed aristocracy) affiliated with the Scottish Rite masonic order *(escoceses)*, while the professional classes (largely lawyers, doctors, smaller merchants, middle-grade officers, and lesser prelates) constituted the membership of the York Rite masons *(yorkinos)*. A third element, the iconoclastic advocates of economic and social transformation (unemployed politicians, lower-ranking officers, soldiers, tradesmen, and shopkeepers), were the radical fringe of Mexican liberalism.[92] After independence the first two groups habitually aligned, as they had done in 1810, to suppress revolution from below and frustrate radical populist objectives. Such rapacious behavior perpetuated corporate privilege at the expense of institutional development and national integration.

One of these corporations, the army, possessed a monopoly of force that enabled it to dictate national priorities in the post-independence republic. After 1814 the viceroyalty had been progressively militarized through the application of tactics and techniques introduced by veterans of the guerrilla campaigns against French occupation of Spain. The royalist army's harsh imposition of martial law and utter disregard for civilian political authority helped nurture personal satrapies that regional army commanders sought to preserve in the post-independence era. Government efforts to create a politically neutral national army subservient to civilian authority were repeatedly subverted by the centrifugal impulses of sectionalism. Besides promoting political instability and perpetuating economic prostration, failure to institutionalize a genuine national army jeopardized Mexico's fledgling sovereignty during the profusion of internal and external exigencies that plagued the nation for the next three decades.

CHAPTER 2

The Army in the Early Republican Era, 1822–33

The 35,000-man army that engineered Mexico's independence was an amalgamation of insurgent and royalist forces cobbled together by Agustín de Iturbide with the lure of rapid promotions and other military remuneration. Integration of these diverse factions into a national army capable of transcending individual special interests became one of the new government's most immediate priorities. Independence had strengthened the position of creole officers by vacating the highest military ranks, which heretofore had been the exclusive preserve of peninsular Spaniards. Although compelled to share these billets with selected Europeans and a handful of former insurgents, creoles constituted the overwhelming majority of the new officer corps.[1]

As commander-in-chief of the armed forces, a position awarded him by the five-man Council of Regency, Iturbide was entitled to appoint all officers in the grade of brigadier and higher and to exercise direct control over any military schools or training centers to be established in the future. Iturbide chose to reward those officers whose loyalty and commitment to his cause were most instrumental in its success. He designated Pedro Celestino Negrete, a Spaniard, to head the army and selected Anastasio Bustamante, Luís Quintanar, Vicente Guerrero, Manuel de la Sota Riva, and Domingo Luaces as field marshals. Other key appointments included the Marqués de Vivanco, Melchor Álvarez, and José Antonio Andrade to the rank of brigadier with letters (a transitory grade, one level above brigadier), and José Joaquín de Herrera, Nicolás Bravo, Joaquín Parres, José Antonio Echávarri, Miguel Barragán, and Juan Obregoso as brigadiers. Iturbide also promoted between three and five hundred enlisted men despite their distinct lack of qualification for the stations to which they were being elevated.[2] Besides adding to the fiscal burden of an already destitute nation, such indiscriminate promotions engendered serious animosity among former insurgent leaders Vicente Guerrero, Guadalupe Victoria, and Nicolás Bravo, who believed they had not been accorded a fair share of the martial remunerations. These quasi-independent regional warlords considered their commands personal satrapies that could be ordered about only with their concurrence.[3]

In an effort to centralize governmental authority, Iturbide divided the country into six commandancies-general and assigned trustworthy senior army commanders to exercise both military and political jurisdiction. Besides filling roles vacated by royalist bureaucrats, this arrangement provided the supreme general *(generalisimo)* with reliable subordinates at the provincial level, where government control was least consolidated.[4] Additionally, regular infantry formations were reorganized into eight regiments and renamed to eliminate any vestige of past affiliation with the royalist army. Each of the new units, except the Guardia Imperial, comprised two battalions. The latter was limited to a single battalion, to enable its ranks to be filled with soldiers of exceptional quality.[5] Selected militia formations also were incorporated into the federal army, much to the chagrin of those militiamen unfortunate enough to have been on active duty at the time of this decision. These reforms were intended to revitalize a military establishment whose discipline and proficiency had waned steadily since the end of hostilities. But shattered unit cohesion and harsh treatment of soldiers by an increasingly authoritarian and indifferent officer corps conspired to nullify any gains these initiatives might have achieved. Desertions proliferated in direct proportion to the intolerability of service in the ranks.[6]

Government inconsistency in meeting its military payroll obligations in a timely manner also accelerated the desertion rate. Flooded mines, abandoned estates, and diminished customs receipts, the legacy of ten years of highly destructive civil war, deprived the government of revenues sufficient to provide essential services and defray the cost of its military establishment.[7] Despite modest force-level reductions during the first six months of independence, military expenditures still consumed nearly 85 percent of the nation's meager fiscal resources. The obligation to integrate former insurgents into the national army and tend to the needs of royalist soldiers awaiting repatriation to Spain conspired against reducing the military budget by an amount large enough to alleviate this burden.[8] Additionally, vigorous opposition from his newly appointed captains-general deterred Iturbide from acceding to proposals from civilian political leaders to downsize the army to levels more consistent with available revenues and national security imperatives. Failure to resolve this matter satisfactorily alienated both factions and contributed to Iturbide's downfall.[9]

Perceiving an erosion of political popularity, the generalisimo's proponents introduced a plan to solidify his authority by replacing the Constituent Congress with a monarchy.[10] This initiative garnered the support of those senior military leaders who believed that their corporate interests would be better served by such an arrangement. General Negrete and a majority of the former insurgents denounced the scheme, but lacking the strength to dispute the majority, they chose to wait for a better opportunity. The lone exception among the ex-guerrillas was Guerrero, whom Iturbide had co-opted with promotion to field marshal and command of the southern military district. The proposal was also endorsed by the ecclesiastical establishment, government employees whose job security depended upon Iturbide's uninterrupted tenure, and a large segment of the general population, among whom Iturbide was still regarded as a liberator.[11]

On the night of May 18, 1822, an adroitly orchestrated demonstration by troops from the 1st Infantry Regiment persuaded most members of Congress that resistance to Iturbide's coronation was both futile and inimical to their interests. Under military and popular pressure, Congress sanctioned the emperor's election the following day.[12] The generals backed the gambit to guarantee political leadership compatible with their institutional goals; as long as Iturbide retained power, the resources to satisfy corporate expectations would be forthcoming. Except for Brigadier Felipe de la Garza's short-lived uprising in September, 1822, the generalisimo enjoyed momentary allegiance from his senior military leaders.[13]

Iturbide's peremptory arrogation of political power failed to alleviate the fiscal prostration inhibiting national economic regeneration. In 1822, expenditures exceeded revenues by 30 percent, with the military establishment devouring the bulk of those monies the government was able to collect.[14] Despite an existing federal deficit, the budget for 1823 appropriated a total of 20,328,470 pesos, 9.76 million of which was earmarked to maintain a standing army of 35,218 men.[15] The relentless economic decline, especially as it began to affect the military, undermined support for the emperor and occasioned defections among previously loyal senior army officers.

The first to renounce fealty was the twenty-eight-year-old military commander of the port of Veracruz, Antonio López de Santa Anna, who was resentful at not having been appointed governor and captain-general of the entire province. Santa Anna believed his role in the defeat of Spanish general Francisco Lemaur's ill-conceived attempt to reassert metropolitan authority in Veracruz merited more substantive recognition than he had been accorded.[16] An increasing number of complaints of misconduct and rumors of conspiratorial activities involving General Lemaur finally compelled the emperor to relieve Santa Anna of command and order him to the capital. But the ambitious *veracruzano* ignored the mandate and returned instead to the port city. On December 6, 1822, he issued the Plan of Vera Cruz reaffirming the three guarantees set forth in the Iguala manifesto and calling for the restoration of the Constituent Congress.[17] The Plan of Vera Cruz was subsequently endorsed by former insurgents Bravo and Guerrero, whose long-standing frustration over perceived inequities in the apportionment of promotions and other military perquisites finally found an avenue through which it could be vented.[18]

The emperor responded to his insubordinate adversary's treachery by dispatching General Echávarri with several loyalist battalions to bring Santa Anna to heel. After a lopsided engagement near Jalapa on December 21, 1822, which cost Santa Anna most of his infantry, Echávarri drove the disheartened rebels back to Veracruz, where he invested the city. The following month, General José Gabriel Armijo defeated Guerrero's troops at Almolonga, badly wounding the insurgent chief, who was left for dead by his fellow insurrectionists.[19] Suppression of these uprisings appeared to mark the end of the first serious military challenge to Iturbide's reign. But within the Masonic lodges, fervent republicans Miguel Ramos Arispe and José Mariano Michelena were drafting a program to supplant the monarchy entirely. At the heart of what would become the Plan of Casa Mata was a provision to convene an entirely new congress to delineate the nation's future political organization. Significantly, no mention was made of a republic, an omission that effectively masked the true nature of the document. The plan garnered notable support among the prominent military chiefs, who were enticed by the prospect of greater regional autonomy and the chance to influence national politics. Fed up with the protracted and ineffectual siege, General Echávarri, along with his principal subordinates, Brigadiers Luís Cortazar and José María Lobato, signed and issued the Plan of Casa Mata on February 1, 1823.[20]

Echávarri's endorsement of the plan precipitated an avalanche of defections from other provincial military commanders who had hedged their bets until the outcome of events was sufficiently clear. By mid-March most of the army had turned against the emperor, including Negrete, who recently had superseded Guerrero as commander of the South.[21] Unable to surmount the forces of regionalism and convinced that continued civil war would further enervate his already crippled nation, Iturbide abdicated on March 19, 1823, and voluntarily expatriated.[22] Twelve days later the restored Congress reconvened and appointed a Supreme Executive Power, consisting of Negrete, Victoria, and Bravo, to exercise political authority until a national constituent assembly could be gathered to promulgate a new constitution.

Iturbide's decision to renounce his crown was driven more by political than military considerations. He had defeated both insurrections and, until mid-February, retained the loyalty of most major army commands. It was the emperor's unwillingness to coexist with the new Sovereign Congress demanded by his adversaries and the loss of centralized political authority to provincial deputations that dissuaded him from remaining on the throne.[23] The Casa Mata arrangement convinced senior army commanders to forsake the monarchy because it accommodated both provincial autonomy and decentralized military command, a compelling arrangement for ambitious *caciques* inclined to further the interests of specific clienteles. Whatever their motivations, acceptance of the Casa Mata formula by such a disparate aggregation of military constituencies signified a definitive rejection of centralized government.[24]

Events at Casa Mata unleashed forces of regionalism that had been restrained by the euphoria of independence, shattering the tripartite constituency that had brought Iturbide to power. Reinstitution of forced loans alienated the ecclesiastical establishment, and growing chaos drove the creole aristocracy to seek the insularity of its landed estates, depriving the government of its most promising source of political leaders. That void was filled quickly by ambitious military officers who saw political power as the most expeditious means of preserving corporate integrity.[25] Vigorous protection of institutional privileges superseded the army's professional obligation to safeguard national interests. Tenuous centralized military authority soon gave way to regionalized commands, fostering an environment conducive to *caciquismo*. Iturbide's abrupt abdication ended the military's brief interval of subordination to centralized governmental authority. Henceforth the army would assume the role of chief political arbiter in the bitter and protracted ideological struggle between federalism and centralism.[26]

The new Congress that convened in the wake of Iturbide's abdication was intensely republican. The emperor's former advocates realigned with moderate republicans in a coalition that precluded the *borbónicos,* monarchist proponents of a Spanish prince on the Mexican throne, from reestablishing a European-style monarchy. In this political reordering, radicals perceived the republic as a vehicle for social progress and supported a strong state that would limit privilege and intervene on behalf of the urban lower classes.[27] Moderates preferred a weak state with unrestricted economic enterprise and some limitations upon the Church. They were uncomfortable with an unfettered republic, which they feared would parrot Jacobin France, but accepted independence to avoid the cycles of revolution and reaction endemic in Europe. Conservatives supported a strong state in which a centralized bureaucracy enforced a hierarchical social structure that resisted social mobility and preserved existing privilege.[28] This political differentiation ultimately devolved into a contest between moderates and conservatives over centralized versus decentralized government, in which radicals affiliated with both factions.

Besides fostering political instability, such parochialism also manipulated the composition and behavior of the post-independence army. Generally, former insurgents gravitated toward radical political groups, while ex-royalists manifested conservative inclinations. Moderates attracted adherents from both camps in small but relatively even numbers. Such political affiliations exerted a powerful influence upon the military's institutional development: the permanent army harbored primarily former royalists of conservative persuasion, while the state militias became refuges for liberally inclined ex-guerrillas. Not surprisingly, political leaders attempted to exploit these distinctions to their own advantage, engendering adversarial relationships between the state militia and permanent army that did little to further a stable polity.[29]

During the republic's first three decades, the average tenure in office for the national executive elite was only ten months. For all but two years and seven months of that interval, an army officer served as chief executive. The political careers of army officers were usually more prolonged than their civilian counterparts, but particular terms of office for each were generally the same. Military affiliation seems to have helped leaders gain political office but evidently afforded no significant retention advantage. Service-related leadership experience or access to coercive armed force probably gave officers the edge over civilian presidents and cabinet ministers, who lacked such training.[30]

Minister of War José Joaquín de Herrera, a thirty-one-year-old veracruzano, was determined to professionalize the military by institutionalizing the concepts of civilian primacy and politically neutral public service. In 1823 he proposed to Congress a series of sweeping reforms that included founding a military academy *(Colegio Militar)* at San Carlos de Perote and creating a forty-two-member general staff *(estado mayor del ejército)*. Besides advising the war ministry on matters pertaining to the administration of all three service branches, the general staff was charged with collecting topographical information, developing war plans, providing for the defense of the nation, and insuring that military science and tactics constituted the core curriculum of the Colegio Militar.[31] A prerequisite written examination for general staff appointment helped preserve the officer corps' predominantly conservative composition by excluding most former insurgents and upwardly mobile pretenders from the ranks. Because the infusion of Spanish and insurgent officers whose ranks were often self-conferred left the army significantly rank-heavy, remedial action was needed to redress the imbalance. Lieutenant generals and field marshals were purged from the rank structure, and the number of division and brigade generals on active duty was limited to twelve and eighteen, respectively.[32]

Guadalupe Victoria's well-intentioned attempt to impose meaningful force reductions was thwarted by Spain's refusal to acknowledge Mexican independence and the omnipresent danger of regional disturbances. By 1825, statutory military strength had escalated to 62,552 men, with 22,534 of those billets allotted to the permanent army *(permanentes)*. The remainder were apportioned among the active militia *(activos)*, a federally funded reserve intended to reinforce the permanent army during national emergencies. The peacetime and wartime manning levels of the permanent battalions were 823 and 1,223, respectively, while prescribed strengths of active militia units varied with the location and mission of each formation.[33]

Actual operating strengths were substantially lower than legal authorizations, especially within the active militia. Despite legislation requiring states to maintain at statutory manning levels the *activo* units posted within their territorial jurisdictions, federal neglect and the general unpleasantness of militia duty conspired to keep these units chronically understrength. The fact that *activo* ranks were commonly filled with regular army deserters and other societal miscreants did little to promote recruitment and retention.[34] The war ministry's annual report for 1826 reflected only 32,161 troops on the rolls, a deficit of 26,794 men, the majority of whom were *activos*. Even these figures misrepresented the number of soldiers who could reliably be assembled for exigencies. Assigned strength was regularly depleted by desertion and illness, preventing the army from ever marshalling the number of soldiers its muster rolls purported to show. Moreover, many commanders intentionally neglected to purge deserters from their manning rosters to enable uninterrupted collection of their pay.[35]

As the prospect of hostilities with Spain continued to rise, recruitment supplanted downsizing as the government's top military priority.[36] Despite its pejorative connotations and inequitability, the permanent army still relied upon the *leva* as the principal means of acquiring troops from each state. The mere rumor of an impending levy was sufficient to trigger a mass exodus of eligible males from the targeted community. Apparently not much had changed from the late colonial period, when recruiting initiatives engendered similar reactions.[37] Such negative regard for military service led the states to impress vagrants, criminals, and sundry other misfits, who were rounded up and shipped off to military encampments, some in chains, others incarcerated at each stop until reaching their final destination.[38]

Some states even went so far as to prioritize specific societal elements for conscription. In Oaxaca, for example, the legislature stipulated that the state's quota be filled by vagrants and dangerous individuals first, followed thereafter by disorderly persons and single men from families that could spare them. Those unfortunate enough to be conscripted into the army were mostly of Indian and mestizo racial extraction, although a small number of *pardos* (Mexicans with some African blood) could also be found among the rankers. In a few peripheral regions, such as Yucatán, entire units of pardos were still maintained in vestigial segregation reminiscent of the colonial period. By utilizing such coercive measures to fill the ranks, the army came to resemble a large penal institution, a characteristic that did little to enhance its competence and reputation as a legitimate fighting force.[39] In his annual state of the military report presented to Congress in January, 1827, Minister of War Manuel Gómez Pedraza urged revamping the conscription statute because it was "unsuitable for forming a disciplined army." Deprivation of liberty, he continued, simply leads to "demoralization, disobedience, indolence, desertion, and in the end, complete moral depravity of the soldier."[40]

To make military service more attractive to rankers, Congress preserved the privileges inherent in the *fuero militar.* Officers continued to possess both criminal and civil *fueros* at all times, while enlisted soldiers enjoyed just the criminal *fuero* unless engaged in active military operations. The *fuero* was a mixed blessing, however, as military courts could be even harsher than their civilian counterparts, particularly if the defendant happened to be a proponent of the political faction not in power at the time. Other vestigial privileges, such as the *bagages,* which empowered an officer in transit to appropriate horses or mules from any citizen, and the *tesorería de ejército,* through which officers were authorized to collect certain revenues, were abolished by the Congress in 1826.[41]

Despite these inducements and constructive reforms, incessant desertion kept the army chronically understrength and poorly trained. Low salaries and increasingly erratic paydays contributed significantly to manpower attrition.[42] To sustain their commands, generals often were forced to draw upon their personal credit or exact involuntary loans from the local customshouse using the unpredictability of uncompensated troops as a thinly veiled threat.[43] Soldiers addressed their plight by selling clothing, equipment, or anything else of value they could find within their respective installations. The farther the garrison from the core districts of Mexico, the worse this situation became. In the peripheral regions of Sonora, California, New Mexico, and Texas, soldiers were reduced to raiding the commissary, selling firewood, or hunting wild game to survive. Under such circumstances, it is small wonder that ordinary denizens spurned government incentives and sought to avoid military service at all costs.[44]

These hardships were common knowledge among Mexico's citizenry, most of whom equated military induction with incarceration, since it virtually guaranteed their families would be left without means to provide for themselves.[45] Not much, it seems, had been learned over the preceding sixty years regarding the inducements and safeguards necessary to create and sustain a viable military force. This dearth of institutional memory and disregard for the lessons of the past significantly impeded the new republic's ability to create a politically neutral professional military willing to subordinate its corporate interests to those of the realm.

Federal legislation enacted in December, 1827, empowered the states to institute their own ordinances regulating civic militia organization and operations and placed these forces under the governor's control. In turn, the state governments made the *ayuntamientos* responsible for meeting recruiting quotas and administering the civic militia, a procedure that often filled the ranks with the least desirable elements of society.[46] Described by British representative Richard Pakenham as being composed of "the very dregs of the people, without discipline or subordination, and ready to take advantage of any opportunity to plunder and commit excesses," the *cívicos* were despised by the local population and derided by the permanent army.[47]

Originally envisioned as a force to be employed against bandits, protect public facilities, and escort prisoners, the *cívicos* became instead politically partisan instruments that the state governors readily employed to resist federal attempts to influence regional interests. In Zacatecas the 17,000-man civic militia approached the federal army in size, making Governor Francisco García a powerful factor with whom to be reckoned on the national political scene.[48]

Such radicals as José María Luís Mora and Lorenzo de Zavala championed the *cívicos* as a means of attenuating praetorianism in the permanent army. Not surprisingly, senior military leaders perceived the state militias as a direct threat to their privileged position and vigorously opposed their creation. Conservatives sided with the generals, favoring a large standing army and abolition of the civic militia. Between these two extremes, the moderates advocated curtailing the federal army's power while limiting the size of civic militia units and restricting participation to the privileged classes. The factious and persistent *cívico* controversy continued to inflame political sensitivities and debilitate military preparedness even as Mexico confronted a genuine threat to its territorial sovereignty. What remained of the Mexico City *cívicos* finally was disbanded by President José Joaquín de Herrera in 1845, purportedly to enable the men to return to their homes and occupations. But the real motive behind its disestablishment was more likely the president's fear that the militiamen might ultimately turn on him.[49]

To facilitate military command and control, the nation was reconfigured into twenty-four commandancies-general roughly approximating the intendancies and territorial boundaries extant in 1823. Each of these geographical jurisdictions was subordinated to a commandant-general who reported directly to the minister of war and exercised authority over all persons within his domain possessing the *fuero militar*. Such an arrangement abetted the centrifugal impulses of sectionalism and politicized the army by subjecting large numbers of soldiers to a highly personalized and localized command relationship.[50]

The preponderance of permanent army and active militia formations was garrisoned near the nation's frontiers and coastal regions where national vulnerabilities were perceived to be greatest.[51] Some 3,300 of these permanent troops were assigned to presidial companies posted along the northern frontier, where Indian raiders and foreign interlopers posed an immediate and discernible security concern. Chronic penury, however, rendered maintenance and repair of the region's presidios low priority, and forced a reduction in the number of permanent presidial companies from thirty-two to twenty-nine.[52] To make up the shortage, the government organized fifteen active militia companies that were to remain inactive except when called upon to supplement the regular garrisons to which they had been assigned.[53] Occasionally it also was necessary to station military forces in the mining communities *(reales de minas)* to preserve order among disgruntled miners, an exigency that diverted troops from essential training and employed units as instruments of social control.[54]

Mexican soldiers of the early republican era were armed with obsolescent and generally unreliable flintlock muskets *(fusiles)*, carbines *(tercerolas)*, and pistols *(pistolas)* of British manufacture. These weapons were available in quantities sufficient only to permit their dissemination down to the highest priority *activo* units. Civic militias were armed and equipped at the expense of their respective states, and many militiamen carried their personal weapons. Selected permanent army formations also were outfitted with a hodgepodge of brass and iron cannon, ranging from 16- to 24-pounders, powder for which was locally manufactured at Chapúltepec and Santa Fé.[55]

Minister of War Gómez Pedraza reported to Congress in January, 1828, "Neither the machinations of the country's enemies, nor writing injurious to the government, nor the seduction of gold have been able to corrupt the morale and the discipline of the army: the soldiers, firm in their task and without listening to a voice other than that of the levy, march to wherever the government sends them." This sanguine assessment masked a progressive deterioration of order and discipline within the army, caused by the failure of reform initiatives to professionalize the institution.[56] Absent a code of professional ethics to guide behavior, military leaders grew increasingly less hesitant to impose upon the country the political tenets and convictions to which they subscribed.

As ideologically differentiated as any other organization in republican Mexico, the army harbored an assortment of officers of both centralist and federalist persuasion. Such prominent federalists as Guerrero, Juan Álvarez, and Bravo tended to have common insurgent roots, while leading centralists, such as Bustamante, Mariano Paredes y Arrillaga, and Manuel de Mier y Terán, generally were career soldiers whose formal military training made them better tacticians and general staff officers. Some officers were merely opportunists whose loyalty was extended to the political faction that could best accommodate their immediate needs. Of this latter group, Santa Anna is the foremost example. While Gómez Pedraza, a former royalist and deputy to the Spanish Cortes, also embraced political affiliations of convenience, he remained steadfastly moderate from 1828 on.[57] Such politicization within the army bred parochialism that superseded national interests and enervated both the country and the military institution.

The army's transformation into executor for the political agenda of the dominant party was accelerated by the collapse of constitutional government occasioned by the cuartelazo de la Acordada on November 30, 1828.[58] The crisis precipitated when former insurgent Vicente Guerrero refused to accept the results of the 1828 presidential election, which he had lost to Gómez Pedraza. Incited by the machinations of radical Finance Minister Lorenzo de Zavala, the Mexico City garrison seized the Acordada armory on December 2 and pronounced for Guerrero. The defection of the federal district's two principal military commanders left President Victoria virtually defenseless, forcing him to come to terms with his opponents and accept Guerrero as his successor.[59]

The Acordada coup inspired a mob of some five thousand hooligans to attack and pillage, on the afternoon of December 4, the shops housed in the central plaza's Parián Building. A commercial emporium of Spanish merchants, the Parián symbolized a lingering foreign presence in Mexico as well as an unwelcome source of local competition for Mexican artisans.[60] The melee persisted until evening, when Lieutenant Colonel Alejandro Zamora and a battery of artillerymen dispatched by General Lobato fired cannons in the direction of the rioters, inflicting a reported two thousand casualties. Although the tumult lasted for only a few hours, the yorkino-inspired lower classes ruled the streets of Mexico City for several days thereafter, forcing the city's *hombres de bien* (Mexicans of high station) to remain sequestered in their homes for fear of injury or insult. The specter of class warfare raised by this alarming display of uncontrolled fury engendered conservatism among elites from both political factions, converging opinion on the need for strong armed forces to discourage a recurrence of this outburst.[61]

The disturbing memory of the Parián episode may temporarily have eclipsed partisan bickering over the army, but popular resentment of resident Spaniards, most of whom were import merchants, remained unabated. Loathed by the masses for their wealth and influence, Spaniards became convenient scapegoats for a deteriorating economy. Lorenzo de Zavala's adroit political exploitation of abiding anti-Spanish sentiment culminated in edicts on March 20 and May 10, 1829, directing the expulsion of all Spaniards excepted from previous legislation. This indignity motivated Ferdinand VII, who still harbored hopes of reestablishing Spain's colonial empire, to order an expeditionary force assembled in Havana for the purpose of reoccupying Mexico.[62]

On July 6, General Isidro Barradas and a contingent of some 3,500 veteran Spanish soldiers and marines set sail for Mexico's Gulf coast. Mexican authorities were not unaware of Spain's bellicose intentions: a variety of sources had been providing a steady flow of credible intelligence regarding intensified military activity in Cuba. Santa Anna was sufficiently alarmed to recommend forming a "división de Reserva" to be garrisoned near the capital or Puebla, to respond to Spanish disembarkations wherever they might occur. The captain of an American frigate that reached Veracruz from Havana early in July substantiated the buildup, prompting Santa Anna to warn Minister of War Francisco Moctezuma in early July that "there is no longer any doubt of the departure from that Cuban port, of the Spanish expedition against the Mexican Republic."[63] Two weeks later, Colonel Feliciano Montenegro sent word from his diplomatic post in New Orleans that a Spanish expedition had set sail from Havana on July 6 en route to Veracruz.[64] Preoccupied with pressing domestic issues, the Mexican government simply was unable to capitalize on such fortuitous intelligence. That omission contributed to an improvised and ineffective military response when hostilities finally broke out.

Between July 27 and 29, Barradas made an unopposed landing at Cabo Rojo and immediately marched his 2,800 troops on Tampico, some fifty-three miles to the north. The first response to the Spanish incursion came from General Felipe de la Garza, commandant-general of the Eastern Interior States, within whose military jurisdiction Tampico lay. Once apprised of Barradas's destination, de la Garza mustered all available forces and departed his headquarters at Soto la Marina on July 31. But his motley assemblage of militiamen was no match for the Spaniards, who forced their way across the Río Pánuco and occupied Tampico on August 6.[65] The Spanish Vanguardia Division, however, was not equipped for conquest and, except for a brief foray on August 19 to acquire supplies from nearby Altamira, remained confined to the city.

Inspired by reports from expatriate *peninsulares,* Spanish authorities believed that most Mexicans still pined for the viceregal era and would rally to the imperial standard if afforded a reasonable opportunity. Accordingly, Barradas issued a proclamation from the captain-general of Cuba that announced, among other things, reimposition of a viceroyalty and prohibition of commerce with other ports.[66] His aspirations were quickly dispelled when Mexican citizens, whose antipathy and paranoia toward Spain had intensified over time, spurned his supplications. Instead, blatant Spanish aggression engendered new life in the moribund Guerrero government, to whom Congress granted extraordinary wartime powers.[67]

The invasion furnished a cause around which the nation could unite, diverting attention from unpleasant domestic issues and providing a fortuitous opportunity for the ever-vigilant captain-general of Veracruz to advance his political fortunes. Unfurling his remarkable aptitude for creating improvised armies, Santa Anna hurriedly assembled an expeditionary force by impressing units within his jurisdiction and confiscating transports until 1,644 men and twelve boats had been collected.[68] Mexico had rostered at this time, 23,041 permanent army troops and 22,084 *activos* out of a federal statutory strength of 59,492. The combination of poor transportation arteries and decentralized command and control, however, precluded the timely mobilization of these scattered forces to confront the invading Spaniards.[69]

Advancing by land and sea to the Río Pánuco, Santa Anna learned of the Spanish raid on Altamira and decided to attack the forces left behind (some six hundred men from the Royal Bourbon Battalion). Instructing de la Garza to employ his Tamaulipas Division to disrupt the Spanish withdrawal from Altamira, Santa Anna began crossing the river at 1:30 A.M. on August 21 with 1,000 men, intent upon capturing the *fortín de la barra,* a key fortified position protecting the approach to Tampico. The river crossing, however, was compromised when one of the *cívicos* inadvertently discharged his firearm, precipitating an eruption of indiscriminate firing that disrupted the attackers. The alerted Spaniards easily repulsed an ill-conceived and clumsily executed frontal assault, killing seventeen Mexicans and wounding fifty-four in the engagement. As Santa Anna gathered additional forces to renew the attack, Barradas and his 1,800 soldiers returned from their Altamira adventure, forcing the general-in-chief to abandon this course of action.[70] Instead, Santa Anna decided to invest the city and let starvation and disease exact their pernicious toll before attempting another attack. Replacing de la Garza with the more reliable and resourceful General Mier y Terán, the general-in-chief ordered the Tamaulipas Division to contain the Spaniards north of the river, while his forces prevented any movement to the south.

Barradas had never intended to seize Mexico by force; his mission was to foment a general uprising by convincing its disenchanted inhabitants to embrace reincorporation into the Spanish empire. Consequently, except for the brief raid on Altamira, he remained inactive throughout the occupation of Tampico, relying on his mere presence to invigorate the masses. Such passivity enabled the Mexicans, for whom time was a lesser consideration, to operate at will outside the confines of the invested city. Each passing day, disease and starvation took an increasing toll of the Vanguardia Division, while the besiegers were able to resupply and reinforce their positions at will.[71] This standoff was finally interrupted by a violent hurricane that inundated the region on September 8, causing extensive damage to fortifications and destroying food and ammunition stocks on both sides. The substantial logistical losses sustained by the Mexicans introduced an element of urgency that convinced Santa Anna to conclude the campaign without further delay.

In the early morning hours of September 11, a force of nine hundred Mexican soldiers mounted eleven separate assaults on the *fortín de la barra,* none which penetrated beyond the outer parapet. Although unsuccessful, the relentless onslaughts were sufficiently enervating to bring about the Spaniards' unconditional capitulation.[72] The Spanish prisoners were disarmed and dispersed to various proximate villages until sufficient transport could be assembled to accommodate their evacuation to Havana. Difficulty in acquiring the requisite shipping delayed repatriation of the final group until December 11, and of the 3,500 Spaniards put ashore at the end of July, only 1,792 made it back to Cuba.[73]

The Mexican triumph over the veteran Spanish formations bestowed upon the Army of Operations a level of national pride and patriotism not experienced since the Independence War. "Henceforth Your Excellency," Santa Anna confidently proclaimed to Minister of War Moctezuma, "the nations will see that Mexicans are worthy of Liberty and that there is no human power that can rob them of their sacred Independence; they will see that the Spanish army that has dared to invade our Republic, has perished one part in the hands of our brave [soldiers], and the rest have departed, capitulated, confounded and disarmed from our territory, never more to return to profane it."[74] The invasion's demise also presented a unique opportunity for nonpartisan heroism that enabled Santa Anna to emerge from the shadow of the independence era protagonists, elevating him to national prominence in his own right. In recognition of his singular contribution to the nation, the national Congress bestowed the title Well-deserving of the Country (Benemérito de la Patria), an accolade he would not hesitate to exploit at every subsequent opportunity.[75]

Political factionalism resumed even before the Spanish crisis concluded. Having become president by virtue of a mutiny and his predecessor's lack of resolve, Guerrero had minimal backing, even among federalists. With the middle and upper classes united in opposition to Zavala's proposed progressive income taxation, and with the military unhappy because of their pay was in arrears, what little support Guerrero had managed to muster rapidly eroded.[76] Using as a pretext the president's refusal to surrender the extraordinary wartime faculties conferred by Congress, Vice President Anastasio Bustamante embraced the Plan of Jalapa on December 4 and took command of the 3,000-man Army of the Reserve, which had been assembled in Jalapa the previous August to bolster gulf coast defenses against subsequent Spanish landings.[77] During the night of December 22–23, General Luís Quintanar's 7th Infantry Regiment pronounced for the *jalapistas* and occupied key installations in Mexico City. Defection of the capital garrison drove the final nail into Guerrero's coffin. Abiding by the will of Congress, Guerrero resigned the presidency the following day and retreated to his southern hacienda, where he continued to enunciate his federalist convictions.[78]

Guerrero remained idle until late 1830, when he joined forces with Juan Álvarez in an attempt to overthrow the centralist government. His pronouncement elicited a vigorous loyalist military response that quelled the disturbance and captured its leader. In January, 1831, Guerrero was put to death in a solitary Dominican monastery outside Oaxaca, outraging a large segment of the Mexican population, who never forgave Bustamante for the incident. The cacique's execution was unusual in that vanquished rivals were habitually treated with uncommon leniency. The fraternal bond between military officers made exile the customary punishment, and that was seldom permanent. In this case, however, his death may have been a warning from the landowning, clerical, and military elite that socially and racially inferior men should not aspire to the presidency. These elites had not forgotten the racial and social connotations of the Independence War.[79]

By subscribing to this coercive change of government, the army again manifested a predilection toward political intervention whenever its corporate interests could be advanced. On this occasion, however, the generals were endorsed by a majority of Mexicans of differing political persuasions who were fed up with the incompetence and policy inconsistencies of the incumbent regime. Guerrero's ouster ended the era in which the former insurgent heroes of the Independence War monopolized the presidency. With few exceptions, Mexico's chief executives would henceforth be creole veterans of the royalist army.[80]

Tainted by illegitimacy and endangered by armed resistance in multiple provinces, Bustamante was obliged to accommodate the caprices of the army commanders who brought him to power. Despite a serious deficit in federal revenues for 1830, he increased the number of general officers on active duty from thirty to fifty. Among those promoted to brigade general was Luís Cortazar, the former royalist chosen by Iturbide to dissolve the

Congress of 1822. Possessed of great charisma, enormous personal wealth, and the complete loyalty of the Guanajuato garrison, the thirty-five-year-old *guanajuatense* was ideally positioned to become a regional arbiter of significant influence.[81]

Such officious pandering, however, did not dissuade Minister of War José Antonio Facio from introducing measures intended to restore discipline and rationalize the military bureaucracy and command structure. Complaining that the states filled their mandated replacement quotas with "vicious and useless men who are unable to serve and readily desert with their clothing and equipment," Facio demobilized a considerable number of active and civic militia units and disestablished Mexico's nascent navy. The former task was simplified by the fact that even the *cívicos'* liberal advocates had become disenchanted with the disorder and lack of discipline permeating these formations.[82]

Even such modest reforms fell victim to the intrigues of partisan politics, which drew the army progressively into the business of state, to the detriment of military preparedness. Instead of tending to matters of national security, military forces became embroiled in a systematic campaign to further government centralization by curbing state political autonomy. Increasingly, army units were employed to supervise local elections, disseminate propaganda, participate in regional industrial and agricultural projects, and remove state governors opposed to conservative Minister of Internal and Foreign Affairs Lucas Alamán's policies of political consolidation.[83]

By 1832, Bustamante's machinations had driven his political opponents into an expedient alliance with Santa Anna, who proffered himself as a champion of federalism.[84] More concerned with baneful government policy changes than opprobrious personalities, growing numbers of army garrison commanders, including Governor Francisco García, leader of the powerful Zacatecas militia, embraced Santa Anna's antigovernment coalition. The steady defection of loyalist forces obliged Bustamante to seek an armistice.[85] Signed on December 23, 1832, by the leaders of both adversarial factions, the Pact of Zavaleta permitted Manuel Gómez Pedraza to serve out the remainder of his original presidential term, at the conclusion of which elections would determine a successor. Observance of the accord occasioned Santa Anna's election to the presidency on April 1, 1833, with radical ideologue Valentín Gómez Farías as vice president.[86] Shrouded in his newly acquired federalist mantle, the president chose to remain at Manga de Clavo and delegate to Gómez Farías authority and responsibility for implementing the military and clerical reforms intended to transform Mexico into a modern, secular state. The civil war of 1832 produced a victory for the traditional federalist states and demonstrated to *hombres de bien* that there would be no return to the coercive politics of the Bustamante regime. Temporarily ascendant, the liberals were prepared to utilize an activist state to implement the kind of progressive reforms of which Zavala had only dreamed in 1829.[87]

The calamitous civil war of 1832 exacted a particularly ruinous toll on both the permanent army and the active militia. Before its onset, permanent manning rosters registered 19,667 men under arms; by April, 1833, however, Minister of War Joaquín Parres reported to Congress that the army could muster only 9,509 of its statutory strength of 22,056 men. Moreover, an inspection of the active militia could account for only 5,209 of the 38,513 troops purportedly carried on the muster rolls of that component, offering further evidence of the deteriorated state of military preparedness.[88] Parres was convinced that the situation could be remedied only by "offering the citizen advantages in the military service that he would find preferable to another occupation; and making him cognizant of the punishment for leaving [without authorization] as so many do today."[89] But bureaucratic inertia and fiscal prostration stymied the initiatives needed to check desertions and restore discipline to the ranks.

Bustamante's distress afforded acting President Gómez Farías an opportunity to render the army permanently incapable of subsequent interference in national political affairs. At the forefront of his federalist antimilitary agenda were proposals to reconstitute the civic militia in the federal district and territories, restation the preponderance of the regular army along the frontiers and coastal peripheries, and redirect all constabulary duties to the enhanced *cívicos*. Additionally, infantry and cavalry formations were to be downsized, the artillery, engineer, and sanitation corps professionalized, promotions meritized, and rank seniority codified. These force-reduction mandates exempted the northern frontier, where relentless Indian hostilities required retention of twenty-nine permanent presidial companies augmented by fifteen companies of *activos*. Six presidial companies also were retained in Alta and Baja California, to protect lives and property in those distant provinces.[90]

The general intent of this latest reform initiative was to attenuate the discriminate political coercion wielded by the permanent army since independence. It was also meant to transform the civic militia into a countervailing military force capable of deterring such pretensions. Gómez Farías and his allies, however, lacked the institutional strength to surmount the traditional elements of Mexican political power.[91] Despite the propitious circumstances, Gómez Farías could no more impose a radical regime upon the nation than Alamán had been able to resurrect one of viceregal stature.

The premeditated assault on ecclesiastical and military privilege propelled the Church into the military camp and engendered pronouncements in the garrisons of Morelia (on May 26) and Tlálpam (on June 1), the leaders professing support for catholicism and clerical and military *fueros*. General Gabriel Durán, who led the Tlálpam uprising, assured Santa Anna, who had resumed the presidency on May 15, 1833, that his intent was only to restore order and preserve the status of the army, not depose the president.[92] Santa Anna responded to these crises by issuing a proclamation condemning the perpetrators *(pronunciados)* and securing congressional authorization to take personal command of the army. Mobilizing a reaction force of 1,500 troops, he set out from the capital on June 2 to subdue the dissidents.[93] His untimely egress at such a critical juncture occasioned concern among the liberals, whose anxieties were not alleviated when an abortive uprising of soldiers garrisoned near the national palace took place just four days after the president's departure. Suspicions of some nefarious plot in the making received added grist when news reached the capital that the president had been taken prisoner at Juchi after refusing to join General Mariano Arista's mutineers.[94]

Speculation over Santa Anna's motives in this episode is considerable and varied. It is possible that he was embroiled in the conspiracy from the outset and backed out when he determined that military support was insufficient to insure the venture's success. He may also have used his alleged detention as a ruse by which to assess the rebellion's prospects for success. When widespread support failed to materialize among senior military leaders, Santa Anna likely concluded that the insurrection would falter and threw in his lot with the winning faction. By his own account, Arista believed that Santa Anna would accept an invitation to join the rebels.[95]

Fortuitously, Santa Anna "escaped" his putative captors and made his way back to the capital, where he resumed his post as chief executive. Forthwith he dispatched General Pedro Lemus to bring the rebels to heel; on July 1, however, Arista defeated Lemus in a sharp engagement near Tepeaca, forcing the president to assemble a 2,000-man contingent of regulars that he personally led out of the capital nine days later. After a protracted pursuit, Santa Anna finally cornered his elusive adversary at Guanajuato on October 8. The customary lenient terms of surrender offered by Santa Anna persuaded Arista to capitulate, bringing an end to this latest round of military adversarialism.[96] Such generosity, however, applied only to personnel implicated in the rebellion. The army and militia units that had rallied to the insurrectionist cause were disestablished and purged from the national military force structure, a development endorsed by Santa Anna because it removed dissidents who posed a threat to him personally as well as to the government.

The immediate crisis alleviated, Congress resumed its military-reform agenda. Intent upon reducing the permanent army to a level at which it no longer could influence provincial activities or intervene in governmental affairs, the liberals proposed legislation disbanding six of twelve infantry and ten of the twelve cavalry regiments and deactivating all three artillery brigades. Such force reductions in the permanent army would have diminished proportionately the requirement for both field-grade and general officers, giving Congress an opportunity to purge from the ranks individuals of questionable political loyalty. Additionally, all commandancies-general were to be abolished, relegating to the states the authority previously vested in those military jurisdictions.[97]

With Congress poised to enact such unprecedented antimilitary legislation, Santa Anna invoked his emergency powers to reorganize the army in a manner much less detrimental. While the army sustained some cuts (mostly by abolishing units that had participated in the most recent rebellion), the commandancies-general and extant unit postings remained unaffected. Santa Anna's preemptive action thwarted congressional intentions to subordinate the army to the *cívicos* by reducing its size and curtailing its jurisdictional authority.[98] The liberals did manage to enact the *ley del caso,* a convenient mechanism enabling the government to exile anyone considered a threat to public safety or welfare. The president signed this edict into law and immediately availed himself of the opportunity to cashier a few of his most implacable foes.[99]

Eager to exculpate himself from any direct responsibility for this latest round of radical-inspired legislation, Santa Anna, who had resumed the presidency on October 27, resorted to the now-familiar pretense of needing a respite from office to recover his health. Congress willingly accommodated the president's entreaty by granting a six-month leave of absence beginning November 26.[100] From his estate in Veracruz, Santa Anna carefully monitored, through General José María Tornel, the increasingly vitriolic conservative reaction to the radical reforms. After entertaining numerous appeals to rescue the country from the disintegration toward which it appeared inexorably headed, he judged the timing suitable for a return to national prominence and reclaimed his executive post on April 24, 1834.[101]

Santa Anna moved cautiously at first, suspending only the most deleterious of the anticlerical statutes already enacted and avoiding a direct break with the radicals. The president's judicious approach marginalized Gómez Farías, compelling him to curtail further legislative initiatives injurious to the Church and tone down the sweeping reorganizational proposals emanating from the Military Affairs Committee. Progressive reversal of the radical legislative agenda provoked armed resistance within the strongly federalist states of Querétaro, San Luís Potosí, Guanajuato, and Jalisco. But without the backing of Zacatecas Governor Francisco García, who had no wish to see his state subjected to a repetition of 1832, loyalist army units quickly disarmed dissident *cívicos* and restored order.[102] Santa Anna maintained this facade of political moderation throughout 1834, reaching accommodation with congressional radicals who were so inclined. The election of a more moderate Congress in January, 1835, and growing public sentiment in favor of centralism, however, convinced him that the time was right to request another leave of absence from the presidency. Empowering Miguel Barragán as chief executive on January 28, Santa Anna once again withdrew to Manga de Clavo, where he continued to monitor, through Minister of War Tornel, the new Congress's progressive dismantling of federalism.[103]

One key piece of legislation promulgated by the new Congress reduced the size of state, territorial, and federal district civic militias to one militiaman per 500 residents. Perceived as a direct attack upon state sovereignty, the law prompted Zacatecas Governor Francisco García to mobilize 4,000 militiamen. Santa Anna, who previously had deferred a move against the powerful Zacatecas militia until his position in the other states had been consolidated, responded by ending his seclusion to take personal command of government forces being assembled to deal with the crisis. On May 11, near Guadalupe, Santa Anna's army dealt the Zacatecas militia a resounding defeat, eliminating the last significant resistance to the new conservative government.[104] The Hero of Tampico followed up his victory by sacking the capital city and leading his army on a triumphant procession through Aguascalientes, Querétaro, Jalisco, and Michoacán.

Santa Anna's decisive victory secured centralism as the dominant political ideology for the ensuing decade. The political transition was completed in April, 1836, when the new Congress supplanted the federalist Constitution of 1824 with the conservative Siete Leyes (Seven Laws). Among other things, the Siete Leyes instituted a highly controlled and complicated system of indirect presidential election, extended the presidential term from four to eight years (with immediate reelection eligibility), and transformed the states into military departments whose chiefs would be named by the president. To preserve political leadership for the elite, the new charter added property qualifications and minimum annual income levels for presidential and congressional candidates (ranging from 4,000 pesos for a presidential contestant to 1,500 pesos for those aspiring to the chamber of deputies).[105] In concert these measures helped create the foundation necessary for the political centralism that prevailed during the first half of the 1840s.

The army emerged from this bizarre episode of machiavellian intrigue generally unscathed by the relentless radical attacks upon its entitlements and status. As in 1821, when reform initiatives emanating from the liberal Spanish Cortes threatened the status quo, the military hierarchy, ecclesiastical caste, and landed aristocracy closed ranks to safeguard their respective corporate interests. Despite their contempt for Santa Anna's unprincipled behavior, many senior army leaders embraced his anti-federalist movement, discerning that it offered the best means of preserving their traditional station. Santa Anna shrewdly and patiently exploited the volatile political climate until conditions so unsettled the vested interest groups that he could shed his convenient federalist mantle and confidently reemerge as the nation's conservative savior. Annulling nearly all the previously enacted radical legislation, he ushered in a political regime nearly as reactionary and centralistic as that he had helped depose in the civil war of 1832. But Santa Anna's attempt to acquire dictatorial powers was thwarted both by stubborn opposition from the traditionally liberal northern states and by misgivings in the country's fiscal and economic constituencies, who considered his motives opportunistic and self-serving.[106]

Despite consuming a disproportionate share of federal revenues since independence, the permanent army had little to show for its extravagance. Units remained poorly trained, ill-equipped, and increasingly personalized. Absent a bond of national fealty, the army remained a collection of provincial constabularies more concerned with preserving regional autonomy than defending national interests. Many prominent generals had emerged as formidable caciques whose priority lay in maintaining a government with which they shared ideological compatibility. The army of the early republican era, therefore, comprised little more than self-aggrandizing and factitious local legions that cooperated only when collective corporate interests were at risk. Except for the abortive Spanish "invasion" of 1829 and relentless Indian incursions along the northern periphery, the army had yet to experience a serious challenge to Mexican territorial integrity. The preponderance of its operational experience involved confrontations with rival military factions, usually over an issue of sectional or ideological hegemony, and these were relatively bloodless affairs, generally resolved through mediation and compromise. When the smoldering impasse in Texas finally came to a head in October, 1835, the government was unable to mobilize from among its standing formations an expeditionary army of sufficient size and readiness to bring the rebellious Texans quickly to heel. By necessity, therefore, the restoration of order devolved upon the country's most prominent caudillo, Antonio López de Santa Anna.

CHAPTER 3

The Texas Revolution, 1835–36

The conservative Constitution of 1836 provoked federalists throughout Mexico, but nowhere was this reaction more clamorous than in Texas, a loosely administered province historically resistant to centralized authority. In the early 1820s the Mexican government granted impresario contracts to Moses Austin to settle Texas with colonists of diverse national origin. Despite government efforts to promote resident loyalty, protestantism, slavery, language, and a compelling desire for self-rule conspired to estrange the sparsely settled territory. The steadily growing population of Anglo-American colonists harbored little affinity for centralized government, especially one with which they shared neither linguistic nor cultural commonality. Agitated by the intrigues of Mexican federalists and encouraged by the United States, whose vision of Manifest Destiny included annexation of Texas, the movement for total separation from Mexico gained adherents and momentum.[1]

Government intransigence in matters of local autonomy and the military's coercive removal of acting President Valentín Gómez Farías were the catalysts necessary to provoke Texan independence activists into open rebellion. The rapid deterioration of provincial security that followed prompted an alarmed Mexican Congress to authorize military intervention to restore order. Command of the expeditionary army sanctioned for this purpose was entrusted to Antonio López de Santa Anna, who had been biding his time at Manga de Clavo since crushing the Zacatecas militia in May.

From the outset, the new general-in-chief faced imposing challenges to organizing and equipping an army of operations. An impecunious treasury, the rebellions of 1832 and 1833, and radical-inspired antimilitary legislation had conspired to render the permanent army ineffective as a dependable and deployable armed force. Especially damaging was the purging of veteran formations with independence era experience. They had possessed a semblance of national identity, absent in the green units that entered Texas. "An old soldier," professed Minister of War Tornel, "is a treasure because he is the teacher of recruits, and because without veteran cadres, one cannot organize new corps that can be usefully employed, particularly in offensive war."[2] When hostilities erupted near Gonzales on October 2, 1835, Mexico was caught without a standing army capable of mounting a timely and effective response.

In March, 1835, army personnel records listed 38,715 troops available for duty, of whom 18,219 were *permanentes.*[3] To the general-in-chief's consternation, however, he quickly discovered that only 3,500 of those rostered could readily be assembled for the Texas expedition. This disparity was caused in part by the government's decision to retain an inordinate number of the army's permanent formations in the core districts for possible commitment against a recrudescence of federalist revolutionary activity. As he had demonstrated during the Spanish invasion of 1829, Santa Anna possessed a remarkable facility for improvising armies with minimal governmental assistance, and this undertaking was no exception.[4] On this occasion, though, he would have to contend with the added burden of traversing nearly six hundred miles of mostly uninhabited and inhospitable terrain, an impediment not heretofore encountered. Logistics, not training, became the overriding consideration as he and his subordinates set about organizing an army of operations that would return the defiant Texans to the Mexican fold.

In the midst of intensive military preparations, Santa Anna was distracted by an unwelcome development in Texas. On October 28, 1835, Brigade General Martín Perfecto de Cós, the newly appointed commander of Mexican military forces in the rebellious province, had been roughly handled at Concepción by a hastily gathered band of Texan sharpshooters led by James Bowie. Cós was forced to seek refuge within the confines of Béjar, which the Texans then besieged, and his situation became more precarious with each passing day.[5] To relieve his beleaguered brother-in-law, Santa Anna ordered the military commander of Zacatecas, Brigade General Joaquín

Ramírez y Sesma, to collect the Morelos Battalion at Laredo, arming them with the surplus materials he carried, and to draft "those useful men familiar with firearms . . . incorporating them into the rank and file as auxiliary volunteers to enlarge the Division."[6] The commandant-general was also directed to give no quarter to the foreigners waging war against the Mexican nation, because they "have violated all laws and do not deserve any consideration. . . . They have audaciously declared a war of extermination against the Mexicans and should be treated in the same manner."[7] Concerned that the equivalent grades of Cós and Ramírez y Sesma would encumber the existing command relationship, Santa Anna appointed Division General Vicente Filisola second commander-in-chief on December 8 and instructed him to proceed to Béjar forthwith to assume overall command of Mexican forces in Texas.[8]

The Italian-born Filisola had begun his distinguished military career in 1804 with the Regimiento Fijo de Buenos Aires and later fought with the guerrillas resisting the French occupation of Spain. Reassigned to the royalist army in New Spain, he participated in the government's counterinsurgency campaigns until joining Iturbide's Ejército Trigarante. By the time of the Spanish invasion of 1829, he was a brigadier general commanding the Reserve Army. Thereafter he held various commissions to include captain-general of Guatemala, commandant-general of Michoacán, México, and Puebla, general-in-chief of the Army of the South, and inspector general of permanent infantry and cavalry forces. During the War with the United States he would command the Querétaro Division and serve thereafter as president of the Supreme War and Marine Tribunal.[9]

Filisola caught up to Ramírez y Sesma on December 19 as the latter was attempting to cross the surging Salado River, but unbeknown to either of these officers, Cós had capitulated ten days earlier and was in the process of withdrawing the remnants of his command to Laredo.[10] Cós's evacuation of Texas added an unpleasant wrinkle to Mexican plans to subdue the insurgency, for Santa Anna now faced a hostile environment devoid of friendly forces. Nevertheless he chose Béjar as his initial objective because he could expect more cooperation from its predominantly Mexican inhabitants than from settlements elsewhere in the province.

The Ministry of Finance appropriated a half-million pesos to underwrite the venture. Because none of these funds was immediately available, the general-in-chief was obliged to borrow 47,000 pesos from the secular church, 30,000 of which he immediately dispatched to Filisola to pay the troops and procure supplies.[11] Santa Anna intended to repay the ecclesiastical note via involuntary loans levied upon the departments of Guanajuato, Jalisco, and Zacatecas supplemented by import taxes derived from the customs houses at Matamoros and Tampico. Subsequently a 400,000 peso loan was negotiated with the commercial house of Rubio and Errazu, but on terms so unfavorable that its consummation was strongly opposed by the Mexican Congress.[12]

With the funding dilemma temporarily resolved, the general-in-chief directed his attention to the matter of assembling, organizing, and training the forces necessary to execute the campaign. The Army of Operations was formed into a fifty-officer general staff, to plan and supervise tactical and logistical operations, and five maneuver elements, each commanded by a general officer. The five maneuver elements included the Vanguard Brigade under Ramírez y Sesma (1,541 men and eight cannon); the 1st Infantry Brigade (1,600 men and six cannon), commanded by Brigade General Antonio Gaona; the 2nd Infantry Brigade (1,839 men and six cannon) commanded by Brigade General Eugenio Tolsa; Urrea's division (641 men and eight cannon), under Brigade General José Urrea; and the Cavalry Brigade (437 men) commanded by Brigade General Juan José Andrade.[13] Conscripts levied from various military units scattered about the country filled the ranks of the infantry, cavalry, and artillery units. A little more than half the army's total strength of 6,018 troops was derived from active militia and presidial forces; the balance came from permanent army formations. To the considerable detriment of operational effectiveness, commanders consistently ignored the keen reconnaissance skills of the frontier-savvy *presidiales*.[14]

In general the troops were poorly equipped, shoddily clothed, and undernourished, and the majority exhibited a distinct lack of enthusiasm for the enterprise they were about to undertake. Most infantrymen were armed with the *fusil,* a 9.7-pound, flintlock-operated, smoothbore musket of British manufacture that fired a monstrous half-ounce, .753-caliber lead ball with an effective range of about seventy yards. Nicknamed the Brown Bess *(morena licha)*, it was the same British East India Pattern weapon that had seen widespread use during the Napoleonic Wars. Though generally a sturdy and reliable weapon in the hands of disciplined troops, the Brown Bess muskets issued to the Mexican army had been condemned previously by the British. The British Baker Rifle, a 9.2-pound, muzzle-loading, flint ignition firearm with seven lands and grooves that permitted its .614-caliber projectile to be fired with relative accuracy out to 200 yards, was issued to select light infantrymen known as *cazadores*.[15] Cavalrymen were similarly armed, except that they carried a wooden lance and a sword or saber in addition to the Pagent carbine, a shorter-barreled, lighter version of the smoothbore musket that could be reloaded on horseback. The artillery available to the Army of Operations was a mélange of antiquated pieces ranging in size from 4- to 12-pounder cannon supplemented by a few high-trajectory 7-inch howitzers.

The enormous distance that this army of 6,000 men was required to traverse to reach its theater of operations made logistics a matter of utmost concern. The nature of the terrain was such that settlements were few and far between, and water and forage exceedingly scarce. Cognizant of these obstacles, Santa Anna directed his commanders to stockpile two months' rations and prepare to live off the land.[16] Hundreds of oxen and mules were required to move the army's supplies and artillery. Although oxen needed considerably less forage than mules and could be consumed if necessary, they possessed inferior speed and endurance and could be worked for only eight hours a day. Reliance on such modes of transport rendered the army especially vulnerable to the vicissitudes of impressed muleteers who were prone to desert at will, particularly if their pay was not forthcoming in a timely manner.[17] Any shortage of teamsters required the diversion of military manpower to assume those duties, a contingency that depleted available line strength.

Preventive health care and treatment of injuries were supposed to be vested in the Military Health Corps *(Cuerpo de Sanidad)*, but that chronically understaffed and ill-equipped branch never was able to fulfill its statutory mission. As a result the Army of Operations experienced serious medical supply and treatment deficiencies throughout the campaign.[18] In the absence of assigned doctors, the army relied heavily upon *curanderos* to render primary nursing services. These remarkable herb healers, some of whom were more practically skilled in medicine than many trained physicians, were a part of the contingent of *soldaderas* who customarily accompanied the army on campaign. Mainly soldiers' wives and girlfriends, the *soldaderas* performed essential sewing, cooking, maintenance, and foraging duties, without which it would have been exceedingly difficult for the army to operate.[19] *Soldaderas* ministered to enemy wounded as well, took up residence with foreign armies, and served as consorts for foreign officers. At this juncture, no real sense of nationalism existed that would have bound them exclusively to Mexico. While more than 1,500 women and children accompanied the Army of Operations to Béjar, fewer than 300 actually reached their final destinations; thirst, starvation, and the rigors of multiple sustained marches over difficult terrain exacted a terrible toll on the *soldaderas*.[20]

The fundamentally Napoleonic tactics espoused by the Army of Operations leadership featured the heavy use of infantry in linear formations to deliver both mass and shock. Santa Anna, who idolized Napoleon but possessed only a superficial understanding of his military principles, visualized a strategy in which the Texans would be engaged in a series of set-piece battles, in which the volley fire, mass, and mobility of the Mexican army could be maximized.[21] He intended to capitalize on the advantage enjoyed by Mexican infantry and cavalry in the open field, while avoiding wooded areas that afforded cover and concealment to Texan sharpshooters. Such precaution is evident in the orders issued to Ramírez y Sesma on the eve of his departure to relieve Cós at Béjar:

> Should the enemy present himself to offer battle, you will first of all examine the position he has taken. If it proves so much to his advantage that you consider it unlikely that you can defeat him, then you will avoid attacking him and manage your maneuvers to entice him to fight on different ground. . . . If the enemy should present battle on open ground, you will waste no time in forming the lines so that his fire and maneuvers can always be anticipated by your own. Your well located artillery should deliver the first destructive blows. The cavalry in two columns will attract the enemy's attention to the flanks at the rear, taking advantage of any weakness or negligence to support the action; a sound maneuver when the enemy's cavalry is no match for ours.[22]

The Army of Operations, however, was composed predominantly of inexperienced conscripts, who would have required extensive training to execute linear tactics proficiently. Because the army possessed neither the time nor the resources to accomplish such a formidable task, it was compelled to begin the recovery of Texas with soldiers possessing only rudimentary tactical skills.[23]

If training and equipment levels in the Mexican army were less than ideal, conditions in the ranks of its opponent were notably worse. The Texan army was little more than an undisciplined militia supplemented with volunteers from the United States. It seldom exceeded 1,200 troops and was dispersed in small detachments, none larger than 400.[24] Short of funds, food, clothing, and weapons and unschooled in the intricacies of conventional tactics, the Texans had little choice but to embrace the role of highly mobile light infantry. Especially fearful of being caught in the open by

Mexican cavalry, the rebels made extensive use of woodlines, entrenchments, and movement during hours of reduced visibility to compensate for their paucity of massed firepower and limited mobility. Aimed rifle fire from protected positions became the tactic of choice to defeat volley fire supported by artillery and cavalry, particularly after the insurrectionists' success against Cós at Concepción.[25] Such tactical imperatives predominated throughout the revolution, with the Mexicans dominating the western prairies while the Texans prevailed in the eastern woodlands, where the advantages of light infantry could be exploited. One of the most important tactical lessons emanating from this war was the surprising lethality of individually aimed Texan rifle fire compared to the volley musketry of massed Mexican infantry formations.[26]

By January, 1836, the units formed in San Luís Potosí, Coahuila, and Nuevo León had converged on Saltillo to prepare for the forced entry *(entrada)* into Texas. The loss of Béjar obliged Santa Anna to modify his original plan, which had General José Urrea advancing upon Goliad via Laredo, while the rest of the army proceeded along a northern axis that crossed the river at Presidio del Rio Bravo (Guerrero). With the expedition's main objective now in enemy hands, Urrea was redirected to Guerrero, where he was to subordinate his forces to General Filisola.[27] The latter, however, already had relocated his command to Laredo, where he linked up with Cós and Ramírez y Sesma.

Noting that the lack of water and forage would impose severe hardship upon the army, Filisola cautioned Santa Anna against using the northern route. As an alternative he suggested assembling the army at Mier, where the agricultural products of Nuevo León and Tamaulipas and the proximity of the port of Matamoros would help alleviate myriad logistical problems. Additionally, such a disposition would better posture the army to seize Goliad, which Filisola considered the campaign's most significant objective. Béjar in fact, was of little strategic value to either the Texans or their opponents, but Santa Anna considered it politically imperative to drive out the Texans while the rebels were seduced by the putative impregnability of the Alamo. Seizing San Patricio and Goliad would have isolated Béjar, enabling its circumvention without a fight.[28] Obsessed with avenging Cós's humiliating capitulation, however, Santa Anna dismissed his deputy's advice and directed Ramírez y Sesma to march his brigade to Guerrero. Concurrently he ordered Cós to Monclova to rest and refit and instructed Urrea to remain at Saltillo.[29] Santa Anna's indifference to Filisola's sound advice was a serious operational error that subjected an already weary segment of the army to unnecessary movement across inhospitable terrain. Difficult for veteran professional soldiers, such marches were nearly intolerable for raw conscripts whose commitment to this crusade was less than overwhelming.[30]

The general-in-chief's final concept of operation called for Béjar to be enveloped by columns converging along two separate axes of advance. In the north the Vanguard Brigade (Ramírez y Sesma), the 1st Infantry Brigade (Gaona), the 2nd Infantry Brigade (Tolsa), the Cavalry Brigade (Andrade), and the command group would cross the Rio Bravo at Guerrero and proceed to Béjar by the most expeditious route. Along the southern axis, Urrea's division was to advance from its Matamoros cantonment and approach Béjar via Goliad.[31] Designated as the army's advance guard, Ramírez y Sesma was instructed to incorporate "one hundred men from the presidial companies gathered at [Guerrero], selecting from among those better armed and mounted," and depart that location for Béjar on February 12. Having lived the majority of their lives on the periphery defending their homes against Indian raiders, most *presidials* "knew the terrain like the palm[s] of their hands" and were extraordinarily proficient scouts. But the army leadership disdained these crass frontiersmen and consistently failed to exploit their invaluable skills.[32]

The main body's march to the Rio Bravo was one of extraordinary hardship for the soldiers of the Army of Operations. Unusually foul weather, coupled with inadequate water, food, and forage, imposed upon the army conditions so unbearable that increasing numbers of soldiers abandoned the enterprise while still relatively close to home. Alarmed by this exodus, Santa Anna instructed Filisola to insure the military commandant of Monclova complied with his orders to maintain active patrols along routes most likely to be used by deserters. Additionally the ministry of war issued new regulations governing the apprehension and punishment of deserters in an unavailing attempt to stem the hemorrhage.[33]

Many soldiers who stuck with their units suffered from chronic dysentery and other debilitating ailments. On February 13 a severe snow storm left 16-inch drifts that killed a number of oxen and accelerated desertions, especially among contract wagon drivers. Accustomed to the gentle climate of Yucatán, Urrea's predominantly Mayan recruits were particularly vulnerable to such environmental extremes, suffering six exposure deaths on February 25 alone.[34] Hostile Comanches added to the misery of the march by raiding the column for provisions and livestock, attacking ranchos where stores had been pre-positioned and dispatching skulkers and stragglers. The general-in-chief had been under the impression that the Plains Indians would

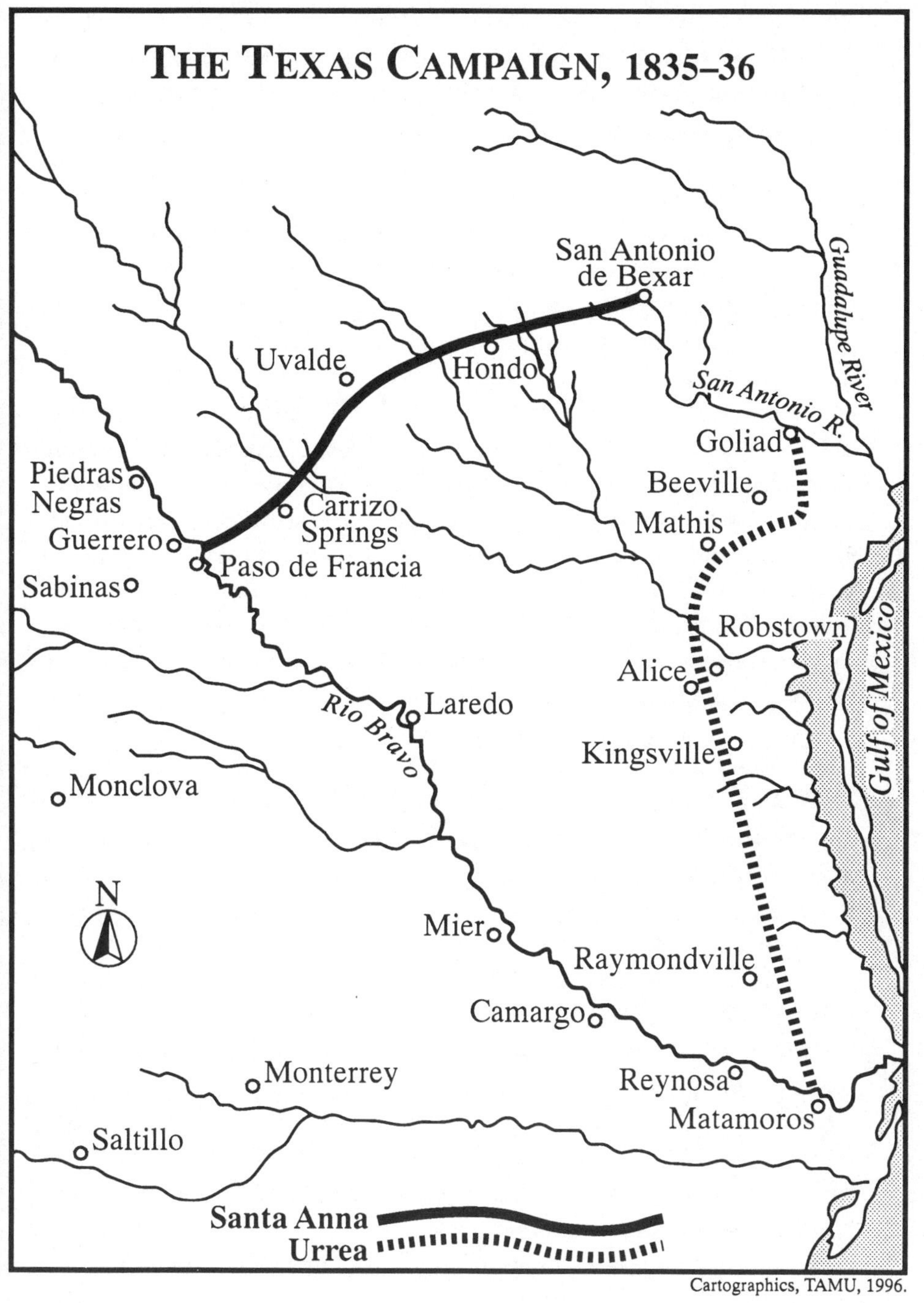

Cartographics, TAMU, 1996.

ally with the Mexicans, but it seems that the spoils to be derived from both contenders inclined them toward opportunistic neutrality.[35]

Santa Anna and the command group closed on Ramírez y Sesma's Vanguard Brigade near the Rio Frío on February 19 and traveled in its company for the next three days, until reaching the boundary delineating Coahuila from Texas. At this juncture the army was strung out over some three hundred miles, and the route was littered with stragglers, animal carcasses, and discarded equipment.[36] Although long forced marches over the vast, nearly uninhabited desert exacted a terrible toll on the unprepared and inadequately provisioned soldiers, residents of the few settlements along the way saw their meager farms pillaged at will by soldiers and *soldaderas* alike.[37]

As the Army of Operations approached Béjar, the newly elected commander, Colonel James Bowie, the former leader, Colonel William Barret Travis, and 150 Texan defenders worked furiously to fortify the Alamo. The two leaders dispatched numerous appeals for reinforcements, the most readily available source of which was Colonel James W. Fannin's 420-man contingent at Goliad. General Sam Houston, however, was deceived as to the true Mexican objective. Convinced that Santa Anna would strike first at Goliad, he refused to release any of Fannin's troops to reinforce Béjar. The Vanguard Brigade entered the city unopposed on the afternoon of February 23 and announced its presence by hoisting a scarlet flag (signifying "no quarter") from the belfry of San Fernando Church. This provocative display evoked cannon fire from the Alamo, which continued intermittently until nightfall and resumed the following morning as the Mexicans began siege preparations.[38]

In later years the impetuous Ramírez y Sesma became the target of considerable criticism for his failure to take the unsuspecting garrison by surprise, thereby obviating the need for a costly assault. "General Sesma," Almonte contends, "did not advance to reconnoitre because he expected an advance of the enemy which was about to be made according to the accounts given by an enemy spy who was caught."[39] Because the Alamo defenders already had been alerted to his proximity by a small reconnaissance element that spotted the Vanguard Brigade near las lomas de Alazán earlier that morning, Ramírez y Sesma's impassivity may have been the most prudent course of action after all.

While awaiting arrival of the Army of Operations' main body, Ramírez y Sesma opened a random cannonade upon the Alamo, which elicited only a meager response from its defenders, who were conserving ammunition pending the arrival of reinforcements from Goliad. The timely appearance of

Urrea's division on February 27, however, forced Fannin to recall the 350-man force dispatched the day prior to reinforce the Alamo. Urrea's success illustrates the soundness of Santa Anna's original operations plan. By advancing along two axes, the general-in-chief compelled the Texans to split their seriously depleted forces in the face of a superior enemy, rendering them vulnerable to defeat in detail.[40]

When Santa Anna reached Béjar later that day, he notified Minister of War Tornel that his assault of the Alamo would "occur at least with the arrival of the First Brigade which is presently seventy leagues distant from here." He also indicated that he would move on Goliad, Brazoria, and other fortified positions between Béjar and the Sabine River (the recognized boundary with the United States) so that these could be secured prior to the rainy season.[41] The March 3 arrival of 1,000 reinforcements from the 1st Brigade and the Cavalry Regiment elevated Mexican troop strength in Béjar to 2,590 men and further demoralized the Alamo's beleaguered defenders.[42]

Originally a Franciscan mission, the Alamo compound comprised a variety of buildings including a convent, a roofless church, a barracks and a mill. Although boasting an outer wall six to nine feet high and 18 to 42 inches thick, the Alamo was not really a fortress in the classic sense. Despite the efforts of Cós, James C. Neill, and William Barret Travis to enhance its defensibility, the badly deteriorated structure possessed no redoubts and was inherently difficult to secure, especially with such a small garrison. By virtue of its location on a slight rise, however, the Alamo did enjoy unobstructed fields of fire commanding the approaches in every direction.[43]

The general-in-chief planned to assault this objective at 4:00 A.M. on March 6, with four columns advancing along separate axes. The cavalry under Ramírez y Sesma was positioned south of the Alamo to block any attempted escape. Santa Anna's decision to attack in closed-up linear formation rendered his soldiers' muskets considerably less effective and provided superb targets for the Texan sharpshooters even in the reduced predawn light.[44] Mexican assault forces moved into attack position undetected and lay on their arms until 5:30, when a bugler sounded the call to attention followed by the *degüello* (no quarter). The soldiers responded with shouts of "Long live the fatherland" *("Viva la patria")* and quickly closed in on the walls of the Alamo, suffering appalling losses from close-range discharges of grape and solid cannon shot.[45] Within fifteen minutes the majority of the attacking infantry had scaled the north and south walls and were inside the compound engaging knots of retreating Texans desperately seeking refuge inside the long barracks. Frenzied close-quarters fighting continued for another hour, until all defenders were either killed or captured. David Crockett and six other Texans unfortunate enough to have been apprehended were summarily executed in compliance with Santa Anna's *degüello* edict. Only a few women and children and Travis's slave Joe were spared.[46]

Overwhelming force enabled the Mexicans to prevail over their vastly outnumbered opponents, but at a cost to the attackers of between 500 and 600 casualties. In his after-action communique to Minister of War Tornel, the general-in-chief reported Mexican losses as 70 killed and 300 wounded while exaggerating Texan strength at 600 defenders.[47] Santa Anna's decision to conduct a frontal assault without first subjecting the Alamo to an intensive and sustained artillery bombardment reflects his impatience, disdain for Texan defenders, and disregard for basic tactical precepts. Colonels José Enrique de la Peña and Carlos Sánchez Navarro take Santa Anna to task for failing to employ massed artillery fires to open a breach in the outer wall of the mission complex. "Another victory like this," lamented Sánchez Navarro, "will take us to the devil."[48]

In Mexico City the anti-liberal newspaper *El Mosquito Mexicano* lauded the general-in-chief's victory and expressed confidence that peace soon would be restored throughout the republic. The pro-federalist press, however, was markedly less enthusiastic, fearing that such veneration would only reinforce Santa Anna's growing autocratic power.[49] The polemical reporting in the competing presses deferred publication of an unbiased version of the Alamo engagement. Meanwhile, most Mexicans rejoiced in the euphoria of victory, at least until events at San Jacinto brought them back to reality.[50]

The lack of doctors and medical supplies exacted a severe toll upon wounded Mexican soldiers, a situation for which Santa Anna was justifiably excoriated. His callous indifference to the plight of the wounded was exacerbated by the venal behavior of a few senior commanders who appropriated the spoils of the battle to themselves while denying their own troops even the meanest necessities. "There are no hospitals, medicines, or doctors," Colonel Sánchez Navarro recorded in his diary, "and our wounded are the ones who suffer; there are neither mattresses upon which they can lie, nor blankets with which to cover up, despite the fact that in the occupation of Béjar three or four tents were taken from the enemy, one of which is now called 'the Government tent,' where everything sold is expensive and requires cash."[51]

Such insensitive leadership was one of the principal factors contributing to the inability of the Mexican army to develop the unit cohesion and loyalty necessary to function effectively under disordered conditions such as at

San Jacinto. This deplorable situation prompted Congress to enact legislation in August, 1836, revitalizing the Cuerpo de Sanidad. The law also appropriated funding for adequate medical stores and authorized assignment of a surgeon to fixed hospitals or provisional field facilities of each permanent army and active militia corps. Unfortunately, mere recognition of this problem did not translate into its resolution, as the army's medical capability improved only slightly in the ensuing decade.[52]

By March 11, all of Santa Anna's remaining elements had closed on Béjar, consolidating the Army of Operations for the first time since leaving Monclova. The dearth of friendly population coupled with the scarcity of locally available supplies and forage, however, obliged the general-in-chief to accelerate his departure from Béjar.[53] For the next phase of his Texas campaign, Santa Anna divided his army into four components. Three were to sweep east along separate axes and clear Texas all the way to the Sabine. On the northern axis, Gaona was directed to proceed with 700 soldiers via Bastrop to Nacogdoches. In the center, Ramírez y Sesma, with 800 men, was instructed to advance via Beason's Crossing toward San Felipe de Austin. Urrea, reinforced by Colonel Juan Morales's 500-man Jiménez Battalion, was ordered to seize Goliad and continue south to Matagorda, where he was to establish a maritime resupply point. The fourth element, under General Andrade's command, remained at Béjar to secure the city. The overall intent was for the three maneuver elements, consisting of some 2,000 soldiers, to reunite in the vicinity of San Felipe de Austin, where an updated estimate of the situation would determine subsequent courses of action.[54] The wide divergence of these columns indicates that the general-in-chief had little idea of the size, strength, and disposition of his opponent and was relying upon a reconnaissance-in-force to find and fix the main contingent of Texan rebels. Collection and use of tactical intelligence, never a strong attribute of the Mexican army, was one singular weakness of this campaign.

One location where Texan insurgents were known to be concentrated in force was Goliad, and Santa Anna entrusted the elimination of this position to his most competent divisional commander. Born to a military family at the presidio of Horcasitas in 1797, José Urrea had begun his army career at age eleven as a cadet in the presidio of San Rafael de Buenavista. He participated in the royalist counterinsurgency campaigns before finally embracing the Plan of Iguala in 1821. Removed from military service for being on the losing side of Nicolás Bravo's 1827 Tulancingo *cuartelazo,* which sought to impose a form of federalism on the country, he was later restored to active duty by virtue of his performance against the invading Spaniards in 1829 and his seconding of the Plan of Jalapa. After being promoted to brigade general in 1835, he was assigned to Durango with orders to organize a military force to counter the growing Apache menace in that district. Shortly thereafter, he received orders to join Santa Anna's Army of Operations. "El señor General don José Urrea," wrote Colonel Sánchez Navarro, "was without doubt the General who most distinguished himself in the Texas campaign." Urrea's performance also elicited equally meritorious praise from the general-in-chief.[55]

Annihilation of the Alamo garrison convinced the Texans to consolidate their scattered forces under Houston's command and withdraw to the east, where prevalent woodlands provided the concealment necessary to render their guerrilla tactics considerably more effective.[56] Trading space for time and hoping to overextend the Mexicans, Houston ordered Fannin to evacuate Goliad and fall back on Victoria. The indecisive Texan colonel, however, delayed evacuating his command until March 19, when the contingent previously dispatched to Refugio to evacuate American settlers had been recovered.[57] After covering just six miles, Fannin unaccountably halted for an hour, enabling the pursuing Mexicans to overtake his command in the open prairie near Coleto Creek. General Urrea immediately deployed his cavalry to cut the Texans off from a nearby woods, which would have provided indispensable cover and concealment, and maneuvered his dragoons into positions surrounding their makeshift square. After a series of inconclusive but costly probes, Urrea suspended operations until his artillery, reinforcements, and additional ammunition could be brought forward under cover of darkness. The next morning a brief cannonade announced renewal of the attack and convinced Fannin, who was outnumbered seven to one, to ask for terms. Urrea replied by offering terms of surrender at the discretion of the Mexican government, conditions that the encircled Texan had little recourse but to accept.[58]

Urrea appealed to Santa Anna in an effort to spare the lives of the captives but was reminded of the December 30, 1835, decree of the Mexican Congress that mandated the execution of all foreigners taken in battle or bearing arms against the nation.[59] Santa Anna attempted to consign the burden of responsibility for prisoner disposition to the Congress, but paragraph 9 of his December 7, 1835, instructions to Ramírez y Sesma contained very explicit language regarding the treatment of enemy captives: "The foreigners who wage war against the Mexican Nation have violated all laws and do not deserve any consideration, and for that reason, no quarter will be given them as the troops are to be notified at the proper time. They have audaciously declared a war of extermination against the Mexicans and should be treated in the same manner."[60]

Fannin's troops and the remnants of Colonel William Ward's Georgia Battalion, captured near Dimitt's Landing on March 22, were returned to Goliad and placed under the jurisdiction of Colonel Nicolás de la Portilla. After receiving orders from Santa Anna to execute the prisoners and contradictory instructions from Urrea to see to their welfare, Portilla advised the latter that he had decided to proceed with the executions. Of the 445 captives, Portilla spared only 8 who, he believed, were not under arms. The remainder were removed from the fortress at Goliad on March 27 (Palm Sunday) and summarily shot.[61] In the confusion that followed, some three dozen of the condemned Texans managed to escape, but the consensus of most witnesses is that between 330 and 385 were gunned down in cold blood. Despite Santa Anna's attempts to justify his actions under the *degüello* edict, this carnage was roundly denounced by most of his principal subordinates. Moreover its ultimate and unintended effect was to draw the United States indirectly into the fight.[62]

Convinced that Fannin's decimation and Houston's withdrawal signaled the end of the Texas campaign, Santa Anna ordered the Cavalry Brigade back to San Luís Potosí and adjusted the movements of his remaining maneuver elements to accommodate the new operational environment. To this point, Santa Anna's military planning had been reasonably sound. But his decision to disperse his forces violated the principles of concentration and economy of force and gave a beaten enemy the opportunity to recover. Colonels Peña and Sánchez Navarro, two of his more perceptive subordinates, decried the recklessness of this venture. Rather than drawing to a close, these officers believed, the Texas campaign was just beginning.[63]

Leaving Filisola to tend to logistical matters, the general-in-chief departed Béjar on April 8 bound for San Felipe de Austin, on the west bank of the Brazos River, where he intended to establish a new command post. Four days later he linked up with Ramírez y Sesma at Beason's Crossing.[64] Enticed by rumors of the rebel cabinet's presence in Harrisburg, Santa Anna assembled a 950-man composite force from the Matamoros, Guerrero, México, and Toluca Battalions, and set out to capture this prize. Reaching Harrisburg on April 15, the Mexican commander was chagrined to discover that his quarry had fled only a few hours prior to his arrival. However, after learning that Houston's army was in the vicinity of Groce's Landing, he resolved to cut off and crush his opponent, thereby ending the rebellion in one final engagement. His brash pursuit culminated on April 20 near the junction of Buffalo Bayou and the San Jacinto River.[65] In a wooded area bounded by Peggy Lake and the New Washington Road, the general-in-chief ordered his weary soldiers to encamp. Suspecting that Houston's forces were nearby, Santa Anna opted to await the arrival of 500 reinforcements and two artillery pieces, which he previously had directed Filisola to dispatch under General Cós's command, before deliberately engaging the enemy.[66] Houston, meanwhile, redeployed his 910-man force from Groce's Plantation, where it had been refitting, to Lynchburg on the San Jacinto River. Aiming to catch the overconfident and inattentive Mexican column off guard, he laagered his troops in a thicket adjacent Buffalo Bayou until the enemy had taken up positions in a sparsely wooded area near Peggy Lake. After skirmishing inconclusively on April 20, the Texans seized the initiative at 3:30 P.M. the next day. Burning Vince's Bridge, the only route of egress across White Oak Bayou, Houston launched a multidirectional assault that stunned and routed his foe in a wild melee that lasted fewer than eighteen minutes. Despite posting three elite units *(compañías de preferencia)* to observe the area where the rebels were known to be camped, the entire cantonment was caught unprepared. More than 650 Mexicans, among them General Manuel Fernández Castrillón, to whom the camp's security had been entrusted, were killed in the initial onslaught or the ensuing massacre perpetrated by furious Texans intent upon avenging the Alamo and Coleto. Of the six hundred or so who managed to escape across Peggy Lake, most were apprehended over the next two days.[67]

In yet another display of opprobrious behavior that seemed to characterize his leadership under adverse circumstances, Santa Anna fled the battlefield disguised as an enlisted soldier *(soldado razo)*. Apprehended the following day by a band of Texans pursuing fugitives, Santa Anna was identified when his fellow prisoners recognized him and began shouting *"El Presidente!"* Once identified, Santa Anna was taken to General Houston, to whom he officially surrendered. Subsequently Santa Anna directed Filisola to "order general Gaona to countermarch to Béjar and await orders . . . and advise general Urrea to withdraw his division to Guadalupe Victoria."[68] Three days later he dispatched a second message to Filisola, in which he ordered all Mexican forces evacuated to Matamoros, a decision prompted in part by growing food shortages and deteriorating medical care for the wounded. In compliance, Filisola assembled the principal commanders and organized a strategic withdrawal to Guadalupe Victoria that was completed by May 14.[69]

That same day, Santa Anna signed a treaty with President David G. Burnet, in which he agreed not to take up arms against the Texans nor encourage other parties to do so. Additionally, private property was to be returned, prisoners exchanged, and the Mexican Army of Operations withdrawn to the western bank of the Rio Bravo. In a second secret accord, Santa Anna pledged to try to "prepare the Mexican Cabinet to receive a peace commission" from Texas for the purpose of recognizing the province's independence and establishing definitive boundaries, in return for which he was to be granted immediate release.[70] Before he could set sail, however, a mob of angry Texans removed him from the ship upon which he had embarked and demanded his execution. Though his life was spared by Houston's clemency, Santa Anna remained incarcerated in Texas for the balance of the year.

The Army of Operations contended with logistical and training deficiencies, but the Texas campaign was doomed to failure by inadequate planning, flawed execution, and consistent underestimation of enemy capabilities and intentions. Destruction of insurgent military forces, not seizure and retention of population centers, should have been the campaign's overriding operational objective. Once the Mexicans had gained control of Goliad and San Patricio, Béjar's original strategic significance disappeared. With Béjar isolated, a small residual force could easily have contained the Alamo defenders, freeing the preponderance of the Army of Operations for immediate employment against rebel forces in the interior of the province.[71] By choosing to expend his limited resources on a largely symbolic objective, Santa Anna lost momentum and forfeited the element of surprise that his very difficult and ably conducted cross-country march had achieved. Even his impetuous decision to attack on March 6 rather than await the arrival of his heavy artillery from Monclova wasted the advantage afforded when Urrea's fortuitous arrival at Goliad preempted the Alamo's reinforcement. During the planning conference for this attack, Generals Cós and Castrillón, and Colonels Joaquín Orisñuela (Aldama Battalion) and José María Romero (Matamoros Battalion), suggested delaying until the 12-pounder siege cannon were available to open a breach in the mission walls. But neither Santa Anna nor Ramírez y Sesma was disposed to wait.[72] Such impatience and lack of foresight cost the general-in-chief one-quarter of his available command in a battle that need not have been fought.

The relatively easy victories at Béjar, San Patricio, and Coleto lulled Santa Anna into a sense of complacency and overconfidence that affected his subsequent tactical decision-making. In pursuing the rebels along four separate axes of advance with only vague knowledge of their strength and disposition, the general-in-chief violated the principle of concentration and exposed his forces to defeat in detail. When his elusive quarry finally reappeared in the woody marshes of Buffalo Bayou, only one-quarter of the Mexican army was present to meet the assault, and that was employed with appalling negligence. Had Santa Anna maintained his forces intact and acquired a realistic appreciation of the enemy's capabilities and intentions, he likely would have defeated Houston and suppressed the Texas Revolution, at least for the moment. But the prevailing attitude among most Mexican senior officers toward the Texans and their insurrection was one of denigration and derision: "This will be no more than a military review," retorted General Castrillón to the implication by Colonel Sánchez Navarro that the Texans would give the Mexicans no end of headaches. "[D]o you believe that those miserable wretches will fire even one shot?"[73] Such contemptuousness played an instrumental role in the San Jacinto calamity.

Despite the losses sustained at San Jacinto, the Army of Operations still had 4,078 effectives in Texas and controlled most of the territory from the Brazos River westward.[74] Why then did Santa Anna abandon the campaign? Because operations dependent upon foraging are self-limiting by their very nature, logistics certainly were among the general-in-chief's overriding concerns. An army living off the land must keep moving to survive; remaining static for too long risks exhausting local food supplies. In Texas, forage was deficient to begin with and the Texans scorched much of what was available. "For reasons of supply alone," argues James Presley, "it appears that it was only a matter of time before the Mexican army would be forced to retire beyond the Rio Grande."[75] An equally plausible explanation is that Santa Anna could no longer envision a rapid end to the campaign once the insurgents had gained a signal victory; such events tend to attract new adherents, rejuvenate enthusiasm, and galvanize commitment to a cause. Quite possibly he finally recognized the futility of trying to subdue a predominately non-Mexican population coveted by an increasingly imperialistic United States. He also had been absent from Mexico City for a considerable period and may have perceived a need to bolster his deteriorating political fortunes.[76] In the long run, chronic political instability and fiscal impecuniousness likely would have precluded consolidation of Mexican authority even if Santa Anna had prevailed. In all probability the isolation of Texas from Mexico's core districts, its rapidly expanding Anglo population, and the growing aggressiveness of the United States eventually would have wrested the province from Mexican control.

Abandonment of the Texas campaign squandered an admirable performance by an inexperienced conscript army that had endured severe hardship and sustained heavy casualties.[77] For all the national treasure expended upon the army since independence, however, Mexico should not have had to raise an expeditionary force from scratch to confront this territorial exigency. The nation's costly investment in its military establishment should have produced at least a core of technically and tactically proficient veteran formations around which a larger force could rapidly have been assembled, equipped, and trained. But political divisiveness and sectional rivalry had rendered the permanent army's standing formations little more than local constabularies responsive chiefly to their respective warlords. As a result, Santa Anna was compelled to lead into Texas an improvised army comprising mainly conscripts who harbored little interest or enthusiasm for the venture into which they had been impressed.

The loss of Texas engendered such bitter and pervasive political factionalism throughout the ensuing decade that the government could not extricate itself from the endless recriminations over culpability for this national tragedy. Congress nullified Santa Anna's treaties with the Texans on May 20, declaring that Mexico would "vigorously" continue the struggle to reclaim its lost territory.[78] The anti-liberal newspaper *El Mosquito Mexicano* tried relentlessly to stir up sentiment for a renewal of the Texas campaign. But entrenched regionalism superseded nationalism as the disparate Mexican population spurned further attempts to mobilize support for what was viewed as an increasingly meaningless crusade.[79] Inevitably, the military was drawn into these partisan conspiracies, supporting one side or the other in a succession of *cuartelazos* that disrupted government and obstructed implementation of fiscal reforms essential to national economic development. Minister of War Tornel declared his resolve to prosecute the war even if it led to hostilities with the United States. But the pro-federalist northern state governors were disinclined to contribute scarce resources to strengthen a federal army that might instead be employed to repress their autonomy.[80] The Texas question and its attendant political ramifications also distracted the army from analyzing the mistakes of the Texas campaign and introducing appropriate institutional reforms. When United States military forces crossed the Nueces River in 1846, the Mexican army was only marginally better postured to contend with that territorial violation than it had been a decade earlier in Texas.

CHAPTER 4

The Army in the Decade of Centralism, 1834–45

Ironically the loss of Texas actually enhanced the army's near-term political standing as consensus for the immediate recovery of Texas temporarily abated ideological divisiveness. The government promptly announced its determination to recapture the lost province and set about refitting the army toward that end. The Army of Operations was withdrawn to the Rio Bravo, reinforced with 2,000 troops from the federal district, and redesignated the Army of the North, with general headquarters at Matamoros. Cleared of all charges regarding his decision to withdraw the Army of Operations from Texas, Filisola was appointed the new commander in May, 1837, relieving Nicolás Bravo, whose precarious health precluded further frontier service.[1]

The task of rebuilding the army, however, required a substantial outlay of funds that the national treasury simply could not accommodate. Despite imposition of new taxes, expenditures quickly exceeded revenues, frustrating plans for a timely reconquest.[2] Additionally, serious disturbances in San Luís Potosí and Sonora diverted government attention and consumed military resources that otherwise could have been applied to the Texas initiative. In concert, funding constraints, equipment shortages, recruiting difficulties, leadership discontinuity, and domestic turmoil thwarted efforts to mount a resolute and opportune campaign.

Santa Anna, meanwhile, had been released from confinement and in November, 1836, allowed to go to Washington to plead his case before President

Andrew Jackson. Meeting with Jackson in January, 1837, he reportedly offered to cede Texas to the United States in return for a "fair" consideration. Because Santa Anna no longer was an official representative of the Mexican government, and because the United States had received no such offers from the legally constituted regime, Jackson rejected the proposal.[3] Politically disgraced, but still popular within the military, Santa Anna returned to Mexico the following month and retired to Manga de Clavo.[4] Soon, however, the political fortunes of this remarkably resilient caudillo were resurrected by the endeavors of France to exact outstanding debts from a recalcitrant and penurious nation. The French blockade and subsequent invasion in December, 1838, provided a fortuitous opportunity for Santa Anna to redeem his reputation and rise again to the pinnacle of national prominence. It also eclipsed, at least temporarily, Mexican preoccupation with Texas.

The crisis arose over the issue of past debts owed by Mexico to France, losses incurred during the 1828 Parián Riot being the putative pretext for the claim.[5] The primary motivation for French intervention, however, was not collection of debts past due, but protection of the rights of its citizens residing in Mexico. Loss of income from declining import and export duties, coupled with liabilities incurred during the abortive Texas campaign, prompted the Mexican government to "resort to extraordinary levies on capital wherever it could be found."[6] The forced loans that followed fell particularly heavily on the foreign community, of which the French constituted the second largest element. Adamant that the Mexican government would not be allowed to fleece French subjects at its convenience, Baron Antoine Louis Deffaudis, the imperious French Chargé d'affaires, urged his government to use armed force to pressure Mexico into compliance.

Frustrated by Mexican intransigence, France dispatched a naval squadron, two 60-gun frigates and five brigantines under the command of Post Captain François Bazoche, to blockade the ports of Veracruz and Tampico, a strategy designed to force the issue by depriving Mexico of the revenues generated by its two most lucrative customs houses. Upon arrival at Sacrificios on March 21, 1838, Bazoche advised the Mexican government that in addition to the 600,000 peso indemnification, France also demanded the removal of certain objectionable officials from public office and extension of most-favored-nation trade status.[7] When Mexico rejected the exorbitant French demands, Bazoche and Deffaudis declared the country's ports in a state of quarantine on April 16, but refrained from attacking Ulúa until these punitive measures had been given a chance to achieve their intended purpose.

In the interim, Bazoche succumbed to the *vómito* and was replaced by Rear Admiral Charles Baudin, an officer with impressive military credentials who had lost an arm in Napoleon's service while fighting the British. Empowered with plenipotentiary authority to negotiate a settlement on behalf of his government, Baudin reached Sacrificios on October 26 accompanied by a formidable naval squadron of twenty-six vessels bearing 4,300 combatants.[8] Finding that Bazoche's tiny fleet had been able to maintain the blockade only at Veracruz, the admiral quickly acknowledged the propriety of a diplomatic resolution. Coincidentally, federalist uprisings in Michoacán, Puebla, and Sonora, and José Urrea's confiscation of Tampico customs revenues, rendered Mexican government leaders more amenable to arbitration.

In his first meeting with Foreign Minister Luís Gonzaga Cuevas at Jalapa on November 17, Baudin offered terms that eliminated the demand for removal of offending Mexican public officials but increased the indemnity to 800,000 pesos, presumably to defray the cost of both French naval expeditions. Not surprisingly, on November 27, Cuevas rejected the proposal, whereupon Baudin returned to his flagship and advised General Manuel E. Rincón, the fifty-four-year-old Perote native recently appointed military commander of Veracruz, that he intended to commence hostilities.[9] Early that afternoon, Baudin began a heavy bombardment of San Juan de Ulúa that continued until evening, when the French warships were withdrawn to protected anchorages for the night. The cannonade tore large gaps in the soft coral walls of the decaying fortress, dismounted several batteries, and exploded most of the ammunition stores.[10]

The escalating crisis presented Santa Anna with a serendipitous opportunity to rehabilitate his tarnished reputation and restore himself to national prominence. Arriving in Veracruz two days before the onset of hostilities, he tendered his services to General Rincón, who accepted the offer and instructed Santa Anna to assess the capability of Veracruz to withstand a determined French assault.[11] After conferring with General Antonio Gaona, the Ulúa commander, Santa Anna counseled Rincón to surrender the fortress and declare the city's neutrality. Rincón concurred and, the following day, Gaona delivered Ulúa to Baudin, who permitted its defenders to retire with honors. The general also agreed to a convention authorizing retention of a 1,000-man Mexican garrison in Veracruz and allowed the French fleet to reprovision on shore without opposition. Furious at the outcome of this episode, Bustamante repudiated the agreement, declared war against France, and issued a decree expelling all French subjects within two weeks. He also replaced the discredited Rincón with Santa Anna and ordered both Rincón and Gaona court-martialed. Santa Anna, who had returned to Manga de Clavo, hastened back to Veracruz on December 4, where he conferred with General Mariano Arista, recently arrived from Matamoros with Army of the North reinforcements, regarding measures to defend the port city.[12]

Responding to Bustamante's declaration of war, Baudin ordered three separate raiding parties of French marines to execute a surprise landing intended to capture both Santa Anna and Arista, thereby preventing a potentially devastating naval bombardment of the city. On December 5, under cover of an early morning fog, a column led by François Ferdinand d'Orleans, Prince of Joinville, just missed apprehending Santa Anna (who escaped by climbing over the rooftops) but did capture Arista, whom they found asleep in his lodgings. The French raiders then advanced to the barracks of la Merced, where they exchanged a warm fire with the defenders until the arrival of Baudin brought an end to that action. Lacking both the means and inclination to occupy the city, and all other missions having been accomplished, the admiral ordered Joinville back to the quay.[13]

Santa Anna used the time consumed by Joinville's impetuous foray to rally a contingent of Mexican troops, who engaged the invaders as they withdrew to their awaiting longboats. In the ensuing melee, grapeshot from a cannon covering the French reembarkation, killed Santa Anna's horse and mangled his left leg so badly that it required amputation below the knee. Despite these injuries, Santa Anna jubilantly notified War Minister José María Tornel that "Mexican arms secured a glorious victory in the plaza; and the flag of Mexico remained triumphant: I was wounded in this last effort and probably this will be the last victory that I shall offer my native land."[14] This incident endowed Santa Anna with the qualities of a martyr and restored the reputation he had squandered at San Jacinto, setting the stage for the caudillo's return to national political prominence. There appeared to be a "universal conviction," British Chargé d'affaires Richard Pakenham reported, "that [the Mexicans] have distinguished themselves by an heroic resistance to unjust oppression, and that they come out of the conflict with far more honor than their assailants."[15]

Although many Mexicans endorsed the expulsion of French citizens from Mexico, prominent federalists accused Bustamante of having purposefully allowed the confrontation to escalate in order to solidify centralist political power. To pressure Bustamante into renewed negotiations, Baudin astutely opened a well-publicized dialogue with the refractory José Urrea and lifted the blockade of Tampico, enabling the federalists to collect customs revenues.[16] Despite his aggressive posturing, federalist opposition and Mexico's collapsing economy obliged Bustamante to reopen negotiations with Baudin in February, 1839. Facilitated by the able mediation of Richard Pakenham and French eagerness to settle the affair, Mexican plenipotentiaries Manuel Eduardo de Gorostiza and Guadalupe Victoria concluded a treaty on March 9 in Veracruz. The treaty restored Ulúa to Mexico in the same condition as when it was seized and granted most-favored-nation status to both belligerents. A separate convention signed that same day required the Mexican government to pay $600,000 to indemnify the claims of French nationals made prior to November 26, 1838, and stipulated that all remaining disputes be submitted to third-country arbitration.[17]

In retrospect, France might have been better off consenting to mediation in the first place. The resulting treaty neither satisfied the compelling issue of retail trade nor guaranteed the absolute protection of French citizens from forced loans. Payment of the indemnity was the only discernible remuneration France had to show for its endeavors, and even that compensation was not entirely unqualified. Baudin's expedition not only failed to improve the status of French nationals in Mexico; it aggravated the circumstances upon which their affluence depended. The blockade harmed French merchants as much as it did Mexican, and the financial disorder and political agitation that followed in its wake inflicted further hardship upon the French colony.[18]

As the French threat receded, a recrudescence of federalist-inspired uprisings in the peripheral districts jeopardized Mexico's tenuous political stability. In late 1838 and early 1839, serious disturbances rocked the departments of Tamaulipas, Michoacán, Sonora, and Sinaloa, adding considerable distress to the government's already overextended resources.[19] The most alarming of these pronouncements occurred in November, 1838, when Generals José Urrea and José Antonio Mejía seized Tampico. The truculent Urrea had been appointed commandant-general of Sonora in recognition of his conspicuous service during the Texas campaign. However, displeased at not having been named governor as well, Urrea embraced federalism in December, 1837, and the following spring led a military column into neighboring Sinaloa intending to coerce that region into the federalist fold.[20] Bustamante countered by dispatching General Mariano Paredes with a military contingent large enough to crush the rebels. After successfully eluding Paredes for months, Urrea finally was brought to battle near Mazatlán in May, 1838, defeated, and forced to seek refuge in Durango. Making his way to Tampico, he and Mejía, who had just returned from New Orleans where he had been living in exile since his abortive attempt to capture Tampico in 1835, fomented a rebellion in October that coincided with the French blockade of Mexico's Gulf Coast.[21]

The Urrea-Mejía uprising led Bustamante to order 1,100 troops from General Valentín Canalizo's division at Matamoros to march on Tampico. On November 30, Canalizo launched a frontal attack on the city but was beaten back with the loss of 500 government soldiers.[22] The diversion of troops from the Matamoros garrison offers a pointed example of how domestic upheavals adversely affected initiatives to enhance peripheral security. The principal mission of that garrison was to protect the Rio Bravo frontier against both Texan and Apache incursions. The business of suppressing *cuartelazos* distracted from that task and impeded any serious efforts to reimpose Mexican control over Texas.

Canalizo's defeat accelerated disorder throughout Tamaulipas and contiguous regions, prompting Bustamante to seek permission from the supreme executive *(supremo poder conservador)* to take personal command of the campaign against the *tamaulipeco* insurgents. Appointing Santa Anna interim president on March 18, 1839, Bustamante left the capital the following day bound for San Luís Potosí, where General Mariano Arista was assembling an army comprising the Iguala Regiment and troops from the Matamoros and San Luís garrisons.[23] Before Arista could invest Tampico, however, the renegade generals adroitly force-marched their soldiers south to threaten the strategic Puebla-Veracruz road. Santa Anna reacted to this turn of events by deploying 500 troops from the Federal District to isolate Urrea and by calling out General Valencia's 1,600-man Puebla garrison to contend with Mejía.[24]

On May 3, in the vicinity of pueblo de Acajete and hacienda de San Miguel Lablanca, Valencia's troops decisively defeated Mejía's rebels in a fierce engagement that cost the participants some 600 casualties. Captured near Puebla, Mejía was summarily executed on Santa Anna's orders, presumably because he was considered a traitor for having conspired with the Texan secessionists in 1835. The elusive Urrea managed to flee to Tampico, where he lingered until General Mariano Arista's attack forced the city's surrender on June 5. Escaping once more, Urrea remained a fugitive until October, when he was finally captured in Tuxpan. The intractable general languished in Mexico City's dungeon of the Inquisition until federalist supporters engineered his escape on July 15, 1840.[25]

Santa Anna deftly exploited this latest interim presidency to rehabilitate his reputation, especially within the army. Adept at deriving maximum notoriety from the most mundane issues, Santa Anna and his disciples skillfully manipulated the press to extol the caudillo's virtues while denigrating his rivals. Following the Acajete triumph, for which he took maximum credit, Santa Anna was hailed as the Hero of Tampico, Veracruz, and Acajete; significantly, no mention was made of Texas. On May 8 he returned to a hero's reception in the capital, a clear indication that he finally had surmounted the mortifying stigma of the Texas campaign.[26] Despite such accolades, Santa Anna evidently believed that he had not yet amassed the military and political backing to confront Bustamante directly. Opting to wait for a more propitious opportunity, on July 10, 1839, he relinquished the acting presidency to Nicolás Bravo and returned to the serenity of Manga de Clavo.[27]

On July 17, after a four-month hiatus in San Luís Potosí, Bustamante returned to Mexico City and reclaimed the chief-executive post. To his dismay he found the government's financial condition markedly worse than before his absence. In combination the French blockade, proliferating insurrections, endemic banditry, and Indian depredations had exacted a severe toll upon an already impecunious federal treasury. The president's political standing also had been eroded severely by his lackluster performance in the Tamaulipas campaign, the renewed popularity that the Veracruz and Acajete episodes conferred upon his chief rival, and the dearth of discernible progress toward the recovery of Texas.[28]

In a preemptive effort to neutralize federalist clamor and placate public sentiment over the festering Texas question, in January, 1840, Minister of War Juan Nepomuceno Almonte expressed to Congress the administration's determination to resolve the issue: "The necessity and importance of restoring the lost part of that territory is undeniable, and likewise it is evident that to get it, no sacrifices can be omitted however costly they may be."[29] Transforming rhetoric into action, Bustamante expedited implementation of military reforms sanctioned by Congress during the previous two years. Laws promulgated on June 13 and November 30, 1838, authorized an increase in statutory federal army strength to 60,000, of which 33,000 were earmarked for the *permanentes.* Concomitantly the permanent army was reorganized into twelve infantry regiments of two battalions each and eight separate companies; eight cavalry regiments of two squadrons each, one separate squadron in Yucatán and one separate company in Tabasco; and three brigades of foot artillery and one brigade of light (mounted) artillery.[30]

This same legislation also provided for a new army general staff to centralize direction, preserve discipline, establish strict funds accountability, develop effective organizations, and plan for the future. Headed by a division general assisted by eight colonels and eight lieutenant colonels, the *plana mayor del ejército* absorbed the functions previously vested in the inspectors-general of infantry and cavalry, who had superseded the original general staff in 1828. Charged with verifying the regulatory compliance of all infantry and cavalry units, the inspector-general system had never performed as expected.[31] Concurrently a new series of mandatory reports was introduced to help keep the new general staff apprised of each major command's activities. These administrative and command and control enhancements led Almonte to propose increasing the number of brigade and division generals to fourteen and twenty-four, respectively.[32]

To furnish the expanded army with "scientific officers of proven honor, capable of introducing into the ranks useful knowledge and rigid customs," statutory enrollment at the Colegio Militar was expanded from 100 to 200 cadets. Doubling student capacity, however, overlooked the more critical issue of recruitment and retention. Since opening its doors in 1823, the military academy had never attracted enough candidates to fill all available seats. By 1831 the Colegio Militar had just thirty-one students, and these were housed in the run-down ex-convent of Betlemitas, accommodations unlikely to impress prospective applicants. Legislation promulgated in November, 1833, mandated the Colegio Militar's relocation to Chapultepec, but insufficient funding postponed that move until October 1841. In the interim, in September, 1838, the academy was removed to the equally dreary Casa de Arrecogidas. Rigid entrance standards and a lack of enthusiasm for military service among eligible males conspired to keep enrollment suppressed. Because the army officer corps desperately needed the professional socialization that only the Colegio Militar could provide, consistent failure to meet enrollment quotas had a particularly detrimental effect upon long-term professionalization of the army officer corps.[33]

Subsequent legislation authorized activation of a branch school *(escuela de aplicación)* to provide post-commissioning advanced technical and tactical training for artillery and engineer lieutenants and captains. Subordinated initially to the Colegio Militar, the *escuela de aplicación* represented the Mexican army's first tentative experiment with a tiered professional military educational system.[34] Within two years, responsibility for the institution was transferred to the Ministry of War, where it remained until the outbreak of hostilities with the United States. To the detriment of young army officers, however, the branch school concept never gained widespread acceptance and therefore failed in its objective to furnish the officer corps with the technical skills central to modernization.[35]

To spur enlisted recruitment, an annual lottery *(sorteo)* superseded the detested *leva,* which invariably had filled the ranks with criminals and malcontents since its inception. Conducted on the last Sunday of October, *sorteo* eligibility was limited to all bachelors and childless widowers between the ages of eighteen and forty who met established health and height prerequisites. Selectees were obligated to a six-year term that, with certain reservations, could be served by a paid substitute.[36] To make army service more attractive, a new system of accounting *(contabilidad)* was introduced to administer the military pay system and insure that soldiers received the weapons and equipment necessary to perform their missions successfully.[37] These recruiting enticements were complemented by normal schools *(escuelas normales)* set up in each corps to educate soldiers and return them to society with an awareness of their obligations as Mexican citizens. Unfortunately, because these educational facilities "had not produced the advantages that the government legislation had intended," Tornel, who succeeded Almonte as Minister of War, ordered them closed in 1846 as a cost-cutting measure.[38]

These earnest attempts at military reform notwithstanding, resource constraints and domestic disturbances precluded systematic and comprehensive implementation. Not surprisingly, those garrisons farthest removed from the core districts received the least attention. All along the northern frontier, steadily deteriorating presidial garrisons no longer could protect neighboring frontier communities from Indian attacks. The presidios themselves had fallen into disrepair, and the troopers lacked the weapons, clothing, and horses to carry out their missions effectively. In the Department of Chihuahua, Comanche and Mescalero Apache raids reduced formerly rich properties to "immense deserts," prompting the settlers to negotiate a peace accord with the Gila Apaches *(Jileños)* aimed at exploiting irreconcilable tribal enmities. Further south, Comanche penetrations generated so much anxiety in Durango, Zacatecas, and San Luís Potosí that armed settlers were mustered to serve as presidial auxiliaries.[39]

Minister of War Almonte was convinced that the only way to salvage the situation was to reequip the presidials completely, pay them with regularity, and institute consistent war-making policy. "The most certain means to make war upon such a cruel enemy," he advised Congress, "is that established in the Regulation of September 10, 1772 . . . because designated within are the actions which must be taken to reduce them to peace and avoid the grave damages they inflict upon the populations."[40] Truculent rhetoric, however, had little meaningful impact upon the intensity of Indian hostilities. In Coahuila, residents feared that an alliance between Comanches and Texans would enable the latter to occupy the contiguous borderlands, from which Mexican settlers had been driven. The recent *tamaulipeco* uprising heightened anxieties further by impeding "the general-in-chief of the Army of the North from dedicating his attention exclusively to repressing such a ferocious enemy." Although suppression of federalist unrest cleared the way for renewed offensive operations against hostile Indians in Tamaulipas, Nuevo León, and Coahuila, a serious punitive campaign could not be organized until the middle of 1841, and that accomplished very little.[41]

Political discontinuity, sectional disturbances, and proliferating Indian hostilities were increasingly perceived as evidence of Bustamante's inability to govern. Mexican citizens were further alienated by a series of progressive tax increases imposed in a futile attempt to service the national debt, operate the federal bureaucracy, and pay the military. Particularly irritating to domestic and foreign merchants alike was the fact that the *derecho de consumo,* a levy on imports, had escalated from 5 to 15 percent in 1839, bringing total taxes on imports to a suffocating 49.5 percent.[42] Unable to raise sufficient revenues through direct or indirect taxation, the president resorted to escalated borrowing, a baneful venture that put his government increasingly at the mercy of the infamous *agiotistas.* These financial speculators lent money to the government at high interest rates in return for guaranteed repayment from projected customs duties, thereby locking the government into an endless cycle of debt and borrowing, extrication from which was virtually impossible.[43]

Government insolvency affected especially the military, which went unpaid for months at a time. Forced to curtail weapons and equipment purchases and skimp on the maintenance necessary to keep its military installations in a reasonable state of repair, the Ministry of War was unable to pursue even modest modernization initiatives. Army ranks, moreover, continued to be filled by conscripted vagrants, criminals, and other societal malcontents who readily deserted when faced with the prospect of being posted to the far reaches of Yucatán, Tabasco, or the Texas frontier.[44] The recently inaugurated *sorteo,* intended to make conscription less discriminatory, simply had too many exemptions and exceptions to achieve that goal. Anyone with enough money could purchase a substitute or bribe his way off the selection roster. Even the army's traditional immunity from public criticism was seriously eroded by the Texas and Veracruz debacles and relentless Indian depredations in the North. *El Mosquito Mexicano,* a prominent anti-liberal newspaper of the time, lamented "the grossness, ignorance, viciousness and criminal behavior" that now seemed to characterize large segments of the military rank and file.[45]

Mounting discontent over Bustamante's regressive and ineffective policies culminated on July 15, 1840, when the 5th Infantry Regiment and the *activo* regiment, Comercio de México, pronounced against the government. Marching from the San Hipólito Barracks to the former Inquisition building, the rebels liberated the redoubtable José Urrea and then seized the national palace, where a surprised Bustamante was taken prisoner. With the national palace in rebel hands, Urrea invited inveterate federalist Valentín Gómez Farías to assume political leadership of the movement for the "Regeneration of the Mexican Republic."[46] The insurrection, however, could not succeed without backing from General Gabriel Valencia, who commanded the capital military garrison.

Born in Mexico City, Valencia began his military career in 1810 as a cadet in the Provincial Cavalry Regiment of Tulancingo. He participated in the royalist counterinsurgency campaigns before embracing Iturbide's Iguala manifesto, following which he served in several positions of increasing responsibility, including chief of staff to General Nicolás Bravo during the Texas campaign. Designated army chief of staff in 1839, Valencia later served as commander of the Army of the North, during which assignment he directed the ill-fated Mexican defense of Padierna.[47] Unimpressed by the rebels' chances of success, Valencia turned a deaf ear to Urrea's entreaty and occupied the *ciudadela* with the loyalist forces at his disposal. This would not be the last time Valencia's actions were instrumental to the outcome of a *cuartelazo*.

Fighting erupted at 2:00 P.M. and continued for the next twelve days, causing widespread damage and inflicting hundreds of casualties, most of whom were noncombatants killed or wounded by indiscriminate artillery fire.[48] "The cannon are roaring now," recorded Señora Frances Calderón de la Barca, an astute observer of contemporary events. "All along the street people are standing on the balconies, looking anxiously in the direction of the palace, or collected in groups before the doors, and the *azoteas,* which are out of the line of fire, are covered with men. They are ringing the tocsins—things seem to be getting serious."[49]

The rebels persevered until July 27, when Urrea suddenly opted to negotiate a formal surrender. The motivation behind the capitulation is unclear, but the lack of anticipated support from influential federalists and regional military commanders, fear of uncontrolled social upheaval, and the knowledge that Santa Anna was en route with a relief force probably quenched any thought of prolonging the contest.[50]

Unlike previous attempts to oust an incumbent Mexican president, this coup produced civilian casualties and property destruction on an unprecedented scale. "Some houses have become uninhabitable," relates Señora Calderón, "glass, pictures, clocks, plaster, all lying in morsels about the floor, and air-holes in the roofs and walls, through which these winged messengers of destruction have passed." Such appalling violence and fears of a repetition of "the scenes of pain and weeping" produced by the attacks on property during the Parián riot, clearly deterred federalist sympathizers from embracing the revolt.[51]

Despite the carnage and devastation, the insurrectionists were accorded the customary lenient terms of capitulation. The government agreed to spare the lives and property of those who had taken up arms against it and allow military or government employees who had supported the rebellion to retain their jobs. Such generosity was not, however, extended to the 5th Infantry Regiment, which had spearheaded the attempted coup. That formation was purged from the force structure and replaced with a new light-infantry regiment, one battalion of which was assigned to the capital, and the other scattered over Coahuila, Nuevo León, and Tamaulipas.[52]

Although unsuccessful, the federalist pronouncement of 1840 laid the foundation for Bustamante's downfall the following year. By the summer of 1841 the president had lost the support of all social classes, especially the merchants and landowners who had financed his ascension to power. A 30,000 peso contribution from disgruntled Guadalajara merchants was sufficient to persuade Mariano Paredes, Jalisco's preeminent caudillo, to take the lead against Bustamante. On August 8, 1841, a contingent of 700 rebels marched upon Guanajuato, beginning what was in effect a centralist revolt against centralism.[53] In the capital, Gabriel Valencia once again played the role of swingman in determining the outcome of this latest episode of political coercion. On this occasion, however, he threw the support of his 1,200-man garrison behind Paredes.

Bustamante responded by exacting from Congress a grant of extraordinary faculties and using that authority to organize loyalist resistance. For the next ten days, both factions consolidated their respective positions while sympathetic local merchants kept Valencia supplied with food and cash to pay his troops.[54] During this interlude, Señora Calderón noted, "The soldiers, in the day-time amuse themselves by insulting each other from the roofs of the houses and convents. Yesterday [September 11], one of the president's party singled out a soldier in the citadel and shot him, and then began to dance the *Enanos*, and in the midst of a step, *he* was shot, and rolled over, dead."[55]

On September 14, Generals Luís Cortazar, commandant-general of Guanajuato, and Fernando Franco, military commander of Zacatecas, along with dauntless southern caciques Nicolás Bravo and Juan Álvarez, declared for the rebels, precipitating similar defections from senior army commanders in Aguascalientes, Durango, Querétaro, and San Luís Potosí.[56] Biding his time in Veracruz until the outcome of the uprising was assured, Santa Anna finally discarded his facade of neutrality and occupied the Perote fortress with troops he had been readying, ostensibly as a Yucatán expeditionary force, and issued his Plan of Perote.[57]

Paredes, meanwhile, continued to advance upon the capital in a festive procession, the passage of which attracted the attention of the ever-vigilant Señora Calderón. "The infantry," she noted on September 27,

> was in a very ragged and rather drunken condition—the cavalry better, having *borrowed* fresh horses as they went along. . . . The sick followed on asses, and amongst them various masculine women, with *sarapes* and *mangas* and large straw hats, tied down with coloured hand-kerchiefs, mounted on mules or horses. The sumpter mules followed, carrying provisions, camp-beds, etc.; and various Indian women trotted on foot in the rear carrying their husbands' boots and clothes.[58]

The less-than-intimidating appearance of Paredes's rebels notwithstanding, desertions and collapsing morale rendered the capital's defenders even worse. In a last-ditch effort to retain power, Bustamante declared his conversion to federalism and called for restoration of the Constitution of 1824. But this transparent ploy failed to enlist the necessary support, and in the wake of a *pronunciado* attack on October 3 that routed loyalist defenders, the president surrendered what little remained of his military and agreed to the terms set forth in the Bases de Tacubaya.[59]

Through flexibility and political acumen, Bustamante had survived the incessant foreign crises, federalist pronouncements, and political intrigues that tormented Mexico between 1837 and 1841. However his alienation of the nation's financial and economic entrepreneurs brought an end to his regime. Eager for a form of government that would better accommodate their commercial interests, such businessmen were not averse to purchasing the military forces necessary to bring about that change. The separation from Mexico of Texas, Yucatán, and Tabasco roused military animosity toward a government they held responsible for these ignominious and humiliating territorial losses and rendered nominally loyal senior leaders amenable to coercive political change.[60]

On October 9, 1841, while Bustamante prepared for expatriation to Europe, the Council of Representatives appointed by Santa Anna elected the *caudillo* to yet another term as provisional chief executive, inaugurating what was in effect a government of the military and for the military.[61] In appointing Gómez Pedraza, Francisco García, and Crispiniano del Castillo as ministers of Foreign Relations, Treasury, and Justice, respectively, the new president endeavored to form a cabinet of conciliation. Coincidentally, however, he placed steadfast *santanista* Tornel at the helm of the war ministry, a rather neat arrangement that enabled the new regime to detail only officers of their choice to the commandancies-general and other influential posts. Nor did Santa Anna neglect his key supporters; Paredes was elevated to division general, and Luís Cortazar and Julián Jubera were advanced to brigade general.[62]

To mollify the refractory southern caciques the president granted Juan Álvarez and Nicolás Bravo a measure of de facto sovereignty by promising to create an independent territorial jurisdiction from the southern half of the Department of Mexico. Bravo remained steadfast, but the recalcitrant Álvarez abided government dictates only until 1844, when perceived impingements upon his regional prerogatives propelled him into the antisantanista camp. Appointment as commandant-general and governor of Sonora convinced former Texas campaign divisional commander and erstwhile rebel José Urrea to embrace the Tacubaya principles. Urrea's gubernatorial commission, however, displaced ardent centralist and archenemy Manuel María Gándara, immersing the department in four years of civil strife that cost an inordinate number of lives and diverted resources from economic development.[63]

With order restored and his allies momentarily placated, Santa Anna turned his attention to strengthening federal authority in the periphery, the achievement of which hinged on centralized operational control and modernization of the army. An undertaking of this magnitude entailed substantial expenditures to procure modern armaments, overhaul logistical systems, expand permanent army formations, and institute functional command and control procedures. Modest savings could be accrued by avoiding military campaigns against domestic adversaries, but these clearly were insufficient to defray anticipated outlays. To acquire the additional revenues needed, the president increased real estate and property taxes and imposed particularly onerous levies upon the archdiocese, always his favorite source of contingency funds.[64] These confiscatory measures abrogated the implicit alliance between a military president and the landed aristocracy that had been maintained since independence, drastically shrinking Santa Anna's base of support while augmenting his dependence upon the army. The federal income generated by these supplementary levies did, however, fund the activation of new permanent regiments in the departments of Querétaro, Michoacán, Veracruz, Jalisco, Oaxaca, Puebla, and México, the ranks of which were filled by means of a new *leva* that even some *hombres de bien* could not elude.

Despite the concerted effort to consolidate federal authority, relentless political squabbling continued to divert government attention from peripheral district concerns. Such conspicuous neglect affected especially the distant territory of Yucatán, whose fiercely pro-federalist residents hovered perpetually on the brink of insurrection. In February, 1840, a secessionist rebellion succeeded in driving General Joaquín Rivas y Sayas's understrength military garrison into the plaza de Campeche, where dwindling food supplies forced its surrender three months later. Overwhelmed with disturbances in Tampico, Tamaulipas, and Chihuahua, and lacking a naval force of any consequence, the government could do little to aid the beleaguered loyalists.[65]

Not until August, 1842, did Santa Anna take steps to reestablish government control of the recalcitrant province. On the twenty-sixth of that month a nominal expeditionary force composed of the Zacatecas and México *activo* battalions disembarked on the Isla del Carmen, which government troops secured following a brief skirmish with rebel defenders. On October 13, after receiving 1,000 reinforcements from the 2nd and 8th Infantry Regiments, Brigade General Juan Morales, a forty-year-old infantry officer from Puebla, invaded the Yucatán peninsula at Champotón but made no significant headway.[66] Even with the added reinforcement of General José Vicente Miñón's 2,720-man 2nd Brigade two weeks later, government forces still were unable to suppress the rebellion. Recognizing the futility of further military operations, Santa Anna acceded to an arrangement by which the province was granted virtual autonomy and exempted from new taxes and military recruitment levies.[67]

The de facto secession of Yucatán precipitated a corresponding declaration of independence from Tabasco, which at that time the federal government was equally powerless to influence. Not until June, 1843, was the

Ministry of War able to assemble, equip, and deploy an expeditionary force of a size sufficient to suppress the secessionists and restore order. Command of the campaign was entrusted to General Pedro de Ampudia, a veteran of Mexico's frontier army. Born in Havana in 1805, Ampudia arrived in Mexico just in time to join the Ejército Trigarante. Promoted to the rank of brigade general as recompense for his services in the 1829 campaign against Spanish General Isidro Barradas, he subsequently served in various capacities until being assigned divisional command in the Army of the North.[68] By July 11 the ruthless Ampudia had recaptured Tabasco and sent rebel leader General Francisco Sentmanat fleeing to safety in the United States.

After almost a year in exile, Sentmanat attempted to reenter the province with a force of just 70 men, augmented by 200 rifles for distribution to local sympathizers. Departing New Orleans on May 27, 1844, aboard the United States schooner *William A. Turner,* Sentmanat disembarked his rebels on the beaches of Tabasco after a brief standoff with the Mexican brigantine *Veracruzano Libre.* Ampudia responded to the incursion by dispatching a contingent of 100 infantry and 22 cavalry that engaged the invaders near the village of Jalpa on June 13, seizing all but a handful who managed to escape into a nearby woods. Sentmanat was apprehended the next day and summarily executed in accordance with the presidential decree of July 17, 1843. Thirty-eight of the 42 insurgents captured were accorded the same fate as their leader. As a deterrent to potential partisans, Ampudia ordered the severed heads of Sentmanat and 14 companions boiled in oil and their skulls prominently displayed in iron cages on the walls near the public square in San Juan Bautista. This brutal act earned Ampudia a not-undeserved reputation for cruelty, for which U.S. Army Brigadier General William Jenkins Worth dubbed him the "Culinary Knight."[69]

The loss of Yucatán and Tabasco, coupled with government failure to fulfill its pledge to recover Texas, engendered discontent among senior army commanders, who interpreted these ignominious developments as further evidence of inveterate executive weakness. With military allegiance waning and the newly elected Congress dominated by the liberal "disorganizing faction of 1833," Santa Anna chose to distance himself from the increasingly contentious proceedings. Appointing Nicolás Bravo substitute president on October 26, 1842, he withdrew to the insularity of Manga de Clavo, where he and Minister of War Tornel began a well-conceived campaign to bring about the dissolution of Congress and its replacement with a more compliant legislature.[70]

Under Tornel's skillful orchestration, an increasing number of senior military commanders were persuaded to join the growing chorus of centralists demanding wholesale changes to the ongoing constitutional project. Liberal intentions to abolish all immunities from civil law especially disquieted army leaders, who considered such legislation a flagrant attack upon martial prerogatives. The centralist crusade against the Congress of 1842 climaxed on December 19, when the Celaya Battalion, an element of Valencia's capital garrison, occupied the congressional building, forcing the deputies to withdraw to the home of Francisco Elorriaga.[71] In its wake, Bravo convened a Council of Notables *(junta de notables)*, whose ninety-two members were predominantly older military officers, landowners, and clerics "distinguished by their knowledge and patriotism." For the next four months this singularly unrepresentative assemblage of conservative elites strove to produce a political system that would completely reorganize the nation and eliminate the need for further constitutional reform.[72]

The fundamentally conservative and centralistic constitution emanating from this carefully concocted parody of representative government on June 12, 1843, strengthened executive authority by abandoning the fourth-power concept and vesting regional authority in governors chosen by the president from lists prepared by elected assemblies. It also declared Roman Catholicism to be the exclusive state religion and retained military and ecclesiastical *fueros,* while completely ignoring human rights and equality.[73] Under the new charter, known as the Bases Orgánicas, Santa Anna was elected by the departmental assemblies to a five-year presidential term on November 1. Rather than take up chief executive duties forthwith, however, he chose to delegate that responsibility to loyalist Valentín Canalizo and linger at el Encero, where since October 4 he had taken refuge from the vicissitudes of the national capital. This charade persisted until June 4, 1844, when pervasive discontent over rampant venality, escalating taxes, and dwindling military resources reached the point at which the *caudillo* judiciously reclaimed the reins of executive authority.[74]

As the central government grappled with ideological factionalism, secessionist movements, and Indian depredations, the Army of the North was engaging in limited-scale offensive strikes to keep alive Mexican claims on Texas. In February, 1842, Army of the North commander Mariano Arista ordered General Rafael Vázquez and 500 picked men to launch a surprise attack against Béjar.[75] Departing Matamoros on February 23 with a force of 241 regulars and 150 presidials, Vázquez reached his objective by March 5 but was discovered en route by "an evil Mexican from Laredo" who alerted the garrison. Having lost the element of surprise, Vázquez elected to negotiate a surrender following which he occupied the city, inflicting little damage to property or person, before returning to Matamoros.[76]

Santa Anna was most displeased with the results of this expedition, which he expected to "take by surprise and capture or put to the knife the garrison of adventurers who had taken possession of that town, as well as Goliad and Cópano." Terming the foray "a grave military failure" for having permitted the Texans to escape, Minister of War Tornel ordered Vázquez to present himself in Mexico City without delay to answer for his actions. Arista was in turn, reprimanded for "qualifying as glorious deeds a failure that merited the most severe penalty according to the strictest military laws." The castigating tone of this confidential dispatch so infuriated Arista that he turned over interim command of the Army of the North to General Isidro Reyes (commandant-general of Coahuila) and departed Matamoros in May, 1842.[77]

As a show of Mexican military force, Tornel ordered a follow-up raid to occupy Béjar and clear all "adventurers" from the west bank of the Guadalupe River between Goliad and Cópano. This expedition was to last no longer than one month, and General Reyes cautioned the commander, General Adrian Woll, not to join any action "without insuring that the enemy is weaker than us, and to the extent possible, care should be taken in armed clashes not to have them occur in wooded terrain, nor in fortified points."[78] Still smarting from the San Jacinto experience, Mexican army commanders were understandably leery of engagements in heavily wooded areas.

The French-born Woll began his military career at age eighteen in Napoleon's army. Emigrating to the United States in 1815 he enlisted in the United States Army, serving as Winfield Scott's field adjutant before joining liberal Spanish adventurer Francisco Javier Mina's ill-fated Mexican expeditionary force in 1816, which he survived by expatriating himself to New Orleans for a respectable period. His return to Mexico and subsequent contribution to Santa Anna's 1829 Tampico expedition, earned him a regular army commission as a lieutenant colonel. Promoted to brigade general in 1832, he served as Santa Anna's quartermaster for the Texas campaign, following which he was reassigned to Matamoros as commander of the Army of the North's 2nd Division.[79]

Woll's expedition reached Béjar without incident on September 10 and entered the city at four-thirty the following morning after posting detachments to block the principal routes of egress. In a redoubt near the center of town the Mexicans encountered a force of some 150 Texans, who after a thirty-minute exchange of fire, agreed to surrender unconditionally. The defenders, half of whom escaped in the confusion and early morning fog, suffered twelve killed and three wounded. Woll's losses amounted to one dead and twenty wounded.[80] Consolidating his position in Béjar, Woll carried out the prescribed reconnaissance of the Guadalupe River. Satisfied that his mission had been accomplished, he prepared to return to Matamoros. But the sudden appearance of a large contingent of mounted Texans on September 18 interrupted his departure. Moved to action the Mexicans chased the Texans into a wooded area adjacent the Salado Creek, some twelve miles east of Béjar. In the descending darkness a coordinated cavalry charge and infantry assault finally put the Texans to flight, but the engagement cost Woll 29 dead and 58 wounded. Texan losses were reported at 180 dead and 15 captured. Two days later, Woll struck his tents and began a return march to the Rio Bravo. Except for a brief encounter with the advance guard of a pursuing force of 600 Texans, the Mexicans reached their destination without further incident.[81]

The Mexican forays into Texas did not go uncontested for long. On December 7, 1842, an 800-man contingent of Texans occupied Laredo without opposition and, ten days later, followed up that success by seizing Guerrero. The Army of the North responded to these incursions by redeploying 470 of Pedro de Ampudia's 1st Division soldiers from Matamoros to Mier, the next likely Texan objective. Bolstered with 163 auxiliaries from Colonel Antonio Canales's command, Ampudia set out after the Texans on December 24 but returned that same day without having found them.

On the evening of December 25, having learned of the Mexican military presence at Mier, Texan commander General William S. Fisher launched an attack that secured the outskirts of the town but could penetrate no farther. The following morning, Ampudia positioned his cavalry between the Texans and their river-crossing sites, deployed his infantry to harry the intruders from the front, and committed his reserves to the enemy's flanks. Pressed from all sides "and realizing that they would be put to the knife at the first signal," Ampudia called upon the Texans to capitulate. After some deliberation, General Fisher acceded and delivered into Mexican hands 242 prisoners and a sizable quantity of weapons.[82] Ampudia's success at Mier prompted his elevation to command of the Army of the North on January 27, 1843. Within two months, however, he vacated that position to take over the expeditionary force being formed to suppress Francisco Sentmanat's Tabasco rebellion.

An armistice signed on February 15, 1844, suspended these cross-border incursions until repudiated by Santa Anna when he resumed the presidency in June.[83] Resolved to prolong the confrontation, the president elevated faithful *santanista* Valentín Canalizo to command the Army of the North. His appointment confirmed, Canalizo proceeded to San Luís Potosí on June 13 to assemble an army of operations with troops requisitioned from San Luís, Aguascalientes, Zacatecas, Jalisco, Michoacán, Guanajuato, and Querétaro. Military preparations, however, were interrupted by Santa Anna's abrupt vacation of the presidency on September 12, a development obliging Canalizo to return to the capital and resume his acting chief executive duties.[84] Mariano Arista succeeded Canalizo as commander of the Army of the North, but the government's inability to provide adequate funding and the refusal of the commandants-general to release the forces earmarked for this campaign, ultimately led to its cancellation.

Intended to inflict maximum damage and humiliation at minimal cost, these limited-objective incursions into Texas were manifestations of Mexico's lingering obsession with its erstwhile province. Unable to assemble and sustain the military force necessary to threaten Texan independence seriously, the Mexican government attempted to maintain a facade of belligerency through raids that accomplished little other than expanding the army's casualty rolls. As Mexico's lone sentinel along the Rio Bravo, the 3,000-man Army of the North bore the brunt of such fantasies. Inadequate training, materiel shortages, wretched living conditions, and prolonged intervals without pay notwithstanding, these hardy frontier veterans managed to perform their border security mission with commendable diligence and surprising success.[85]

Mexican bitterness over Texas was further aggravated by United States President John Tyler's unsuccessful attempt to push a treaty of annexation through the Whig and Abolitionist-dominated Senate. Reckoning that a potential showdown over Texas would generate the consensus necessary to advance his bid for broader executive powers, Santa Anna proclaimed that the passage of any act incorporating Texas would be considered tantamount to a declaration of war. The Mexican Congress, however, was decidedly more pragmatic about the nation's chances for recovering the lost province, and its members were becoming increasingly receptive to British offers to guarantee the territorial integrity of California in return for Mexican recognition of Texan independence. It was also apparent that the resources necessary to reoccupy Texas were nonexistent and that such an enterprise surely would drag the country into a full-scale war with the United States, for which it was dreadfully unprepared.[86] While the Congress approved modest tax increases and authorized conscription of 30,000 additional soldiers, the legislators adamantly rejected the president's request for a 10 million peso forced loan. Mexican public opinion, they realized, clearly demanded accountability for taxes that already had been collected to finance the interminable Texas conflict.[87]

Incessant regional instability, economic stagnation, and fiscal immoderation kept the national treasury penniless and ultimately cost Santa Anna the support of the political factions upon which his power rested. His intemperate spending made inevitable the imposition of new taxes to sustain military and governmental operations, alienating his landowning and ecclesiastical constituencies, upon whom the heaviest tax burden fell. Most of the revenue generated from these new levies, moreover, was frittered away on executive opulence and other comparably nonproductive pursuits. Little was applied toward military modernization or the infrastructural development necessary to create a self-sustaining, income-generating economic base. By mid-1844 the Church and the landed aristocracy had reached their respective limits as sources of supplemental revenue. Additionally, Santa Anna's apparent acquiescence to territorial losses and ill-advised decision to replace popular Minister of War Tornel with ardent *santanista* Isidro Reyes estranged fealty within the army.[88] Faced with overwhelming political opposition and divested of his traditional bases of support, Santa Anna's centralist regime was teetering on the brink of collapse.

Patiently waiting in the wings for just such a manifestation of weakness was General Mariano Paredes, who harbored an array of long-standing personal grievances against Santa Anna. Particularly vexing was an incident that had occurred the previous March: Paredes was appointed governor and commandant-general of the Department of Mexico only to be peremptorily relieved of those posts and briefly incarcerated by acting president Valentín Canalizo following an inebriated confrontation with General José Mariano Salas.[89] Before committing himself to such an irreversible course of action, Paredes methodically surveyed the other major regional commanders to determine their receptivity to a coercive change of government. On November 2, 1844, convinced he had sufficient backing to insure success, Paredes denounced the incumbent regime for its heavy taxes, unresolved territorial issues, and misuse of public funds and mobilized the military forces he had been assembling to accompany him to his new post in Sonora.[90]

Four days later, apprised of Paredes's pronouncement, Santa Anna gathered the troops he had taken with him upon vacating the presidency in September and departed Jalapa to suppress the rebellion. Arriving at Guadalupe Hidalgo on November 18, he paused to collect stragglers and incorporate additional troops from that district. Continuing on to Querétaro, he again halted his advance on November 24 to reorganize and prepare for further operations.[91] Meanwhile, on December 6 the political crisis in Mexico City was resolved without a shot being fired, José Joaquín de Herrera having persuaded Canalizo to yield the presidency voluntarily. In the aftermath of this "three hour revolution," Congress declared Herrera interim president and voted to strip Santa Anna of his authority as army commander-in-chief.[92]

Upon learning that the Congress had ordered him to relinquish command to General Pedro Cortazar and report to the capital to answer the charges against his provisional administration, Santa Anna advanced menacingly toward Mexico City. Galvanized into action by this turn of events, the government urged Paredes to march on the capital forthwith and summoned General Bravo from the south to coordinate the city's defenses. Coincidentally the commandants-general of Querétaro, Michoacán, San Luís Potosí, Zacatecas, Aguascalientes, and Guanajuato were ordered to place their forces at Paredes's disposal. Reaching the capital on January 5, 1845, Paredes's 4,000 soldiers soon were joined by Bravo's 1,420 and Álvarez's 2,000, bringing to nearly 15,000 the total number of troops with which Santa Anna would have to contend.[93]

The steady influx of defenders convinced Santa Anna to bypass the capital and proceed directly to Puebla, where he anticipated raising additional forces. Instead he found that city mobilized in opposition and well prepared to defend itself. Between January 2 and 10 he launched a series of uncoordinated probes that General Ignacio Inclán's defenders repelled with significant losses to the attackers. With desertions increasing daily and scant prospect of near-term success, Santa Anna abandoned the siege on January 11 and withdrew toward the coast in the company of 500 cavalry. Judging the situation hopeless, General Juan Morales and 5,149 of his infantrymen went over to the government, and the remaining cavalry submitted to General Álvarez.[94] On January 15, Captain Amado Rodríguez and his auxiliaries apprehended a fugitive Santa Anna near the village of Jico. Convicted of treason and sentenced to life-long exile, the ex-president was confined in the Perote fortress for four months. Following his release, on June 3 he set sail for Havana, where he remained in exile until the following year, when he connived his way back to Mexico.[95]

José Joaquín de Herrera's selection as chief executive was attributable more to widespread discontent with Santa Anna than to any genuine enthusiasm for him personally. Born in Jalapa in 1792, Herrera joined the royalist army in 1809 as a cadet in the Regiment of the Crown and participated in many counterinsurgency campaigns against Hidalgo and Morelos before embracing the Iguala manifesto. Subsequently he served as commandant-general of several states and minister of war in 1834 and again in 1836, after which he remained militarily inactive and out of politics for almost the entire decade of centralism.[96] Herrera inherited a government on the brink of bankruptcy and with meager prospects for acquiring alternative sources of revenue. Convinced that federal outlays could be pared significantly through military reform, the new president instructed Minister of War Pedro García Conde to develop proposals for a sweeping institutional overhaul.

An engineer and former director of the Colegio Militar, who understood the dynamics of military modernization, the thirty-nine-year-old Sonoran attributed the army's chronic weakness and inefficiency to organizational flaws that inhibited training and fomented regionalism. "The system of disseminating the national army in pueblos, cities and department capitals," García Conde asserted, "has produced deplorable results: the isolation of small factions among large populations, has made it impossible for them to become accustomed to war maneuvers; and what is more, distracted in the midst of these amusements, the officers and soldiers contracted habits that were hardly military."[97] Such conditions adversely affected the state of military discipline, led to the abandonment of duties and training, and made it nearly impossible to bring large units together for coordinated military campaigns. Moreover, much of the crime plaguing large cities could be attributed to soldiers who left their garrisons armed and at odd hours of the night. As a remedy, García Conde proposed regrouping scattered permanent army formations into single-garrison divisions, where units could train routinely under the supervision of "experienced, loyal and patriotic generals."[98] Reducing the number of quasi-independent regional commands and consolidating military authority, he believed, also would attenuate parochialism and discourage *cuartelazos.*

In the first major jurisdictional reordering in twenty years, García Conde supplanted the twenty-two commandancies-general with four military divisions and five commandancies-general, the latter encompassing the country's northern and southern peripheries, where virtual states of war persisted with the indigenous population. Territorial responsibility was allocated to each of the military divisions as follows: 1st Division (Toluca)—México, Querétaro, and Michoacán; 2nd Division (Jalapa)—Puebla, Veracruz, Tabasco, and Oaxaca; 3rd Division (Lagos)—Jalisco, Zacatecas, Aguascalientes, San Luís Potosí, and Guanajuato; 4th Division (Monclova)—Coahuila y Téxas, Nuevo León, and Tamaulipas. The five commandancies-general encompassed New

Mexico, Chihuahua, and Durango; Sonora and Sinaloa; Baja and Alta California; Yucatán; and Chiapas. A subsequent adjustment created a fifth military division to which responsibility for New Mexico, Durango, and Tamaulipas was assigned. This territorial arrangement remained unchanged through the war with the United States.[99]

Military and civil authority in the departments was separated, felony prosecutions returned to civilian magistrates, a merit-based promotion system introduced, and the inordinate officer-to-enlisted ratio rectified. The general staff was brought up to the strength specified in the legislation of October 30, 1838, and assigned responsibility for verifying compliance with standing regulations and orders.[100] The Colegio Militar's three-year curriculum was revamped to include mathematics, chemistry, physics, artillery, fortifications, architecture, astronomy, and land surveying. Additionally cadets were required to learn French and English and study modern tactics. The expanded technical curriculum reflected the influence of the French military educational system, in which artillery and field fortifications traditionally had received primacy. Overall the goal of the Colegio Militar was to provide the permanent army with forty to fifty new ensigns *(alférezes)* each year.[101]

Approval by the United States Congress on March 3, 1845, of a joint resolution offering annexation to Texas, reanimated the moribund civic-militia debate. With the entire army committed to the recovery of Texas, the radicals argued, the country needed a reserve to maintain internal security and furnish battle-casualty replacements. García Conde concurred in principle with this assessment, adding, "As a reserve, the active militia is insufficient, as it is composed solely of a limited number of regiments, battalions and squadrons, in complete discordance with what it ought to have as a national reserve." Near-constant mobilization had put *activo* service "on a par with line infantry," and its training, replacement, and equipment needs were now virtually identical to those of the permanent army. The minister of war proposed supplanting the active militia with a national guard *(guardia nacional)* that could augment the regulars in times of crisis and attend to sectional matters outside the permanent army's purview without impinging upon local industrial and agricultural productivity.[102] Initially, concern that the radicals might mobilize such a force to drive him from office dissuaded Herrera from endorsing the national guard concept. But the Texas union vote in July, 1845, provided the impetus to overcome his resistance.

Commanded by local authorities the unpaid volunteers of these new national guard units were to be assembled only in the event of foreign invasion or some comparable national emergency, as determined by the federal executive. The enabling legislation for this initiative, however, imposed such rigid eligibility criteria that few citizens actually qualified for service. As a result, outside the capital itself, only a handful of units were ever activated.[103] García Conde's military reforms were both pragmatic and visionary, but political factionalism and regional obstinacy thwarted their opportune implementation. Moreover, too little time remained for Mexico to transform its fragmented and politicized army into a cohesive and proficient fighting force capable of repelling a determined invasion by its well-endowed northern neighbor.

The amalgamation of ideological rivalry, regional segregation, national penury, domestic instability, and external crises preoccupied and debilitated the Mexican army throughout the decade of centralism. Chronically on the brink of bankruptcy, the federal treasury seldom could appropriate funds sufficient to meet the army's logistical needs. Moreover, too much of what was allocated eventually found its way into the personal coffers of senior officers. Besides inhibiting timely mobilization and training cohesion, the physical separation of units helped politicize the army by entrenching the personalized leadership of local military commanders. Attempts by the federal government to abridge regional autonomy met vigorous resistance from the affected *caciques,* often engendering *pronunciamientos.* Periodic peasant uprisings and relentless Indian hostilities further depleted the federal till and kept military formations perpetually engaged in a constabulary role. Relegated by these interminable domestic confrontations to service as an instrument of social control, the army could never acquire the proficiency, unit coherence, and nationalistic ardor that constitutes the bedrock of an effective fighting force.

Sporadic foreign challenges to territorial sovereignty spawned exigencies that dissipated the nation's military and financial resources even further. Because permanent army formations were either too dispersed or too poorly prepared for timely response, such external crises required assembly of an army of operations from scratch. Rugged topography and rudimentary transportation arteries prevented standing units from deploying rapidly to endangered areas and, once there, from being sustained with a reliable flow of logistical commodities. Soldiers were compelled to live off the land or sustain themselves with near-worthless government drafts. Such wretched living conditions constituted just one of many palpable reasons why Mexicans of eligible age equated military service with incarceration. Such low regard for martial duty filled army ranks with disruptive, indolent, and untrainable conscripts prone to desert at the first opportunity. As deteriorating relations with the United States pushed Mexico ever closer to war, the Herrera regime scrambled to bring its chronically ignored and misutilized frontier military formations to a state of readiness that offered a reasonable chance of defeating a resolute invasion. But the endemic and enervating political chaos of the decade of centralism had rendered the nation's military establishment incapable of preserving territorial integrity.

CHAPTER 5

The War with the United States: The Northern Campaign, 1846

Determined to add Texas to the American union, President James K. Polk applied a process of graduated pressure designed to bring about Mexican acquiescence. But this gambit failed to appreciate that the loss of Texas remained an unacceptable affront to Mexican national dignity and honor. Despite Mexico's precarious financial condition, government leaders consistently rejected all offers of pecuniary settlement from the United States. Even political officials who acknowledged the futility of pursuing reincorporation were compelled by public opinion to maintain a facade to the contrary. Such intransigence was motivated in part by the notion that, should war occur, United States preoccupation with Britain over Oregon would enhance Mexico's chances of reclaiming Texas. The diplomatic impasse emanating from these mutual miscalculations led ultimately to open hostilities the outcome of which cost Mexico nearly one-half its national territory.[1]

The causes of the Mexican-United States War have been the subject of considerable research and scholarly articulation. In essence there are two schools: those who place the blame on Mexico and those who condemn the United States as the principal culprit. Among the former is the eminent historian Justin H. Smith, who asserts that "hostilities were deliberately precipitated by the will and act of Mexico." His position has been assailed by Glen W. Price, who counters that "Smith's work in all its argument that pertained to the origins of the war, was simply preposterous as history." Seymour V. Conner and Odie B. Faulk argue, in their reasonably balanced synthesis of the war, that "the annexation of Texas precipitated a reaction among patriotic zealots in Mexico which produced war—California, Polk, Manifest Destiny, claims, Nueces boundary notwithstanding."[2]

Not surprisingly, Mexican historians incline toward a more parochial viewpoint, the majority tending to exonerate their own country. Mexico is not without culpability in the events that led to armed conflict with the United States, but the preponderance of evidence supports the position persuasively argued by Glen Price.[3] Clearly it was President James K. Polk's avowed intention to secure the Rio Bravo as the recognized international boundary and acquire possession of both Upper California and New Mexico. Whether these objectives were attained through negotiation or by force was not of overriding concern. The contentious nature of Mexican politics and the country's chronic insolvency simply made the task that much easier to achieve.

Knowing that Mexico lacked the military strength to retake Texas, President Herrera was inclined to extend official recognition to the nascent republic in return for a pledge to remain independent of the United States. However, the new chief executive's diplomatic initiatives were subverted by United States Congressional approval to admit Texas into the union and subsequent Texan ratification of that legislation.[4] Still bent on averting hostilities, Foreign Minister Manuel de la Peña y Peña advised United States Chargé d'affaires John Black that the Mexican government was "disposed to receive the commissioner *[comisionado]* of the United States who may come to this capital with full powers from his government to settle the present dispute in a peaceful, reasonable and honorable manner."[5]

For this delicate role, Polk appointed John Slidell, a capable Louisiana lawyer and eminent Spanish language scholar. The United States emissary arrived in Mexico City on December 8 and presented his credentials to Peña y Peña, but the Council of Government rejected them, and Slidell was forced to withdraw to Jalapa and await new instructions. Meanwhile, deliberately leaked news of these tenuous preliminary diplomatic activities precipitated a public remonstrance that only intensified when it became known that Slidell brought, not proposals to settle the Texas dispute, but offers of indemnification for relinquishing New Mexico, Upper California, and all territory between the Bravo and Nueces Rivers. "A few months more," railed the radical newspaper *La Voz del Pueblo,* "and we will have no country at all!"[6]

Mexican public opinion at this time was sanguine regarding the nation's prospects for success in an armed confrontation with the United States. A majority of educated citizens believed that the United States Army was weak, that American volunteers would not fight outside their own borders, and that growing regional animosity over the issue of slavery rendered the United States politically unstable. Outwardly, many Mexicans expressed confidence that in the event of war, such glaring deficiencies would insure a national triumph. Among this same element, however, were those who harbored a private sense of impending doom.[7]

While Herrera continued to pursue a diplomatic solution to the Texas question, the public clamor for action induced him to begin placing the country on a war footing. American annexation of Texas had added to the Mexican army's missions the burden of defending an exposed and ill-defined northern border against a potentially hostile and unpredictable adversary. The redefined strategic landscape forced the war ministry to bolster its military garrisons along the Rio Bravo. Accordingly the President ordered Mariano Paredes's Army of the Reserve to the Texas frontier to reinforce Arista's Army of the North against the eventuality of an incursion by General Zachary Taylor's Army of Occupation, presently ensconced at Corpus Christi. Paredes, however, refused to comply, rejoining that he "did not have the resources and supplies to make the long march and that he must protect the merchants in his area going to the fairs."[8]

Incensed by such flagrant insubordination, Herrera ordered Paredes to relinquish command to General Filisola and report in person to the capital. Instead, Paredes began lining up the military support necessary to overthrow the government. On December 14 he published his Plan of San Luís Potosí, which accused the president of trying to "dissolve the army" by destroying its source of income, treating with an envoy regarding the disposition of national territory, and engendering chaos and anarchy.[9] The ensuing defection of General Valencia, once again the swingman, left Herrera with insufficient military strength to suppress the *pronunciados*. Reconciled to defeat, Herrera resigned the presidency on December 30, admonishing the mutineers that "the consequences of this civil war will not fall upon my government, whose conduct has done nothing to provoke it."[10]

Like many of his contemporaries, the forty-nine-year-old Paredes had begun his military career as a cadet in a royalist army regiment, participated in the counterinsurgency campaigns against Hidalgo and Morales, and finally joined Iturbide's Ejército Trigarante. By the time he was promoted to brigade general in 1832, he already had acquired a reputation as an ardent centralist. He was petulant and haughty, character traits that likely retarded his ascendancy in rank. His appointment as commandant-general of Jalisco in 1838 afforded him an opportunity to consolidate his centralistic political ideology within that largely conservative department. His subsequent election as interim president by a junta of two representatives per department was the culmination of a three-week uprising that demonstrated once again the military's unattenuated propensity for removing unpopular chief executives. In this latest episode, however, the attendant political instability debilitated the nation's most proficient fighting force just as the border confrontation with the United States was heating up.[11]

Polk responded to the Mexican government's rebuff of John Slidell by extending United States military protection in Texas all the way to the Rio Bravo. On January 13, 1846, Secretary of War William L. Marcy instructed Taylor to:

> advance and occupy, with the troops under your command, positions on or near the east bank of the Rio del Norte, as soon as it can be conveniently done with reference to the season and the routes by which your movements must be made. . . . It is not designed, in our present relations with Mexico, that you should treat her as an enemy; but should she assume that character by a declaration of war, or any open act of hostility towards us, you will not act merely on the defensive, if your relative means enable you to do otherwise.[12]

This blatant show of force was calculated to reinvigorate the mediation process, but Polk's advisors had underestimated the depth of popular animosity in Mexico and the implacable political opposition to territorial compromise. The Slidell mission merely aggravated tensions by pursuing an agenda designed to purchase the territories in question rather than reach a mutually acceptable accommodation.[13]

Confident that Mexico would neither invade Texas nor declare war, Polk adamantly opposed reducing demands for territorial concessions. He expected his emissary to employ gradual coercion to negotiate nothing less than an immediate boundary settlement favorable to the United States. Polk's adverse impressions of Mexico were reinforced by renewed political dissension inspired by Santa Anna's inveterate scheming.[14] Colonel Alejandro J. Atocha, a confidential agent for the exiled caudillo, reportedly advised Polk in February, 1846, that in return for $30 million, the former president was amenable to a Rio Bravo boundary and territorial concessions encompassing both California and New Mexico. He also suggested that the United States convey the impression that Santa Anna was coerced into the agreement by blockading Veracruz and advancing a military force to the Rio Bravo. Although there is no irrefutable evidence that Polk was influenced by Santa Anna's machinations, subsequent military actions closely replicate Atocha's original proposals.[15]

Determined to pursue an end that Mexican stubbornness clearly indicated could not be achieved through negotiation, Polk opted for a military solution.[16] Taylor's Army of Occupation was ordered into the disputed territory, prompting the Mexican government to reinforce its endangered Matamoros garrison with a contingent of 2,200 troops led by General Pedro de Ampudia. Taylor's encroachment also elicited from President Paredes on March 21 a cautiously worded manifesto that endeavored to placate anti-American sentiment in Mexico without offending the United States.[17] Despite his previous remonstrances against Herrera's diplomatic initiatives, Paredes realized that Mexico was neither militarily nor fiscally prepared to take on the United States in armed conflict. But efforts to pursue a negotiated settlement were seriously impeded by his obdurate declarations of Mexican territorial sovereignty.[18] Polk's strategy of graduated pressure had succeeded in pushing the Mexican president into a corner where political realities rendered extrication exceedingly difficult. However, in his assumption that military coercion would persuade Paredes to exchange national territory for cash, the American president badly miscalculated. Given a choice of war or territorial concessions, Mexican political and military leaders responded not logically but patriotically, however improbable the prospects of success.[19]

The Mexican army poised on the brink of armed conflict with the United States listed a paper strength of 18,882 permanent troops, which were scattered about the country in a multitude of regional garrisons. Organized into twelve infantry regiments (of two battalions each), eight regiments and one squadron of cavalry, three artillery brigades, five foot artillery companies *(compañías fijas de pie)*, one dragoon brigade, and one battalion of sappers, these units answered more to their regional commanders than to federal military authority. The *permanentes* were supplemented by 10,495 *activos* apportioned into nine infantry and six cavalry regiments. Presidial companies reported 1,174 additional troops, but War Minister Almonte acknowledged that the *presidiales* existed "in name only."[20]

The general staff, despite its reconstitution in 1838, remained incapable of the coordination and supervision necessary to endow the army with centralized direction. Moreover, previous attempts at recruitment reform had failed to eradicate the detested *leva,* and the ranks continued to be filled with reluctant conscripts hauled off to the nearest *cuartel,* where harsh discipline spurred desertions on a massive scale.[21] The quality of the force was not enhanced when Paredes decreed, on April 23, 1846, that all persons lacking visible means of support were to be arrested, tried, and mustered into the army if convicted of vagrancy.[22] Such unremitting turbulence and the contentious attitude of the soldiers themselves made effective training virtually impossible.

The troops also were inadequately fed, erratically paid, and poorly clothed and equipped. Most infantrymen still carried the *morena licha,* the .753-caliber, smoothbore, flintlock musket of British manufacture that predated the Texas Revolution. Cavalrymen were armed with the same lances, sabers, and carbines *(tercerolas)* used during the previous decade. Although somewhat better trained, artillerymen had to contend with antiquated Griveaubal cannon of various calibers that imposed upon the army's fragile logistic system an unremitting problem of carriage repair and ammunition resupply. At the outbreak of hostilities, Mexico had just 140 cannon capable of operating in the field, and some of those were too dispersed to be readily available.[23]

In the absence of designated government depots, the army had to obtain its supplies from nearby communities or forage off the land. Because local procurement most often was compensated via unredeemable drafts on the treasury, the troops frequently went hungry, encouraging desertions, mutinies, and larcenies. The Mexican military posture in 1846 clearly demonstrates that previous reform initiatives had done very little to rectify the organizational, logistical, and training deficiencies responsible in large measure for the Texas debacle. Despite the pervasive trauma of that humiliation, military preparedness continued to suffer from political adversarialism and regional instability, with disastrous consequences for national territorial sovereignty.

In contrast to Mexico, the United States possessed the industrial capacity, political stability, and economic prosperity to mobilize, equip, and sustain a more technically and tactically proficient military apparatus. In 1845 the United States Army comprised just fourteen regiments the majority of which were deployed in small garrisons along the Indian and Canadian frontiers. Taylor's Army of Occupation appropriated two-thirds of these standing formations, about 3,922 men, and constituted the largest force assembled since the War of 1812.[24] The army's preoccupation with Indian fighting and related constabulary duties provided ample small-unit tactical experience for junior leaders but no opportunity for senior commanders to master the large-scale maneuvers necessary to engage European-style armies on a conventional battlefield. By focusing his training program on battalion-level tactics and drill, Taylor's army acquired incrementally the skills necessary to perform on parade with respectable competence.[25]

The Americans also enjoyed advantages in armaments and logistical systems. Lightweight, multiple-caliber cannons capable of firing solid shot or a variety of fragmentation rounds gave the Unites States Army a decisive edge in artillery firepower the employment of which was pivotal to most major battles. The .69-caliber, single-shot, smoothbore, muzzle-loading musket carried by American infantrymen, however, was not significantly different from the Brown Bess with which most Mexican soldiers were armed, just newer and more reliable. Although some volunteers brought along their personal firearms (Hall breech-loading rifles, Whitney rifles, and Jencks carbines), they were slower to load than a musket and therefore unsuitable for the close-order formations necessary to concentrate firepower in the attack.[26] Steamships and railroads afforded rapid transport and dependable resupply of large tactical formations when the Mexican army still employed mules and oxen-drawn wooden carts as its principal logistical platforms. This technological superiority helped compensate for initial troop-strength imbalances and tactical inadequacies extant at the outbreak of the war.[27]

Departing Corpus Christi on March 8, Taylor's army closed up on the Rio Bravo without incident twenty days later and immediately began fortifying the area directly opposite Matamoros. General Francisco Mejía, commanding Mexican forces pending the arrival of Pedro de Ampudia from San Luís Potosí, countered by establishing strong points along the river that subjected American units to enfilading fires.[28] Mejía previously had dispatched a small contingent of Mexican troops to the Arroyo Colorado in an unavailing attempt to delay Taylor's approach and buy some time until reinforcements arrived. Outnumbered, the Mexican troops quickly withdrew without hindering the American advance in the least.[29]

On the political front, meanwhile, the Mexican president responded cautiously to Taylor's trespass. "I do not decree war against the government of the United States of America," Paredes solemnly announced. "But the defense of Mexican territory which United States troops are invading is an urgent necessity, and my responsibility before the nation would be immense if I did not order the repulse of forces which are acting as enemies; and I have so ordered. From this day defensive war begins, and every point of our territory which may be invaded or attacked will be defended by force."[30] The warmongering liberal press and its federalist allies assailed Paredes's declaration of a defensive war as "defeatist and recreant." Those responsible for actually waging the conflict, however, prudently abstained from such inflammatory rhetoric.

Ampudia reached Matamoros on April 11 accompanied by reinforcements that brought the garrison's strength to 5,200 men. Despite the welcome arrival of additional troops, Ampudia's appointment was received "with positive regret in Matamoros by many persons who had a decided hatred for the man."[31] Minister of War Tornel astutely defused this simmering conflict by reinstating Mariano Arista as Army of the North commander and directing Ampudia to suspend all offensive operations pending the arrival of his superior.[32]

Born in San Luís Potosí, the stocky, red-haired, forty-four-year-old Arista began his military career in the militia of that province in 1817 and later served with the Lanceros de Veracruz. After embracing the Plan of Iguala he was promoted to lieutenant colonel in 1822 and reached the rank of brigadier ten years later. Exiled to the United States in 1833 for his affiliation with the abortive anti-federalist revolt of that year, he returned to Mexico in 1839 and promptly was dispatched to subdue Urrea's Tampico rebels. In 1843 he was appointed Army of the North commander, but his failure to endorse Paredes's Plan of San Luís Potosí led to his removal. The threat of war, however, compelled Paredes to strengthen his political base in the north, a task that made Arista's reinstatement to the Army of the North a *sine qua non*. Unfortunately, Ampudia, for whom Arista harbored a deep-seated antipathy, was retained as second-in-command, fomenting dissension that did not abet the Mexican war effort.[33]

For some time, Arista had been reporting to the minister of war serious shortcomings in the combat readiness of his command.[34] Substantive measures necessary to remedy these deficiencies, however, were repeatedly deferred for lack of funds. The Army of the North's deplorable condition notwithstanding, the growing threat to Matamoros compelled Arista to seize the initiative. On April 25 he sent General Anastasio Torrejón across the river with a force of 1,600 cavalrymen to cut Taylor off from his base at Frontón Santa Isabel and force him into a set-piece battle on terrain of Mexican choosing. The next day, Torrejón ambushed a sixty-three-man detachment of United States 2nd Dragoons near rancho de Carricitos, killing eleven, wounding six, and capturing most of the rest, including the unit commander, Captain Seth B. Thornton.[35] Two days later, another of

Torrejón's squadrons surprised a contingent of Texas Rangers, killing five and taking four more prisoners. With the east bank secured, the Mexican cavalrymen took up positions at the Longoreño crossing below Matamoros to cover the passage of Arista's main body.[36]

Leaving Mejía with 1,350 troops to secure Matamoros, Arista crossed the remainder of his army on May 1 and immediately surrounded Fort Brown, an earthen embrasure recently erected by Taylor's men. Once he ascertained that the bulk of the American force had been withdrawn to protect its vulnerable supply line to the *frontón,* Arista split his own force. Leaving Ampudia's 1,230-man brigade to invest the fort, the Mexican general positioned his remaining elements astride the main road at Palo Alto on May 8 to intercept Taylor's return.[37] Distributing his forces in this manner left Arista with 3,270 troops, a force roughly equivalent to that possessed by his American counterpart. Rather than concentrate his entire army at the point of decision as prescribed by accepted tactical doctrine, however, Arista dispersed nearly half his command to positions that bore very little relevance to the success of his operation plan.[38]

Arista interspersed his infantry and artillery forces in two parallel lines along a one-mile course that bisected the Santa Isabel road. Torrejón's cavalry brigade was stationed near the center of the formation, and a contingent of some four hundred mounted irregulars under General Antonio Canales's command was assigned responsibility for the Mexican left wing.[39] Arista envisioned a double envelopment of the American flanks, but neither of his cavalry commanders had conducted an adequate reconnaissance of the marshy intervening terrain, and their attempted maneuver was repulsed by concentrated infantry volley fire and canister shot from Taylor's well-sighted artillery.[40] With his flanking maneuver stymied, Arista ordered an assault upon the artillery positions that were tearing large gaps in the immobile lines of Mexican infantry. But smoke from a raging grass fire obscured the battlefield, impeding the coordination needed for his inexperienced troops to execute this difficult tactical maneuver. Hopelessly intermingled and suffering heavy losses, the attacking formations retreated in disarray.[41] Nightfall brought an end to the contest, affording both sides a welcome respite to consolidate their forces in more defensible positions.

American artillery was the decisive factor in this engagement. Taylor's cannoneers serviced their pieces with greater tactical precision and speed than did their ill-trained opponents.[42] While American batteries ravaged Arista's stationary ranks of massed infantry, poorly coordinated Mexican counterfire fell harmlessly outside its intended target grid. Ammunition for the obsolescent Mexican cannon, mostly solid copper shot, was so slow in its trajectory that the American troops generally were able to avoid the projectiles with relative facility. "The combat was long and bloody," Arista related in an inordinately optimistic after action report, "[T]he enemy threw about three thousand cannon shots from two in the afternoon, when the battle commenced, until seven at night, when it terminated,—six hundred and fifty being fired on our side. The national arms shone forth, since they did not yield a hand's-breadth of ground, notwithstanding the superiority in artillery of the enemy, who suffered much damage."[43]

Mexican casualties amounted to 252 men killed, wounded, and missing; American losses were reported as 5 killed, 48 wounded, and 2 missing.[44] The Mexican wounded were evacuated to Matamoros by cart, where their presence undermined the morale of that city's defenders, or were abandoned on the battlefield to succumb unattended. Clearly, battle-casualty management remained a significant weakness in the Mexican army, very little advancement having been realized since the dreadful experience of the Texas campaign.[45]

The large caliber and low muzzle velocity of weapons used in this war inflicted horrible wounds in which the projectile usually remained in the body rather than passing through. Bullets often carried debris such as pieces of uniform or accoutrements into the wound, retarding healing and promoting infection. With no known means of halting the spread of infection, gangrene, osteomyelitis, and pyemia generally were treated with amputation, and peritonitis caused a high fatality rate among soldiers sustaining stomach wounds.[46] The absence of antiseptics and the generally unsanitary conditions of field hospitals propagated infection even more rapidly, costing wounded soldiers their lives or the loss of a limb. Where amputations were involved, the lack of anesthesia subjected the wounded to excruciating pain.[47]

The following morning (May 9) Arista withdrew his army to the Resaca del Guerrero, a 200-meter-wide depression that perpendicularly intersected the road to Matamoros. Located some three miles from the Rio Bravo, this long, erratic chaparral-shrouded site offered superior defensibility.[48] Convinced that Taylor would not immediately attack such an imposing position, Arista delegated command to General Rómulo Díaz de la Vega and confidently repaired to his tent to attend to some administrative duties he considered pressing.[49] Taylor, however, did not tarry in pursuing his retiring foe, and by three in the afternoon his army had drawn up along the *resaca* in battle formation. The ensuing engagement quickly degenerated into a series of small-unit contests as the thick chaparral precluded the visual continuity required to maintain battle-formation integrity. The fighting continued inconclusively until Arista's left flank foundered, unhinging the defense and turning the Mexican army out of its positions. The disorder on the left infected the largely unengaged right, which collapsed precipitously into a full-blown retreat that did not abate until the bulk of the army had escaped across the river.[50]

Once again superior American artillery had played the decisive role, sundering the ranks of Mexican infantry while dragoons rode down Arista's immobile cannoneers.[51] Also contributing to the outcome were incompetent leadership, faulty tactical disposition, inadequate training, and inferior equipment. Additionally, the personal animosity between Arista and Ampudia crippled the command-level cooperation essential for successful tactical operations on a linear battlefield. Preponderant responsibility for the defeat, however, must be borne by Arista, whose soldiers paid the price for his overconfidence and underestimation of both the intent and the capability of his opponent.

After collecting his scattered forces and reassessing the tactical situation, Arista concluded that his army lacked the manpower, ammunition, rations, and funds to sustain the defense of Matamoros.[52] A *junta de guerra,* convened to decide subsequent courses of action, resolved to evacuate the battered Mexican army to Linares, a small city some seventy miles to the north. The retreat, which began on May 17, imposed great hardship upon the soldiers, who went without sustenance or medical care for the entire journey. Scarcity of transportation compelled the Mexicans to abandon substantial equipment, weapons, and supplies and to forsake some four hundred wounded to the mercy of Taylor's forces, who entered the city the following day. Despite such difficulties, many of the army's generals found the means to bring along most of their personal comfort items.[53] Arista reached Linares on May 28 with only 2,638 of the 4,000 troops who made it back to Matamoros, and he remained there until June 4, when orders arrived directing him to relinquish command of the Army of the North to General Mejía. Paredes needed a scapegoat to appease those affronted by the recent debacles, and Arista's removal was the most expeditious means of apportioning blame.[54]

In Washington, meanwhile, Taylor's report of Thornton's ambush induced Polk to send to the United States Congress on May 11 a "war message," declaring his intent to escalate hostilities. "War exists," Polk's message stated in part, "and notwithstanding all our efforts to avoid it, exists by the act of Mexico herself. We are called upon by every consideration of duty and patriotism to vindicate with decision, the honor, the rights, and the interests of our country."[55] After two days of partisan and acrimonious debate, Congress issued an official declaration of war and followed up with legislation authorizing 50,000 volunteers to serve one year or until the war ended, and appropriating $10 million to finance the venture.[56] Paredes responded to the latest American provocation by asking the Mexican Congress to reciprocate in kind, but that legislative body acceded only in granting authorization to repel the invaders. The initial stages of the war would unfold under inordinately restrictive legal auspices.[57]

Despite his proclamation of war, Polk had not entirely discarded the potentiality of resolving the conflict through Santa Anna's intervention. On May 13 he instructed Commodore David Conner, commanding the fleet blockading Veracruz, "If Santa Anna endeavors to enter the Mexican port, you will allow him to pass freely."[58] Polk followed up this initiative in July by dispatching John Slidell's nephew, Commander Alexander Slidell Mackenzie, to verify with Santa Anna what he had been told earlier by Atocha. When the special agent's report corroborated Atocha's information, Polk decided to proceed with this course of action.[59] On August 16, Conner notified Polk, "I have allowed him to enter without molestation. . . . I could easily have boarded the *Arab*, but I deemed it most proper not to do so, allowing it to appear as if he had entered without my concurrence."[60] In acceding to the caudillo's unmolested return, Polk was wagering that even if Santa Anna failed to regain power and negotiate a favorable treaty, his mere presence would be highly disruptive. Ironically, once restored to power, Santa Anna quickly abandoned any pretense toward negotiations and took charge of the army being assembled in San Luís Potosí to halt the American incursion.

With Taylor poised to move on Monterrey amidst mounting federalist agitation in the northern departments, Veracruz, Acapulco, and Guadalajara, Paredes requested congressional authorization to assume personal command of the army. Appointing Nicolás Bravo acting president, Paredes departed the capital on August 1 with some three thousand troops from the Army of the Reserve.[61] In his absence, General José Mariano Salas, a forty-three-year-old Mexico City native still smarting from the March, 1843, unpleasantness with Paredes, immediately usurped governmental authority. Two weeks after having himself declared acting chief of state on August 6, Salas issued a decree restoring the Constitution of 1824 and replaced the departments with states, effectively bringing down the final curtain on the decade of centralism.[62]

Salas, though, was little more than an expedient and expendable figurehead; Paredes's ouster had been cleverly orchestrated by Valentín Gómez Farías, and the latter moved quickly to consolidate his position.[63] For some time, Gómez Farías had been negotiating with Santa Anna for the military backing necessary to install a federalist regime. By May, 1846, the conspirators had reached an agreement in principle, setting in motion yet another machination for the extra-constitutional removal of an unpopular chief executive. His advocates in place, Santa Anna returned from exile the following week and, after his customary respite at el Encero, reentered the capital on September 14 amidst cheering throngs who considered him the only national leader capable of stemming the tide of Yankee imperialism.[64] Salas was permitted to continue in office as acting chief of state until December 23, when the Congress elected Santa Anna and Gómez Farías interim president and vice president, respectively.[65] As in 1833–34, mutual need, not ideological affinity, motivated cooperation between the federalists and Santa Anna. With their traditional northern strongholds threatened by foreign military occupation, the federalists embraced collaboration as the only pragmatic means of resisting the United States aggression.

In addition to diverting attention and resources from the war effort, political turbulence in the capital disrupted command continuity in the Army of the North at a pivotal period. Francisco Mejía, who had replaced Arista in the wake of the Palo Alto and Resaca calamities, was himself superseded by Pedro de Ampudia.[66] On August 29 the new commander reached Monterrey accompanied by three 8-pounders and three brigades of infantry, bringing the garrison's strength to 7,303 men. At first, Ampudia endorsed his predecessor's defensive arrangements, but subsequently, just as Taylor approached the city, he ordered alterations that left the defenders without a coordinated plan.[67] Santa Anna, who considered Monterrey indefensible, urged the Army of the North commander to withdraw to Saltillo. Ampudia, however, replied that the time required to demolish the fortifications, the adverse affect of withdrawal upon troop morale, and the likelihood of the abandoned region joining forces with Taylor mitigated against evacuation at such a crucial moment.[68]

Extending his defenses as far forward as possible, Ampudia posted General Torrejón's cavalry brigade in Marín, where it was supposed to force the Americans into a premature and presumably damaging engagement. However, his first glimpse of the enemy, on September 18, sapped what little ardor the irresolute Torrejón might have possessed for this venture. Without firing a shot he ordered his command back to Monterrey, enabling Taylor to close upon his objective without sustaining the attrition that Torrejón's covering force should have inflicted. Inside the city, animosity between Ampudia and his subordinates, intensified by the endless revision of defensive preparations, had engendered "a state of uncertain anxiety."[69]

Taylor had at his disposal some 6,220 troops to attack a fortified city composed primarily of single-story, flat-roofed, thick-walled, stone-and-adobe dwellings arrayed along linear streets that provided excellent fields of fire for the Mexican defenders. The constricted urban environment, however, limited the utility of Ampudia's forces, which included an inordinate number of cavalry formations. Taylor's concept of operation envisioned isolating the Mexican garrison by interdicting the road to Saltillo and following with a double envelopment to bring about its capture.[70] The attack began in a downpour at dawn on the twenty-first, with Brigadier General William Jenkins Worth's brigade dispersing Colonel Mariano Moret's Guanajuato Regiment in a sharp engagement that left the Americans in control of the vital artery to Saltillo, effectively eliminating any hope of outside assistance.[71] At the opposite end of the city, Brigadier General John A. Quitman's brigade captured the Tenería redoubt in a fierce fight during which that garrison's commander is reported to have deserted his troops by leaping into the adjacent river. Taylor pressed his attack into the city until halted at the puente de Purísima by resolute Mexican infantry and artillery fire. But Ampudia's dilatory pursuit enabled the Americans to withdraw in good order, thereby forfeiting an opportunity to inflict a defeat so decisive that it might have impeded the campaign.[72] For his part, Taylor had little to show for the 394 casualties his inadequately planned and poorly coordinated attack had cost the Americans on the first day of this battle.

Hostilities resumed the following morning (September 22) with a successful American assault upon the Obispado heights, which United States artillery then occupied and used to bombard enemy fortifications throughout the city. Mexican troops evicted from the heights sought refuge in the city, where their arrival infused among the defenders "a silent fear that comes before defeat." In response to these reverses, Ampudia abandoned all remaining outposts and concentrated his entire army in the center of the city, where the advantages of a restrictive urban environment could be exploited.[73] The next day, Taylor's forces occupied the strongholds vacated by Ampudia during the night and pressed their attack toward the Plaza Mayor, blasting through the common walls of adjacent houses to avoid deadly sniper fire in the streets. The battle raged furiously until nightfall, when Taylor disengaged, apparently anxious that his forces not become entangled in the city after dark.[74]

Sensing impending failure, Ampudia sent an envoy to arrange a meeting with the American commander to discuss capitulation. Early on the morning of September 24, General Worth concluded an armistice with the Mexican commander that delivered the city into American hands while allowing the commissioned officers to retain "their side-arms; the infantry their arms and accoutrements; the cavalry their arms and accoutrements; the artillery one field battery, not to exceed six pieces, with twenty-one rounds of ammunition." Ampudia agreed to retire "beyond the line formed by the pass of the Rinconada, the city of Linares, and San Fernando de Pusos," and the Americans would not "advance beyond the line specified [above] before the expiration of eight weeks, or until the orders of the respective governments can be received."[75] Between September 25 and 28 the largely intact Army of the North relocated to Saltillo, where it remained for the next month. Ordered to San Luís Potosí in November, it would constitute the core of the army being formed by Santa Anna to drive the Americans out of northern Mexico.[76]

Polk, who had low regard for Taylor, was incensed at the notion of an armistice and ordered its summary abrogation. Absent any realistic appreciation of the situation, he believed that if Taylor had captured Ampudia's army and advanced further into the country, "[I]t would have probably ended the war with Mexico." But Taylor's tired and demoralized army had sustained 487 casualties and was in no condition to continue the fight. Ammunition was critically low, and the troops were ill-prepared for the tough urban fighting that a forced entry of the city would have entailed.[77]

The Army of the North likely could have held off the Americans for a significantly longer period. They had suffered 367 men killed and wounded, about five percent of the engaged force, and still retained the most strategic and defensible sectors of the city. With determined leadership the battle could have been prolonged considerably and the attackers made to pay dearly for any gains. But the timorous Ampudia, who was "not endowed with despatch and energy," lacked the mettle for an arduous fight. Consequently the Army of the North endured yet another defeat in which the conspicuous gallantry and élan of its soldiers was nullified by the ineptitude of its senior officers.[78]

While the Army of the North was yielding Monterrey, Mexican sovereignty in New Mexico was being dismantled by Brigadier General Stephen

Watts Kearny, a fifty-two-year-old veteran of the western frontier. Following a grueling two-month, 856-mile trek from Fort Leavenworth, Kearny's 1,658-man volunteer Army of the West reached the outskirts of Santa Fe on August 16, 1846.[79] Forewarned of the American approach, New Mexico governor Manuel Armijo had assembled a composite military force of some 3,000 presidials, militia, and raw recruits with which to block Kearny's passage through the narrow confines of Apache Canyon. But powerful commercial links with St. Louis and the province's estrangement from the federal government had conspired to erode enthusiasm for the venture. Anticipating failure the feckless Armijo disbanded his forces and fled to Chihuahua on August 17 in the company of 90 dragoons. Near El Paso del Norte he encountered Colonel Mauricio Ugarte, commandant-general of Chihuahua, who was en route to Santa Fe with 400 reinforcements. When apprised by Armijo that the city was occupied by 6,000 American troops, Ugarte abandoned his mission and hastened back to Chihuahua.[80]

American attempts to establish a provisional government in New Mexico met strong opposition in the province's northern reaches, where a resistance movement that had gone underground resurfaced with a vengeance in 1847. Early in the morning of January 19, insurgents led by Pablo Montoya, a Mexican peasant, and Tomasito Romero, a Pueblo Indian, killed Governor Charles Bent and five other American officials in Taos, jeopardizing American rule in that region. Learning of the revolt the next day, Colonel Sterling Price assembled 479 men and several cannon and force-marched them through the bitter cold toward La Cañada. Upon arrival, the Americans engaged and defeated some 1,500 insurgents, and five days later they routed a second contingent of 700 rebels. On February 3, Price stormed the Taos Pueblo, where a residual rebel force was ensconced. In a bloody four-hour battle that cost the Americans 7 killed and 45 wounded, Price seized the pueblo and captured or dispersed the rebellion's leaders. While guerrilla resistance in northern New Mexico was never completely extinguished, Price's Taos Pueblo victory brought to an end the most serious challenge to American sovereignty in that region.[81] The Mexican federal government's failure (or inability) to integrate New Mexico into the nation's political, social, and economic fabric rendered this distant province relatively easy pickings for the United States Army.

With New Mexico secured, Kearny was ordered to California with a force of 300 dragoons to bring that province into the American fold. While Kearny's expedition was en route, Commodore John D. Sloat seized Monterey and San Francisco without opposition on July 7 and 9, respectively, establishing a United States claim to California and laying the basis for occupying the rest of the province.[82] Three weeks later, Sloat, whose health was in decline, transferred command of operations ashore to Commodore Robert F. Stockton and prepared to return home. A smart but arrogant and selfish career officer thirsting for glory, Stockton immediately antagonized the local population, obviating aspirations for a peaceful transition. By October 1 the excesses of his forcefully imposed civil government had precipitated a revolt in southern California that drove the Americans out of Los Angeles.[83]

Meanwhile Kearny, who had elected to proceed to his destination despite news of Sloat's achievements, reached Warner's Ranchería (Agua Caliente) on December 2, in the midst of the insurrection. The 100 dragoons who had stayed with him provided enough additional military force to enable the beleaguered Americans to suppress the insurgents and recapture Los Angeles on January 10, 1847.[84] In little more than six months a small American military force had occupied and pacified all of upper California, a remarkable accomplishment attributable to Mexico's tenuous hold on the most remote of its territories. Preoccupied with events unfolding around Saltillo, the federal government had neither the will nor the means to influence developments on the nation's periphery. As a matter of policy, moreover, Santa Anna had deliberately concentrated the country's military assets under his direction and disregarded what he considered "non-essential territory."

Believing his political fortunes rested upon assuming personal leadership of the military, Santa Anna turned the government over to Gómez Farías and departed the capital on September 28 with some 2,500 regulars. Arriving two weeks later in San Luís Potosí, he relieved Ampudia and set about reorganizing the demoralized assemblage of raw recruits, unhappy conscripts, disgruntled veterans, and criminals into an army capable of driving the Americans from northern Mexico. Mackenzie's mission and growing antiwar sentiment in the United States convinced Santa Anna that a single victory over Taylor would be enough to bring about a peace agreement favorable to Mexico.[85]

To fill the army's vacant ranks, federal authorities announced a national levy of 30,000 troops. Quotas were assigned to each state, and every Mexican citizen between the ages of 16 and 50 was alerted for service. But the national government had no mechanism to enforce mobilization on a national scale, and Santa Anna was forced to rely on the voluntary cooperation of the states to provide the requisite manpower.[86] In character with the fractious nature of the politicized Mexican military establishment, only

Guanajuato, Jalisco, Querétaro, San Luís Potosí, Aguascalientes, and the Federal District furnished their specified contingents, and these arrived raggedly outfitted and badly armed. When Taylor notified Santa Anna that hostilities would resume on November 13 and three days later occupied Saltillo, the reorganization of the Army of the North took on greater urgency.[87] The liberal press also was beginning to carp loudly about the delay in employing the large military force that was consuming a disproportionate measure of the nation's dwindling resources.[88] Through his customary energy and resourcefulness, however, the general-in-chief surmounted these liabilities, recasting San Luís Potosí into a bustling war town where disparate groups of soldiers and recruits were molded into an army and supplies were stockpiled for the forthcoming campaign.

To secure his exposed northern flank and position forces for a deeper penetration of Mexico, Taylor sanctioned Brigadier General John E. Wool's proposal to relocate his 2,000-man division from Monclova to Parras.[89] Wool's presence in Monclova was the outcome of the first Chihuahua expedition, which had been initiated the previous July in conjunction with Kearny's New Mexico campaign. Setting out from San Antonio, Wool's mostly volunteer soldiers encountered negligible opposition from the predominantly pro-federalist inhabitants of the region traversed during their long overland trek. The Americans reached Monclova on October 29 only to learn that the Chihuahua garrison had fallen back to Durango. Since Chihuahua no longer possessed tactical significance, Wool suggested advancing his division to Parras to expedite a subsequent drive into Durango or Zacatecas. Taylor concurred, and Wool put his division on the road to Parras, which he occupied on December 5 after an arduous twelve-day forced march of 180 miles. Within two weeks, however, Wool received new orders directing him to proceed to Saltillo and reinforce that garrison against the growing likelihood of a Mexican attack.[90]

Mexican interest in Saltillo as a military objective gained momentum when a copy of the order reassigning Worth's regulars from Taylor's command to Winfield Scott's impending Veracruz expedition came into Santa Anna's possession on January 6, 1847. Acquired during the ambush of an American courier, this document provided up-to-date information on American troop strength and dispositions in that city.[91] Discerning from this fortuitous bit of intelligence that Taylor's position had been weakened considerably, Santa Anna decided to capitalize on the unexpected American vulnerability. He intended to seize Saltillo by luring the enemy out of the city's fortifications onto the nearby plateau, where Mexican numerical superiority would offset the training and armament advantages the Americans enjoyed. Coincidentally, José Urrea, with 6,700 cavalry and mounted irregulars was directed to interdict the supply route to Matamoros and threaten Taylor's rear. Santa Anna believed that rendering Taylor's Army of Occupation ineffective would permit the Mexican war effort to focus exclusively upon Scott's anticipated invasion in the south.[92]

The force that departed San Luís Potosí between January 27 and February 2 numbered between 20,653 and 21,553 effectives and counted thirty-nine pieces of artillery, ranging in caliber from 4- to 16-pounders.[93] As usual the Army of the North accommodated a large contingent of *soldaderas.* Because the war ministry could not reliably furnish Mexican soldiers with rations, clothing, or medical care, *soldaderas* filled the void, helping sustain the force and, in the process, stemming desertion.[94] The 240-mile winter trek across barren desert terrain exacted a severe toll upon the ill-clothed and malnourished soldiers. Shoes fell apart, weapons rusted, and pre-positioned rations were rendered inedible by the incessant precipitation. The intense cold that, one survivor noted, "tormented them indescribably" caused many exposure casualties, and the freezing rain and paucity of wood for warming fires convinced numerous others to abandon the enterprise at the first opportunity.[95]

On February 20, when the army reunited at the hacienda de la Encarnación, a muster revealed that deaths, desertion, and straggling had pared its strength by nearly four thousand men, some thirty percent of the force. Nevertheless, to a member of the Kentucky cavalry squadron captured at Encarnación by General José Vicente Miñón's advanced guard, the Army of the North still cut an impressive figure:

> We met the great army . . . twenty thousand strong, and marching in four divisions. First came his splendid park of artillery of fifty guns; then a body of five thousand infantry; then a huge body of cavalry; then infantry and cavalry, together in large bodies; then Santa Anna in person, seated in a chariot of war drawn by eight mules and surrounded by his staff elegantly and gorgeously equipt; then he fluttered on his rear a bevy of wanton women; and lastly, covering his rear, his baggage train in the midst of which were five mules loaded with chicken cocks from the "best coups" of Mexico.[96]

What the army enjoyed in quantity, however, it lacked in quality. Consumed with clothing, equipping, paying, and feeding their troops, army leaders neglected the basic tactical training essential to battlefield success. Moreover, chronic supply shortages led Santa Anna to issue what equipment was on hand to the *regimiento de Húsares* and other favored formations, creating dissension that affected morale adversely.[97]

Two more days of marching brought the army to la Angostura, a narrow valley flanked by mountains and deep-cut arroyos, that afforded formidable protection to the American defenders ensconced in its reaches.[98] Santa Anna's scheme of maneuver called for the divisions of Generals Francisco Pacheco and Manuel María Lombardini to make the main attack against the American center on the plateau, while General Ignacio Mora y Villamil's composite force seized the Angostura Pass and Ampudia's *cuerpo ligero* threatened the American left. General Miñón's cavalry brigade was instructed to establish itself near Saltillo and cut off the expected enemy retreat.[99]

Before advancing his forces, the general-in-chief afforded Taylor an opportunity to surrender: "You are surrounded by 20,000 men and according to all probability, you cannot avoid the defeat and destruction of your troops; but since you are deserving of my personal esteem, I advise you that you may surrender at discretion with the assurance that you will be treated with all the civility of the Mexican character." "Sir:" Taylor responded in the polite parlance characteristic of that era, "In reply to your note of this date, summoning me to surrender my forces at discretion, I beg leave to say that I decline acceding to your request."[100] His surrender imperative rebuffed, Santa Anna opened hostilities at 3:30 P.M. with an assault by Ampudia's *cuerpo ligero* on the left wing of the American position. Taylor quickly parried the threat by extending his line, and the engagement broke off at nightfall with minimal damage to either participant.[101]

Around 8:00 A.M. the next day the *cuerpo ligero*, now reinforced with 1,500 additional light infantrymen and a battery of 8-pounders, resumed its assault upon the American left. Shortly thereafter the divisions of Lombardini and Pacheco launched the main effort against Taylor's center on the plateau.[102] The attack was repulsed with considerable loss to Lombardini's command. As the Americans attempted to exploit this advantage, however, Colonel William A. Bowles misinterpreted the displacement of a nearby artillery battery and ordered the 2nd Indiana Regiment to withdraw, opening a large gap through which Santa Anna quickly pushed Pacheco and Lombardini. General Wool responded to this exigency by shifting artillery to the menaced sector. This action and the timely arrival of the 2nd Illinois and 2nd Kentucky Regiments broke the momentum of Pacheco's advance and deflected Lombardini's thrust to the left. In the fog of battle, however,

Cartographics, TAMU, 1996.

Torrejón's cavalry brigade and Ampudia's *cuerpo ligero* turned the left flank of the American line, gaining the rear in great strength and disrupting the defense. At this moment (about 9 o'clock in the morning) the Mexicans might have prevailed had their cavalry been poised to intercept the badly disorganized Americans. But the brigades of General Julián Jubera and the gerontocratic Miñón were roaming ineffectually about Taylor's rear areas at Buena Vista and Saltillo, respectively, and could not respond in time to interfere with the enemy's ability to reorganize on successive defensive positions.[103]

Before Santa Anna could exploit his success, Taylor returned from Saltillo with the Mississippi Regiment, which he positioned to block the *cuerpo ligero*. Joined by the 3rd Indiana and Captain Braxton Bragg's artillery battery, the reconstituted defense effectively contained the Mexican penetration. Santa Anna continued to press his attack by reinforcing his success on the American left; however, so replete was the Angostura battlefield with alternate defensive positions that merely pushing the Americans off one hill was insufficient to create a breakthrough. Relentless pressure was needed to deny the enemy time to reconstitute along successive lines of defense, and Santa Anna's troops could not maintain the requisite momentum.[104] The general-in-chief attempted one final assault upon the American center, but galling double-canister fire decimated the ranks of General Francisco Pérez's brigade and a sudden thunderstorm sapped from his exhausted soldiers what little strength and impetus remained. By 5:00 P.M. the final Mexican drive had run its course.

Santa Anna acquitted himself reasonably well during the battle, reportedly losing one horse to gunfire while riding between positions and encouraging his soldiers. But evidently he believed his army had reached the point of ineffectuality and elected to break contact rather than risk decisive defeat.[105] After a council of war with his subordinate commanders that evening, he ordered a general withdrawal to the hacienda de Aguanueva, where the army could be securely reprovisioned and reorganized. The limited number of oxcarts made it necessary to triage the wounded, evacuating only those determined to have the best chance of recovery. Aguanueva became a veritable "hospital of blood," where those who survived did so in excruciating pain, anguished further by proximity to the amputations being performed on their comrades. Wounded whom the available transport could not accommodate were simply abandoned to the elements and prowling predators until Taylor's forces came to their relief the following morning.[106] Even those soldiers who straggled into Aguanueva found no fresh water or shelter, only enormous confusion engendered by officers attempting to restore order to a battered and demoralized army.

Angostura cost the Mexican army 591 killed, 1,037 wounded and 1,854 missing, among whom 294 subsequently turned up as prisoners of war. Taylor reported his losses as 267 killed, 456 wounded and 23 missing.[107] Santa Anna held the tactical initiative throughout the engagement, as Taylor, with a preponderantly volunteer force, was satisfied simply to parry the moves of his adversary. Once again, American light artillery played a decisive role in the outcome, shifting rapidly about the battlefield to check Mexican infantry advances at critical moments.[108] This fight, however, was primarily a succession of small-unit actions in which individual initiative and the tactical and technical acumen of leaders acting on their own volition were keys to success. In that regard the American junior officers were infinitely better prepared than their Mexican counterparts. Unaccustomed to such latitude, Mexican officers and sergeants were incapable of capitalizing upon fortuitous tactical opportunities, and in the fluidity of the Angostura battle, that was a recipe for failure. In his only offensive campaign of the war, Santa Anna had authored a tactically sound plan, but he had neither the imaginative leaders nor the resourceful soldiers to execute it successfully.

American retention of the battlefield enabled Taylor to declare victory. Such assertions, however, failed to deter Santa Anna from reporting the outcome as a great Mexican triumph, an impression enthusiastically endorsed at the time by Mexican public opinion.[109] In justifying his decision to quit a battlefield he claimed to have won, Santa Anna maintained that his troops had not eaten or slept in forty-eight hours and were dying of thirst, hunger, and fatigue: "After a march of twenty leagues, sixteen of which were without water, without other nourishment except a single meal eaten at the hacienda de [la] Encarnación, [the army] endured two more days of fatigue, fighting, and ultimately triumphing. With all of that, our physical force was spent."[110] He also intimated that his withdrawal was intended to lure Taylor out of his defenses onto more open terrain, where the Mexican cavalry could operate with greater maneuverability. Once his troops had been fed and rested, Santa Anna asserted, he would return to the business of finishing off Taylor's army.[111]

Resumption of hostilities by the Army of the North was not a far-fetched notion. Taylor's army was battered, and the provisions stockpiled at Saltillo would have provided the stores necessary to sustain such a campaign. Never one to entertain risky propositions, however, Santa Anna was unwilling to hazard the nation's most experienced military force in an unpredictable and fruitless engagement with Taylor. The Americans, he correctly surmised, were sequestered in the northern reaches of the country and could have little influence upon the outcome of the war. After conferring with his principal subordinates the general-in-chief ordered a full-scale withdrawal to San Luís Potosí, commencing February 26, 1847.

The 265-mile return march was another harrowing two-week nightmare during which the Army of the North lost nearly half its remaining strength to desertion and disease. Rations pre-positioned along the way had putrefied; this and consistently brackish water infected the troops with severe, often fatal, dysentery. On March 12, forty-four days after the first contingent had departed for Angostura, the beleaguered Army of the North dragged itself into San Luís, whose appreciative citizens accorded the soldiers a "triumphal reception." What the Americans failed to accomplish at Angostura they achieved in the Mexican retreat; an utter rout on the battlefield would have been far less costly than the losses sustained during the return to San Luís Potosí.[112]

Not long after his arrival, growing political disturbances in the capital distracted the general-in-chief from the pressing task of reconstituting the Army of the North. The radical assault on ecclesiastical mortmain, which Santa Anna had encouraged as a means of blackmailing the Church into financing the war, now threatened to alienate that institution's pecuniary benevolence entirely. These relentless attacks on the Church also disquieted four of the capital's national-guard battalions, whose socially well-to-do members, known as *polkos* because of their fondness for that dance, fiercely opposed radical anticlericalism. Unable to mollify or disarm the dissident militiamen, Gómez Farías ordered their units to Veracruz on February 22 to bolster that city's defenses. Four days later that apparently politically motivated directive provoked a mutiny of the 1,000-man Independencia Regiment, which was soon joined by the Hidalgo, Mina, Victoria, and Bravos Battalions. Although the rebellion inflicted few casualties, it precipitated a month-long stalemate that preoccupied the government and diverted attention from events rapidly unfolding in Veracruz.[113]

Determined to rescue the Church from the radicals and regain its allegiance and financial beneficence, Santa Anna delegated command of the Army of the North to General Ignacio Mora y Villamil and set out for Mexico City with 5,000 of his fittest troops. Meeting with rebel representatives on March 21 at Guadalupe, Santa Anna urged both factions to declare a cease-fire and resolve their differences pacifically. The day after having secured pledges from loyalist commander Valentín Canalizo and insurgent leader General Matías Peña y Barragán, the caudillo entered the capital and resumed the presidency at the behest of an ambivalent Congress. Backed by the *polkos* and soldiers who accompanied him from San Luís Potosí, he annulled the radicals' ecclesiastical property confiscation law of January 11, 1847, and on April 2 he removed Gómez Farías by abolishing the office of interim vice president.[114] These political machinations temporarily averted concern for the near-term implications of Angostura's abandonment. But such partisan divisiveness in the face of armed external aggression seriously impaired the army's ability to repulse the impending American invasion of Veracruz and both abetted and expedited the subsequent penetration of the Mexican heartland.

CHAPTER 6

The War with the United States: The Eastern Campaign, 1847

As Santa Anna's army disengaged from Angostura, Colonel Alexander W. Doniphan's 1st Missouri Mounted Volunteers were disposing of Mexican forces to the north of Taylor. Doniphan's 856-man expedition had departed Valverde, New Mexico, between December 14 and 18, 1846, intending to link up with General Wool in Chihuahua. En route they defeated a formation of 500 Mexican presidials and militiamen during a 30-minute Christmas day engagement at Temascalitos (El Brazito), opening the way to El Paso. After receiving reinforcements from Santa Fe, Doniphan resumed his march to Chihuahua on February 8. Meanwhile, General José Antonio Heredia, the military chief *(jefe militar)* of Chihuahua, deployed some 2,800 men in impressive fortifications along the Rio Sacramento to contest the American incursion.[1] After reconnoitering this imposing defensive array, Doniphan opted for an indirect approach. In a bold maneuver on the morning of February 28, his troops forced their way around the Mexican left, turning the defenders out of position and rendering the entire line untenable. The next day the triumphant Missouri Volunteers paraded into Chihuahua, where they lingered until setting out on April 25 to join General Wool at Saltillo.[2]

While Doniphan's operations alleviated security concerns over the Army of Occupation's vulnerable northern flank, Taylor adamantly refused to move without an additional 2,000 regular army troops. Increasingly disenchanted with the conflict, Taylor would have resigned forthwith had it not been for the adverse personal publicity that act likely would have engendered.[3] For the time being, though, he was content to remain in Saltillo and focus his attention on Urrea's vexatious guerrillas, who were routinely interdicting his tenuous supply lines. Relieved of any lingering obligation to prosecute the northern campaign, Taylor finally requested leave from Secretary of War Marcy and, on November 25, 1847, relinquished command to General Wool.[4]

The strategic isolation of Taylor's army coupled with Foreign Minister Manuel Crescencio Rejón's rebuff of the most recent American peace proposal, convinced Polk to open a second front to the southeast. By striking directly at the seat of political power, the American president hoped to bring about a rapid Mexican capitulation. Relegating the northern campaign to a holding action intended to tie up the Army of the North, Polk ordered the insertion of a second expeditionary army along the Gulf coast of Mexico.[5] On November 23, 1846, Secretary Marcy directed General Winfield Scott to "repair to Mexico, to take command of the forces there assembled, and particularly to organize and set on foot an expedition to operate on the gulf coast, if on arriving at the theater of action you shall deem it to be practicable."[6]

The proposed lodgement required a suitable coastal site through which the army could be resupplied or withdrawn as necessary, and Veracruz satisfied these criteria nicely. Scott's invasion force, comprising the regular divisions of Brigadier Generals William Jenkins Worth and David E. Twiggs and several newly formed volunteer regiments under Brigadier General Robert Patterson, arrived off Antón Lizardo on March 4.[7] In keeping with Jomini's precept of the indirect approach, Scott chose to disembark at Playa Collado, some two and one-half miles southeast of Veracruz. Prior reconnaissance showed the site to be undefended, and the nearby Isla de Sacrificios afforded the fleet a secure anchorage. Additionally, Scott's choice of the Collado beachhead nullified the 1,030-man garrison and 159 cannons of San Juan Ulúa. Disembarkation operations began at 5:00 P.M. on March 9 and proceeded without interruption until all scheduled assault waves had been landed. Evidently Brigade General Juan Morales, who had 3,360 effectives to defend the city's badly deteriorated fortifications, overestimated the size of the American invasion force and elected not to put his command at risk opposing the landing.[8] Nevertheless, the confusion and delay inherent in an undertaking as elaborate as an amphibious operation, afforded Morales ample time to establish defenses from which the initial waves could have been roughly handled. His lack of aggressiveness enabled Scott to put nearly 10,000 soldiers on the beach by midnight without sustaining a single reported casualty.[9]

Once the lodgement was secured, the Americans invested Veracruz from the landward side by extending a cordon from Collado to Vergara. Scott elected to besiege the city rather than attempt a direct assault because the latter "would no doubt be equally successful, but at the cost of an immense slaughter on both sides, including non-combatants."[10] On March 22, with his investment complete and artillery in place, Scott called on Morales to surrender the city. When the latter refused, Commodore Matthew C. Perry's offshore naval batteries opened an intensive bombardment that soon was joined by the land-based siege cannon and 10-inch mortars. The defenders retaliated with haphazard counterbattery fire, but the overwhelming number of guns coupled with generous quantities of ammunition enabled the Americans to gain and maintain fire superiority.

The relentless and indiscriminate pounding caused great structural damage and exacted an appalling toll on defenders and noncombatants alike. "From the gate of La Merced to the Parish," *Diario del Gobierno* reported, "not a single house was uninjured. The greater part of them was destroyed and the streets were impassable from the rubbish. . . . There was no light, and there was no passing by the sidewalks, for fear the balconies would fall."[11] Concluding that further resistance was futile, but unwilling to be held accountable for surrendering the city, Morales relinquished command to General José Juan Landero at midnight on March 26 and withdrew to Ulúa.

Landero, widely regarded as a *santanista,* then convened a junta that "in consequence of there being ammunition for only a three-hour fire, and no provisions except those given out by the ayuntamiento," agreed to capitulate.[12] Scott's surrender terms paroled the entire garrison, allowed officers to retain their arms and personal property, guaranteed protection to local residents, and permitted evacuation of Veracruz with full military honors. The surrender document was ratified on March 28, and the Americans took possession of the city the following day. After designating General Worth military governor, Scott notified Marcy that, "The flag of the United States of America floats triumphantly over the walls of this city and the castle of San Juan d'Ulloa *[sic]*."[13]

Declaring the surrender shameful and ignominious, Santa Anna ordered both Morales and Landero incarcerated in San Carlos de Perote. Such public consignment of blame served to obfuscate the fact that the government had done virtually nothing to strengthen the city's defenses despite credible intelligence of an impending invasion. As early as January 14, 1847, Santa Anna warned the minister of war, "The enemy have embarked about three hundred men and several cannon at Tampico to join their squadron off Vera Cruz, probably intending to attack Vera Cruz or Alvarado. Send an express to the Commandant General of Vera Cruz instructing him to be on the lookout."[14] Compelling evidence notwithstanding, Veracruz received neither the military nor the financial assistance necessary to afford a reasonable prospect of success against a determined attack. Evidently Santa Anna believed he could simply contain the besiegers until the *vómito* had exacted its pernicious toll, as he had done to the Spanish invaders eighteen years earlier at Tampico.[15]

Once again artillery played a decisive role in the Mexican defeat. However, unlike Angostura, where Taylor's highly mobile "flying artillery" was instrumental to success, the outcome at Veracruz was determined by Scott's massed employment of heavy Paixhan siege cannon to pummel the city's decaying fortifications.[16] The demoralizing effects of five days of relentless bombardment, coupled with the perception that the government had abandoned the city to its fate, engendered hopelessness among residents and defenders alike. Mounting personnel and property losses eroded the will to resist until morale crumbled entirely.[17] Unable to match the large-caliber American guns and short of serviceable ammunition, the defenders were condemned to eventual capitulation absent some measure of outside succor. Timely relief, however, was obstructed by the partisan divisiveness that continued to paralyze the Mexican political system, even in the face of impending national disaster.[18]

The fall of Veracruz engendered considerable consternation in the previously insulated capital; for the first time its residents began to discern their vulnerability to enemy occupation. Conceding the gravity of recent events, Santa Anna ordered General Valentín Canalizo to Jalapa to establish an operational base for the recently activated Army of the East and steadily dispatched units to that location as they became available.[19] Landero had ordered the units evacuating Veracruz to proceed to Orizaba, Jalapa, Córdoba, Tuxpan, and Alvarado and await further instructions. In constituting the Army of the East, Santa Anna reincorporated many of these soldiers, their parole-granting oath of nonbelligerency notwithstanding.[20]

Obtaining permission from the Congress to take personal command of the army, Santa Anna turned over the government to General Pedro María Anaya and on April 2 set out for el Encero, where he established his provisional headquarters.[21] During a reconnaissance four days later, the general-in-chief selected a dominating hill, known as el Cerro del Telégrafo, as the principal location from which to oppose Scott's advance upon the capital. Despite protestations from Lieutenant Colonel Manuel Robles Pezuela, his highly regarded engineer and a future Mexican president, that el Telégrafo was unsuitable for a defensive position, Santa Anna remained insistent.[22] His obduracy was motivated in part by the belief that his occupation of this position would keep the Americans in the yellow-fever zone.

Situated along the national highway between Veracruz and Jalapa, Cerro Gordo (so named for a proximate village) is bordered on the right (south) by a deep canyon through which flows the Río del Plan and on the left (north) by dense vegetation and difficult, though less obstructive, terrain features. The general-in-chief's concept of operation arrayed General Luís Pinzón, General José María Jarero, and Colonel Badillo with nineteen guns and 1,800 troops on the right wing, along three fingers that protruded between the river and the road and dominated the approach to the ravine. Like several of his contemporaries the forty-six-year-old Jarero had managed to resuscitate a blemished career. In December, 1833, a court-martial found the Jalapa native guilty of dereliction for having led government forces to defeat at Chilpancingo the preceding month. Briefly incarcerated for his misdeed, Jarero regained favor by supporting the prevailing side in subsequent political factionalism. As a reward he was given successive commandancies-general in Aguascalientes (1841), Jalisco (1842), Sonora (1846), and México (1847). Such cursory punishment for infractions committed by senior Mexican army officers was not unusual; those responsible for their adjudication realized that the tables might be turned at any time.[23]

In the center of the position, Santa Anna posted General Rómulo Díaz de la Vega with six guns and 1,400 men to interdict the road where it entered the ravine. On the left wing, el Telégrafo was occupied by 100 men and four cannon under General Ciriaco Vázquez. General Canalizo's cavalry was held in reserve at the ranchería de Cerro Gordo for employment as the tactical situation dictated. All told, Santa Anna had between ten and twelve thousand men with which to oppose Scott's advance.[24]

What appeared to be a strong position was in fact highly vulnerable. The strength of the defense could be avoided by turning its left flank. Additionally, Cerro Gordo's location on the fringes of the *tierra caliente* subjected Mexican soldiers to insect infestation, water shortages, and inadequate provisions. Not surprisingly this level of discomfort exacerbated morale problems among the troops, most of whom were raw recruits already intimidated

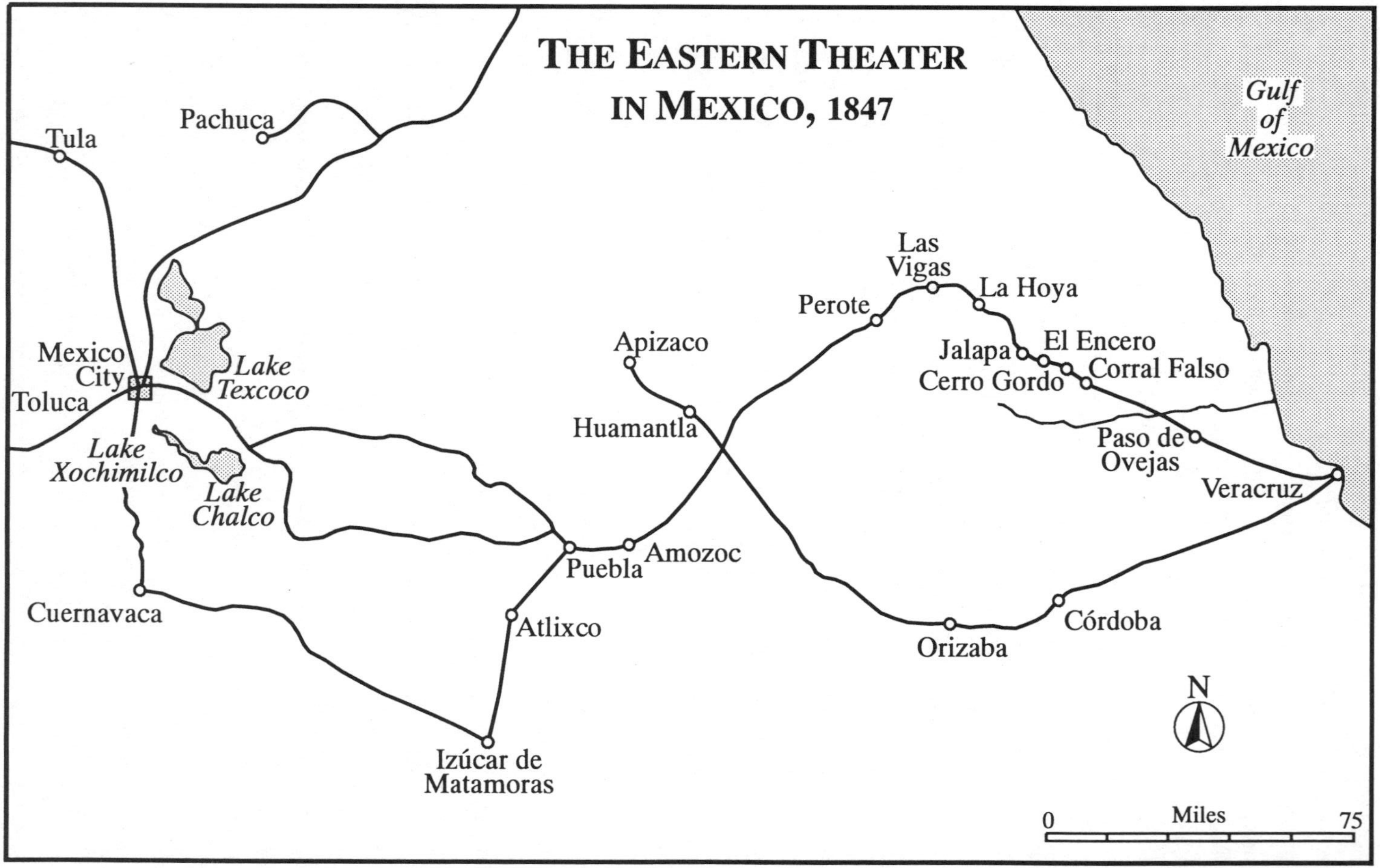

THE EASTERN THEATER IN MEXICO, 1847

Gulf of Mexico
Tula
Pachuca
Mexico City
Toluca
Lake Texcoco
Lake Xochimilco
Lake Chalco
Cuernavaca
Izúcar de Matamoras
Atlixco
Puebla
Amozoc
Apizaco
Huamantla
Perote
Las Vigas
La Hoya
Jalapa
El Encero
Cerro Gordo
Corral Falso
Paso de Ovejas
Veracruz
Orizaba
Córdoba
N
0 Miles 75

Cartographics, TAMU, 1996.

by the perception of Yankee invincibility, or enervated veterans suffering from a variety of ailments.[25]

As Santa Anna was leaving Mexico City for el Encero, Scott set his army in motion toward Jalapa, a city above the yellow-fever line that harbored forage and draft animals. By April 12 the American army had reached the Plan del Río and established a base camp two miles from the Mexican defenses obstructing its westward passage. Five days later, during a reconnaissance of el Cerro de la Atalaya, elements of Twiggs's division stumbled upon Vázquez's troops on nearby el Telégrafo, initiating a nasty fight that consumed the better part of the afternoon and inflicted some two hundred Mexicans casualties.[26]

Despite the interest in the left demonstrated by this encounter, Santa Anna remained preoccupied with the right, where he expected the main attack to develop. After analyzing the intelligence collected from this mission, Scott told his subordinate leaders, "The enemy's whole line of entrenchments and batteries will be attacked in front, and at the same time turned, early in the day, to-morrow—probably before ten o'clock, A.M."[27] Twiggs's division, now ensconced on la Atalaya, was ordered to seize el Telégrafo and cut the national road; Brigadier General Gideon Pillow's brigade, of Patterson's volunteer division, would assault the three fingers; and Worth's regulars were to follow Twiggs, exploiting any opportunities that might arise.[28]

The battle recommenced the next morning (April 18) with a heavy cannonade of el Telégrafo by American artillery pieces that had been dragged up la Atalaya during the night. Under cover of this fire, Twiggs's division, led by Colonel William S. Harney's volunteer brigade, moved along a trail somehow unknown to the Mexicans and attacked el Telégrafo from its vulnerable left flank. The fighting raged furiously, with both sides incurring heavy casualties. In a display of courage rare among Mexican senior officers during this battle, General Vázquez fell mortally wounded while attempting to rally his troops. The sudden appearance of Brigadier General Bennet Riley's brigade from yet another direction forced the already unnerved defenders out of their positions.[29]

As Riley's troops pursued the panicked Mexicans down the backside of el Telégrafo, Brigadier General James Shields's volunteer brigade bypassed the strong point and attacked the Cerro Gordo base camp, routing Canalizo's reserve corps and cutting the Jalapa road. The loss of both el Telégrafo and the national highway unhinged the entire position and sent the terrified soldiers streaming back through the narrow defile leading to Jalapa and safety, “pressed forward every instant by a new impulse, which increased the confusion and disgrace of the ill-fated day.”[30] Even General Pillow’s belated and inept attack on the Mexican right wing was salvaged by successes elsewhere on the battlefield. Cut off from the rest of the army, Generals Pinzón and Jarero surrendered their largely intact commands. After being subjected to more than three hours of appalling violence the nascent Army of the East ceased to exist as an organized fighting force.[31]

Cerro Gordo was predominantly an infantry fight, in which the relentless assault of hilltop fortifications carried the day. The piecemeal, non-mutually supporting defensive positions chosen by Santa Anna against the advice of his chief engineer officer made the attacker’s task simpler and immeasurably less risky. Unlike the plains of Angostura, the rough terrain of Cerro Gordo precluded rapid displacement of artillery to the centers of gravity, especially along the main thrust of the American attack.[32] Under such conditions the defenders, their guns already emplaced and sited, should have enjoyed fire superiority. But that advantage was nullified by tactically unsound disposition and clumsy servicing of the pieces. Worn out by long road marches and the enervating climate, the aggregation of ill-trained, poorly equipped, and disillusioned Mexican troops could not muster the tenacity that had made the battles of the northern campaign much closer contests.

In the wake of defeat, Santa Anna headed for el Encero, leaving Pedro de Ampudia and Joaquín Rangel to collect as much of the routed army as possible. But American cavalry impeded his egress, forcing the general-in-chief to wander about the countryside for three days before finally reaching Orizaba, where remnants of the scattered Mexican army were slowly trickling in.[33] After recovering from the shock of Cerro Gordo and regaining his composure, Santa Anna conveyed to the minister of war his plans for subsequent operations:

> It seems that the enemy, taking advantage of his triumph and the perturbation in which the villages find themselves, proposes to continue all the way to this capital; but I am dictating measures to organize here a respectable force, over which general Antonio León already exercises command, and your excellency may assure the president ad interim, that with the addition of some auxiliaries who may be received from the outlying States or from the supreme government, I will be able to harass the enemy’s rear in a sensible manner, while his destruction is achieved. I have already issued orders to general Canalizo

to use his cavalry to protect the Perote fortress, and to general Gaona to put [the fortress] in the best state of defense, meanwhile I am reinforcing [the garrison].[34]

Santa Anna's professed intentions notwithstanding, General Canalizo and the largely intact Mexican cavalry had abandoned San Carlos de Perote. When Worth's troopers entered the fortress two days later, they found 54 serviceable guns and mortars of various calibers, 11,065 cannon-balls, 14,300 bombs and hand-grenades, and 500 muskets. In addition to this ordnance, the Americans also discovered Mexican generals Landero and Morales, whom Santa Anna earlier had imprisoned for surrendering Veracruz.[35] Worth's occupation of Perote extinguished any realistic prospect of reestablishing a defensive line east of Puebla.

The general-in-chief's next moves were influenced by political as well as operational considerations. With a presidential election looming, Santa Anna needed a more proximate location from which to influence its outcome. Puebla satisfied this requirement, and the four thousand troops who had found their way to Orizaba were redeployed there on May 11.[36] Finding the city in a state of extraordinary agitation and its citizens greatly demoralized by the news of Cerro Gordo, Santa Anna decided to abbreviate his stay. Considering the attitude of the inhabitants and the city's virtual indefensibility, the general-in-chief advised the minister of war that he had "determined to depart for San Martín Tesmelucan the following day [May 14] with the troops of my command divided into brigades."[37]

Scott, meanwhile, was biding his time in Jalapa, waiting for his adversary to make the first move. Upon learning Santa Anna's destination, he set Worth's division in motion toward Puebla, where he believed pro-clerical and anti-*santanista* sentiment would expedite its capture. En route, in a message dated May 12, Worth apprised the city leaders that the rights and property of citizens would be respected if his entry were unopposed.[38] Santa Anna responded by sending a contingent of cavalry to engage what he believed to be an isolated brigade of Worth's command. But his soldiers found more than they bargained for and were driven off after an inconclusive skirmish at Amazoc. Three days later, Worth's 4,200 troops entered the city uneventfully, followed two weeks thereafter by the remainder of the American expeditionary force. With his army now reduced to 7,000 men by the departure of seven volunteer regiments whose brief terms of enlistment had expired, Scott prudently chose to remain in Puebla until he received enough replacements to mount a swift and victorious drive on the capital.[39]

The Cerro Gordo calamity reanimated *moderado*-radical tensions that had lain dormant since Santa Anna's defusing of the Polko Revolt in March. Suppressed resentment, and discontent arising from repeated military failures, exploded in a bevy of accusations as Santa Anna became the focus of Mexican anger and frustration. Charges of cowardice and military incompetence were levied against the caudillo for having abandoned the battlefield, and allegations of treasonous negotiations with the enemy resurfaced.[40] A few radicals called for an immediate end to the war. However the *moderados* were in control, and a majority of them resolved, not without trepidation, to defend the capital. Invoking emergency wartime powers granted by Congress, Acting President Anaya subjected every citizen to conscription for military duty or work on fortifications and expelled from endangered areas any persons suspected of sympathizing with the enemy. A state of siege was declared in the capital on May 1, and five days later, Santa Anna was appointed general-in-chief of the federal district.[41]

Despite statutory proscription against the chief executive's serving simultaneously as commander-in-chief of the armed forces, Santa Anna returned to Mexico City on May 18 and resumed the presidency two days later.[42] Appalled by this turn of events, *El Monitor Republicano* cynically announced, "The man of La Angostura, of Cerro Gordo, of Amazoc, weary of destroying Mexicans on the field of battle, comes home tranquilly to find repose in the Presidential chair."[43] Ignoring such invective, Santa Anna took personal charge of defensive preparations and directed his prodigious energies toward gathering yet another army to defend the capital. Troops were solicited from the outlying states, the Army of the North summoned from San Luís, and arms and ammunition procured from local foundries. Having regained a measure of optimism, those Mexico City residents who had not already removed themselves to the countryside, responded to the caudillo's entreaties with an uncharacteristic display of patriotic zeal.[44]

Lacking the troops and equipment to defend the city's entire perimeter, Santa Anna decided that the most practicable alternative was to fortify the elevated roads and causeways that traversed the contiguous marshlands. The most likely target of the American advance was el Peñón Viejo, an imposing 450-foot lava hill commanding the road between Ayotla and the capital. The general-in-chief assigned General José Joaquín de Herrera to command el Peñón's defenses and detailed his talented engineer, Lieutenant Colonel Robles Pezuela, to design and construct its fortifications. The seven thousand Mexican troops who converged on this position created an instant demand "for the building of groceries, eating houses, stores and liquor shops, and at once a portable city sprang from the earth." The entire affair took on the air of a carnival as the citizens from the city ventured out to witness the spectacle.[45] The vulnerable southern flank, considered Scott's second most probable target, was protected by Nicolás Bravo's Army of the Center, headquartered at Mexicalzingo. In the north, no advanced defenses existed; only rudimentary works centered around the gates *(garitas)* of Nonaloco, Vallejo, and Peralvillo. At the height of this preparatory activity, more than one thousand civilian laborers were engaged in constructing fortifications.[46]

The general-in-chief's concept of operation was fundamentally defensive in nature. It envisioned holding strong points along the perimeter with less-reliable national guard units and using permanent army formations as a mobile reserve to bolster the most-threatened sector. From its staging area at Texcoco, General Valencia's Army of the North was expected to fall upon the flank of the American army as it approached the city's outer defenses.[47] Juan Álvarez's 2,762-man Army of the South was responsible for defending the line from Mexico City to Acapulco and interdicting Scott's communications with Puebla. Commanded by Santa Anna himself, the Army of the East, reconstituted with some two thousand *permanentes,* eight thousand national guards and the remnants of Cerro Gordo, was deployed in strong points along the outer perimeter. All told, the general-in-chief had between 20,000 and 25,000 men with which to defend the capital.[48]

This latest army was composed primarily of national guardsmen from the economically advantaged elements of Mexican society. Gone were the conscripted Indians who filled the ranks of previous armies; now it was creoles and mestizos who would shed their blood defending the patria.[49] Like their Indian counterparts, these militiamen were ill-equipped and poorly trained. But they were strongly motivated to fight and ultimately proved to be the capital's most steadfast defenders.

Preferring to avoid a forced entry of Mexico City, an undertaking likely to generate heavy casualties, Polk assigned to Scott's army Nicholas P. Trist, the State Department's egotistic chief clerk. The president empowered Trist, a fluent Spanish speaker, to exploit any manifestation of Mexican interest in mediation and apprised Scott that "Mr. Trist is clothed with such diplomatic power as will authorize him to enter into agreements with the government of Mexico for the suspension of hostilities."[50] But Scott's relations with Trist were at first so puerile and epistolary that the latter was compelled to enlist the support of British Minister Charles Bankhead to communicate with the Mexican government. Despite his standoff with Scott,

Trist was able to initiate a dialogue with Santa Anna regarding American proposals for peace. But the arrival from San Luís Potosí of Army of the North commander Gabriel Valencia, an implacable foe of negotiations, scuttled this preliminary maneuvering and ended any prospect that the capital might be spared the ravages of combat.[51]

While Trist pursued these mediation initiatives, Scott pressed on with his military preparations. Among the four avenues of approach to the capital under consideration was el Peñón, the position upon which the Mexicans had anchored their defense. To Santa Anna's consternation, though, the American commander elected to bypass that heavily defended strong point entirely and march instead on Tlálpam (also known as San Agustín), where the southern shores of lakes Chalco and Xochimilco afforded his right flank natural protection. Except for an annoying but uneventful demonstration by Álvarez's cavalry, the American army reached its destination on August 16 without further incident.[52]

Scott's continued adherence to Jomini's maxim of the indirect approach achieved a measure of operational surprise that turned Santa Anna's entire defensive alignment. The strongest fortifications had been rendered useless, and the American army was now arrayed along the most vulnerable point in the capital's defense. Santa Anna responded by redeploying most of the el Peñón defenders to selected locations on the southern front, leaving only Herrera with one brigade to man the strong point.[53] Within the city, General Anaya reported, "Many families had departed; the doors and balconies were closed; and the echo was heard at a great distance of the tramp of the soldiers."[54] The residents, it seems, had already discerned the impending disruption of their serenity.

After consolidating Tlálpam, Scott advanced Worth's division toward San Antonio, which he intended to use as a staging area for a follow-on attack of Tacubaya, and ordered Twiggs to approach this same objective from the west via San Angel. Learning of these movements on August 17, Valencia shifted his Army of the North to a cluster of hills overlooking the rancho de Padierna, where he would be positioned to block Twiggs's advance. Like Santa Anna at Cerro Gordo, Valencia ignored the advice of his chief engineer and elected to establish his defense on a promontory that, while commanding the road to Tacubaya, neglected to obstruct several negotiable approaches into his position.[55]

Santa Anna disapproved of Valencia's dispositions and ordered his political nemesis and nominal subordinate to remove his infantry to Coyoacán and artillery to Churubusco, where they would be better postured to react to an American advance along either main artery.[56] Valencia, however, refused to comply, asserting that the Americans would attack:

> two natural points at the same time which are San Antonio and Churubusco, and the one defended by the army under my command; at one he will present a false attack, while the other will be made with total tenacity; but if one of these [points] is found abandoned upon commencing his move, he will suspend his movement under cover until his forces, making a violent march, are repositioned to strike an exposed flank and envelop your position.

The general-in-chief did not press the issue, merely noting his subordinate's responsibility for the consequences of his recalcitrance.[57]

Meanwhile, Scott's reconnaissance elements found San Antonio heavily defended and approachable only along a constricted causeway. This impasse encouraged Captain Robert E. Lee and Lieutenant Pierre G. T. Beauregard to search for a passage across the Pedregal, an intervening outcropping of hard lava whose ravines, crags, and fissures made its negotiation exceedingly treacherous. The engineers discovered a path to the top of the barrier, and at Scott's direction began constructing a road that would enable the army to approach Tacubaya via San Angel. Leaving Worth's regular and Brigadier General John Quitman's volunteer divisions at Tlálpam, Scott ordered Twiggs and Pillow to move their commands across the Pedregal and secure San Angel. After passing through the obstacle, Pillow's lead elements ran into Valencia's troops in positions blocking the road to Tacubaya. This unexpected encounter brought on a general engagement that, at this juncture, Scott neither anticipated nor desired.[58]

At 2:00 P.M. on August 19 the American artillery opened a brisk fire on General José María Mendoza's exposed cannon, driving the pieces from their advanced position and wounding General Anastasio Parrodi in the process. Torrejón's cavalry countered with an unsuccessful and costly charge in which Brigade General José Frontera, the forty-nine-year-old commander of the 2nd Cavalry Regiment, went down with a musket ball to the chest. Valencia then appealed for reinforcements to Santa Anna, who responded by putting Francisco Pérez's 3,000-man brigade on the road toward Padierna. Flanking artillery fire from the Pedregal, however, impeded Pérez's progress, and the ardor of his soldiers was further dampened when they were engaged by Valencia's troops, who mistook them for Americans.[59] These hindrances induced Santa Anna to recall the relief force, a decision that likely forfeited an opportunity to smash a significant portion of the four brigades that already had crossed the Pedregal and now were trapped between the general-in-chief and Valencia. But the Mexican army's capacity to exploit such fortuitous circumstances was severely circumscribed by vacillating leadership and wretched unity of command. Darkness abated the action, permitting the weary Mexican defenders, who had not eaten all day, to seek respite from the cold rain that had begun to fall. At 2:00 A.M., Valencia received a message from Santa Anna instructing him to spike his guns, destroy his ammunition, and withdraw. Believing his opponent to be near collapse and recognizing the negative personal implications inherent in retreat, the Army of the North commander again chose to disobey his superior.[60]

As these events transpired, Brigadier General Persifor F. Smith, of Twiggs's division, took charge of the four isolated brigades now gathered at San Jeronimo. At 3:00 A.M. he led three of these into a ravine that offered a concealed route into the rear of Valencia's line. When Twiggs's artillery opened fire from the Pedregal at 6:00 A.M., Smith's brigades assaulted the inattentive and demoralized Mexicans, some of whom already had begun to slip away as the precariousness of their situation became apparent. The stunned defenders were routed in a violent seventeen-minute fight that inflicted 700 casualties and accounted for 813 prisoners, including deputy army commander Jóse Mariano Salas and 3 subordinate general officers. American losses were reported at 60 killed and wounded but may have been as high as 300.[61]

Santa Anna attempted to bolster the Padierna defenders but was obliged to abandon that initiative when the unbridled retreat of Valencia's disintegrating army impeded his reinforcements. With the tactical situation now irretrievable, the general-in-chief dispatched orders redeploying his remaining formations to positions blocking entry into the capital. Pérez's brigade was withdrawn to the Churubusco bridgehead, Rangel's brigade was reestablished in the *ciudadela,* and Bravo's command was directed to retire from San Antonio to the garita de Candelaria.[62]

Capitalizing on his opponent's desperate plight, Scott unleashed Worth upon the badly rattled national guardsmen of the Hidalgo and Victoria battalions, who swiftly evacuated San Antonio in headlong flight toward the capital. Their arrival at the constricted Churubusco bridgehead at the same time as Pérez's troopers provided abundant targets that American artillery exploited with deadly accuracy. Once across, however, Pérez's brigade turned about and established a strong defensive position around the bridgehead that obstructed the American advance for the next hour.[63]

Scott sensed victory and impetuously ordered Twiggs to assault the convent, a partially fortified stone edifice defended by 1,500 to 1,800 men of the Independencia and Bravos national-guard battalions and a contingent of American deserters known as San Patricios. However, he had reckoned neither with the strength of that defensive position nor with the tenacity of General Manuel Rincón's defenders, and for the first time in the war an American attack was stymied. Reacting to this setback, Scott ordered Shields to cut off the Mexican defenders by interdicting the road to Mexico City near hacienda de los Portales. By 4:00 P.M. the combination of Worth's persistence, dwindling Mexican ammunition, and Santa Anna's withdrawal of the 4th Ligero from Pérez to counter the enemy presence in his rear, enabled the Americans to force the bridgehead and link up with Shields.[64]

With the bridgehead under American control, Twiggs advanced on the convent, where the defenders held out until their ammunition stocks were exhausted. The tactical situation now hopeless, Rincón's stalwart troopers reluctantly laid down their arms. Among the 1,259 Mexicans taken prisoner at the convent were 85 members of the San Patricio Battalion *(Legión de Estrangeros)*, a unit composed for the most part of American deserters who for one reason or another had opted to fight on the Mexican side.[65] Fifty of these captured deserters subsequently were convicted by courts-martial as traitors and hanged. Sixteen others were more fortunate, receiving fifty lashes, incarceration, and branding for their crimes.[66]

The consecutive defeats at Padierna and Churubusco offer further evidence of the army's inability to develop and execute a coordinated tactical plan. Mexican forces occupied strong defensive positions and enjoyed relative superiority in the correlation of forces. The rivalry and mistrust between the general-in-chief and Valencia, however, doomed to failure whatever prospects of success the defense of Padierna might have nurtured. Poor leadership continued to nullify the occasional episodes in which Mexican soldiers fought bravely and tenaciously. Moreover, at this point in the campaign even the most zealous patriots could see that an American occupation of Mexico City was inescapable.[67]

For his part, Scott lost control of the battle when he ordered his forces to pursue the withdrawing Mexicans without conducting an adequate reconnaissance or insuring that his subordinate commanders clearly understood his intent. His underestimation of enemy strength, disinclination to abandon the fight, and decision to conduct a frontal attack produced heavy casualties that might have been avoided by a more judicious approach.

Nevertheless, sensing that he had Santa Anna reeling, Scott followed his instincts, surmounting some of the city's most imposing fortifications. Sustained pressure might conceivably have yielded an even more decisive triumph, but the Americans were tired, and persistence likely would have disintegrated what little discipline remained.[68]

Padierna and Churubusco were devastating setbacks to the Mexican army's attempt to keep the Americans out of the capital. Not only were critical defensive positions lost, but a significant portion of the army had been utterly routed and irretrievably demoralized. In the first real test of senior military leadership within viewing range of the capital's inhabitants, the officers were found wanting, and popular confidence in the army plummeted drastically.[69] These circumstances prompted Santa Anna to convene a council of his ministers to determine subsequent strategy. In light of the battered condition of the army, they agreed to pursue a truce through the offices of Spanish Minister Plenipotentiary Salvador Bermúdez de Castro and British Consul General Evan K. Mackintosh.

Recognizing that his army was also in need of respite, on August 21, Scott notified Santa Anna of his willingness "to sign, on reasonable terms, a short armistice." In reply, Minister of War Lino José Alcorta, advised the American commander that "the president and general-in-chief . . . accepts the proposal to hold an armistice session."[70] The next day the two Mexican representatives sat down in Tacubaya with U.S. Army brigadier generals John Quitman, Persifor Smith, and Franklin Pierce to arrange the details of an armistice. The document emanating from this meeting imposed a cessation of hostilities within thirty leagues of the capital that would remain in effect "as long as the commissioners of the two governments may be engaged in negotiations or until the commander of either of the two armies gives formal notice to the other of the cessation of such, and with forty-eight hours anticipation of the resumption of hostilities." In the interim it prohibited erecting offensive or defensive fortifications and advancing troops into the lines already held by their opponent but allowed for the free passage of supplies into and out of the capital.[71] Ratified by Santa Anna on August 24, the armistice was intended to serve as a forum for the initiation of full-scale peace negotiations.

On September 1, Mexican delegates José Joaquín de Herrera, Ignacio Mora y Villamil, José Bernardo Couto, and Miguel Atristán met with Nicholas Trist in Atzcapotzalco to hear what kind of peace proposals the Americans had to offer. Trist was broadly empowered to act on behalf of the best interests of the United States, while the Mexican commissioners were restricted merely to receiving any such proposals and conveying them to Congress.[72]

Trist offered a treaty that created new boundaries separating Texas, New Mexico, Alta and Baja California, and part of northern Sonora from Mexico and guaranteed in perpetuity the right of free passage across the Isthmus of Tehuantepec. In return for these concessions the United States agreed to waive all claims for war reparations, assume liability for all foreign demands against Mexico, and provide a cash settlement the precise amount of which was left blank for the time being. The Mexican government's categorical rejection of these terms ended the negotiations and prompted Scott to notify Santa Anna that he intended to terminate the armistice effective September 7.[73] Santa Anna warned his counterpart that "yours will be the responsibility before the world, which readily discovers on whose side lie moderation and justice" and retaliated by resuming offensive operations against American troops bivouacked on the outskirts of the city.[74]

Availing himself of the respite afforded by the peace talks, the general-in-chief set about realigning his defense using as an anchor el Cerro de Chapultepec, a dominant feature of the terrain crowned with a large stone castle that had housed the Colegio Militar since 1841. He repositioned his forces to cover each of the principal approaches to Chapultepec, one of which was a rambling cluster of buildings known as el Molino del Rey. Located one thousand meters from the Castillo de Chapultepec, at the western end of the walled park, Molino del Rey comprised a complex of two massive stone buildings. Five hundred meters to the northwest, separated by a dry aqueduct thirty meters behind which was a thick wall of maguey plants *(magueyal)*, stood another sturdy stone edifice known as the Casa Mata. Both structures fell within the range fan of the Chapultepec artillery.[75]

The mill complex was manned by the brigades of Generals Joaquín Rangel and Antonio León; 1,500 *permanentes* of Francisco Pérez's brigade defended the Casa Mata; and the intervening terrain was held by General Simeon Ramírez's command reinforced with seven cannon arrayed in the *magueyal*. About a mile to the east, across a deep ravine, Juan Álvarez readied 3,000 cavalrymen at the hacienda de los Morales to fall upon the American left flank. The defense was well prepared, with commanders marking the limit of effective musket fire to enable their troops to know precisely when to begin engaging the enemy. Interlocking fields of fire and downward-sloping terrain further enhanced the defensive advantages of this imposing position.[76]

Based upon spurious intelligence reports that Molino del Rey was an active brass cannon foundry, Scott decided to make that facility his next objective. His scheme of maneuver called for Worth's division to assault the mill complex, while Twiggs's division feinted toward the south in an attempt to fix Mexican reinforcements in place. Because Santa Anna already expected the main effort to be directed at the Niño Perdido and Candelaria *garitas*, Scott's concept of operation achieved the level of tactical surprise envisioned.[77]

Worth opened the attack at 5:45 A.M. on September 8, and his troops were promptly repulsed by Ramírez's massed artillery fires and a vigorous counterattack from Lieutenant Colonel Miguel María Echeagaray's 3rd Ligera Battalion of Pérez's brigade, which had just arrived on the scene. Neither the general reserve nor Ramírez's own troops were committed to reinforce this success, and Echeagaray was compelled to withdraw to the Casa Mata, losing some of his soldiers to friendly fire in the process.[78] After reorganizing his brigades, Worth renewed the attack against both the Casa Mata and the mill complex. As the battle became general, Santa Anna ordered Álvarez to charge the American flank, but his nominal subordinate demurred, contending that he lacked artillery support and that his horses could not traverse the intervening ravine.[79] Major Edwin V. Sumner's 270 dragoons had no difficulty traversing this putative obstacle at the same point designated by Santa Anna for the Mexican cavalry crossing, but even if Álvarez had been right, his cavalry could have dismounted and fought as infantry, providing reinforcements that might have made a difference in the outcome. It would seem that the old cacique's cavalry never became an influencing factor because he was content to be an observer rather than a participant.[80]

The contest soon degenerated into the kind of autonomous small-unit actions that significantly handicapped the inadequately trained and incompetently led Mexican soldiers. Relentless pounding by American heavy siege artillery and tenacious room-to-room combat finally forced the defenders out of their positions and into a fighting retreat toward the woods around Chapultepec. The mill-complex defenders subdued, Worth's soldiers turned their fire on the Casa Mata and, with timely assistance from Captain James Duncan's artillery battery, soon overcame all resistance from that quarter, too. After two hours of sustained fighting, the Americans controlled the entire battlefield; however, the heavy casualties incurred in the process (one-quarter of the attacker's strength), rendered this a "dearly bought" victory.[81]

The battle for Molino del Rey lacked centralized direction and control, so the Mexicans never could bring to bear the full potential of their available combat power. Each element was left to fight on its own volition, and as has been observed in other battles in which this same phenomenon prevailed, the Mexicans were decidedly disadvantaged. After reviewing the defenses and ordering enough confusing last-minute changes to compromise the position's integrity, Santa Anna removed both himself and a sizeable contingent of troops to the garita de Candelaria, which he still believed would be the target of Scott's main effort. As the battle was joined, the general-in-chief made his way over the five miles to Molino del Rey, but by the time he arrived (9:30 A.M.), the tactical situation was beyond redemption.

Despite coming into possession of a copy of Scott's operation order a few hours after it was issued, Santa Anna failed to exploit this serendipitous bit of intelligence, apparently believing it to be a fabrication. He later claimed that his decision to withdraw troops from Molino del Rey was prompted by credible evidence indicating that Scott intended to enter the capital via the Niño Perdido and Candelaria gates.[82] In the absence of a supreme commander, to coordinate the defense and direct adjustments in response to the developing situation, Mexican forces were employed piecemeal, or not at all, forfeiting their numerical superiority and positional advantage. Skillful tactical employment of artillery contributed to the American triumph, but this was fundamentally a small-unit infantry fight in which individual fortitude and enterprise prevailed.

In the wake of victory, American units collected their wounded and withdrew to Tacubaya to prepare for the next engagement. Once reconnaissance confirmed that the preponderance of Mexican forces was still concentrated around the southern accesses, Scott decided to penetrate the capital via the Belén and San Cosmé *garitas,* because they were "less unfavorable approaches" than those to the south.[83] The scheme of maneuver supporting his plan called for Pillow's division, which had surreptitiously reoccupied Molino del Rey under cover of darkness, to make the main attack against Chapultepec while the divisions of Quitman and Worth conducted supporting attacks against the Belén and San Cosmé gates, respectively. Twiggs's division remained in front of the southern *garitas* "to maneuver, to threaten, or to make false attacks, in order to occupy and deceive the enemy."[84] For his plan to succeed, Scott's forces had to surmount the defenses of el Cerro de Chapultepec.

This seemingly daunting task was abetted by the faulty disposition of Mexican forces. Still persuaded that the southern approaches remained the Americans' main objective, Santa Anna reinforced the garita de Candelaria with General Mariano Martínez' brigade and ten artillery pieces. Rangel's brigade with five guns and General Andrés Terrés' composite force with

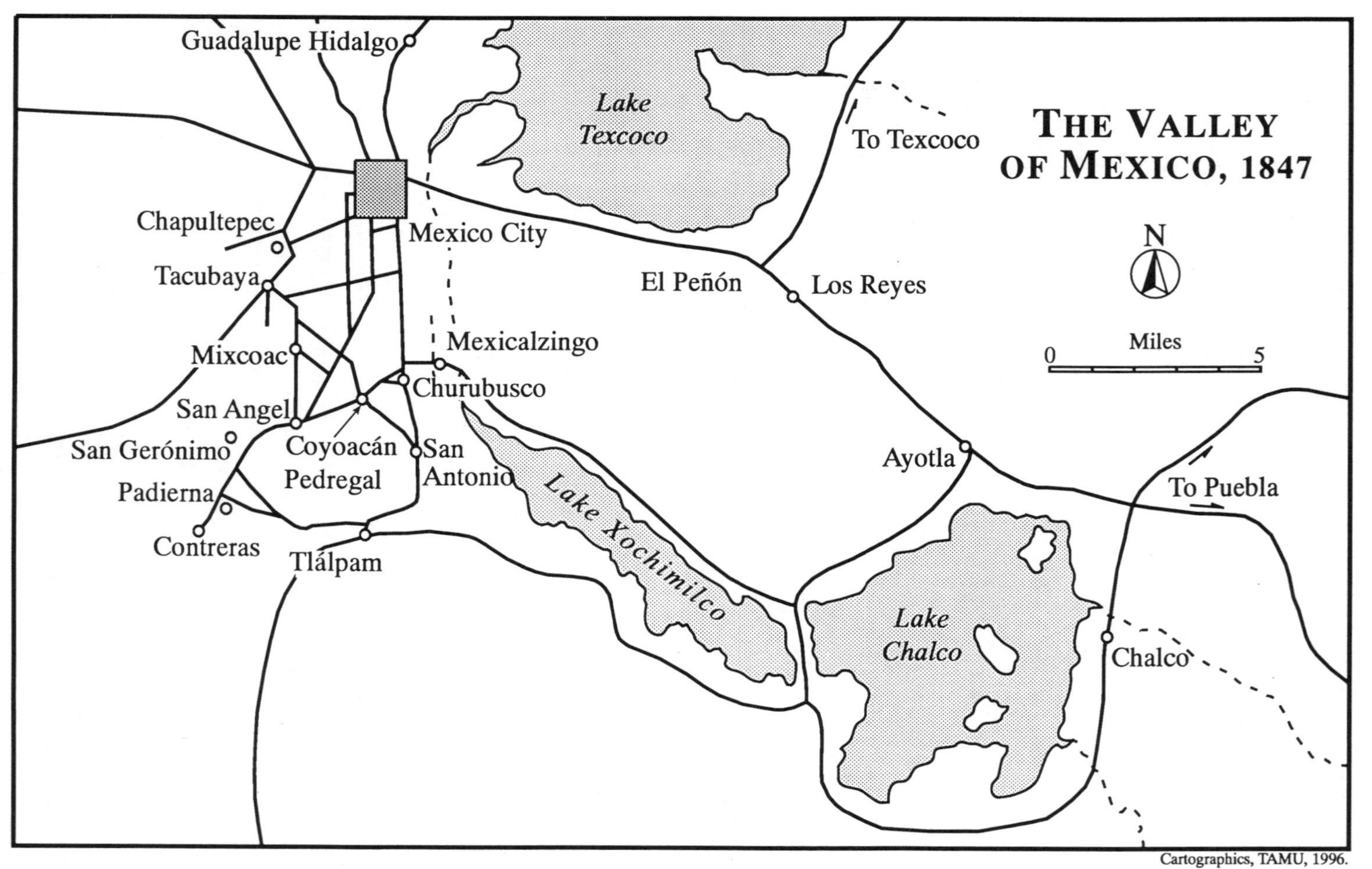

THE VALLEY OF MEXICO, 1847
N
Miles
0
5
Lake Texcoco
To Texcoco
Guadalupe Hidalgo
Chapultepec
Mexico City
Tacubaya
El Peñón
Los Reyes
Mexicalzingo
Mixcoac
Churubusco
San Angel
San Gerónimo
Coyoacán
Pedregal
San Antonio
Padierna
Contreras
Tlálpam
Lake Xochimilco
Ayotla
To Puebla
Lake Chalco
Chalco
Cartographics, TAMU, 1996.

three cannon were posted to the San Cosmé and Belén *garitas,* respectively. Despite Nicolás Bravo's estimate that an effective defense of Chapultepec required 2,000 soldiers, Santa Anna committed just 832 of his available troops, the majority of whom were national guardsmen from the Querétaro, Mina, Union, Toluca, and Patria battalions, and seven cannon to defend the castle and its environs. The 10th Infantry Regiment and 46 Colegio Militar cadets ranging in age from thirteen to twenty, constituted the balance of General Bravo's troop strength.[85] The general-in-chief recognized the tactical significance of Chapultepec to the integrated defense of the city, but his emphasis on the southern strong points left that garrison inadequately manned. As Scott's real intentions became evident, Santa Anna attempted to rectify his error; Mexican forces, however, were too widely dispersed for a timely and coordinated response. Scott later noted, "The stratagem against the south was admirably executed throughout the 12th and down to the afternoon of the 13th, when it was too late for the enemy to recover from the effects of his delusion."[86]

At first light on September 12, Scott commenced a withering thirteen-hour, 2,000-round artillery bombardment of the castle, exacting a significant toll on both the edifice and its defenders. Still confused over the direction of the main American thrust, Santa Anna vacillated in dispatching the additional forces demanded by General Bravo until the following day, when he finally sent the 400-man *activo* San Blas Battalion to occupy the nearby woods *(bosque).* Motivated by the precariousness of their situation, Bravo's troops labored throughout the night to repair the damage caused by the sustained cannonade and strengthen their position. The main approaches to the castle were obstructed by three large mines; but these were never activated, either because their trains were cut or because ignition was overlooked in the heat of battle.[87]

Hostilities resumed the next morning with a furious two-hour artillery preparation. As these fires lifted, at about 8:00 A.M., Pillow's division sallied from Molino del Rey and quickly gained a foothold on the lower reaches of the hill. But the attack faltered in the face of fierce opposition, and the Americans were driven to ground until the arrival of reinforcements restored their momentum. With skirmishers systematically picking Mexican defenders off the parapets, the attackers worked their way progressively up the slope. Meanwhile, in the *bosque* to the east, Pillow's right wing engaged and virtually annihilated the San Blas Battalion, clearing the way for a general assault upon the castle. In a final push, the Americans scaled the walls and gained control of the castle in bloody hand-to-hand fighting with the stubborn defenders, among whom were the Colegio Militar cadets. Six of these youths were killed in action, 3 wounded, and 37 taken prisoner. Among the latter were future generals Miguel Miramón and Manuel Ramírez de Arellano.[88] Convinced that further resistance would only invite more bloodshed, General Bravo capitulated around 9:30 A.M. His surrender precipitated a vitriolic exchange of recriminations with Santa Anna over culpability for the loss of Chapultepec. After prolonged contention and public invective, Bravo was completely exonerated.[89]

With the castle and gateway batteries now in American hands, Scott pressed the attack toward the city, advancing Worth and Quitman to the San Cosmé and Belén *garitas,* respectively. Quitman encountered tenacious resistance from the Morelia Battalion defending the Belén *garita,* which he overcame only when depleted ammunition stocks forced General Andrés Terrés to withdraw his troops into the *ciudadela.* When Santa Anna arrived with reinforcements, he severely upbraided the timorous seventy-three-year-old Barcelona native, whom he found sheltered in a nearby doorway, punctuating the chastisement with a blow to Terrés's face.[90]

Meanwhile, Quitman, whose mission was to conduct only a supporting attack, pressed on the heels of an enemy he believed "to have been conquered and driven out of the garita." A volunteer general whose command had not been presented an opportunity for glory during previous encounters, Quitman was obsessed with distinguishing himself and repeatedly ignored attempts to curtail his forward progress. His indiscretion was greeted with "a shower of iron" and vigorous counterattacks from the *ciudadela* that kept the attackers at bay while inflicting heavy losses.[91]

Fortunately for the Americans, Worth's main attack succeeded in dislodging Rangel from positions on the San Cosmé causeway, forcing him to reconstitute his defense around the *garita.* Realizing at last that this was the Americans' main thrust, Santa Anna reinforced the severely wounded Rangel with additional troops and artillery, and ordered Torrejón's cavalry to strike the attacker's exposed flank. This accretion halted the Americans only momentarily, as they soon managed to flank the new position and enter the city behind its defenses. To avoid entangling his command in a hostile urban environment after dark, Worth suspended his advance at 6:00 P.M. and established night defensive positions in proximity to the gate.[92]

With the outer defenses breached, his army disorganized and demoralized, and the populace uncooperative in efforts to defend the city, Santa Anna convened a junta in the *ciudadela* in which Generals Alcorta, Lombardini, and Pérez concurred that a continued defense of the capital would be unavailing. Satisfied that Mexican honor had been upheld, and wanting to avoid a destructive bombardment, Santa Anna declared "that this same night the city must be evacuated, and I name Sr. Lombardini General-in-chief and General Pérez his second."[93] Between 8:00 and 9:00 P.M., Santa Anna and most of the remaining cavalry formations departed the *ciudadela* for the nearby village of Cuautitlan, followed several hours later by the infantry under the command of General Herrera, in all some nine thousand soldiers. The Americans entered the capital the following day, took possession of the national palace, and set about the business of suppressing residual resistance and establishing occupation rule.[94]

The American subjugation of Mexico City concluded a remarkable and audacious campaign in which Scott's expeditionary force had marched inland from Veracruz and defeated at every encounter a Mexican army more than twice its size. As in the northern campaign, artillery played a significant role in the outcome of the various battles. Here, however, heavy siege guns made the greatest difference, not the highly mobile "flying artillery" so instrumental in the American victories at Palo Alto, Resaca, and Angostura. The relentless pounding of Mexican positions at Veracruz, Molino del Rey, and Chapultepec shattered the coherence of the defense and sapped the defenders' will. Hamstrung by antiquated weapons, logistical inadequacies, and training deficiencies, Mexican artillery could not generate the counterfire necessary to neutralize the American guns.

The contribution of artillery notwithstanding, the battles of the eastern campaign were principally infantry affairs the outcome of which was determined by individual initiative and small-unit leadership. Schooled by years of campaigning against elusive Indian guerrillas on the western frontier, American junior officers were accustomed to extensive tactical latitude and decentralized decision-making under high-stress conditions. The rarity of such qualities within the Mexican army significantly disadvantaged its units when the fighting degenerated into the amorphous confusion that characterized the disjointed engagements at Padierna, Churubusco, Molino del Rey, and Chapultepec. All too often, gallant individual and collective performances by Mexican soldiers were nullified by the irresolute and indifferent leadership of their officers and Santa Anna's capricious and uncoordinated operational direction.

Indulged by government largess since independence, how had the army failed so miserably in its efforts to repel Scott's invasion? The Indians comprising most of its ranks were potentially good soldiers and, despite inadequate training and obsolescent weapons, fought bravely in those few instances in which they were competently led. Debauched by three decades of self-glorification and political manipulation, their officers lacked the exemplary leadership, technical skill, and concern for individual welfare to transform this raw material into proficient soldiers, endowed with nationalistic ardor.

Successive pronouncements thwarted military professionalism and brought to power competing groups of self-interested officers who considered the army an instrument of corporate aggrandizement rather than of politically neutral public service. Abetted by rugged physical geography and primitive transportation arteries, intrinsic localism perpetuated affiliation with regional caciques whose competing agendas destabilized and prostrated the nation.[95] A firsthand observer of the conflict and harsh critic of the military, José Fernando Ramírez denounced the generals as: "cowards, ignoramuses, and men wholly devoid of even one spark of personal honor. Judged by their ability, they scarcely would make good sergeants. Judged by their character they are what one of our hapless poets has said of them: Tortoises in the country, Vultures in the city."[96]

Defeat, however, cannot be attributed exclusively to military ineptitude: the dearth of national resistance to the American penetration of the Mexican heartland also played a role. The social inequities stratifying the nation engendered a lack of interest in the conflict. Existing outside the mainstream of governmental and economic activity, the large mass of Indian peasants perceived the American incursion "with the same indifference that they formerly viewed the invasion of Spanish troops."[97] The heterogeneous character of Mexican society and the abuses extant since the colonial era combined to create widespread apathy toward events not impacting directly on the inhabitants' domain. The only active role Indian peasants played in national public affairs was "to serve as soldiers in the army which they are obliged to do by force."[98] Ideological divisiveness and sectional rivalry spawned a military institution incapable of waging war successfully against a nation with the political stability and economic resources of the United States. The American victory, however, was abetted significantly by the lack of national consensus against the invaders and the paucity of patriotic spirit mobilizing the population at large. With foreign occupation a reality, the nation's military and political leaders now had to set aside their ideological differences and form a common front to remove the American presence as expeditiously as possible.

CHAPTER 7

Postwar Reorganization and Reform, 1848–52

Santa Anna's exodus bestowed responsibility for governing the capital upon the Mexico City *ayuntamiento*. Order, the council realized, could be restored most expeditiously by facilitating Scott's entry and cooperating in the reestablishment of civil government. Accordingly, a three-man delegation was appointed to convey to Scott a proposal for conditional surrender. The delegates, however, found the American commander disinclined to entertain terms until all hostile acts against his troops had desisted completely. The *ayuntamiento* obliged by issuing two general cease-fire decrees that, when punctuated with Scott's punitive use of artillery, brought all but sporadic guerrilla resistance to an end by September 17.[1]

Disdaining the *ayuntamiento's* pragmatism, Santa Anna denounced its putative collaboration with the enemy and excoriated the first magistrate *(alcalde mayor)*, Manuel Reyes y Veramendi, for his reprehensible conduct.[2] In spite of his public bombast, Santa Anna was privately disheartened by recent events and eager to relinquish the reins of civil authority. On September 16 he announced his resignation as president of Mexico and handed over interim chief-executive duties to the chief justice of the Supreme Court, Manuel de la Peña y Peña, a moderate who had served previously as foreign minister.[3] The interim president immediately established a provisional headquarters in Toluca and set about convening a national congress in the city of Querétaro. Although nearly a month transpired before the requisite quorum could be gathered, by November a semblance of national federal authority had been restored. Moderado domination of this ad hoc assembly, however, precipitated a bitter power struggle with the radicals that hindered peace negotiations and retarded postwar recovery.[4]

After evacuating the capital, Santa Anna split what remained of his army in two, directing Herrera to proceed to Querétaro with most of the artillery and trains while he led the infantry and cavalry toward Puebla. Apprised of a popular uprising in the capital, Santa Anna turned his forces about, intending to exploit the purported resistance. However, learning that the disturbance was not widespread and soon would be contained by the Americans, he again reversed course and resumed his march to Puebla.[5] Predictably, such desultory countermarching fomented a rash of desertions among soldiers exasperated with a cause that clearly was lost and that engendered excesses in every community through which the army passed: "In the towns they endeavored to sack stores: in the shops and eating-houses they consumed whatever eatables they found, without paying for them; and no consideration restrained them from satiating their hunger and satisfying their needs."[6] More a mob than an organized military force, this remnant army left in its wake a trail of desolation and outrage that antagonized citizens, helping to quell whatever anti-American sentiment they might have harbored.

Santa Anna's disintegrating formations reached Puebla on September 23 and linked up with General Joaquín Rea's 2,500 irregulars and national guardsmen, who had been investing the city for the past ten days. After failing to convince Colonel Thomas Childs to surrender, Santa Anna declared Puebla to be in a state of siege and, for the next two weeks, engaged in a series of ineffectual skirmishes that accomplished little other than maiming more Mexican soldiers and depleting the surrounding countryside of its already meager food supplies. Such hollow posturing finally was abbreviated by the approach of General Joseph Lane's relief column from Veracruz, which compelled the general-in-chief to redirect most of his 4,000 besiegers to intercept the new threat.[7]

Forewarned of Santa Anna's intention to ambush his column near el Pinal de Puebla, Lane shifted his advance toward Huamantla, where, on October 9, he surprised and easily drove off a contingent of 500 Mexican hussars *(húsares)*. In the wake of this latest misfortune, Santa Anna withdrew the remainder of his army to Querétaro, allowing Lane's brigade to proceed unmolested to Puebla, where the Americans fought their way through Rea's guerrillas and broke the siege on October 13.[8] The Puebla debacle convinced interim president Peña y Peña to order Santa Anna to turn over his formations to General Manuel E. Rincón and report to Querétaro to stand court-martial. After some deliberation the caudillo reluctantly complied and withdrew to Tehuacán, where he remained until the following May, when he was forced once again into exile.[9]

Meanwhile, Secretary of War Marcy had augmented Scott with 2,957 troops from Taylor's static northern command, bringing the Army of Occupation's total strength to 15,250. These reinforcements were intended to provide the American commander with the capability to "carry on further aggressive operations; to achieve new conquests; to disperse the remaining army of the enemy in your vicinity and prevent the organization of another."[10] To maintain order within the capital itself, recently appointed military governor John Quitman established commissions to adjudicate crimes committed by unruly American soldiers. For matters concerning Mexican nationals, Quitman delegated judicial authority to the existing bureaucracy, which remained largely intact.[11]

While American occupation authorities were reasonably indulgent and benign, the perceived autonomy and contentiousness of the *moderado*-administered Mexico City *ayuntamiento* increasingly strained relations. Persifor F. Smith, a scholarly lawyer who succeeded the irascible Quitman as military governor, finally dissolved the recalcitrant municipal council, clearing the way for the election of radical assemblymen whom, at that juncture, the United States clearly favored. Francisco Suárez Iriarte, a radical from Toluca, took over as first alcalde, initiating a program to decentralize power that eliminated all *fueros* and revised the tax code to make it more equitable and direct.[12] Despite advocating continuation of the war, the new municipal assembly managed to cooperate with the American occupation authorities.

This relationship stood in marked contrast to that of the fledgling national government in Querétaro, whose radical minority vigorously contested *moderado* efforts to formulate an agenda for substantive peace negotiations. Such a curious dichotomy lends credence to the notion that the radicals of the Mexico City *ayuntamiento* were more interested in consolidating their political power than in prosecuting the war. They wanted the United States out of Mexico but not until their authority had been successfully established in the Federal District and its environs, creating in essence a semi-independent state over which they exercised total control.[13] Such divergent intentions seriously compromised Mexico's bargaining position at the forthcoming peace negotiations.

Nicholas Trist had attempted to restart peace talks in October, 1847, but Peña y Peña's interim government lacked the consensus necessary to engage in meaningful colloquy. The following month, Pedro María Anaya, a fifty-two-year-old moderate from Huichapan, succeeded Peña y Peña as provisional president, clearing the way for negotiations. Anaya appointed his predecessor foreign minister with full authority to open a dialogue and named Bernardo Couto, Miguel Atristán, and Luís Gonzaga Cuevas commissioners to the peace talks.[14] On November 16, however, Trist received instructions recalling him to Washington. After considerable deliberation and encouragement from both Mexican officials and American occupation authorities, he decided to ignore these orders and press on with the peace process.[15]

Formal negotiations opened on January 2, 1848, but within a week, Anaya's provisional term expired, forcing Peña y Peña to resume the acting presidency until a congressional quorum could be assembled to sanction a constitutional successor. This unanticipated delay further aggravated an already frustrated Trist, who threatened to suspend the talks unless an agreement was reached by February 1. The ultimatum inspired the commissioners to accept a draft treaty that they then forwarded to Peña y Peña at Querétaro.[16]

Pressure from new British Chargé d'affaires, Percy W. Doyle, and a Gómez Farías-inspired uprising of pro-war radicals in San Luís Potosí convinced the timid Peña y Peña to sanction the agreement without modification. The following day (February 2) the commissioners signed the Treaty of Guadalupe Hidalgo.[17] Under its provisions, Mexico renounced all claims to Texas north of the Rio Bravo, Alta California, and the New Mexico territory (which included portions of Colorado, Utah, Arizona, and Nevada) in return for direct monetary compensation in the amount of $15 million. Additionally the United States agreed to assume the $3,250,000 in claims held against the Mexican government by American citizens, and Mexican nationals residing in the ceded territories would have their rights protected and might become American citizens if they desired.[18]

On February 29, General William O. Butler, who recently had superseded Scott as commander of occupation forces, agreed to an armistice suspending hostilities pending the outcome of the treaty-ratification process.[19] The terms of this accord preserved the extant occupation zone and returned municipal elections, taxation, and public administration to Mexican control. The *moderados,* toward whom Butler now inclined, acted quickly to dissolve the radical-dominated municipal assembly and appoint in its stead the one that had existed under Reyes y Veramendi's leadership. This development concluded the power struggle between national and municipal government that had undermined Mexico's bargaining position throughout the negotiation process.[20]

The treaty's harsh terms were loudly decried by the Mexican public, particularly those who had clamored for continuance of the war. Such remonstrances were prolonged by Mexico's inability to assemble in a timely manner the national congressional quorum necessary to consummate ratification. When the Congress finally did convene, both the Chamber of Deputies and the Senate voted on May 9, 1848, to ratify the document, the radicals' fervent protestations notwithstanding.[21] While the exchange of ratifications on May 30 officially brought the war to a close, the unpopular treaty inflamed latent political tensions and obstructed national reconciliation for some time.

Cessation of hostilities paved the way for the ascendancy of José Joaquín de Herrera to the nation's postwar presidency.[22] The new chief executive faced a profusion of daunting national reconstruction tasks: economic recovery, institutional resurrection, governmental reorganization, and military revitalization, each of which demanded forceful political determination and resources from a nearly bankrupt treasury. Before he could address these issues, however, Herrera first had to fend off a political challenge from the inveterate conspirator Mariano Paredes, who was once again instigating provincial unrest.[23] Confident that he had amassed the necessary regional military support to prevail, Paredes denounced the Treaty of Guadalupe Hidalgo and, on June 1, proclaimed his Plan of Aguascalientes. This latest incarnation of Paredes's "plans" opposed recognizing the Herrera government. In the absence of federal authority, the plan declared, the states should resume their sovereignty until the best form of government to replace the contested administration could be determined. The governors, Paredes went on, should appoint the commanders of their respective state militias until a new government could be formed, and the permanent army should remain orderly and conform to the dictates of the ranking general seconding the plan (conveniently Paredes himself).[24]

Committed to removing its forces from Mexico and therefore unwilling to intervene on behalf of any faction advocating the treaty's repudiation, American occupation authorities reproved Paredes's *cuartelazo*. United States Commissioner Nathan Clifford counseled Secretary of State James Buchanan to back Herrera. "The present administration is republican in the strictest sense," he admonished, "and the first constitutional government that Mexico has enjoyed for many years."[25]

While Paredes managed to reach agreement with the military commander of Guanajuato, enabling the unopposed occupation of that nearby city, his efforts to enlist the support of other commandants-general were unavailing. Most considered him an unprincipled opportunist whose extra-constitutional ouster of Herrera in 1845 eliminated what little hope Mexico might have had to resolve pacifically its territorial dispute with the United States. Herrera meanwhile worked to bolster the fidelity of uncommitted states and designated the venerable veteran general Anastasio Bustamante to assume command of loyalist forces. With the backing of Generals José Vicente Miñón, Pedro Cortazar, José María Yáñez, and Manuel María Lombardini, Bustamante advanced upon the *alhóndiga,* where the pronunciados had established a stronghold.[26]

After having failed to dislodge the rebels with an attack on July 8, Bustamante launched an assault ten days later that routed the defenders after prolonged and bloody fighting. This defeat, coupled with the capture of the Spanish priest and popular wartime resistance leader Celestino Domeco de Jarauta, led Paredes to abandon his army early the following morning. Left leaderless, the demoralized rebels capitulated on July 19, ending the first serious armed resistance to Herrera's nascent regime. Paredes eluded capture for several months, eventually finding refuge in a Mexico City convent, where he remained until his death on September 7, 1849.[27]

Paredes's abortive pronouncement accentuated the need for military revitalization. Devastated and nearly leaderless, the country's entire postwar army had been reduced to 7,413 officers and men, of whom only about 6,000 were fit for duty. This meager force had just forty-eight pieces of artillery, ammunition for which was scattered throughout the various states. In May, 1848, Minister of War Pedro María Anaya apprised Congress that the army "is not only incapable of fulfilling the objectives of its institutions, but is so reduced in number that it cannot even maintain internal order."[28] Anaya added that the states had refused to respond to the government's appeal for 16,000 replacements to rebuild the army's shattered formations. "From these results," he continued, "the line battalions, instead of increasing, have diminished considerably, because desertion is so general, and to avoid it one must maintain the soldiers in rigorous lock-up."[29]

The dearth of cohesive military formations encouraged instability throughout the realm. "In the rest of the States of the Federation and in the Territories," Anaya declared, "nothing, absolutely nothing exists capable of attending to internal security, nor to resist the hostilities of a foreign enemy."[30] Eruptions of rural violence in Chiapas, Oaxaca, and the Sierra

Gorda, Indian incursions into Zacatecas and Durango, and endemic banditry along the Veracruz-Puebla highway—symptoms that spilled over into contiguous regions—intensified anxieties in the already apprehensive countryside. Security concerns were fueled further by Anaya's belief that the Sierra Gorda rebels "had entered into relations with the enemy invader and had asked him for assistance to continue making war against the [Mexican] government."[31] Coordinated pacification campaigns, however, were preempted by Lieutenant Colonel Rafael Téllez's uprising in Mazatlán and a disturbance in Tamaulipas authored by inveterate rebel General José Urrea.[32]

These proliferating challenges to federal authority prompted Herrera to undertake a series of sweeping military reforms designed to professionalize the army and institutionalize civilian primacy. To direct this formidable initiative, the president chose the dynamic and well-regarded war veteran General Mariano Arista.[33] In turn, the new war minister appointed General Manuel Andrade, a forty-eight-year-old veteran cavalry officer from Puebla, to head a commission of senior officers tasked to analyze General Pedro García Conde's provident military reorganization plan of 1845 and submit recommendations for its adaptation and implementation. García Conde's plan was itself a permutation of the comprehensive proposals conceived in 1838 but never fully implemented. Finishing its work on April 11, 1849, the Andrade Commission forwarded to the president its recommendation to adopt García Conde's plan with only minor adjustments.[34]

While the Andrade Commission went about its duties, Congress enacted legislation on November 4, 1848, reducing authorized army strength to 10,000 men, increasing salaries, and revamping recruitment procedures so that army units would no longer be regarded as "presidios of criminals or accumulations of disgraced men taken casually or by force."[35] In order to fill the reorganized army's ranks with suitable volunteers, Congress assigned each state a quota based upon the ratio of one soldier for every 600 inhabitants. The government endeavored to generate interest and attract candidates by awarding a ten peso enlistment bonus, furnishing uniforms, and paying entry-level salaries ranging from 15 to 17 pesos a month for infantrymen and sappers, respectively. Noncommissioned-officer pay scales at that time ranged from 26 to 30 pesos per month, and division generals earned 417 pesos.[36]

Despite such incentives, the states did not meet their mandated assessments because the revived state militias were competing for manpower and because the federal government failed to secure legislation enabling competent and qualified rankers to earn commissions. Arista assured the Congress that, although the elimination of conscription had produced a smaller army (only 5,649 troops at the onset of 1850), that force comprised "honorable citizens who possess the aptitude for a military career." "Soldiers now serve on their own volition," he added optimistically, "and have career aspirations because they are promptly paid, adequately fed, properly clothed and effectively trained."[37]

Since independence, army officers had received little systematized and codified training, relying instead upon heroic leadership to accomplish their tactical and operational missions. This lack of formal military education diminished their utility as trainers and mentors for the junior officers who represented the future leadership of the Mexican army. "Ignorance and revolutionary audacity," Arista admonished, "could be superseded only by organization and formal military education."[38] To build the professionally socialized officer corps the postwar army so desperately needed, Arista reopened the Colegio Militar on June 17, 1848. Using the Cuartel del Rastro on the Plaza de San Lucas as a temporary facility, until Chapultepec could be repaired, he incorporated scientific and mechanical courses into the academy's curriculum and intensified tactical and gunnery instruction. Entrance exams now regulated admission, and advancement depended upon successful completion of standardized proficiency tests.[39]

Also introduced in an effort to improve the officer corps' overall quality were specific eligibility criteria for general staff duty and merit promotions contingent upon competitive examination. Henceforth, Arista promised, promotions and assignments would be based on achievement rather than political influence, and every effort would be made to reward those whose performance was extraordinary. "The government will fill the vacancies that result in the army," he explained, "by rotating unassigned officers in the rank corresponding to the vacancy, and by immediately promoting eligible officers from within the corps. Toward this end for each three vacancies that occur, two will be covered with the first [procedure], and one with the second."[40] Although they were laudable in purpose and design, the reforms neglected to reinstate the post-commissioning branch schools or establish a war college to prepare senior officers for the intricacies of general staff operations and the organizing, coordinating, and sustaining of large maneuver forces. The absence of tiered military education perpetuated the void in officer corps professional socialization and impaired attainment of branch-specific technical proficiency.[41]

With respect to organization, tactics, training, and weapons, Mexican army leaders continued to regard France as the preferred military model. Accordingly the Herrera administration contracted with the French government to purchase for the permanent army's immediate needs, 80,000 pesos worth of long-range, standardized-caliber, fulminant muskets, rifles, and carbines. To preclude hostile blockades from restricting access to armaments, the Mexican government also acquired from France manufacturing equipment that would enable Mexico to achieve domestic self-sufficiency in small-arms production.[42]

Small-arms deficiencies were relatively easy to rectify, but field-artillery shortfalls were another matter entirely. In 1850, Mexican army inventories reflected a total of 106 mobile artillery pieces *(artillería de campaña)* ranging in caliber from 8- and 12-pounder bronze cannon to 24-pounder bronze howitzers, of which only 31 were compatible with the recently adopted French system. The remaining 75 serviceable pieces were relegated to the military colonies for frontier defense or melted down and recast in foundries retooled to produce cannon only of calibers suitable to the new system. At the same time an effort was launched to remount stationary cannon *(artillería de plaza)* that had been dismounted and to repair the forts in which they were housed. Of 444 such cannon and mortars scattered about the country, 96 (22 percent) were unserviceable.[43]

To help maintain public order and enforce the law, on July 15, 1848, Congress enacted legislation reorganizing the national guard into local and mobile militia formations. The mobile militia could be deployed for up to six months outside the confines of its home state; the local militia was restricted to service within its own territorial boundaries. Militiamen were paid by the states only when activated, during which time their compensation was equal to that accorded the regular army. "To defend the nation's independence, sustain its institutions, preserve public tranquility and enforce the laws and authorities established for them," all physically fit men between the ages of eighteen and fifty-five, except doctors, servants, police, federal employees, and members of the permanent army, were now subject to conscription by lottery.[44] The state militias served at the pleasure of their respective governors; the president directed the activities of units assigned to the Federal District and territories.

In September, 1849, Congress authorized an additional thirty-four mobile militia companies to bolster defenses along the northern frontier. Equipped by the states but paid by the federal government, the 1,900 men ultimately recruited for these formations were allocated among the seven northern frontier states, with Coahuila receiving 300, Durango 400, and the remaining five states 240 men each. Congress also sanctioned the *guardia de policía,* a provincial law-enforcement organization intended to protect travelers from bandits and administer prisons in the Federal District.[45] Although it was comprehensive, this latest round of enhancements did little to abate the attacks upon vulnerable frontier settlements. Like their predecessors, these new militia companies were too scattered and poorly equipped to intercept hostile intruders effectively. Indian raiders simply bypassed the militia posts and refused to subject themselves to engagements under unfavorable conditions.

The rejuvenated national guard now represented the only other organized military force in Mexico, as the inability or unwillingness of the states to fill their prescribed active militia manpower quotas had all but extinguished that element. Only the Tampico Battalion (ninety-three men) and two companies from Alvarado and Acayúcan (ninety-six men collectively) remained in the force structure as designated *activo* units.[46] Arista was pragmatic in accepting the demise of the active militia as an operational component of the military establishment. From its inception in 1825, the concept had never worked as envisioned because the citizen soldiers comprising these units customarily were retained on extended active duty, blurring the distinction between full-time and part-time service. Competition for manpower among the three military components also helped insure that each would suffer chronic shortages, with the active militia eventually becoming the least attractive service alternative. Despite such liabilities, Arista believed that peripheral jurisdictions disquieted by chronic unrest still could benefit from the presence of an active militia battalion. Accordingly he advocated that in Yucatán an organization be established that was modeled after the one in Tampico and led by permanent-army officer veterans of the Caste War currently stationed in that turbulent province.[47]

The general intent of Herrera's military reforms was to create a small, efficient, well-equipped army at a sustainable cost to the nation. Through Arista's aggressiveness and congressional acquiescence, significant strides were made toward achieving many of those objectives. The reforms improved military education and training, reduced the officer-to-enlisted ratio, attenuated some of the more egregious inequities affecting rankers, curtailed special privileges, and made the entire military establishment more affordable. By 1850, Herrera's military budget request was just 6,280,449 pesos, a sum into which had been factored mandatory salary reductions for all personnel except those who had served in the war with the United States.[48]

Even cumulatively, however, these inclusive measures could not engender a cohesive national army. While the military was in fact leaner and more efficient, it remained scattered about the country in small garrisons, unskilled in the complexities of coordinated large unit operations and influenced by the caprices of regional caciques. García Conde's concept of consolidated divisional posts had not been realized, and the institution still suffered from a lack of national identity and purpose.[49] The army, moreover, was unable to extricate itself from the ideological adversarialism that continued to infect Mexican politics. Herrera's well-intentioned effort to depoliticize the army ultimately failed because the latent causes of political instability and attendant military interventionism remained as virulent as ever. In the final analysis this latest experiment in military reform was frustrated by the progressive resurgence of liberal-conservative antagonism.

Besides political resistance, Herrera's military reforms had to contend with a litany of regional disturbances the most pressing of which was a revolutionary agrarian movement in the Sierra Gorda, a region of rugged mountains and hot valleys protruding into the states of Guanajuato, Querétaro, and San Luís Potosí. Discontent among the resident Pames and Jonás Indians had been brewing for some time over the increased privatization of communal forest lands *(tierras baldías)* the exploitation of which constituted their traditional livelihood.[50] The enactment of legislation in January, 1847, authorizing the government to dispose of 15 million pesos worth of mortmain property furnished the spark necessary to ignite the fury of those natives whose communal lands the new law affected.[51] State militias suppressed the uprising in short order, but preoccupation with the American invasion precluded the federal government from attending to the root causes of discontent and afforded the rebels a respite in which to recover and recruit additional adherents. As the movement reconstituted, the charcoal makers *(carboneros)* and wood cutters *(leñadores)* were joined by army deserters, bandits, and disgruntled peons from nearby haciendas. By early 1848 the insurgency had revitalized under the leadership of Eleuterio Quiróz, a former muleteer from the hacienda de Tapanco in San Luís Potosí. Vehemently opposed to the treaty being proffered by the United States, Quiróz expediently affiliated with Mariano Paredes' Plan of Aguascalientes and began attacking haciendas bordering the Sierra Gorda. The government's initial response was to extend amnesty, even to army deserters, and attempt to co-opt Quiróz and those of his leaders "who are influential and considered necessary" with cash stipends of 10,000 and 5,000 pesos, respectively. But neither the cash nor the amnesty had the desired effect, and hostilities continued to escalate.[52]

Amnesty and bribery having failed, Herrera ordered Anastasio Bustamante, the seasoned sixty-eight-year-old commandant-general of Guanajuato, to crush the insurgents with overwhelming military force.[53] Among the commanders Bustamante selected for this mission were Colonels José López Uraga, Angel Guzmán, and Tomás Mejía, the third having just the year before led an abortive antigovernment uprising in a region contiguous to the Sierra. Several years later, Mejía again would incite rebellion in the Sierra Gorda, an infraction for which the inveterate conspirator finally was incarcerated.[54]

Operating in cooperation with designated contingents of state militia, federal forces garnered some initial successes until, on February 10, 1849, Lieutenant Colonel Leonardo Márquez pronounced in favor of the restoration of Antonio López de Santa Anna. A battalion commander in Guzmán's brigade, Márquez had, up until that point, acquitted himself with distinction.[55] For the next eight days, Bustamante was forced to suspend his counterguerrilla campaign to deal with Márquez's *cuartelazo,* a diversion that enabled the Sierra rebels to seize Rio Verde and other strategically important points.[56] Herrera reacted to these unwelcome developments by reinforcing government forces with the Tampico and Monterrey Battalions and requesting 2,000 additional national guardsmen from the contiguous states. These reinforcements enabled the federal commanders to secure the most vulnerable haciendas, forcing the rebels to venture farther from their sanctuary to find undefended targets.[57]

The revolt continued on until October, 1849, when government soldiers captured Quiróz during his desperate attempt to seize San Luís Potosí. A military tribunal found the insurgent chieftain guilty of treason and sentenced him to be executed within two months. His most zealous supporters were resettled in military colonies along the northern frontier, where their aggression could be channeled into more constructive endeavors.[58] Herrera gave promotions and bonuses to permanent army personnel who helped suppress the rebellion, and to national guardsmen he extended eligibility for land grants in the military colonies being established in the Sierra Gorda and along the northern frontier. To settle 480 military colonists and 600 *vecinos* in the new colonies, the government appropriated 84,457 pesos.[59]

Postwar military reform was further encumbered by a resurgence of armed conflict in Yucatán. Over time, agricultural production there had shifted to large henequen plantations owned by the predominately white landed elite *(dzules)*, progressively alienating Mayan communal lands. This transition left many laborers outside the region's monocultural economic system and fueled latent racial enmity. Pent-up animosity finally erupted in violence on

July 29, 1849, initiating a vicious insurgency that seriously threatened provincial integrity.[60] Government anxiety over the fate of the endangered province intensified when it became known that the British were clandestinely providing arms and ammunition to the insurgents in an attempt to estrange Yucatán further from Mexican sovereignty.[61] Steadily deteriorating conditions prompted Herrera to dispatch General José Manuel Micheltorena with an expeditionary force of 4,000 soldiers in February, 1850, to subdue the rebels. A former commandant-general of California and veteran of the Angostura campaign, the forty-eight-year-old oaxaqueño was a competent leader, though neither an innovator nor a risk-taker. Through a combination of amnesty and relentless pressure that afforded the insurgents little respite, Micheltorena managed, by July, to recapture Valladolid and Tihosuco and drive the rebels into the interior. Despite measurable progress, the commandant-general was unable to crush the insurrection completely. Hampered by desertions of national guard troops fed up with overdue pay, inadequate rations, and years of dispiriting warfare, the government offensive ground to a halt.[62] The diversion of scarce military resources to suppress the Sierra Gorda uprising and the pronouncements of Paredes and Márquez combined to deprive the Yucatán expeditionary force of the assets necessary to bring that conflict to a swift and congruous conclusion. The government's inability to provision its forces adequately, moreover, inspired soldiers to pilfer maize from the most proximate Indian fields. Such illegal confiscations of limited indigenous food supplies prolonged the war by alienating an otherwise neutral element of the population.

By the spring of 1851, the prevailing stalemate in Yucatán prompted War Minister Arista to replace Micheltorena with General Rómulo Díaz de la Vega, a forty-seven-year-old veteran engineer officer with a reputation for resilience and resourcefulness. In an effort to resolve the conflict expeditiously, Arista gave his new commandant-general extraordinary authority. He also provided the means necessary to rebuild the expeditionary force, in the expectation "that by paying the troops with regularity, they will not have recourse to despoil the Indians of their provisions."[63] This represented a significant policy change from a "war of extermination to that of submission," which from the onset permitted a reduction in confrontations with the insurgents and opened the possibility for constructive dialogue.

In May, 1851, a sanguine Díaz de la Vega informed Arista that "the Indians gathered in the aforementioned forests declare that there is a positive desire among the eastern rebels to return to government authority, rather necessitated by the shortages of maize they are suffering."[64] Backed by credible armed force, the government's conciliation policy gradually curtailed the level of hostilities. On September 16, 1852, the principal chiefs assembled to sign a convention promising "not to commit any acts of aggression against the white race."[65] At least for the time being, the tempestuous province of Yucatán relinquished its status as one of the ongoing crises distracting government attention from the pressing business of military reform, economic recovery, and political stability.

Besides the Sierra Gorda and Yucatán uprisings, military reform initiatives had to contend with chronic insecurity along the northern periphery. The withdrawal of Taylor's army following ratification of the Treaty of Guadalupe Hidalgo exposed this region to a resurgence of Indian incursions.[66] The permanent presidial companies garrisoned along the frontier had all but vanished, and what remained of the militia was neither adequately equipped nor sufficiently trained to deal with the highly mobile and elusive raiders. Forays into Sonora, Chihuahua, and Durango were inflicting intolerable damage and suffering upon the beleaguered inhabitants of those vulnerable communities.[67] Herrera responded by ordering additional army units into the area to safeguard the most endangered settlements. But Sierra Gorda, Yucatán, and other trouble spots more proximate to the capital devoured the preponderance of the government's limited military resources, leaving most frontier communities to fend for themselves.

Both the president and his minister of war believed that long-term resolution of the intractable frontier problem resided in more extensive colonization. Congress already had earmarked 625,091 pesos from the American war-indemnification award to establish military colonies at strategic points along the frontier and create the thirty to forty mobile militia companies believed necessary to protect the settlements from hostile intruders.[68] Military colonies, however, constituted only one facet of the president's conceptual solution; he also advocated offering "free land and immunity from taxation for a period of six years to foreigners who desire to live in the republic."[69] But congressional fear of a large influx of protestant immigrants scuttled that idea, compelling the war ministry to fall back upon military colonies and presidios as the only achievable pacification vehicles.

Finally, in July, 1848, the pressing issue of military colonies prompted Congress to enact legislation offering volunteers parcels of arable land ranging in size from one to three *fanegas de tierra* in return for a six-year commitment. If the colonist agreed to remain in service for an additional six years, his land allocation was doubled. As further incentive, married settlers were exempted from all taxes, including ecclesiastical levies. This legislation also included an appropriation of 10,000 pesos to purchase gifts for non-hostile Indians, a technique employed by Spain with considerable success during the latter part of the eighteenth century.[70] In fact the concept of the military colony derived in large part from that developed and implemented by Teodoro de Croix during his seven-year tenure as commandant-general of New Spain's interior provinces (see Chapter 1).[71]

Concurrently the northern frontier was reorganized into three geographical segments, each under the jurisdiction of a commandant-inspector carrying the rank of colonel, and a captain was put in charge of each new settlement. By mid-1849, 1,072 colonists had been resettled in eighteen colonies established in the states of Tamaulipas (3), Coahuila (4), Chihuahua (5), Sonora (5), and Baja California (1). However, because it was short on funds and lacked appeal, the project never achieved its proponents' expectations. By 1851, only half the proposed settlements had been founded and the number of recruits was considerably less than what was needed.[72] Mexican citizens, it seems, preferred the relative tranquility and security of the interior to the harsh and dangerous life of the frontier, incentives notwithstanding.

The interminable succession of pronouncements and insurrections vexing most of Herrera's presidential term consigned to failure even the best-intentioned military reforms. Despite what appears to be a genuine commitment to professionalizing and modernizing the army, neither Herrera nor his successor as president, fellow moderate Mariano Arista, achieved those elusive goals. The failure to dissociate military units from their traditional regional affiliations helped perpetuate *caciquismo* and frustrated efforts to create a consciousness of national identity. Furthermore, even though troops in the postwar army were indeed better paid, fed, equipped, and trained, the incentives offered for enlistment and retention fell short of making professional soldiering an attractive alternative to other careers available to Mexican males of eligible military age. And competition from the revitalized state militias further restricted the pool from which the regular army could recruit talented and motivated young men.

Despite the admirable intentions of military reformers, resurgent ideological rivalry perpetuated the army's propensity for interfering in government, especially when its corporate interests appeared to be in jeopardy. Preoccupation with such domestic matters, it seems, quickly superseded the lessons of the recent war with the United States, encouraging the army to reassert its primacy as guarantor of internal security and progenitor of ideologically compatible political leaders. With state governors once again in possession of militias, Arista's moderate regime kept a tight rein on deployable permanent army contingents to contain potential *cuartelazos.* Blame for the ignominious peace treaty still hung like an albatross around the necks of the *moderados,* emboldening conservatives to agitate the political process. Such partisanship provoked a series of mutinies that, in April, 1853, led to yet another Santa Anna presidency. With the caudillo back at the helm for the eleventh and final time, the stage was set for an outbreak of factional violence that engendered circumstances conducive to another foreign occupation.

Conclusion

Sovereignty subtly vitiated the professional army envisioned by New Spain's eighteenth-century viceroys. The residual effects of mass participation, inherited from a decade of brutalizing civil war that militarized the countryside, quickly splintered the expedient coalition of royalists and insurgents that brought an end to Spanish colonial rule. Absent a common enemy and with no acceptable national agenda around which to rally, what little cohesion this incongruous confederation still maintained swiftly abraded. Rather than a unitary armed force, Mexico embarked upon nationhood with a heterogeneous collection of constabularies whose loyalties were overwhelmingly local and intensely personal.

The leadership vacuum occasioned by the extirpation of royal government and the creole aristocracy's eschewal of political participation gave rise in republican Mexico, and elsewhere in Central and South America, to national military leaders distinguished by the manner in which they sought, achieved, and maintained power. After half a century of political exclusion, creole officers yearned for a prominent role in governing the independent nation they helped create. But political aspiration alone was no substitute for apprenticeship. Habituated to centralistic authoritarianism and accustomed to violence, caudillos were predisposed to protect corporate interests through expediency and coercion. Once liberated from the moderating influence of an assertive and politically engaged elite and the constraints imposed by traditional colonial institutions, praetorianism quickly supplanted patriotism.

Repudiation of Mexico's brief experiment with monarchy reordered national political affiliations. In the republican government that superseded Agustín de Iturbide's empire in 1823, radicals championed a powerful state that would limit privilege and intervene on behalf of the urban lower classes. Moderates advocated a weak state with unrestricted economic enterprise and ecclesiastical circumscription. Uncomfortable with an unfettered republic, which they feared would parrot Jacobin France, moderates embraced federalism to avoid the recurrent cycles of revolution and reaction endemic to Europe. Conservatives favored a centralized bureaucracy with an enforced hierarchical structure that resisted social mobility and preserved existing privilege. This ideological differentiation eventually settled into a contest between conservatives and moderates over centralized versus decentralized government, with the radicals represented to varying degrees in both camps.

The contentious and protracted rivalry between centralists and federalists cleaved the army's senior leadership. Ambitious officers sought alliances with whatever political faction best accommodated their corporate expectations and personal aspirations. Former insurgents generally gravitated toward the radical element; ex-royalists embraced the conservative faction. Moderates attracted adherents from both contingents in small but relatively even numbers. These affiliations were never absolute, as Santa Anna demonstrated on more than one occasion, but their intrinsic divisiveness helped determine the military's institutional configuration. Ultimately, the permanent army and active militia came to harbor primarily former royalists of conservative or moderate persuasion, and the state militias became sanctuaries for liberally inclined erstwhile guerrillas.

The establishment of commandancies-general in 1824 accelerated the disaggregation by further decentralizing military authority. By dispersing military formations throughout the country with minimal regard for legitimate national-security imperatives, this jurisdictional arrangement subjected soldiers to the personalized leadership and caprice of regional caciques. The middle-class creole officers heading up these territorial satrapies derived inordinate influence and power from the isolation engendered by a topography so rugged and diverse that it inhibited communications, fostered individualism, and discouraged societal cohesion. Absorbed in their own political, social, and economic advancement, the caciques tenaciously guarded their provincial prerogatives. When challenged, they did not hesitate to employ the coercive means at their disposal to bring about a favorable political outcome.

The growing animosity between national and regional forces destabilized the polity and sundered army professionalization. Attempts by the federal government to impose its will upon the countryside invariably elicited a violent response from those most affected by the perceived encroachment. State governors, commandants-general, and sundry other regional satraps crafted temporary alliances to depose regimes whose policies they deemed inimical to their interests. Once in power, the perpetrators of these *cuartelazos* were at liberty to reorder the government to their liking, at least for a while. The losers generally received light treatment because the adjudicators clearly realized that the tables might be turned at any time. Military personnel files are replete with examples of officers who successfully resurrected their careers after having instigated an abortive mutiny or affiliated with a losing faction.

Among the provincial citizenry the localism that abetted the personal ambitions of regional warlords occasioned widespread indifference to events occurring outside the immediate confines. Fed by social injustice and economic inequity, such apathy made filling permanent army and active militia ranks an onerous and unreliable proposition. Moreover, competition from the state militias further reduced the pool of eligible males from which the army could draw replacements. Military service in either of the federal components was so unpleasant that those who could not evade the despised levy deserted at alarming rates. Unable to attract suitable volunteers, recruiters resorted to indiscriminate conscription that invariably filled army ranks with society's least desirable and most untrainable elements.

Overwhelmed with constabulary duties, the army seldom enjoyed the respite, resources, or direction necessary to achieve a level of operational readiness commensurate with the challenges to territorial sovereignty that plagued Mexico during the first three decades of nationhood. With permanent army and active militia formations chronically under strength, raggedly equipped, and geographically dispersed, the task of countering contingencies fell upon extemporized armies of conscripted peasants led by marginally qualified officers with little personal interest in the well-being of their charges. Poorly motivated, ill trained, and haphazardly provisioned, these improvised armies were significantly disadvantaged when faced with adversity or steadfast opposition.

Government awareness of army deficiencies and limitations did little to engender permanent solutions. Despite real threats to Mexican territorial sovereignty, military and political leaders refused to suspend their partisan agendas for the good of the nation. Neither the Spanish incursion (1829), the Texas secession (1835–36), nor the French intervention (1838–39) persuaded these adversaries to set ideological differences aside long enough to collaborate effectively on the country's pressing security problems. Time and again inveterate parochialism nullified the earnest enterprise of reform-minded patriots to professionalize and modernize the army. The vital issues of centralized command, equitable recruitment, standardized training, soldier welfare, and tiered military education elicited vigorous opposition from caciques who regarded such undertakings as elaborate attempts to limit territorial authority. Their implacable resistance repeatedly abrogated programs that could have produced a professionally socialized and technically proficient officer corps obedient to civilian authority. Clearly, such unfettered military and political contentiousness facilitated the American invasions of 1846–47 and abetted the forfeiture of one-half of Mexico's national territory.

Secessionist movements in the Sierra Gorda and Yucatán, Indian incursions along the northern frontier, and unabated regionalism thwarted the efforts of postwar reformers to create an authentic national army from units that survived the war. Interminable constabulary duties kept the few remaining formations continuously engaged and consumed precious resources that otherwise could have been directed toward training, education, refitting, recruitment, and retention. Inability to disassociate military units from the protectionist inclinations of local warlords perpetuated *caciquismo* and frustrated efforts to revitalize the discredited and disheartened federal army. Determined to maintain their coercive capability to influence political decision making, the caciques stridently resisted any power-limiting ventures. Resurgent ideological factionalism subsumed the lessons of 1846–47, paralyzing the military-reform agenda and creating conditions conducive to another iteration of civil war and foreign intervention.

By 1855, growing anxiety over further American territorial encroachment into northern Mexico effectively blurred centralism as a distinguishing feature between liberals and conservatives. No longer obsessed with federalism, the liberals redirected their energy toward eradicating ecclesiastical political power.[1] Vehement liberal anticlericalism aimed at the complete liquidation of Church property brought on yet another round of civil strife. The ensuing Three Years' War (1857–60) pitted the conservative core against the liberal periphery; the clerical, military, and landowning elite against the Indian peasants of Oaxaca and Guerrero and the *mestizo rancheros* of northern Mexico. Emerging victorious, the liberals inaugurated a reformist agenda the following year that featured as its centerpiece the total separation of Church and state.[2]

The liberal reform program was derailed by chronic indebtedness and economic deterioration, creating conditions for another foreign intervention in 1862 that enabled devoted monarchists to establish a Mexican empire under Hapsburg prince, Archduke Maximilian. French military occupation, however, motivated patriots of both liberal and conservative persuasion to set aside their ideological differences and collaborate in unified resistance against the imperialists. Withdrawal of the French expeditionary army in January, 1867, cleared the way for a full-scale assault by republican army forces that drove Maximilian's monarchists from power and restored Benito Júarez to the presidency. Determined to suppress militarism, Júarez demobilized two-thirds of the 70,000-man republican army and ruthlessly crushed subsequent *cuartelazos* by disgruntled caciques. The Army of Restoration *(Ejército Restaurador)* remained quiescent until Juárez's death and a resurgence of militarism orchestrated by the preeminent Oaxacan cacique, Porfirio Díaz, brought the liberal revolution to an end in November, 1876.[3]

Adroitly exploiting the common bond of loyalty engendered by his heroic resistance to French occupation, Díaz centralized direction of the armed forces, crushed the regional warlords, brought order at the expense of liberty, and opened the way for economic development.[4] His establishment of an authentic national army rendered increasingly irrelevant the state militias and the caciques to whom they responded. Professional militarism was further vitiated by the steady influx of western European military intellectualism and technology, which made raising and equipping an armed force strong enough to challenge the federal government prohibitively expensive for local warlords.[5]

The abatement of *caciquismo,* unfortunately, did not insulate Díaz's federal army from politicization. Progressive use of the military to perpetuate porfirian despotism ultimately spawned an institution incapable of either understanding or coping with the violent social revolution that consumed Mexico between 1910 and 1920. The 29,000-man urban-bound, railway-dependent army, its ranks once more filled with insouciant conscripts, lacked the mobility, initiative, and leadership to defeat the insurgents and destroy their regenerative capacity. Withdrawing to the principal cities and lowlands, the *federales* adopted a static enclave strategy that ceded the countryside to the elusive, highly mobile rebels.[6] By failing to eradicate the local uprisings, Díaz incurred a national revolution that his overextended, undermotivated federal army could not contain. Steady erosion of government morale caused by a succession of rebel victories brought down the *profiriato* on May 25, 1910. For five more years the federal army fought on—until the Constitutional revolutionaries finally finished it as a unitary organization capable of sustaining or removing legitimate governments.[7] Even so, genuine military apoliticization was not achieved until 1940, when Manuel Avila Camacho, by eliminating the military sector from the Partido de la Revolución Mexicana (PRM), breaking up the armed-forces block in Congress, and forcibly retiring most revolutionary generals still on active duty, wrested from the army its last vestiges of political influence.[8]

APPENDIX 1

Status of Mexican Military Forces in 1826

Permanent Army	*Statutory Strength*	*Under Arms*
3 artillery brigades	1,767	1,767
12 infantry battalions	9,876	9,876
12 cavalry regiments	6,703	6,708
34 presidial companies	3,317	3,317
11 mobile infantry and cavalry companies on coasts	1,120	1,120
TOTAL:	22,788	22,788
Active Militia (Statutory)		
12 artillery companies	1,152	
20 infantry battalions in interior	24,240	
13 artillery battalions on coasts	6,600	
6 squadrons and 9 companies of coast guard cavalry	2,475	
15 cavalry companies in interior	1,500	
1 cavalry squadron in Mazatlán	200	
TOTAL:	36,167	
Active Militia (Under Arms)		
4 infantry battalions in interior	4,848	
4 battalions of coast guard infantry	2,000	
12 squadrons and 3 companies of coast guard cavalry	825	
15 presidial cavalry companies	1,500	
1 cavalry squadron in Mazatlán	200	
TOTAL:	9,373	

SUMMARY

Component	*Statutory*	*Under Arms*	*Shortfall*
permanent army	22,788	22,788	0
active militia	36,167	9,373	26,794
total armed forces	58,955	32,161	26,794

Source: Memoria del Secretario de Estado y del despacho de la guerra, 1826, estados 2, 3.

APPENDIX 2

Status of Mexican Forces in 1850

Location	*Unit*	*Strength*	*Total*
México and Cuernavaca	3rd Inf. Battalion	389	
	invalid corps	301	
	foot artillery (two batteries)	90	
	horse artillery (two batteries)	79	
	5th Cav. (two squadrons)	197	
	6th Cav. (one squadron)	97	1153
San Luís Potosí, Guanajuato, and Sierra Gorda	Sapper Battalion	199	
	artillery	88	
	2nd Cav. Corps	127	
	military colonies	183	597
Veracruz and Jalapa	artillery	30	
	7th Inf. Battalion	258	
	active company of Alvarado	54	
	active company of Acayucan	59	401
Perote	6th Cav. (one squadron)	125	125
Tampico	artillery	16	
	8th Inf. Battalion	199	
	active battalion of Tampico	93	308
Tabasco	artillery	44	
	6th Inf. Battalion (two companies)	86	
	7th Inf. Battalion (two companies)	150	280

Appendix 2 (cont.)

Location	*Unit*	*Strength*	*Total*
Yucatán	6th Inf. Battalion	279	279
Acapulco, Jalisco,	artillery	46	
and Colima	artillery	26	72
Sinaloa	artillery	53	
	4th Inf. Battalion	175	228
Matamoros	artillery	12	
	1st Inf. Battalion	141	
	4th Cav. Corps	169	322
Camargo	1st Cav. Corps	188	188
Monterrey	artillery	22	
and the Frontier	military colonies	434	456
Durango	artillery	32	
	5th Inf. Battalion	145	
	3rd Cav. Corps	156	333
Chihuahua	2nd Inf. Battalion	201	
	military colonies	296	497
Western Frontier	military colonies	340	340
Chiapas Frontier	3rd Inf. Battalion (two companies)	70	70
general total of forces in the republic			5,649

Note: Besides the forces cited above, there were in the actual service and pay of the federal treasury, 5 chiefs, 44 officers, and 1,017 national-guard troops of all branches stationed in Veracruz, Acapulco, Sinaloa, Durango, Querétaro, and San Luís de la Paz (*Memoria del Secretario de Estado y del despacho de guerra y marina,* 1850, estado 4).

APPENDIX 3

Prominent Mexican Generals, 1822–52

Name	*Dates/Birth Place*	*Entered Service*	*Rank/Branch*	*Political Post*	*Military Post*
Nicolás Bravo	1786–1854 Chilpancingo, Gro.	1811 insurgent	div. gen. infantry	interim president	army commander
Anastasio Bustamante	1780–1853 Jiquilpan, Mich.	1802 royalist	div. gen. infantry	president	army commander
Guadalupe Victoria	1786–1843 Tamazula, Durango	1811 insurgent	div. gen. infantry	president	army commander
Antonio López de Santa Anna	1795–1876 Jalapa, Veracruz	1810 royalist	div. gen. infantry	president	army commander
José Joaquín de Herrera	1792–1854 Jalapa, Veracruz	1809 royalist	div. gen. infantry	president	minister of war

Appendix 3 (cont.)

Name	*Dates/Birth Place*	*Entered Service*	*Rank/Branch*	*Political Post*	*Military Post*
Vicente Filisola	1785–1850 Riveli, Naples	1804 royalist	div. gen. infantry	governor of Michoacán	minister of war
Manuel E. Rincón	1784–1849 Perote, Veracruz	1811 insurgent	div. gen. infantry	member of Congress	minister of war
Gabriel Valencia	1799–1848 Mexico City	1810 royalist	div. gen. cavalry	member of Congress	army commander
Mariano Paredes y Arrillaga	1797–1849 Mexico City	1812 royalist	div. gen. infantry	president	minister of war
Valentín Canalizo	1794–1850 Monterrey, N. León	1811 royalist	div. gen infantry	interim president	minister of war
José María Tornel y Men.	1789–1853 Orizaba, Veracruz	1813 insurgent	div. gen. infantry	member of Congress	minister of war
Mariano Arista	1802–55 San Luís Potosí	1817 royalist	div. gen. infantry	president	minister of war

Juan Álvarez y Benítez	1790–1867 Atoyac, Guerrero	1810 insurgent	div. gen. cavalry	president	army commander
Manuel Gómez Pedraza	1789–1851 Querétaro	1800 royalist	div. gen. infantry	president	minister of war
José Mariano Salas	1797–1867 Mexico City	1813 royalist	div. gen. cavalry	interim president	army deputy commander
José María Jarero	1801–67 Jalapa, Veracruz	1816 royalist	div. gen. infantry	governor of Puebla	commandant general
Rómulo Díaz de la Vega	1804–77 Mexico City	1821 royalist	div. gen engineer	interim president	commandant general
Pedro María Anaya	1795–1854 Huichapan, Hgo.	1811 royalist	brig. gen. infantry	interim president	minister of war
Pedro de Ampudia	1805–68 Havana, Cuba	1818 royalist	brig. gen. engineer	member of Congress	commandant general
Manuel María Lombardini	1802–53 Mexico City	1814 royalist	brig. gen. infantry	interim president	army commander

Appendix 3 (cont.)

Name	*Dates/Birth Place*	*Entered Service*	*Rank/Branch*	*Political Post*	*Military Post*
Pedro García Conde	1806–51 Arispe, Sonora	1817 royalist	brig. gen. engineer	member of Congress	minister of war
José Urrea	1797–1849 Horcasitas, Sonora	1809 royalist	brig. gen. cavalry	governor of Sonora	commandant general
Juan Nepomuceno Almonte	1803–69 Carácuaro, Mich.	1810 insurgent	brig. gen. cavalry	minister to United States	minister of war
Lino José Alcorta	1787–1854 Veracruz	1813 royalist	brig. gen. infantry	governor of Sinaloa	minister of war
Ignacio Mora y Villamil	1791–1870 Mexico City	1805 royalist	brig. gen. engineer	Armistice Commission	minister of war
José Manuel Micheltorena	1802–53 Oaxaca	1816 royalist	brig. gen. cavalry	governor of California	commandant general
Luís Cortazar	1796–1840 Celaya, Guanajuato	1810 royalist	brig. gen. infantry	governor of Guanajuato	commandant general

Antonio Gaona	1793–1848 Havana, Cuba	1801 royalist	brig. gen. infantry	governor of Puebla	army deputy commander
Antonio León	1794–1847 Huajuapan, Oaxaca	1811 royalist	brig. gen. cavalry	member of Congress	commandant general

Sources: Carreño, ed. *Jefes del Ejército Mexicano en 1847*, 1914; *Diccionario Porrúa de história, biografía y geografía de México*, 1995; Orozco Linares, *Gobernates de México: desde la época Prehispánica hasta nuestros días*, 1985.

NOTES

CHAPTER 1

1. Lucas Alamán, *Historia de Méjico desde los primeros movimientos que preparon su independencia en el año de 1808 hasta la época presente* (Mexico: J. Mariano Lara, 1850), 1:107–108; Lyle N. McAlister, "The Reorganization of the Army in New Spain, 1763–1766," *Hispanic American Historical Review* 33 (February, 1953): 7–9. While more economical, transferring to New Spain responsibility for its own defense entailed risks inherent in arming colonists who ultimately might turn against the mother country. Both the Crown and the viceregal government harbored an inveterate fear of social uprisings by the underclasses, particularly the racially mixed element stigmatized as castes *(castas)*. But the loss of Havana to the British and the unexpected acquisition of Louisiana provided the requisite impetus to supersede such anxieties.
2. Arriaga to Villalba, August 1, 1764, reales instrucciones para el desempeño de los comisiones que S.M. le ha encargado en ese Reyno, Archivo General de la Nación (AGN), Reales Cédulas (RC), vol. 85, exp. 142, para. 17, 35; Oficiales generales que pasan con destino a Nueva España, y sueldos que gozan al año, AGN (RC), vol. 85, exp. 142; McAlister, "Reorganization of the Army," 13–14.
3. Cruillas to Julián de Arriaga, México, January 2 and 7, 1765, AGN, Correspondencia de Virreyes (CV), 2nd series, vol. 10, exp. 985, 990; Lyle N. McAlister, *The "Fuero Militar" in New Spain, 1764–1800* (Gainesville: Univ. of Florida Press, 1957), 3–4; María del Carmen Velázquez, *El estado de guerra en Nueva España, 1760–1803* (México: El Colegio de México, 1950), 63–73; Bernard E. Bobb, *The Viceregency of Antonio María Bucareli in New Spain, 1771–1779* (Austin: Univ. of Texas Press, 1962), 87; McAlister, "Reorganization of the Army," 28–31. On the eve of his departure, Villalba reported 2,341 regulars, 9,244 provincial militiamen, and 1,454 urban militiamen on the colony's military manning rosters. Marqués de Croix (1766–71), however, believed those strengths to be greatly overrated and contended that many deficiencies had to be corrected before the army could be considered operationally effective. Croix to Arriaga, no. 64, México, October 27, 1766, AGN, CV, 2nd series, vol. 11, foja 111.
4. Dictamen del Marqués de la Torre, October 24, 1768, AGN, Indiferente de Guerra (IG), vol. 36b, para. 25–27, 38–39; Villalba to Marqués de Cruillas, México, December 16, 1765, AGN, IG, vol. 151; Christon I. Archer, *The Bourbon Army in Mexico, 1760–1810* (Albuquerque: Univ. of New Mexico Press, 1977), 15; Herbert I. Priestley, *José de Gálvez, Visitador General of New Spain 1765–1771* (Berkeley: Univ. of California Press, 1916), 164–71.
5. Bucareli to Arriaga, México, October 5, 1771, AGN, CV, 1st series, vol. 10, exp. 18; Bobb, *Antonio María Bucareli,* 91–99, 102; McAlister, *Fuero Militar,* 55.

6. Martín de Mayorga to Gálvez, México, October 5, 1780, AGN, CV, 1st series, vol. 6, exp. 748; Archer, *The Bourbon Army,* 20; Velázquez, *El estado de guerra,* 134–35. The regimiento de la Corona, which included a considerable number of Mexican soldiers, was relocated to protect Havana and Santo Domingo, and it provided contingents to reinforce Bernardo de Gálvez's expeditionary forces in Florida and Louisiana.
7. Ricardo Rees Jones, *Real ordenanza para el establicimiento é instrucción de Intendentes de Exército y Provincia en el reino de Nueva España* (Mexico: UNAM, 1984); Archer, *The Bourbon Army,* 21.
8. Dictamen del Coronel Don Francisco Antonio Crespo, Inspector interino de las tropas del Virreynato de Nueva España sobre su mejor arreglo y establicimiento, expuesto al Exmo. Sr. Virrey Dn. Matías de Gálvez, México, July 31, 1784, Bibliotéca Nacional (BN), División de Manuscritos (MS), tomo 173; José Antonio Calderón Quijano, ed., *Los virreyes de Nueva España en el reinado de Carlos IV, (1787–1798)* (Sevilla: Publicaciones de la Escuela de Estudios Hispano-Americanos de Sevilla, 1972), 33; Archer, *The Bourbon Army,* 21–22.
9. Crespo, "Dictamen," para. 147–56; Proyecto militar de 1784: Resumen de fuerzas de los cuerpos provinciales que se proponen, Archivo General de Indias (AGI), México, legajo 2418; McAlister, *Fuero Militar,* 56–59.
10. Antonio Valdés to Flórez, October 20, 1788, Real ordenes que corresponden a la formación de los Regimientos de Infantería fixos . . . y hechas las prevenciones conducientes a su total arreglo en vista del proyecto de Coronel Dn. Francisco Antonio Crespo, AGN, RC, vol. 141, exp. 106; Jorge Ignacio Rubio Mañé, "Política de Virrey Flórez en la Comandancia General de Provincias Internas," *Boletín del Archivo General de la Nación* 24 (1953): 213–57; Velázquez, *El estado de guerra,* 243–45.
11. Calderón Quijano, *Los virreyes de Nueva España,* 93; Jorge Ignacio Rubio Mañé, "Síntesis histórica de la vida del II Conde de Revillagigedo, Virrey de Nueva España," *Anuario de Estudios Americanos* 6 (1949): 451–96.
12. Instrucción reservada que el conde de Revilla Gigedo dió a su sucesor en el mando, marqués de Branciforte (México, Imprenta a Cargo de C.A. Guio, 1831), para. 543–77, 628–46; Reglas que deberán obsevarse para la formación y alistamiento de las milicias de lo interior del reino, May 29, 1794, AGI, Estado, legajo 22; Archer, *The Bourbon Army,* 32.
13. Branciforte to Alange, México, July 30, 1794, AGN, CV, 2nd series, vol. 1, exp. 22; Branciforte to Alange, October 5, 1794, AGN, CV, 2nd series, vol. 1, exp. 81; Calderón Quijano, *Los virreyes de Nueva España,* 549; Archer, *The Bourbon Army,* 34–36.
14. Reglas que deberán observarse para la formación y alistamiento de las milicias en lo interior de reino, May 24, 1784, AGI, Estado, legajo 22; Archer, *The Bourbon Army,* 232.
15. Marqués de Branciforte, May 16, 1795, Bando declarando el cumplimiento de Real Decreto de 9 de Febrero de 1793 sobre el fuero militar de Nueva España, AGN, IG, vol. 13b; Pedro Telmo de Landero to Iturrigaray, no. 1594, July 20, 1807, AGN, IG, vol. 60a; Archer, *The Bourbon Army,* 248–49, 253; McAlister,

Fuero Militar, 15, 87. The prospect of lost revenues dissuaded previous viceroys from removing the ban on enlisting tributaries.

16. Arriaga to Villalba, August 1, 1764, Instrucciones Reales, AGN, RC, vol. 85, exp. 142, para. 36; McAlister, "Reorganization of the Army," 14.
17. Branciforte, May 16, 1795, Bando declarando el cumplimiento de Real Declaración de 9 de Febrero de 1793, AGN, IG, vol. 13b; McAlister, *Fuero Militar,* 6–8, 10–14. Military *fueros* were of two specific types: the *fuero militar ordinario,* pertaining to the regular army, and the *fuero militar privilegiado,* applying only to the militia.
18. Informe de Miguel Bataller, February 9, 1805, AGN, IG, vol. 33; Archer, *The Bourbon Army,* 275–76. For a dissenting opinion, see McAlister, *Fuero Militar,* 14–15, 88–89.
19. Jorge Alberto Lozoya, *El ejército mexicano,* 3rd ed. (México: El Colegio de México, 1984), 21–23; McAlister, *Fuero Militar,* 89. In this context, praetorianism connotes an army above and beyond civilian control, dominated by officer elites who discern officership as an entitlement rather than a profession and whose personal loyalty supersedes national affiliation or allegiance to the military as an institution. For a more detailed discussion of this concept, see Alain Rouquié, *L'Etat Militaire en Amerique Latine* (Paris: Editions du Seuil, 1982), chap. 10.
20. Dictamen que de orden del Exmo. Señor Marqués de Croix, Virrey de este Reyno, expone el Mariscal de Campo Marqués de Rubí, en orden a la mejor situación de los Presidios para la defensa y extención al Norte de este Virreynato, April 10, 1768, AGI, Guadalajara, legajo 511; Lawrence Kinnaird, ed., *The Frontiers of New Spain, Nicolás de la Fora's Description 1766–1768,* Quivira Society Publications (Berkeley: The Quivira Society, 1958), 36–41; Max L. Moorhead, *The Apache Frontier: Jacobo Ugarte and Spanish-Indian Relations in Northern New Spain 1769–1791* (Norman: Univ. of Oklahoma Press, 1968), 16.
21. Reglamento e instrucción para los presidios que se han de formar en la linea de frontera de Nueva España, resuelto por el Rey Nuestro Señor en Cédula de 10 de Septiembre de 1772, in Sidney B. Brinckerhoff and Odie B. Faulk, *Lancers for the King: A Study of the Frontier Military System of Northern New Spain, with a Translation of the Royal Regulations of 1772* (Phoenix: Arizona Historical Foundation, 1965).
22. Enrique Gonzales Flóres and Francisco R. Almada, eds., *Informe de Don Hugo O'Conor sobre el estado de las Provincias Internas del Norte 1771–1776* (México: Editorial Cultura, 1952), 73–76; David M. Vigness, "Don Hugo O'Conor and New Spain's Northeastern Frontier," *Journal of the West* 6 (January, 1967): 31; Moorhead, *Apache Frontier,* 33–35.
23. Charles III to Gálvez, Aranjuez, May 16, 1776, AGI, Guadalajara, legajo 301; Alfred B. Thomas, *Teodoro de Croix and the Northern Frontier of New Spain, 1776–1783* (Norman: Univ. of Oklahoma Press, 1941), 17. Moorhead, *Apache Frontier,* 45; Priestley, *José de Gálvez,* 293.
24. Charles III to Gálvez, enclosing appointment of Croix as commandant-general of the Interior Provinces, Aranjuez, May 16, 1776, AGI, Guadalajara, legajo

301; Thomas, *Teodoro de Croix,* 17–18. Sinaloa and Sonora constituted a single province until 1834.

25. Charles III to Croix, no. 2, San Ildefonso, August 22, 1776, para. 13, 14, enclosed with Pedro de Nava to Marqués de Bajamar, Number 1, Chihuahua, December 2, 1791, AGI, Guadalajara 520 (hereinafter cited as Charles III to Croix, San Ildefonso, August 22, 1776).
26. Luís Navarro García, *Don José de Gálvez y la Comandancia General de las Provincias Internas del Norte de Nueva España* (Sevilla: Publicaciones de la Escuela de Estudios Hispano-Americanos de Sevilla, 1964), 352; Gonzales Flóres and Almada, eds., *Informe de Hugo O'Conor,* 37–38.
27. Croix to Gálvez, no. 458, Arispe, January 23, 1780, Informe General, AGI, Guadalajara 278, para. 117–19, 122 (hereinafter cited as Croix, General Report of 1780).
28. Bobb, *Antonio María Bucareli,* 151–52. Bucareli's lack of financial generosity was quite likely motivated by his opposition to the nascent command.
29. Croix to Gálvez, no. 735, Arispe, April 23, 1782, Acompaña por duplicado la primera parte de sus informes generales, y por principal la Segunda, ofreciendo la oportuna remisión de las restantes, AGI, Guadalajara 279, para. 565 (hereinafter cited as Croix to Gálvez, no. 735, Arispe, April 22, 1782).
30. Croix to Gálvez, no. 595, Arispe, January 23, 1781, Acompaña Informe general sobre establicimiento de milicias a Nueva Vizcaya, AGI, Guadalajara 281-A, para. 76 and carpeta 7 (hereinafter cited as Croix to Gálvez, no. 595, Arispe, January 23, 1781).
31. Croix to Gálvez, no. 891, Arispe, February 24, 1783, Expone lo que se le ofrece en respuesta a real orden de 28 de Junio de 82 en que se le hacen varias prevenciones sobre la guerra, AGI, Guadalajara 284 (hereinafter cited as Croix to Gálvez, no. 891, Arispe, February 24, 1783).
32. Croix to Gálvez, no. 595, Arispe, January 23, 1781, para. 79.
33. *Ibid.*, para. 96–98, 107 and carpeta 9. The unit's clothing and equipment cost 33,600 pesos, while annual salaries consumed 60,120 pesos.
34. *Ibid.*, para. 83–90, 99. These militia units were also earmarked for commitment against potential European encroachment.
35. *Ibid.*, para. 126–29.
36. *Ibid.*, para. 130.
37. Croix to Gálvez, no. 595, Arispe, January 23, 1781, para. 51, 64; Juan Marchena Fernández, *Oficiales y soldados en el ejército de América* (Sevilla: Escuela de Estudios Hispano-Americanos de Sevilla, 1983), 35–36. To encourage recruiting, the king granted Croix authorization to extend the *fuero militar* to all soldiers serving in frontier militia units.
38. Croix to Gálvez, no. 735, Arispe, April 23, 1782, para. 434–35; Moorhead, *The Apache Frontier,* 120–23.
39. Croix to Gálvez, no. 595, Arispe, January 23, 1781, para. 17 and carpeta 7; Croix to Gálvez, no. 735, Arispe, April 23, 1782, para. 421. *Arbitrios* were levied upon the sale of specific items, the amount of which varied by commodity and the financial condition of the affected district.

40. Felipe de Neve to Gálvez, Arispe, December 1, 1783, Informe General, AGI, Guadalajara 520, para. 56.
41. Donald E. Worcester, trans. and ed., *Instructions for Governing the Interior Provinces of New Spain, 1786, by Bernardo de Gálvez,* Quivira Society Publications (Berkeley: The Quivira Society, 1951), 70–71.
42. Informe de Obispo Estéban Lorenzo de Tristán, September 9, 1788, AGN, Civil, vol. 1363, expediente 2; Richard E. Greenleaf, "The Nueva Vizcaya Frontier, 1787–1789," *Journal of the West* 8 (January, 1969): 63.
43. Real Cédula de Consolidación de Vales Reales, December 26, 1804, AGN, Bienes Nacionales (BN), legajo 1667, expediente 6; Brian R. Hamnett, "The Appropriation of Mexican Church Wealth by the Spanish Bourbon Government—The 'Consolidación de Vales Reales,' 1805–1809," *Journal of Latin American Studies* 1, no. 2 (November, 1969): 85–113; Asunción Lavrin, "The Execution of the Law of *Consolidacíon* in New Spain; Economic Aims and Results," *Hispanic American Historical Review* 53 (February, 1973): 27–49.
44. Enrique Lafuente Ferrari, *El Virrey Iturrigaray y los orígenes de la independencia de México* (Madrid: Instituto Gonzalo Fernández de Oviedo, 1941), 42–49; Romeo Flores Caballero, *La contrarevolución en la independencia: Los españoles en la vida política, social y económica de México (1804–1838)* (México: El Colegio de México, 1969), 31–40; Colin M. MacLachlan and Jaime E. Rodriguez O., *The Forging of the Cosmic Race: A Reinterpretation of Colonial Mexico,* expanded ed. (Berkeley: Univ. of California Press, 1990), 300–302. Unlike parish curates and the church hierarchy, who derived their incomes from dues and tithes, the lower clergy depended almost entirely upon monies from these endowments for their livelihood.
45. Alamán, *Historia de Méjico,* 1:192; Flores Caballero, *La Contrarevolución en la independencia,* 41–42; R. A. Humphreys, "Isolation from Spain," in R. A. Humphreys and John Lynch, eds., *The Origins of the Latin American Revolutions, 1808–1826* (New York: Alfred A. Knopf, 1965), 146–47.
46. Timothy E. Anna, *The Fall of Royal Government in Mexico City* (Lincoln: Univ. of Nebraska Press, 1978), xi–xii, 17–20; John Lynch, *The Spanish American Revolutions, 1808–1826* (New York: Norton, 1973), 299; Brian R. Hamnett, "Mexico's Royalist Coalition: The Response to Revolution, 1808–1821," *Journal of Latin American Studies* 12 (May, 1980): 61–62; Lafuente Ferrari, *El Virrey Iturrigaray,* 242.
47. Flores Caballero, *La contrarevolución en la independencia,* 43–45; Alamán, *Historia de Méjico,* 1:244, 267; Lynch, *The Spanish American Revolutions,* 304. Garibay remained in office only until July, 1809, when he was replaced by Archbishop Javier Lizana y Beaumont, who himself lasted less than a year. The *audiencia* ruled from April to September, 1810, when Spain took steps to restore order to government with the appointment of Lieutenant General Francisco Javier de Venégas on September 4, 1810.
48. Alamán, *Historia de Méjico,* 1:305–306; Flores Caballero, *La contrarevolución en la independencia,* 47; Jan Bazant, *A Concise History of Mexico from Hidalgo to Cárdenas, 1805–1940* (Cambridge: Cambridge Univ. Press, 1977), 9–10; Lyle

N. McAlister, "Social Structure and Social Change in New Spain," *Hispanic American Historical Review* 43 (August, 1963): 349–70.

49. Neill Macaulay, "The Army of New Spain and the Mexican Delegation to the Spanish Cortes," in Nettie Lee Benson, ed., *Mexico and the Spanish Cortes, 1810–1822* (Austin: Univ. of Texas Press, 1968), 137; Frank N. Samponaro, "The Political Role of the Army in Mexico, 1821–1848" (Ph.D. diss., State University of New York at Stony Brook, 1971), 9.
50. Archer, *The Bourbon Army,* 300–301; Alamán, *Historia de Méjico,* 1:282–83; Flores Caballero, *La contrarevolución en la independencia,* 46–47.
51. Hugh M. Hamill, Jr., *The Hidalgo Revolt: Prelude to Mexican Independence* (Gainesville: Univ. of Florida Press, 1966), 105–107; Heriberto Frías, *Episodios militares mexicanos: principales campañas, jornadas, batallas, combates y actos heróicos que ilustran la historia del ejército nacional desde la independencia hasta el triunfo definitivo de la republica, Primera parte, Guerra de independencia* (México: Librería de la Vda. de Ch. Bouret, 1901), 20–21; Hamnett, "Mexico's Royalist Coalition," 63.
52. Alamán, *Historia de Méjico,* 1:324; Hamill, "The Hidalgo Revolt," 36, 101; Hamnett, "Mexico's Royalist Coalition," 63–64. A muster of some 12,000 militiamen at Jalapa, Orizaba, and Córdoba in 1806 gave creole activists such as Allende, Michelena, and Aldama an opportunity to evaluate the militia's military potential.
53. Quoted in Hamill, *The Hidalgo Revolt,* 113; Wilbert H. Timmons, "Los Guadalupes: A Secret Society in the Mexican Revolution for Independence," *Hispanic American Historical Review* 30 (November, 1950): 475; Velázquez, *El estado de guerra en Nueva España,* 226–30.
54. John Tutino, *From Insurrection to Revolution in Mexico: Social Bases of Agrarian Violence, 1750–1940* (Princeton: Princeton Univ. Press, 1986), 41–42.
55. D. A. Brading, *Haciendas and Ranchos in the Mexican Bajío: León, 1700–1860* (Cambridge: Cambridge Univ. Press, 1978), 180–83; Tutino, *From Insurrection to Revolution,* 73–74.
56. Eric Van Young, *Hacienda and Market in Eighteenth Century Mexico: The Rural Economy of the Guadalajara Region, 1625–1820* (Berkeley: Univ. of California Press, 1981), 281–82; William B. Taylor, "Landed Society in New Spain: A View from the South," *Hispanic American Historical Review* 54 (August, 1974): 387–413; Tutino, *From Insurrection to Revolution,* 78–79. Brading, *Haciendas and Ranchos,* 194.
57. Tutino, *From Insurrection to Revolution,* 99–100. For a dissenting viewpoint, see Eric Wolf, "The Mexican Bajío in the Eighteenth Century," *Synoptic Studies of Mexican Culture* (New Orleans: Tulane University, Middle America Research Institute, 1957), 192.
58. Brian R. Hamnett, "Royalist Counterinsurgency and the Continuity of Rebellion: Guanajuato and Michoacán, 1813–20," *Hispanic American Historical Review* 62 (February, 1982): 22–23; José María Luís Mora, *México y sus revoluciones* (México: Editorial Porrúa, 1950), 3:37–45.

59. Hamill, *The Hidalgo Revolt,* 175–76; Brading, *Haciendas and Ranchos,* 198–200; Tutino, *From Insurrection to Revolution,* 182–83.
60. Flores Caballero, *La contrarevolución en la independencia,* 48; Hamill, *The Hidalgo Revolt,* 117.
61. Calleja to Venégas, no. 76, October 31, 1810, AGN, Operaciones de Guerra (OG), vol. 169; Christon I. Archer, "La Causa Buena: The Counterinsurgency Army and the Ten Years' War," in Jaime E. Rodriguez O., *The Independence of Mexico and the Creation of the New Nation* (Los Angeles: Univ. of California Press, 1989), 87–90.
62. Archer, *The Bourbon Army,* 299; Lynch, *Spanish American Revolutions,* 308; Hamill, *The Hidalgo Revolt,* 180–81; Frías, *Episodios militares,* 30–41.
63. *Relación que hizo al virrey Venégas al coronel D. Diego Garcia Conde,* in Alamán, *Historia de Méjico,* 1:471–74; Carlos María de Bustamante, *Campañas del general D. Félix María Calleja, comandante en gefe del ejército real de operaciones, llamado del centro* (México: Imprenta del Águila, 1828), 22–24; Hamill, *The Hidalgo Revolt,* 181; Tutino, *From Insurrection to Revolution,* 154–57.
64. *Gazeta Extraordinaria del Gobierno Imperial de México,* November 29, 1810, AGN, OG, vol. 169; Calleja to Venégas, Guanajuato, November 25, 1810, AGN, OG, vol. 169; Tutino, *From Insurrection to Revolution,* 182, 324.
65. Calleja to Venégas, nos. 35, 36, Guanajuato, August 12, 1811, AGN, OG, vol. 190; Calleja, Indicaciones sobre el estado de la insurrección. . . , AGN, OG, vol. 197; Reglamento politico-militar que deberán observar bajo las penas que señala los Pueblos, Haciendas y Ranchos a quienes se comunique por las autoridades legitimas y respectivas. . . , Aguascalientes, June 8, 1811, AGN, OG, vol. 186; Archer, "The Counterinsurgency Army," 90–91, 99; Hamnett, *Roots of Insurgency,* 180–83.
66. Calleja to Venégas, no. 54, October 14, 1811, AGN, OG, vol. 186; Wilbert H. Timmons, *Morelos of Mexico: Priest, Soldier, Statesman* (El Paso: Texas Western Press, 1963), 17–23; Nancy M. Farriss, *Crown and Clergy in Colonial Mexico 1750–1821, The Crisis of Ecclesiastical Privilege* (London: Athlone Press, 1968), 194–99.
67. Calleja to Venégas, no. 26, San Juan Zitaquero, January 20, 1812, AGN, OG, vol. 197; Niceto de Zamacois, *Historia de México desde sus tiempos más remotos hasta nuestros días* (Barcelona: J. F. Parres y Cía, 1876–88), 10:56; Lynch, *The Spanish-American Revolutions,* 316–17; Macaulay, "The Army of New Spain," 135.
68. Quoted in Frías, *Episodios militares,* 269; Calleja to Venégas, no. 151, Mazabario, July 20, 1812, AGN, OG, vol. 197; Timothy E. Anna, "Francisco Novella and the Last Stand of the Royal Army in New Spain," *Hispanic American Historical Review* 51 (February, 1971): 93; Hamnett, "Mexico's Royalist Coalition," 70.
69. Jorge Ignacio Rubio Mañé, "Antecedentes del Virrey de Nueva España, Félix María Calleja," *Boletín del Archivo General de la Nación* 19 (July–September, 1948): 323–30; M. Meade, "Don Félix María Calleja del Rey. Actividades anteriores a la Guerra de Independencia," *Boletín del Archivo General de la*

Nación 1 (1960): 59–86; Timmons, *Morelos of Mexico,* 58; Frías, *Episodios militares,* 145. For a comprehensive analysis of the political career of this remarkable military leader, see Carol Ferguson, "The Spanish Tamerlaine? Félix María Calleja, Viceroy of New Spain, 1813–1816" (Ph.D. diss., Texas Christian University, 1973).

70. José Francés Enríquez to Calleja, Oaxaca, May 8, 1814, AGN, OG, vol. 490; José Francés Enríquez to Calleja, Puebla, March 21, 1815, AGN, OG, vol. 490; Hamnett, "Royalist Counterinsurgency," 24–25; Flores Caballero, *La contrarevolución en la independencia,* 59.
71. Reglamento politico-militar, México, June 8, 1811, AGN, OG, vol. 186; Hamnett, "Royalist Counterinsurgency," 25; Frías, *Episodios militares,* 265; Archer, "The Counterinsurgency Army," 93–94. Spanish officers who fought as insurgents against the French occupation of Spain brought to New Spain the lessons learned from that bitter conflict, adding a new element of brutality to an already vicious environment.
72. Proclamación de D. Felix María Calleja del Rey, Brigadier de los Reales Ejércitos. . . , January 5, 1812, AGN, OG, vol. 196; Hamnett, "Royalist Counterinsurgency," 37–38; Brian R. Hamnett, "Anastasio Bustamante y la Guerra de Independencia, 1810–1821," *Historia Mexicana* 112 (April–June, 1979): 527–31. Resettlement was successful only in areas where small numbers of individuals were affected. Attempts to relocate sizable populations from their ancestral lands merely drove the inhabitants into the rebel camp.
73. Enríquez to José de Castro, Puebla, January 21, 1815, AGN, OG, vol. 278; José Bravo Ugarte, *Historia sucinta de Michoacán* (México: Editorial Jus, 1962–64), 3:48–49; Archer "The Counterinsurgency Army," 98–99; Hamnett, "Royalist Counterinsurgency," 31. Calleja attempted to address the Veracruz dilemma by forming units of lowlanders, who were unaffected by the *vómito.*
74. Justo Sierra, *Evolución política del pueblo mexicano,* 2nd ed. (México: Fondo de Cultura Económica, 1950), 167–68; Hamnett, "Royalist Counterinsurgency," 48; Hamnett, "Mexico's Royalist Coalition," 73.
75. "Controversia entre el obispo de Puebla y el virrey Calleja," *Boletín del Archivo General de la Nación* 4 (September–October, 1937): 658–59; Macaulay, "The Army of New Spain," 146–47; Julio Zárate, *La Guerra de independencia,* vol. 3 of *México a través de los siglos,* edited by Vicente Riva Palacio (Editorial Cumbre, 1953), 520–21.
76. Orden general que debe observar el Ejército del Rey, June 20, 1817, AGN, Historia, vol. 485; Venadito to Ministro de Guerra, no. 761, México, December 31, 1818, AGN, CV, 1st series, vol. 273, fojas 255–62; Hamnett, "Royalist Counterinsurgency," 43–45; Zárate, *Guerra de independencia,* 527.
77. Pascual de Liñán to Venadito, no. 145, Veracruz, April 22, 1819, AGN, OG, vol. 490; Bravo Ugarte, *Historia sucinta,* 3:51–55; Archer, "The Counterinsurgency Army," 104–105; Hamnett, "Royalist Counterinsurgency," 46; Flores Caballero, *La contrarevolución en la independencia,* 61–62.
78. Estado que manifiesta la fuerza de los cuerpos y compañías sueltas de urbanos y Realistas fieles de todos armas auxiliares del Ejército de Nueva España . . . ,

August 31, 1816, AGN, Historia, vol. 485, expediente 19; Samponaro, "Political Role of the Army," 12; Zavala, *Ensayo histórico,* 70–71.

79. Nettie Lee Benson, *La diputación provincial y el federalismo mexicano* (Mexico City: El Colegio de México, 1955), 125–29; Margaret L. Woodward, "The Spanish Army and the Loss of America, 1810–1824," *Hispanic American Historical Review* 48 (November, 1968): 596–97, 606; Anna, *Fall of Royal Government,* 195–96, 198–204; Ladd, *Mexican Nobility at Independence,* 166. Prominent examples of these creole officers, most of whom were of middle-class origin, are Antonio López de Santa Anna, Anastasio Bustamante, and José Joaquín de Herrera.

80. Karl M. Schmitt, "The Clergy and the Independence of New Spain," *Hispanic American Historical Review* 34 (August, 1954): 303–307; William S. Robertson, *Iturbide of Mexico* (Durham, N.C.: Duke Univ. Press, 1952), 8; Bazant, *History of Mexico,* 26; Farriss, *Crown and Clergy,* 248–49; Ladd, *The Mexican Nobility at Independence,* 166; Benson, *La Diputación provincial,* 148–50.

81. Lozoya, *El ejército mexicano,* 24–25; Hamnett, "Mexico's Royalist Coalition," 77–78; Robertson, *Iturbide of Mexico,* 97.

82. Jaime Delgado, "El conde del Venadito ante el Plan de Iguala," *Revista de Indias,* 33–34 (1948): 957–66; Fernando de Gabriel y Ruíz de Apodoca, *Apuntes biográficos de exmo. señor D. Juan Ruíz de Apodoca y Eliza, Conde de Venadito* (Burgos, 1849), 63–77; Zárate, *La guerra de independencia,* 89.

83. Timothy E. Anna, *The Mexican Empire of Iturbide* (Lincoln: Univ. of Nebraska Press, 1990), 10; Anna, "Francisco Novella," 97; Archer, "The Counterinsurgency Army," 106–107; Robertson, *Iturbide of Mexico,* 76; Woodward, "The Spanish Army and the Loss of America," 598–99. Among the most influential royalist officers subscribing to Iturbide's appeal were Anastasio Bustamante, commander of the all-important Bajío district; Brigadier Pedro Celestino Negrete, second in command of regular troops in Nueva Galicia; Colonel Luís Quintanar, commander of Valladolid; Colonel Domingo Luaces, commander of Querétaro; and José Morán, Marqués de Vivanco, second in command of Puebla.

84. Christon I. Archer, "Where did all the Royalists Go? New Light on the Military Collapse of New Spain, 1810–1822," in Jaime E. Rodriguez O., ed., *The Mexican and the Mexican American Experience in the Nineteenth Century* (Tempe: Arizona State Univ. Press, 1989), 23–43; Apodoca, *Apuntes biográphicos,* 115–19; Woodward, "The Spanish Army and the Loss of America," 602; Anna, "Francisco Novella" 92. Venadito, who despised the new liberal regime in Spain, resisted reinstating the Constitution of 1812 in New Spain, thereby antagonizing senior absolutist officers who considered such reforms the last chance to preserve the empire.

85. Renuncia que hace el Exmo Sr. Virrey Conde del Venadito en Novella y encargo de este del mando militar, Archivo Histórico del Ayuntamiento de la Ciudad de México (AHA), Historia en General, legajo 2255, expediente 106; Carlos María Bustamante, *Cuadro histórico de la revolución mexicana* (Mexico: Ediciones de la Comisión Nacional, 1961), 3:268–73; Anna, "Francisco Novella," 99–100. Novella was actually the second ranking officer in the Mexico City

garrison. Field Marshal Pascual de Liñán, his nominal superior, refused to take power in the wake of the coup, and Novella became the "accidental commander," as the rebels were later to characterize him.

86. Jaime Delgado, "La Misión a Méjico de Don Juan de O'Donojú," *Revista de Indias* 35 (January–March, 1949): 25–87; Anna, "Francisco Novella," 105–106.
87. Tratados celebrados en la villa de Córdoba, August 24, 1821, AGN, Impresos oficiales (IO), vol. 60, expediente 100. By endowing creole landowners with the political power denied them throughout the colonial period, this treaty garnered the third crucial element of Iturbide's corporate coalition.
88. AHA, Actas de Cabildo, August 10, 1821, legajo 672; Anna, "Francisco Novella," 107.
89. Francisco Novella, Avisa haverse hecho un armisticio con el Ejército Trigarante por seis días contados desde la ratificación del tratado, 7 de septiembre de 1821, AGN, IO, vol. 44, expediente 77; Anna, "Francisco Novella," 109–11; Robertson, *Iturbide of Mexico,* 125–26.
90. David A. Brading, "Government and Elite in Late Colonial Mexico," *Hispanic American Historical Review* 53 (August, 1973): 389–414; Archer, "The Counterinsurgency Army," 107–108; Hamnett "Mexico's Royalist Coalition," 81; Ladd, *Mexican Nobility at Independence,* 242.
91. Anna, "Francisco Novella," 94; Hamnett, "Mexico's Royalist Coalition," 84–85; Samponaro, "The Political Role of the Mexican Army," 15–16; Woodward, "The Spanish Army and the Loss of America," 592–93, 598–99. With the restoration of Ferdinand VII, ambitious officers could achieve rapid advancement best through proximity to the center of patronage, not by chasing insurgents through the Mexican countryside.
92. Michael P. Costeloe, *La primera república federal en México (1824–1835): un estudio de los partidos políticos en el México independiente* (Mexico: Fondo de Cultura Económica, 1975), 438–39; Hamnett, "Mexico's Royalist Coalition," 84–85.

CHAPTER 2

1. Fernando Escalante Gonzalbo, *Ciudadanos imaginarios: Memorial de los afanes y desventuras de la virtud y apología del vicio triunfante en la República Mexicana* (Mexico: El Colegio de México, 1992), 161–62; Lorenzo de Zavala, *Umbral de la independencia* (Mexico: Empresas Editoriales, S.A., 1949), 143; Josefina Zoraida Vázquez, "Iglesia, ejército y centralismo," *Historia Mexicana* 39 (July–September, 1989): 212–13.
2. Recomendación del Iturbide a la Regencia, Mexico City, December 7, 1821, and Circular de Iturbide, Mexico City, December 8, 1821, Bibliotéca Eusebio Dávalos del Instituto Nacional de Antropología e Historia (BINAH), Colección Antigua, tomo 3, legajo 35; Romeo Flores Caballero, *La contrarevolución en la independencia: Los españoles en la vida política, social y económica de México, 1804–1838* (Mexico: El Colegio de México, 1969), 77; Eduardo Paz, *Reseña histórica del estado mayor mexicano, 1821–1860* (Mexico: Talleres del Estado Mayor, 1907), 3; Frank N. Samponaro, "The Political Role of the Army in

Mexico, 1821–1848" (Ph.D. diss., State University of New York at Stony Brook, 1971), 29–31. Created in September 1821, the Council of Regency was an executive body of five military officers, presided over by Iturbide, responsible for administering the fledgling Mexican empire until a permanent government could be formed.

3. Flores Caballero, *La contrarevolución en la independencia,* 77; Escalante Gonzalbo, *Ciudadanos imaginarios,* 162; Henry George Ward, *Mexico in 1827* (London: H. Colburn, 1828), 1:278.
4. Decreto de la Regencia, Mexico City, October 12, 1821, BINAH, Colección Antigua, tomo 3, legajo 35; Ministerio de Guerra y Marina, *Memoria del Secretario de Estado y del despacho de la guerra* (Mexico: Imprenta a Cargo de Martín Rivera, 1822), 7–8; Timothy E. Anna, *The Mexican Empire of Iturbide* (Lincoln: Univ. of Nebraska Press, 1990), 40; Enrique Olavarría y Ferrari, *México independiente, 1821–1855,* vol. 4 of *México a través de los siglos,* edited by Vicente Riva Palacios (Mexico: Editorial Cumbre, S.A., 1962), 23. The six captaincies-general were apportioned as follows: Nueva Galicia, General Negrete; Puebla, General Luaces (succeeded in short order by General Echávarri); Mexico, General de la Sota Riva; Interior Provinces, General Bustamante; Mérida de Yucatán, General Melchor Álvarez; and the South, General Guerrero. Since Guerrero remained a powerful and popular figure in the South, Iturbide wisely chose not to antagonize a region over which he exercised little effective control by appointing an outsider. Samponaro, "Political Role of the Army," 54.
5. Plana Mayor del Ejército, *Noticia histórica de todos los cuerpos del Ejército Nacional, que desde 1821 han existido y existen actualmente* (Mexico: Imprenta del Aguila, 1845), BN, Colección Lafragua, tomo 303, 14–24; Flóres Caballero, *La contrarevolución en la independencia,* 77–78. While these redesignations eradicated Spanish military antecedents, they also destroyed unit cohesion by fracturing the strong martial bonds that had been formed during the protracted civil war. Many veterans simply returned to their villages rather than serve in the reorganized units.
6. *Gaceta de México,* October 25, 1821; Olavarría y Ferrari, *México independiente,* 42–43; Carlos Navarro y Rodrigo, *Vida de Agustín de Iturbide* (Madrid: Editorial América, 1919), 134.
7. Joaquín Ramírez y Sesma, ed., *Colección de decretos, ordenes y circulares espedidas por los gobiernos nacionales de la federación mexicana desde el año de 1821 hasta el de 1826 para el arreglo del ejército de los Estados Unidos Mexicanos y ordenandos por el teniente coronel de caballería J.R.S.* (Mexico: Martín Rivera, 1827), 111–19; Flores Caballero, *La contrarevolución en la independencia,* 80; Závala, *Umbral,* 150. While most of the royalist army submitted to O'Donojú's acceptance of Mexican independence, General José Dávila and a small group of recalcitrants withdrew into the fortress of San Juan de Ulúa to await Spanish reinforcements. Their presence in that formidable installation obstructed maritime trade and prevented the Mexican government from collecting import tariffs and export taxes, the nation's principal source of revenue at the time.
8. *Memoria del Secretario de Estado y del despacho de la guerra,* 1822, 30; Jan Bazant,

Historia de la deuda exterior de México, 1823–1946 (Mexico: El Colegio de Mexico, 1968), 14–15; Escalante Gonzalbo, *Ciudadanos imaginarios,* 163. Attempts to reimpose forced loans upon Mexico's most affluent economic sector merely encouraged Spanish merchants to repatriate their profits or emigrate to Spain.

9. Flores Caballero, *La contrarevolución en la independencia,* 83; Olavarría y Ferrari, *México independiente,* 44.
10. Lucas Alamán, *Historia de Méjico desde los primeros movimientos que preparon su independencia en el año de 1808 hasta la época presente* (Mexico: J. Marino Lara, 1850), 5:548; José María Bocanegra, *Memorias para la historia de México independiente 1821–1841* (Mexico: Imprenta del Gobierno Federal, 1892–97), 1:62; William S. Robertson, *Iturbide of Mexico* (Durham, N.C.: Duke Univ. Press, 1952), 165.
11. Bocanegra, *Memorias para la historia,* 1:56–57; Lorenzo de Závala, *Ensayo histórico de las revoluciones de México desde 1808 hasta 1830* (Mexico: Manuel N. de la Vega, 1845), 1:124.
12. Decreto del Congreso, Mexico City, May 21, 1822, BINAH, Colección Antigua, tomo 3, legajo 35; Anna, *Mexican Empire of Iturbide,* 64–65; Bocanegra, *Memorias para la historia,* 1:55–57.
13. Alamán, *Historia de Méjico,* 5:414–15; Anna, *Mexican Empire of Iturbide,* 76, 107; Závala, *Ensayo histórico,* 1:140. De la Garza eventually was pardoned by Iturbide and restored to command of Nuevo Santander.
14. Barbara A. Tenenbaum, *The Politics of Penury: Debts and Taxes in Mexico, 1821–1856* (Albuquerque: Univ. of New Mexico Press, 1986), 14–20; Alamán, Historia de Méjico, 5:422; Robert A. Potash, *Mexican Government and Industrial Development in the Early Republic: The Banco de Avío* (Amherst: Univ. of Massachusetts Press, 1983), 18. Total Government revenue for 1822 was 9,328,749 pesos (one-half of the annual average for the decade prior to 1810). Expenditures consumed 13,455,377 pesos.
15. Presupuesto para 1823, Mexico City, December 21, BINAH, Colección Antigua, tomo 3, legajo 35; Ministerio de Guerra y Marina, *Memoria del Secretario de Estado y del despacho de la guerra* (Mexico: Imprenta al Cargo de Martín Rivera, 1823), estado 1; Bazant, *Historia de la deuda,* 15.
16. *Gaceta Extraordinaria del Gobierno Imperial de México,* November 19, 1822; Anna, *Mexican Empire of Iturbide,* 152. On October 27, General Francisco Lemaur, Spain's newly appointed superior political chief *(jefe político)* of New Spain and commander of royalist forces still holding out in San Juan de Ulúa, launched an attack upon Veracruz that was repulsed by the combined forces of Santa Anna and General José Antonio Echávarri, Commandant-general of Puebla. In recognition of their valor, Iturbide promoted the former to brigadier and the latter to field marshal.
17. *Gaceta Extraordinaria del Gobierno Imperial de México,* (1822) December 22, 1822; "Proclamas de Brigadier Santana a los habitantes y tropas de Veracruz," Veracruz, December 2, 1822, University of Texas Nettie Lee Benson Latin American Collection (UTLAC), Santa Anna, *Documentos;* Bocanegra, *Memorias*

para la historia, 1:183–91; Jan Bazant, *Alienation of Church Wealth in Mexico: Social and Economic Aspects of the Liberal Revolution, 1856–1875* (London: Cambridge Univ. Press, 1971), 15–16; Nettie Lee Benson, "The Plan of Casa Mata," *Hispanic American Historical Review* 25 (February, 1945): 45–47. Santa Anna enlisted the support of Miguel Santa María to codify in a political document, the proclamations of December 2. Signed by Santa Anna and Guadalupe Victoria four days later, the Plan of Vera Cruz borrowed much of its substance from the Iguala manifesto.

18. Anna, *Mexican Empire of Iturbide,* 163–64; Carlos María de Bustamante, *Diario histórico de México* [for 1823], edited by Elías Amador (Zacatecas: J. Ortega, 1896), 1:95, 127; Benson, "Plan of Casa Mata," 48; Leonard D. Parrish, "The Life of Nicolás Bravo, Mexican Patriot (1786–1854)" (Ph.D. diss., University of Texas, 1951), 104.

19. Marqués de Vivanco to Iturbide, Puebla, January 29, 1823, BINAH, Colección Antigua, tomo 2, legajo 10; "Trabajos del ciudadano Guerrero por defender su patria," Puebla, May 3, 1823, UTLAC, Genaro García Manuscript Collection; Alamán, *Historia de Méjico,* 5:440; Bustamante, *Diario histórico,* 1:126. Eventually nursed back to health by local peasants, Guerrero's impaired lung caused him chronic difficulty throughout the balance of his life.

20. Acta de Casa Mata, Cuartel General de Casa Mata, February 1, 1823, BINAH, Colección Antigua, tomo 2, legajo 10; Benson, "Plan of Casa Mata," 49–51; Miguel M. Lerdo de Tejada, *Apuntes de la heróica ciudad de Veracruz* (Mexico: Imprenta de Ignacio Cumplido, 1850–58), 2:262. Diminishing stocks of food and ammunition threatened the success of the mission and by inference, Echávarri's military reputation. Fearful of being associated with failure, the Casa Mata formula also furnished a convenient way out of Echávarri's predicament.

21. Iturbide to Negrete, Ixtapaluca, March 2, 1823, in Mariano Cuevas, ed., *El Libertador: Documentos selectos de Don Agustín de Iturbide* (Mexico: Editorial Patria, 1947), 382; Alamán, *Historia de Méjico,* 5:460. Negrete and Echávarri, both of whom were Spaniards, eventually fell victim to anti-Spanish sentiment and were expelled from Mexico in 1827.

22. Iturbide to Manuel Gómez Pedraza, Mexico City, February 11, 1823, in Cuevas, *El Libertador,* 377–79; Anna, *Mexican Empire of Iturbide,* 201–205. Iturbide returned to Mexico on July 17, 1824, landing at Soto la Marina in Tamaulipas, where he was detained by Felipe de la Garza, the same officer he had previously pardoned and restored to command of Nuevo Santander. The next day he was informed that the federal congress law of April 28, 1824, proscribing his return would be enforced. On July 19, he was executed by a four-man firing squad and buried in a nearby parish church. In 1838 his remains finally were repatriated to Mexico City at the order of President Bustamante. Alamán, *Historia de Méjico,* 5:660–69.

23. Anna, *Mexican Empire of Iturbide,* 171; Jóse Bravo Ugarte, *Historia de México: Independencia, caracterización política e integración social.* 2nd ed., rev. (México: Editorial Jus, 1953) 151–52.

24. Brian Hamnett, "Factores regionales en la desintegración del regimen colonial en Nueva España: El federalismo de 1823–1824," in Inge Buisson et al., eds. *Problemas de la formación del Estado de la Nación Hispanoamérica* (Cologne: Bohlau Verlang, 1984), 305–15; Benson, *La diputación provincial,* 90–91.
25. Samponaro, "Political Role of the Army," 68–69, 71–72; Vázquez, "Iglesia, ejército y centralismo," 212–13.
26. Anna, *Mexican Empire of Iturbide,* 203–205, 239; Benson, "Plan of Casa Mata," 45–56; Bocanegra, *Memorias para la historia,* 1:208; Hamnett, *Roots of Insurgency,* 197.
27. Donald Fithian Stevens, *Origins of Instability in Early Republican Mexico* (Durham, N.C.: Duke Univ. Press, 1991), 110–11.
28. *Ibid.*, 111–12.
29. *Ibid.*, 53–54.
30. *Ibid.*, 60, 69–71; Samponaro, "Political Role of the Army," 68–72.
31. *Memoria del Secretario de Estado y del despacho de la guerra,* 1823, 39–40; Lozoya, *El ejército mexicano,* 25–26. In regard to the proposed location of the Colegio Militar, Gómez Pedraza remarked that Perote "was better suited for punishing delinquents, than serving as a residence for youths in whom the country founds its hopes." Juan Manuel Torrea, *La vida de una institución gloriosa. El Colegio Militar, 1821–1930* (Mexico: Talleres Tipografía Centenario, 1931), 17.
32. *Memoria del Secretario de Estado y del despacho de la guerra,* 1823, 10–14, 24–26; Alamán, *Historia de Méjico,* 5:237–38. The military used brevet ranks to reward exceptional performance when lack of vacancies or funding prohibited statutory promotion to the next higher rank. Such officers wore silver rank insignia (instead of gold) and were officially designated *graduados.*
33. Ministerio de Guerra y Marina, *Memoria del Secretario de Estado y del despacho de la guerra* (Mexico: Imprenta del Supremo Gobierno, 1825), 10 and estados 2 and 3. Before 1810 the colonial military establishment, less the Interior Provinces, comprised some 30,000 men, of whom 6,000 were regulars; at the end of the Independence War, that figure stood at about 35,000.
34. Circular de la Secretaría de Guerra y Marina, Sección 1, May 12, 1824, AGN, Guerra y Marina (GM), vol. 18; Ministerio de Guerra y Marina, *Memoria del Secretario de Estado y del despacho de la guerra* (Mexico: Imprenta del Supremo Gobierno, 1826), estado 3.
35. Stanley C. Green, *The Mexican Republic: The First Decade, 1823–1832* (Pittsburgh: Univ. of Pittsburgh Press, 1987), 83; Escalante Gonzalbo, *Ciudadanos imaginarios,* 184; Lozoya, *El ejército mexicano,* 28; Ministerio de Guerra y Marina, *Memoria del Secretario del Estado y de despacho de la guerra* (Mexico: Imprenta del Supremo Gobierno, 1827), 9–10. One illuminating example of this strength discrepancy occurred in 1829, when only 8,000 of 33,373 rostered troops could be assembled to counter the Spanish invasion.
36. *Memoria del Secretario de Estado y del despacho de la guerra,* 1825, 15–16; Vázquez, "Iglesia, ejército y centralismo," 213.
37. *Memoria del Secretario de Estado y del despacho de la guerra,* 1827, 9–10, 16; Escalante Gonzalbo, *Ciudadanos imaginarios,* 176.

38. *Memoria del Secretario de Estado y del despacho de la guerra,* 1827, 9; Escalante Gonzalbo, *Ciudadanos imaginarios,* 177. A law enacted in 1825 compelled the states to maintain a certain number of militia units regardless of population. Puebla, with 800,000 inhabitants, for example, was required to raise one battalion of 1,200 troops, and Querétaro, with just 200,000 residents, had an identical obligation.
39. *Memoria del Secretario de Estado y del despacho de la guerra,* 1827, 9–10; Christon I. Archer, "Pardos, Indians and the Army of New Spain: Interrelationships and Conflicts, 1780–1810," *Journal of Latin American Studies* 6 (November, 1974): 231–32; Green, *The Mexican Republic,* 184–85; Jóse Antonio Serrano Ortega, *El contingente de sangre: Los gobiernos estatales y departmentales y los métodos de reclutamiento del ejército permanente mexicano, 1824–1844* (México: Instituto Nacional de Antropología e Historia, 1993), 50–51.
40. *Memoria del Secretario de Estado y del despacho de la guerra,* 1827, 16.
41. *Ibid.*, 13.
42. Ministerio de Guerra y Marina, *Memoria del Secretario de Estado y del despacho de la guerra* (Mexico: Imprenta del Supremo Gobierno, 1828), estados 2, 3; Escalante Gonzalbo, *Ciudadanos imaginarios,* 164–65.
43. José María Bermúdez, *Verdadera causa de la revolución del Sur, justificándose el que la suscribe con documentos que existen en la Secretaría del Supremo Gobierno del estado de México que los certifica* (Toluca: Imprenta del Gobierno del Estado, 1831), 19; Lionel Hervey to George Canning, December 14, 1824, Mexico, Foreign Office 50/17; *Memoria del Secretario de Estado y del despacho de la guerra,* 1826, estado 1. Salaries at this time ranged from 500 pesos a month for generals engaged in active operations to 11 pesos a month for privates.
44. *Memoria del Secretario de Estado y del despacho de la guerra,* 1825, 19–20; Green, *The Mexican Republic,* 185. Such privations notwithstanding, a soldier's personal attachment to his commander often motivated him to fight with dogged determination when the situation warranted.
45. *Memoria del Secretario de Estado y del despacho de la guerra,* 1827, 9; Serrano Ortega, *El contingente de sangre,* 51–52.
46. Dublán y Lozano, *Legislación mexicana,* 2:49–51; Costeloe, *La primera república federal,* 155–56, 298–99; Serrano Ortega, *El contingente de sangre,* 63–64. The December 29, 1827 law established the size of the civic militia at one percent of the state's population and required all healthy Mexican males to serve in the country's defense.
47. Richard Pakenham to Lord Palmerston, June 11, 1833, Mexico, Foreign Office 50/84; Charles A. Hale, *Mexican Liberalism in the Age of Mora, 1821–1853* (New Haven: Yale Univ. Press, 1968), 142–43; Torcuato S. Di Tella, "The Dangerous Classes in Early Nineteenth Century Mexico," *Journal of Latin American Studies* 5 (May, 1973): 80–81; Serrano Ortega, *El contingente de sangre,* 64–65.
48. Dublán y Lozano, *Legislación mexicana,* 3:38; Pedro Santoni, "A Fear of the People: The Civic Militia in Mexico in 1845," *Hispanic American Historical Review* 68 (May, 1988): 272–73; Frank N. Samponaro, "La alianza de Santa Anna

y los federalistas, 1832–1834: Su formación y desintegración," *Historia Mexicana* 30 (January–March, 1981): 383–84.

49. *El Monitor Constitucional,* January 17, 1845; *El Siglo XIX,* January 23, 1845; Santoni, "The Civic Militia," 270–71, 276.
50. Decreto sobre el establicimiento de comandancias, September 11, 1823, AGN, GM, vol. 26; *Memoria del Secretario de Estado y del despacho de la guerra,* 1823, 24–25; Samponaro, "Political Role of the Army," 151. By 1828, consolidation and reorganization reduced the number of commandancies to twenty-one. *Memoria del Secretario de Estado y del despacho de la guerra,* 1828, 6.
51. *Memoria del Secretario de Estado y del despacho de la guerra,* 1826, 10–11. For a detailed description of Mexican coastal defenses during this period, see Ignacio Mora y Villamil, *Las Defensas de México en 1824,* ed. W. Michael Mathes (Monterrey: Capilla Alfonsina/Bibliotéca Universitaria, 1983).
52. *Memoria del Secretario de Estado y del despacho de la guerra,* 1827, 7–8 and estado 3.
53. *Memoria del Secretario de Estado y del despacho de la guerra,* 1828, 4. A law enacted on March 21, 1826, mandated only twenty-three permanent presidial companies to be apportioned among the states of Chihuahua (6), Sonora y Sinaloa (6), Coahuila y Téjas (7), punta de Lampazos (1), Tamaulipas (2), and Nuevo Mexico (3).
54. Di Tella, "The Dangerous Classes," 87. Among the most fractious of Mexico's population groups, miners were constantly involved in violent altercations, one of the most serious of which occurred at the Real de Monte in June 1827.
55. *Memoria del Secretario de Estado y del despacho de la guerra,* 1827, 10–12 and estado 4; José C. Valadés, *Orígenes de la república mexicana* (Mexico: Editores Mexicanos Unidos, 1972), 132–33.
56. *Memoria del Secretario de Estado y del despacho de la guerra,* 1828, 8–9; "Dos Años en México, o memorias críticas sobre los principales sucesos de la República de los Estados Unidos Mexicanos, desde la invasión de Barradas, hasta la declaración de Puerto de Tampico contra el gobierno del General Bustamante," escritas por un Español, Valencia, 1838, BN, Colección Lafragua, tomo 338, 71 (hereinafter cited as "Dos Años en México"); Olavarría y Ferrari, *México independiente,* 121.
57. "Dos Años en México," 71; Green, *The Mexican Republic,* 83–84, 184; Escalante Gonzalbo, *Ciudadanos imaginarios,* 170. The United States Army at this time was not without similar political affiliations: some officers were committed Democrats; others supported the Whig cause. Officer political activity, however, was generally nonpartisan and focused on pursuit of individual and collective professional objectives. William B. Skelton, *An American Profession of Arms: The Army Officer Corps, 1784–1861* (Lawrence: Univ. Press of Kansas, 1992), 296–97.
58. Ministerio de Guerra y Marina, *Memoria del Secretario de Estado y del despacho de la guerra* (Mexico: Imprenta del Supremo Gobierno, 1829), 1–2; Escalante Gonzalbo, *Ciudadanos imaginarios,* 171.
59. Bocanegra, *Memorias para la historia,* 1:473; Dublán y Lozano, *Legislación*

mexicana, 2:90; Flóres Caballero, *La contrarevolución en la independencia,* 119–20; Joel Poinsett to Henry Clay, no. 57, Mexico City, December 10, 1828, in Despatches from United States Ministers to Mexico, 1823–1906 (M97), National Archives of the United States (NA), Records of the Department of State, Foreign Affairs Section, Record Group 59; José María Tornel y Mendívil, *Manifestación del C. José María Tornel* (Mexico: Impreso por Ignacio Cumplido, 1833), 4–10. President-elect Gómez Pedraza resigned at the end of December and, on March 2, 1829, expatriated himself to England.

60. Silvia M. Arrom, "Popular Politics in Mexico City: The Parián Riot, 1828," *Hispanic American Historical Review* 68 (May, 1988): 251–52; Ward, *Mexico,* 2:610. The masses identified with Guerrero, a dark-skinned, uneducated mestizo who, they believed, would promote social mobility and protect the domestic textile industry, upon which so many lower class citizens depended, from European competition.

61. "Extracto del Diario" enclosed in Charles T. O'Gorman to Blackhouse, Mexico City, December 19, 1828, Mexico, Foreign Office 50/52; Alamán, *Historia de Méjico,* 5:845; Arrom, "Popular Politics in Mexico City," 263–64; Ward, *Mexico,* 2:481; Tornel, *Manifestación,* 8–9.

62. Harold D. Sims, *Descolonización en México; El conflicto entre mexicanos y españoles (1821–1831)* (Mexico: Fondo de Cultura Económica, 1982), 218–19; Eugene Wilson Harrell, "Vicente Guerrero and the Birth of Modern Mexico, 1821–1831" (Ph.D., diss., Tulane University, 1976), 299, 317. The initial expulsion order was promulgated on December 20, 1827.

63. Santa Anna to Ministro de Guerra y Marina, April 20, 1829, ADN, expediente XI/481.3/655; Santa Anna to Ministro de Guerra y Marina, July 5, 1829, ADN, expediente XI/481.3/656, foja 43.

64. Montenegro to Ministro de Guerra y Marina, July 21, 1829, ADN, expediente XI/481.3/655.

65. *El Sol,* August 4, 1829; Alberto M. Carreño, ed., *Jefes del Ejército Mexicano en 1847: Biografías de generales de división y de brigada y de coroneles del ejército mexicano por fines de año del 1847* (Mexico: Imprenta de la Secretaría de Fomento, 1914), lxiii–lxiv; Alfonso Trueba, *Santa Anna,* 3rd ed. (Mexico: Editorial Jus, 1958), 24.

66. Proclamación del Capitán General de la isla de Cuba, Francisco Dionisio Vives, a los habitantes de Nueva España, July 17, 1829, ADN, expediente XI/481.3/665, foja 51.

67. *Voz de la Patria,* January 29, 1830; Jaime Delgado, *España y México en el Siglo XIX* (Madrid: Instituto Gonzalo Fernández de Oviedo, 1950), 1:429, 471; Pakenham to Aberdeen, no. 77, Mexico City, August 26, 1829, Mexico, Foreign Office 50/58. The 1827 expulsion laws and the Arena conspiracy exemplify the tenacity of anti-Spanish sentiment in Mexico.

68. *El Censor,* August 8, 1829; "Dos años en México," 80; Carlos María Bustamante, *Memorias para la historia de la invasión española sobre la costa de Tampico de Tamaulipas hecha en el año de 1829* (Mexico: Valdés, 1831), 3; Miguel A. Sánchez Lamego, *La invasión española de 1829* (Mexico: Editorial Jus, 1971), 60–61.

69. Ministerio de Guerra y Marina, *Memoria del Secretario de Estado y del despacho de la guerra* (Mexico: Imprenta del Supremo Gobierno, 1830), 1 and estados 1, 2.
70. Santa Anna to Ministro de Guerra y Marina, Pueblo Viejo, August 24, 1829, ADN, expediente XI/481.3/665, fojas 38–41; Sánchez Lamego, *La Invasión Española,* 63–67.
71. Santa Anna to Barradas, Pueblo Viejo, September 8, 1829, ADN, expediente XI/481.3/665, foja 178; Sánchez Lamego, *La Invasión Española,* 68–80; Tornel, *Manifestación,* 83.
72. Artículos de Capitulación, September 11, 1829, ADN, expediente XI/481.3/668, fojas 184–86; Joseph T. Crawford to John Bidwell, Tampico, August 29, 1829, Mexico, Foreign Office 50/58; *El Sol,* September 23, 1829; Santa Anna to Ministro de Guerra y Marina, Pueblo Viejo, September 19, 1829, ADN, expediente XI/481.3/669, fojas 36–42; Sánchez Lamego, *La Invasión Española,* 78–79. This engagement cost the Mexicans 135 killed and 167 wounded, while Spanish losses were reported as 104 killed and 66 wounded.
73. Mier y Terán to Ministro de Guerra y Marina, December 12, 1829, ADN, expediente XI/481.3/674, foja 119; Crawford to O'Gorman, Tampico, September 17, 1829, Mexico, Foreign Office 50/60.
74. Santa Anna To Ministro de Guerra y Marina, Pueblo Viejo, September 11, 1829, ADN, expediente XI/481.3/668, fojas 7–8,
75. José Fuentes Mares, *Santa Anna: Aurora y ocaso de un comediante,* 3rd ed. (Mexico: Editorial Jus, 1967), 67; Sánchez Lamego, *La invasión española,* 94–95; Valadés, *Orígenes,* 93.
76. Dublán y Lozano, *Legislación mexicana,* 2:110–12, 116; *El Sol,* September 13, 1829; Green, *The Mexican Republic,* 170–72; Vázquez, "Iglesia, ejército y centralismo," 214.
77. "Dos Años en México," 84–86; Carreño, *Jefes del Ejército Mexicano,* lxxxiii–lxxxiv; Joel Poinsett to Martin Van Buren, no. 191, Mexico City, November 20, 1829, in *Despatches from United States Ministers to Mexico, 1823–1906,* National Archives of the United States (NA), Records of the Department of State, Foreign Affairs Section, Record Group 59; Manuel Rivera Cambras, *Historia antigua y moderna de Jalapa y de las revoluciones del estado de Veracruz* (Mexico: Imprenta de Ignacio Cumplido, 1869–70), 2:556–65.
78. *El Sol,* January 8, 1830; Pakenham to Aberdeen, no. 8, Mexico City, January 9, 1830, Mexico, Foreign Office 50/62. As soon as he learned of Guerrero's capitulation, the ever-vigilant Santa Anna switched allegiances to Bustamante, purportedly to avoid a civil war. Santa Anna to Secretaría de Estado y Relaciones, January 3, 1830, AGN, Gobernación, vol. 90, exp. 8.
79. *Voz de la Patria,* January 21, 1831; Jan Bazant, "Mexico," in Leslie Bethell, ed., *Spanish America After Independence, c.1820–c.1870* (Cambridge: Cambridge Univ. Press, 1987), 134; Samponaro, "Political Role of the Army," 75.
80. "Dos Años en México," 30–35; Hale, *Mexican Liberalism in the Age of Mora,* 106–107; Samponaro, "Political Role of the Army," 133; Stevens, *Origins of Instability,* 53–54. Former insurgents, generally non-whites of humble origin with little formal education, were significantly disadvantaged in national politics

when challenged by creoles experienced in forging alliances of convenience with other powerful groups.

81. *El Fénix de la Libertad,* August 13, 1832; Ministerio de Guerra y Marina, *Memoria del Secretario de Estado y del despacho de la guerra* (Mexico: Imprenta del Supremo Gobierno, 1831), 13; *Registro Oficial,* January 23, 1830; Green, *The Mexican Republic,* 200–201; Escalante Gonzalbo, *Ciudadanos imaginarios,* 171.
82. "Dos Años en Mexico," 41; *Memoria del Secretario de Estado y del despacho de la guerra,* 1830, 7–8; Green, *The Mexican Republic,* 202; Hale, *Mexican Liberalism in the Age of Mora,* 143; Pakenham to Aberdeen, no. 91, Mexico City, September 30, 1829, Mexico, Foreign Office 50/60; Serrano Ortega, *El contingente de sangre,* 53–55. After the Spaniards abandoned the fortress of San Juan de Ulúa, interest in a Mexican navy dissipated rapidly, and by the end of the decade that service no longer existed. For an examination of this issue, see Robert L. Bidwell, "The First Mexican Navy, 1821–1830" (Ph.D., diss., University of Virginia, 1960).
83. Anonymous, Al Excmo. Sr. General de División D. Anastasio Bustamante, BN, Colección Lafragua, tomo 338; *El Fénix de la Libertad,* December 28, 1831; Stanley C. Green, "Lucas Alamán: Domestic Activities, 1823–1835" (Ph.D. diss., Texas Christian University, 1970), 139–40, 152–58, 266.
84. "Dos Años en México," 85; Michael P. Costeloe, "Santa Anna and the Gómez Farías Administration in Mexico, 1833–1834," *The Americas* 31 (July, 1974): 18–19; Hale, *Mexican Liberalism in the Age of Mora,* 72–74.
85. *El Fénix de la Libertad,* May 19, 1832; Cuevas, *El Porvenir de México,* 378; Valadés, *Orígenes,* 216; Vázquez, "Iglesia, ejército y centralismo," 215–16.
86. *El Fénix de la Libertad,* January 20 and April 13, 1833; Costeloe, "Santa Anna and the Gómez-Farías Administration," 20; Fuentes Mares, *Santa Anna,* 77. Ironically, it was Santa Anna who led the coup that deposed Gómez Pedraza from his original presidential term.
87. Santa Anna to Gómez Farías, March 16, 1833, UTLAC, Gómez Farías Papers, 44A/26; *El Fénix de la Libertad,* April 13, 1833; Bustamante, *Diario histórico,* March 23, 1833, cited in Cecil Alan Hutchinson, "Valentín Gómez Farías: A Biographical Study" (Ph.D. diss., University of Texas, 1948), 162.
88. Ministerio de Guerra y Marina, *Memoria de la Secretaría de Guerra y Marina* (Mexico: Imprenta del Supremo Gobierno, 1833), 1, 4, and estados 1–4. Eighteen months of internecine strife had similarly debilitated the army in 1824, but on that occasion, foreign loans had bailed out the government, and a sympathetic president had helped the military recover.
89. *Memoria de la Secretaría de Guerra y Marina,* 1833, 8; Serrano Ortega, *El contingente de sangre,* 66–67.
90. Dublán y Lozano, *Legislación Mexicana,* 2:503–14, 520–21; *Memoria de la Secretaría de Guerra y Marina* (Mexico: Imprenta del Águila, 1833), 8. Prior to this restructuring, permanent army forces comprised twelve infantry regiments, twelve cavalry regiments, three brigades of artillery, twenty-nine presidial companies in the eastern and western interior provinces, and six presidial compa-

nies in Alta and Baja California. *Memoria de la Secretaría de Guerra y Marina* (Mexico: Imprenta del Gobierno Supremo, 1833), 1 and estados 1 and 2.

91. Hutchinson, "Valentín Gómez Farías," 243–45; Ministerio de Guerra y Marina, *Memoria del Secretario de Estado y del despacho de la guerra* (Mexico: Imprenta del Águila, 1834), 5 and estado 1. The liberals reinforced their crusade against the army with anticlerical legislation that removed the tithe on agricultural products, disentailed monastic property, and empowered the state to assume complete control over ecclesiastical patronage. Michael P. Costeloe, *Church and State in Independent Mexico: A Study of the Patronage Debate, 1821–1857* (London: Royal Historical Society, 1978), 129–30; Bazant, *Alienation of Church Wealth,* 25.

92. Gabriel Durán to Santa Anna, June 1, 1833, published in *El Telégrafo,* June 2, 1833; Bocanegra, *Memorias para la historia,* 2:486–87; Vázquez, "Iglesia, ejército y centralismo," 216.

93. *El Fénix de la Libertad,* May 16, 29, 1833; *El Telégrafo,* May 22, 1833; Dublán y Lozano, *Legislación mexicana,* 2:528; Olavarría y Ferrari, *México independiente,* 324.

94. *El Fénix de la Libertad,* June 14, 1833; *El Telégrafo,* May 22, 1833; Bocanegra, *Memorias para la historia,* 2:486–91; Mariano Arista, *Reseña histórica de la revolución que desde 6 junio hasta 8 octubre tuvo lugar en la República en el año 1833 a favor del sistema central* (Mexico: Mariano Arévalo, 1835), BN, Colección Lafragua, tomo 321; Santa Anna, *Mi historia militar y política,* 29–30. Arista, who was Santa Anna's hand-picked second-in-command, embraced Durán's pronouncement on June 8.

95. Arista, *Reseña histórica,* 5–7; Costeloe, "Santa Anna and the Gómez Farías Administration," 31; Frank N. Samponaro, "Santa Anna and the Abortive Anti-federalist Revolt of 1833 in Mexico," *The Americas* 40 (July, 1983): 102–103; Vázquez, "Iglesia, ejército y centralismo," 216–17.

96. Arista to Santa Anna, Guanajuato, October 6, 1833, ADN, expediente XI/481.3/1000, foja 139; Santa Anna to Herrera, Allende, September 23, 1833, published in *El Telégrafo,* September 25, 1833; Costeloe, "Santa Anna and the Gómez Farías Administration," 30; Dublán y Lozano, *Legislación mexicana,* 2:599–600; *El Fénix de la Libertad,* July 13, 1833; *Memoria del Secretario de Estado y del despacho de la guerra,* 1834, 17.

97. Cámara de Diputados, *Dictamen de las comisiones de guerra de la Cámara de Diputados sobre reorganización del ejército permanente* (Mexico: Ignacio Cumplido, 1833), 3–5; *El Fénix de la Libertad,* November 2, 1833.

98. Decreto arreglando el ejército permanente, November 16, 1833, AGN, GM, vol. 36; Decreto reorganizando el cuerpo de Ingenieros, November 16, 1833, AGN, GM, vol. 36; Decreto disolvieron los cuerpos permanentes y activos por haberse sublevado contra la constitución federal, November 15, 1833, AGN, GM, vol. 36; *Memoria del Secretario de Estado y del despacho de la guerra,* 1834, 5–6, 12–13 and estado 1; Serrano Ortega, *El contingente de sangre,* 68–69. The law reduced the infantry to ten regiments and eight mobile companies *(compañías sueltas)*, pared the cavalry to six regiments and one squadron (in

Yucatán), left the artillery brigades and presidial companies intact, cut the number of general officers to eight division and twelve brigades, and authorized the permanent army a total strength of 17,563 men.

99. Arista, *Reseña histórica,* 206–207; Vázquez, "Iglesia, ejército y centralismo," 217.

100. *El Fénix de la Libertad,* November 29, 1833; Dublán y Lozano, *Legislación mexicana,* 2:536, 600–601; Olavarría y Ferrari, *México independiente,* 336.

101. Anthony Butler to Robert Mclane, no. 66, Mexico City, March 27, 1834, in *Despatches from United States Ministers to Mexico, 1823–1906,* NA, Record Group 59; *El Fénix de la Libertad,* April 14, 1834; *El Telégrafo,* May 3, 1834; Bocanegra, *Memorias para la historia,* 2:546; Hutchinson, "Valentín Gómez Farías," 300–303.

102. *El Telégrafo,* June 22, 1834; Bocanegra, *Memorias para la historia,* 2:573–74; Costeloe, "Santa Anna and the Gómez Farías Administration," 39–41; Vázquez, "Iglesia, ejército y centralismo," 221–22.

103. Dublán y Lozano, *Legislación mexicana,* 3:38; Ministerio de Guerra y Marina, *Memoria del Secretario de Estado y del despacho de la guerra* (Mexico: Impreso por Ignacio Cumplido, 1835), 33; "Manifesto del gobernador de Zacatecas a los habitantes del estado" (Zacatecas, April 3, 1835), BN, Colección Lafragua, tomo 393; Reynaldo Sordo Cedeño, "El general Tornel y la guerra de Téxas," *Historia Mexicana* 62 (1993): 937–38; Costeloe, "Santa Anna and the Gómez Farías Administration," 39–41.

104. Elías Amador, *Bosquejo histórico de Zacatecas* (Zacatecas: Talleres Tipográficos "Pedroza," Ags., 1943), 411–22; Callcott, *Santa Anna,* 115–16; Samponaro, "La alianza de Santa Anna y los federalistas," 383–84. Santa Anna had thoughts of continuing on into Coahuila and Texas, but political machinations in Mexico City dissuaded him from pursuing that option.

105. Dublán y Lozano, *Legislación mexicana,* 3:71, 75–78, 89–90. Felipe Tena Ramírez, ed., *Leyes Fundamentales de México, 1808–1971* (Mexico: Porrúa, 1971), 204–48; Costeloe, *The Central Republic,* 99–109.

106. Callcott, *Santa Anna,* 108–109; Fernando Díaz Díaz, *Caudillos y caciques: Antonio López de Santa Anna y Juan Álvarez* (Mexico: El Colegio de México, 1972), 124–27; Hutchinson, "Valentín Gómez Farías," 306; Costeloe, "Santa Anna and the Gómez Farías Administration," 43–44; Vázquez, "Iglesia, ejército y centralismo," 229–30.

CHAPTER 3

1. *El Anteojo,* November 15, 1835; Vicente Filisola, *Memorias para la historia de la guerra de Téjas, por el Sr. General de división y actual Presidente del Supremo Tribunal de guerra y marina de la República* (Mexico: Tipografía de R. Rafael, 1849), 2:193–209; Oakah L. Jones, Jr, *Santa Anna* (New York: Twayne Publishers, 1968), 63; George L. Rives, *The United States and Mexico, 1821–1848: A History of the Relations Between the Two Countries from the Independence of Mexico to the Close of the War with the United States* (New York: Charles Scribner's Sons, 1913), 1:275–76; Vito Alessio Robles, *Coahuila y Téjas, desde la consumación de la Independencia hasta el Tratado de paz de Guadalupe Hidalgo*

(México: Imprenta Universaria Talleres Gráficas de la Nacíon, 1945–46), 2:57–82; Andreas V. Reichstein, trans. Jeanne R. Wilson, *Rise of the Lone Star: The Making of Texas* (College Station: Texas A&M Univ. Press, 1989), 40–42, 127.

2. José María Tornel y Mendívil, *Breve reseña histórica de los acontecimientos mas notables de la nación mexicana desde el año de 1821 hasta nuestros días* (México: Imprenta de Cumplido, 1852), 350–51; Ministerio de Guerra y Marina, *Memoria de la Secretaría de Estado y del despacho de la guerra y marina* (México: Imprenta del Águila, 1839), 12; Reichstein, *Rise of the Lone Star,* 128–32; Reynaldo Sordo Cedeño, "El general Tornel y la guerra de Téxas," *Historia Mexicana* 62 (1993), 940–41.
3. Ministerio de Guerra y Marina, *Memoria del Secretario de Estado y del despacho de la guerra y marina,* (México: Impreso por Ignacio Cumplido, 1835), estados 1 and 2. Statutory strength at this time was 49,634 troops.
4. *El Telégrafo,* November 28, 1835; Ministerio de Guerra y Marina, *Reglamento del estado mayor de ejército que debe operar sobre Téjas* (México: J. Mariano Lara, 1844), 2–10; José C. Valadés, *Santa Anna y la guerra de Téjas* (México: Editores Unidos Mexicanos, 1965), 162–64; Sordo Cedeño, "El general Tornel," 942.
5. *Diario del Gobierno,* November 9, 1835; José Ramón Malo, *Diario de sucesos notables, 1832–1853* (México: Editorial Patria, 1948), 1:104; Stephen L. Hardin, *Texian Iliad: A Military History of the Texas Revolution, 1835–1836* (Austin: Univ. of Texas Press, 1994), 30–35. Texan rebels also seized the Mexican garrisons of Goliad, San Patricio, and Cópano, thereby cutting Cós's overland and maritime communications.
6. Santa Anna to Ramírez y Sesma, San Luís Potosí, December 7, 1835, Referentes a la Campaña Sobre las Colonias Sublevados de Téjas, verificadas el año de 1836, entry number 7, fojas 7v–10v (hereinafter cited as "Referentes"). The original "Referentes" appearing in Santa Anna's order book are reproduced in Richard G. Santos, *Santa Anna's Campaign Against Texas, 1835–1836, Featuring the Field Commands Issued to Major General Vicente Filisola* (Salisbury, N.C.: Documentary Publications, 1968), 102–61. Comprising the permanent army battalions of Matamoros and Jiménez, the provincial militia of San Luís Potosí, and the permanent cavalry regiment of Dolores, Ramírez y Sesma's 1,500-man Vanguard Brigade is illustrative of the peculiar manner in which the Mexican national military command cobbled units together for exigent missions.
7. Santa Anna to Ramírez y Sesma, San Luís Potosí, December 7, 1835, "Referentes" entry number 7, fojas 7v–10v. This paragraph of the instructions is of particular importance, because it subsequently was cited to justify the massacre of the Coleto/Goliad prisoners.
8. Santa Anna to Filisola, San Luís Potosí, December 8, 1835, "Referentes" entry number 3, fojas 4–5. Second commander-in-chief was a title without any meaningful authority whose designate was expected to advise the commander and execute faithfully any orders he might receive.
9. Carreño, *Jefes del Ejército Mexicano,* 27–29.
10. Cós to Santa Anna, rancho de Salinas, December 15, 1835, published in *Diario*

del Gobierno, January 3, 1836; Filisola, *Memorias,* 2:193–209; Alessio Robles, *Coahuila y Téjas,* 2:57–62. Cós surrendered to the besieging Texans on December 10, after four days of bitter house-to-house fighting that left both armies exhausted. See Hardin, *Texian Iliad,* 77–91, for a detailed account of that action.

11. *Diario del Gobierno,* October 29, 1835; Filisola, *Memorias,* 2:280–86; Santa Anna to Filisola, San Luís Potosí, December 14, 1835, "Referentes," entry number 4, foja 5.

12. Antonio López de Santa Anna, "Manifiesto que de sus operaciones en la campaña de Téjas y en su Cautiverio dirige a sus conciudadanos el General Antonio López de Santa Anna" (Veracruz: Imprenta Liberal á cargo de Antonio María Valdés, 1837), 2–8; Frank C. Hanighen, *Santa Anna, the Napoleon of the West* (New York: Coward-McCann, 1934), 81–82; Ramón Martínez Caro, "A True Account of the First Texas Campaign and the Events Subsequent to the Battle of San Jacinto," in Carlos E. Castañeda, trans. and ed., *The Mexican Side of the Texas Revolution* (Dallas: P. L. Turner Co., 1928), 88 (hereinafter cited as Martínez Caro, "A True Account").

13. *Reglamento del estado mayor,* 3–11; Filisola, *Memorias,* 2:333–41. These figures are imprecise, because muster rolls fluctuated daily; nevertheless they provide a relatively realistic approximation of total army strength on the eve of departure.

14. Jesus Sánchez Garza, ed., *La Rebelión de Téxas—Reseña y Diario de la Campaña de Téxas por José Enrique de la Peña* (México: Impresora Mexicana, 1955), 33 (hereinafter cited as Peña, *Diario de la campaña de Téxas*); Jóse Urrea, "Diario de las operaciones militares de la Divisíon que al mando de General José Urrea hizo la guerra de Téjas, Victoria de Durango, 1838," in *Documentos para la historia de la guerra de Téjas* (México: Editorial Nacional, S.A., 1952), 23 (hereinafter cited as Urrea, "Diario de operaciones militares"). Troops were drawn from Matamoros, San Luís Potosí, Dolores, Aldama, México, Toluca, Guadalajara, Tampico, Querétaro, Guanajuato, and Yucatán. Filisola, *Memorias,* 2:292–94, 332–37.

15. Angelina Nieto, Joseph Hefter, and Mrs. John Nicholas Brown, *El soldado mexicano, 1837–1847: Organización, vestuario, equipo y reglamentos militares* (México: Ediciones Nieto-Brown-Hefter, 1958), 57; Major Frederick Myatt, *The Illustrated Encyclopedia of 19th Century Firearms* (New York: Crescent Books, 1979), 16–17, 28–31; James W. Pohl and Stephen L. Hardin, "The Military History of the Texas Revolution: An Overview," *Southwestern Historical Quarterly* 89 (January, 1986): 280–81; Hardin, *Texian Iliad,* 73–75, 99; Valadés, *Santa Anna,* 197–98. A complicated nineteen-step process was required to load and fire the musket; improper procedure, bad weather, or fouled pieces caused frequent misfires.

16. Santa Anna to Filisola, Leona Vicario (Saltillo), January 8, 1836, "Referentes" entry number 10, fojas 11v–12. Santa Anna advanced Filisola some 30,000 pesos for the purpose of procuring sufficient quantities of corn, beans, rice, lard, and salt, an amount not nearly sufficient for the task at hand.

17. Filisola, *Memorias,* 2:323–24; Martínez to Tornel, May 8, 1836, University of

Texas Archives, Barker Transcripts, Part I, p. 122; Martínez Caro, "A True Account," 100–101; James Presley, "Santa Anna in Texas: A Mexican Viewpoint," *Southwestern Historical Quarterly* 62 (April, 1959): 494, 500–502.

18. Filisola, *Memorias,* 2:333–41; *Memoria del Secretario de Estado y del despacho de la guerra,* 1830, 4; Carlos Sánchez Navarro, *La Guerra de Téjas: Memorias de un Soldado,* 2nd ed. (Editorial Jus, S.A., 1960), 137. First conceived in November 1829, the Cuerpo de Sanidad was ignored by senior military leaders until events in Texas substantiated its need.
19. Elizabeth Salas, *Soldaderas in the Mexican Military: Myths and History* (Austin: Univ. of Texas Press, 1990), 29.
20. Salas, *Soldaderas,* 29–30. Both Filisola and Ramírez y Sesma tried to have the *soldaderas* eliminated from the campaign; but more pragmatic authorities in the ministry of defense realized that the army could not sustain itself in their absence and sanctioned continued *soldadera* participation.
21. Michael Robert Green, "El Soldado Mexicano, 1835–1836," *Military History of Texas and the Southwest* 13 (1975): 7.
22. Santa Anna to Ramírez y Sesma, San Luís Potosí, December 7, 1835, "Referentes" entry number 7, fojas 7v–10v. The defeats at Concepción and Nueces Crossing had driven home to Mexican senior leaders the point that fighting Texans on their terms was a recipe for disaster.
23. Peña, *Diario de la campaña,* 8–9. Colonel Peña also notes that the coercive nature of the conscription process produced soldiers disinclined toward and unreceptive to military training.
24. Santos, *Santa Anna's Campaign,* 36–37. The 1,200-man force that had driven Cós out of Béjar in December, 1835, was reduced to 100 by mid-January.
25. Eugene C. Barker, "The Texan Revolutionary Army," *Southwestern Historical Quarterly* 9 (1906): 227; Jerry J. Gaddy, comp. and ed., *Texas in Revolt: Contemporary Newspaper Accounts of the Texas Revolution* (Fort Collins: Old Army Press, 1973), 25–26. Most Texan fighters carried a version of the Kentucky long rifle, a nine-pound, muzzle-loading, flint-ignition firearm that propelled a .614-caliber bullet with relative accuracy to a range of 270 yards.
26. Pohl and Hardin, "Military History of the Texas Revolution," 285.
27. Santa Anna to Filisola, San Luís Potosí, December 20, 1835, "Referentes" entry number 5, foja 5v. This change was prompted by the knowledge that Cós was withdrawing his 700-man force to Laredo, and Santa Anna did not want two of his principal maneuver elements collocated.
28. *Diario del Gobierno,* December 31, 1835; Filisola, *Memorias,* 2:256–69; Pohl and Hardin, "Military History of the Texas Revolution," 288.
29. Santa Anna to Filisola, San Luís Potosí, December 28, 1835, "Referentes" entry number 6, fojas 6–7v; Santa Anna, *Manifiesto,* 7–8, 12. This new disposition extended the army's line of operations from Guerrero through Monclova to Saltillo, where the general-in-chief established his headquarters on January 5, 1836.
30. The odyssey of Colonel José María Romero's Matamoros Battalion provides a good example of such hardship. Dispatched from Saltillo to reinforce Béjar,

the unit reached Béjar via Laredo on December 9, only to be forced to return to Laredo three days later. From there it was redirected back to Saltillo. Santos, *Santa Anna's Campaign,* 21.

31. Urrea, "Diario de operaciones militares," 12. Designating Goliad as Urrea's principal objective somewhat mitigated Santa Anna's specious decision to make Béjar the main focus of his campaign.
32. Santa Anna to Ramírez y Sesma, Monclova, February 5, 1836, "Referentes" entry number 26, fojas 18v–19; Filisola, *Memorias,* 2:324–25. The balance of the Army of Operations was scheduled to depart Monclova between the 8th and 12th of February, with the command group breaking camp on February 12 and linking up with the Vanguard Brigade at some point along the route to Béjar.
33. Santa Anna to Filisola, Monclova, February 7, 1836, "Referentes" entry number 28, fojas 21–21v; Reglas que deben observarse para la persecución y aprehensión de desertores . . , September 25, 1835, published in *Diario del Gobierno,* January 3, 1836; Filisola, *Memorias,* 2:317.
34. Juan N. Almonte, "The Private Journal of Juan Nepomuceno Almonte, February 1–April 16, 1836," *Southwestern Historical Quarterly* 48 (July, 1944): 154; Carlos Sánchez-Navarro, *La guerra de Téjas: Memorias de un soldado,* 2nd ed. (México: Editorial Jus, S.A., 1960), 80; Urrea, "Diario de operaciones militares," 15–18. These Mayan soldiers were further disadvantaged by their inability to communicate effectively in Spanish.
35. Filisola, *Memorias,* 2:353; Presley, "Santa Anna in Texas," 499; Callcott, *Santa Anna,* 129; Valdés, *Orígenes,* 305–306.
36. Sánchez Navarro, *Memorias de un soldado,* 81; Santos, *Santa Anna's Campaign,* 59. Historically the Medina River had been recognized by both the Spanish and Mexican governments as the boundary separating the two provinces, and the Nueces River served the same function between Texas and Tamaulipas.
37. *Diario del Gobierno,* February 22, 1836; Peña, *Diario de la campaña,* 34–35; Salas, *Soldaderas,* 29. Colonel Peña attributes such predatory behavior to the army's attempt to live off the land in an environment that could barely sustain even its few permanent inhabitants.
38. Hardin, *Texian Iliad,* 133; Santos, *Santa Anna's Campaign,* 55–56, 61; Santa Anna, *Manifiesto,* 13; Valadés, *Santa Anna,* 169. The original 150 defenders were joined on February 29 by 32 men from Gonzales, the only reinforcements the beleaguered Texan garrison received.
39. Almonte, "Journal," 16.
40. Urrea, "Diario de operaciones militares," 8–9; Henderson K. Yoakum, Esq., *History of Texas, from its first settlement in 1685 to its annexation by the United States in 1846* (New York: Redfield, 1855), 2:78. Reaching the Nueces River late on the evening of February 26, Urrea easily overwhelmed the small contingent of Texans attempting to defend San Patricio.
41. Santa Anna to Tornel, Béjar, February 27, 1836, "Referentes" entry number 33, fojas 23–24v; Jones, *Santa Anna,* 23. Santa Anna first visited Béjar in August, 1813, as a nineteen-year-old first lieutenant serving under Spanish Brigadier Joaquín Arredondo during the Independence War. The cruelties his superior

inflicted upon the Texan rebels led by Agustín Magee and Bernardo Gutiérrez de Lara left an indelible impression that likely influenced his action a quarter-century later.

42. Almonte, "Journal," 17–18, 22–23; William Barret Travis to the President of the Convention, March 3, 1836, in *Telegraph and Texas Register,* March 24, 1836; Jones, *Santa Anna,* 23; Sánchez Navarro, *Memorias de un soldado,* 82. Despite the intermittent shelling, which continued through March 5, Travis reported that the Texans had "not lost a man" up to that point.
43. Hardin, *Texian Iliad,* 112–16, 128–29; Santa Anna, *Manifiesto,* 13.
44. Almonte, "Journal" 18; Peña, *Diario de la campaña de Téjas,* 254–55; Santa Anna, Order, March 5, 1836, in John H. Jenkins, ed., *The Papers of the Texas Revolution, 1835–1836* (Austin: Presidial Press, 1973), 4:518–19; Valadés, *Santa Anna,* 197–98.
45. Nieto, et al, *El soldado mexicano,* 53–54; Martínez Caro, "A True Account," 105; Peña, *Diario de la campaña de Téjas,* 254–55.
46. Santa Anna to Ministro de Guerra, March 6, 1836, in Jenkins, *Papers,* 5:11–12; *Diario del Gobierno,* March 27, 1836; Peña, *Diario de la campaña de Téjas,* 70; Sánchez Navarro, *Memorias de un soldado,* 84; Martínez Caro, "A True Account," 103–104; Valadés, *Santa Anna,* 200–204. Most accounts of the battle indicate that the executions were carried out by staff officers who had not actively participated in the fighting.
47. *El Cosmopolita,* March 23, 1836; *El Mosquito Mexicano,* March 22, 1836; Peña, *Diario de la campaña de Téjas,* Anexo no. 9, "Final del parte rendido por el general en jefe del ejército de operaciones sobre Téjas, Don Antonio López de Santa Anna, el 6 de Marzo de 1836," 255–56; Jeff Long, *Duel of Eagles: The Mexican and U.S. Fight for the Alamo* (New York: William Morrow and Company, 1990), 259–60. Because most of the corpses were quickly burned to prevent the spread of disease, it is impossible to obtain a completely verifiable number. Most reliable sources place Texan losses at between 182 and 187 killed.
48. Peña, *Diario de la campaña de Téjas,* 71–73; Sánchez Navarro, *Memorias de un soldado,* 85–86.
49. *El Mosquito Mexicano,* March 22, 1836; *El Cosmopolita,* March 23, 1836.
50. For a more detailed examination of this issue, see Michael P. Costeloe, "The Mexican Press of 1836 and the Battle of the Alamo," *Southwestern Historical Quarterly* 91 (April, 1988): 533–43.
51. Sánchez Navarro, *Memorias de un soldado,* 85–86; Martínez Caro, "A True Account," 105; *Memoria de la Secretaría de Estado y del despacho de la guerra y marina,* 1839, 23.
52. Decreto establiciendo el Cuerpo de Sanidad, August 16, 1836, AGN, GM, unnumbered vol.
53. Filisola, *Memorias,* 2:430–31; Presley, "Santa Anna in Texas," 506.
54. Filisola, *Memorias,* 2:400–401; Santa Anna, *Manifiesto,* 15–17.
55. Francisco R. Almada, *Diccionario de historia, geografía y biografía Sonorenses* (Hermosillo: Instituto Sonorense de Cultura, 1990), 806–10; Hardin, *Texian Iliad,* 163–66; Sánchez Navarro, *Memorias de un soldado,* 86–87; Santa Anna,

Manifiesto, 16, 20. Among the most exceptional of Mexico's nineteenth-century military leaders, Urrea would play a prominent, though often contentious, role throughout the decade of centralism and the war with the United States.

56. Pohl and Hardin, "Military History of the Texas Revolution," 300; Yoakum, *History of Texas,* 2:498. On March 2 the Constitutional Convention, meeting at Washington-on-the-Brazos, had formally declared Texan independence and appointed Houston commander of all armed forces.
57. Valadés, *Santa Anna,* 209–17; Urrea, "Diario de operaciones militares," 15–17; Yoakum, *History of Texas,* 2:471–72.
58. Henry Stewart Foote, *Texas and the Texans; or, Advance of the Anglo-Americans to the Southwest Including a History of Leading Events in Mexico, From the Conquest of Fernando Cortes to the Termination of the Texas Revolution* (Austin: Univ. of Texas Press, 1935), 2:228–32; Hardin, *Texian Iliad,* 170–74; Urrea, "Diario de operaciones militares," 20. Urrea surrounded the Texans to prevent their exfiltration during the night.
59. Urrea, "Diario de operaciones militares," 21–23. This decree was rescinded April 14, 1836, and all remaining Texan prisoners had their sentences commuted to imprisonments of varied duration. Decreto de la Secretaría de Guerra y Marina, April 14, 1836, AGN, GM, vol. 5; Dublán y Lozano, *Legislación mexicana,* 3:149.
60. Santa Anna to Ramírez y Sesma, San Luís Potosí, December 7, 1835, "Referentes" entry number 7, fojas 7v–10v.
61. Callcott, *Santa Anna,* 133; Santa Anna, *Manifiesto,* 18.
62. Peña, *Diario de la campaña de Téjas,* 109–12; Sánchez Navarro, *Memorias de un soldado,* 86–87; Urrea, "Diario de operaciones militares," 21.
63. Peña, *Diario de la campaña de Téjas,* 106; Sánchez Navarro, *Memorias de un soldado,* 87; Urrea, "Diario de operaciones militares," 55–56.
64. Santa Anna to Filisola, San Felipe de Austin, April 8, 1836, "Referentes" entry number 38, fojas 28v–29; José C. Valadés, *Orígenes de la república mexicana* (México: Editores Mexicanos Unidos, 1972), 306–307. Santa Anna soon changed his mind and moved Filisola to San Felipe de Austin to establish a provisional capital. Santa Anna to Filisola, San Felipe de Austin, April 8, 1836, "Referentes" entry number 39, fojas 29–30v.
65. José María Roa Bárcena, *Recuerdos de la invasión norteamericana, 1846–1848* (México: Editorial Porrúa, S.A., 1947), 1:353; Pohl and Hardin, "Military History of the Texas Revolution," 300; Santa Anna, *Manifiesto,* 29–30; Valadés, *Santa Anna,* 229, 232.
66. Santa Anna to Filisola, Thompson's Crossing, April 13, 1836, "Referentes" entry number 37, fojas 26v–27; Roa Bárcena, *Recuerdos,* 1:353–54; Santa Anna, *Manifiesto,* 31–32; Valadés, *Santa Anna,* 234–35. Cós reached the encampment early on April 21, with just 300 men, bringing Mexican strength to around 1250.
67. Callcott, *Santa Anna,* 135–36; Carreño, *Jefes del Ejército Mexicano,* cviii–cxi; Hardin, *Texian Iliad,* 209–15; Roa Bárcena, *Recuerdos,* 1:354–55; Santa Anna, *Manifiesto,* 32–33; Yoakum, *History of Texas,* 2:498–502. The Texans were re-

ported to have sustained only six killed and twenty-four wounded, among whom was Houston, whose right ankle was badly mangled.

68. Santa Anna to Filisola, Campo de San Jacinto, April 22, 1836, in Filisola, *Memorias,* 2:481; Roa Bárcena, *Recuerdos,* 1:355–56; Niceto de Zamacois, *Historia de México desde sus tiempos más remotos hasta nuestros días* (Barcelona: J.F. Parres, y Cía., 1876–88), 12:91–92.
69. Peña, *Diario de la campaña de Téjas,* 32; Sordo Cedeño, "El general Tornel," 945–46; Filisola to Ministerio de Guerra y Marina, Guadalupe Victoria, May 14, 1836, in Vicente Filisola, *Representación dirigida al Supremo Gobierno por gral . . . , en la defensa de su honor y aclaración de sus operaciones como general en jefe del ejército sobre Tejas* (Mexico: Ignacio Cumplido, 1836), 68–70.
70. Filisola, *Representación,* 68–70; Callcott, *Santa Anna,* 140–41; Rives, *The United States and Mexico,* 1:357–58; Valadés, *Santa Anna,* 279–81; Santa Anna, "Las Guerras de México con Téjas y los Estados Unidos," in Genero García, *Documentos inéditos o muy raros para la Historia de México* (México: Librería de la Vda. de Ch. Bouret, 1910), 32:58.
71. Pohl and Hardin, "Military History of the Texas Revolution," 288.
72. Almonte, "Journal," 20–21; Green, *El Soldado Mexicano,* 7.
73. Sánchez Navarro, *Memorias de un soldado,* 77. Having experienced firsthand the Texans' tenacity and spirit when Cós was expelled from Béjar, Sánchez Navarro was not among those blinded by such arrogance.
74. Roa Bárcena, *Recuerdos,* 1:356. The disposition at the time Filisola received orders to evacuate Texas was: 1,408 with Ramírez y Sesma at Oldford; 1,165 with Urrea at Brazoria and Columbia; 1,000 with Andrade at Béjar; and sundry small detachments scattered from Cópano to Matagorda.
75. Presley, "Santa Anna in Texas," 509–12.
76. Pohl and Hardin, "Military History of the Texas Revolution," 304–305. The unexpected death of President *ad interim* Miguel Barragán in February, 1836, precipitated a succession crisis that Santa Anna was too far removed to influence.
77. Francisco Bulnes, *Las grandes mentiras de nuestra historia: la nación y el ejército en las guerras extranjeras* (México: Editora Nacional, S.A., 1969), 438; Pohl and Hardin, "Military History of the Texas Revolution," 306.
78. "Manifiesto del Congreso General en el presente año" (México, July 29, 1836), BN, División de Manuscritos, tomo 46; Dublán y Lozano, *Legislación mexicana,* 3:142. The government attempted to recognize the valor of its enlisted soldiers by establishing a military legion, membership in which was intended to "recompense the distinguished actions of the army and navy." Estatuto de la Legión, April 27, 1836, AGN, GM, unnumbered vol.
79. *El Mosquito Mexicano,* June 14 and 24, 1836; Powhatan Ellis to John Forsyth, October 11, 1836, in *Despatches from United States Ministers to Mexico, 1823–1906,* vii, NA, Record Group 59. On May 20, 1836, War Minister Tornel ordered all military units to display a ribbon of black crepe on their flags and guidons as long as Santa Anna remained a prisoner.
80. Ellis to Forsyth, May 19 and June 25, 1836, in *Despatches from United States*

Ministers to Mexico, 1823–1906, vii, NA, Record Group 59; José María Tornel y Mendívil, *Téxas y los Estados Unidos de America en sus relaciones con la república mexicana* (México, 1837), 69; Sordo Cedeño, "El general Tornel," 948–49.

CHAPTER 4

1. *El Cosmopolita,* March 8, 1837; Tornel to José Justo Corro, Mexico City, January 29, 1837, AGN, Archivo de Guerra (AG), vol. 200; Representación dirigida al Supremo Gobierno por el General Vicente Filisola en defensa de su honor . . . , August 23, 1836, AGN, AG, vol. 200; Miguel A. Sánchez Lamego, *The Second Mexican-Texas War, 1841–1843,* trans. Joseph Hefter, Hill Junior College Monograph no. 7 (Hillsboro, Tex.: Hill Junior College, 1972), 1–2; Leonard D. Parrish, "The Life of Nicolás Bravo, Mexican Patriot (1786–1854)" (Ph.D. diss., University of Texas, 1951), 238–39. José Urrea succeeded Filisola as Army of the North commander and was, in turn, replaced by Nicolás Bravo in September 1836.
2. *Diario del Gobierno,* October 16, 1837; Memoria, Ministro de Hacienda, April 12, 1836, 2–3. The following year the treasury minister reported a budget deficit of 18 million pesos, adding that military expenditures alone exceeded anticipated revenues.
3. Convención entre Antonio López de Santa Anna y el Presidente David A. Burnet de la Republica de Téxas, May 14, 1836, AGN, AG, vol. 200; Eugene C. Barker, "President Jackson and the Texas Revolution," *American Historical Review* 12 (July, 1907): 808. During his absence the Congress nullified all agreements entered into by Santa Anna, declared him out of office, and barred him from holding subsequent political or military positions until he submitted to trial for his actions in Texas. Manuel Dublán y José María Lozano, eds. *Legislación Mexicana; ó Colección completa de las disposiciones legislativas expedidas desde la independencia de la República* (Mexico: Imprenta del Comercio, 1876–93), 3:162.
4. Ellis to Forsyth, no. 27, October 11, 1836, *Despatches from United States Minister to Mexico, 1823–1906,* vii, NA, Record Group 59; Wilfred Hardy Callcott, *Santa Anna: The Story of an Enigma Who Once Was Mexico* (Norman: Univ. of Oklahoma Press, 1936), 151–53; José Fuentes Mares, *Santa Anna: Aurora y ocaso de un comediante,* 3rd ed. (Mexico: Editorial Jus, 1967), 153; Enrique Olavarría y Ferrari, *México independiente, 1821–1855,* vol. 4 of *México a través de los siglos,* ed. Vicente Riva Palacios (Mexico: Editorial Cumbre, S.A., 1953), 385.
5. William S. Robertson, "The French Intervention in Mexico in 1838," *Hispanic American Historical Review* 24 (May, 1944): 222–23; José C. Valadés, *Orígenes de la república mexicana* (Mexico: Editores Mexicanos Unidos, 1972), 316–17. Although most Parián businesses had Spanish proprietors, one victim of the 1828 riot happened to be the owner of a French pastry shop, a coincidence that lent the sobriquet "Guerra de los Pasteles" (Pastry War) to the 1838 confrontation.
6. Nancy Nichols Barker, *The French Experience in Mexico, 1821–1861* (Chapel Hill: Univ. of North Carolina Press, 1979), 57–59; Robertson, "The French Intervention," 225. Barker cites outright contempt for Mexico and France's failure

to clearly define its foreign policy objectives as additional factors influencing the decision to employ military force. Barker, *The French Experience in Mexico,* 67.

7. *Diario del Gobierno,* March 27, 1838; P. Blanchard and A. Dauzats, *San Juan de Ulùa [sic], ou rélation de l'expédition Française au Mexique sous les ordres de M. le contre-amiral Baudin* (Paris: Gide, 1859), 229–48; Robertson, "The French Intervention," 228–29.
8. *Diario del Gobierno,* April 9, 1838; Antonio de la Peña y Reyes, *La primera guerra entre México y Francia* (Mexico: Publicaciones de la Secretaría de Relaciones Exteriores, 1927), 58–61; Blanchard and Dauzats, *San Juan de Ulúa,* 260; David Pletcher, *The Diplomacy of Annexation: Texas, Oregon and the Mexican War* (Columbia: Univ. of Missouri Press, 1973), 58–59. Even at full strength, Bazoche's small seven-ship squadron could not possibly have blockaded the Gulf Coast from Matamoros to Veracruz with any degree of success.
9. Baudin to Manuel Rincón, November 27, 1838, AGN, GM, unnumbered vol.; Ashburnham to Palmerston, December 10, 1838, Mexico, Foreign Office 50/116; Barker, *The French Experience in Mexico,* 73–75; Luís Gonzaga Cuevas, *Exposición del Ex-Ministro que la suscribe, sobre las diferencias con Francia* (Mexico: Ignacio Cumplido, 1839), 49–51; Peña y Reyes, *La primera guerra entre México y Francia,* 120–41. Interestingly, the negotiations broke down over the issue of retail trade and not indemnification, a convincing indication that commercial interests were at least as important as compensation for past grievances.
10. Blanchard and Dauzats, *San Juan de Ulúa,* 320–38; E. H. A. Jenkins, *A History of the French Navy from its Beginnings to the Present Day* (London: MacDonald and Jane's, 1973), 290–91.
11. Ashburnham to Pakenham, December 4, 1838, Mexico, Foreign Office 50/116; *Diario del Gobierno,* December 1, 1838; *Memoria de la Secretaría de Estado y del despacho de la guerra y marina,* 1839, 7–8; Rincón to Ministro de Guerra y Marina, Veracruz, December 8, 1838, ADN, expediente XI/481.3/2067; Alberto, M. Carreño, ed., *Jefes del Ejército Mexicano en 1847: Biografías de generales de división y de brigada y de coroneles del ejército por fines del año 1847* (Mexico: Secretaría de Fomento, 1914), cxxii–cxxv, 29–33; Barker, *The French Experience in Mexico,* 75–76, 79.
12. *El Cosmopolita,* December 8, 1838; Carlos María Bustamante, *El gabinete mexicano durante el segundo período de la administración del exmo. señor presidente d. Anastasio Bustamante* (Mexico: J. Mariano Lara, 1842), 1:135; Carreño, *Jefes del Ejército Mexicano.* cxxviii–cxxx; Eugène Maissen, *The French in Mexico and Texas (1838–1839),* translated and with an introduction and notes by James L. Shepherd III (Salado: Anson Jones Press, 1961), 50.
13. *El Cosmopolita,* December 8 and 12, 1838; *Memoria de la Secretaría de Estado y del despacho de la guerra y marina,* 1839, p. 27; Ashburnham to Palmerston, December 31, 1838, Mexico, Foreign Office 50/116; "Manifiesto que hace a sus conciudadanos el General Mariano Arista sobre las circunstancias ocurridas en su prisión y libertad por las tropas francesas," Mexico City, February 10, 1839,

BN, Colección Lafragua, tomo 305; Bustamante, *El gabinete mexicano,* 1:141–45; Maissen, *The French in Mexico and Texas,* 52; Jenkins, *History of the French Navy,* 291. This engagement is reported to have cost the attackers eight killed and sixty wounded (Baudin acknowledged only one killed and two wounded), while the Mexicans sustained nine killed and nine wounded. Lerdo de Tejada, *Apuntes de la heróica cuidad,* 2:467; Pakenham to Sir Charles Paget, HMS Pique, December 31, 1838, Mexico, Foreign Office 50/123.

14. Quoted in *Diario del Gobierno,* December 8, 1838; Decreto del Congreso, February 11, 1839, AGN, GM, vol. 42; Bustamante, *El gabinete mexicano,* 1:141–45; Blanchard and Dauzats, *San Juan de Ulúa,* 457–62.
15. Pakenham to Sir Thomas Harvey, July 20, 1839, Mexico, Foreign Office 50/126, ff., 5–11.
16. Baudin to Urrea, December 22, 1838, published in *Diario del Gobierno,* January 9, 1839; Pakenham to Palmerston, January 26, 1839, Mexico, Foreign Office 50/123; Barker, *The French Experience in Mexico,* 82–83; Bustamante, *El gabinete mexicano,* 1:137–39; Dublán y Lozano, *Legislación mexicana,* 3:564; Robertson, "The French Intervention," 244–45.
17. *Diario del Gobierno,* January 9 and March 15, 1839; Peña y Reyes, *La primera guerra entre México y Francia,* 250–52, 337–43; *Tratados y convenciones celebrados y ratificados por la República Mexicana desde su independencia hasta el año actual, acompañados de varios documentos que les son referentes,* Edición Oficial (Mexico: Gonzalo A. Esteva, 1878), 415–23; Ministerio de Guerra y Marina, *Memoria del Ministro de Guerra y Marina* (Mexico: Imprenta del Águila, 1840), 46–47; Pakenham to Palmerston, May 11, 1839, Mexico, Foreign Office 50/124. The Mexican Congress objected to the reparation provision but ultimately approved the treaty as Mexico's penurious condition offered no other satisfactory alternatives. France ratified the treaty soon thereafter, and on March 28, Baudin returned Ulúa to Mexican control. He was more than happy to evacuate the dank fortress in which one-twentieth of his command had perished from disease in little over three and one-half months.
18. *Diario del Gobierno,* March 15, 1839; Barker, *The French Experience in Mexico,* 85–86; Robertson, "The French Intervention," 251–52.
19. Cecilia Noriega Elío, *El Constituyente de 1842* (Mexico: Universidad Nacional Autónoma de México, 1986), 18; David M. Vigness, "La expedición Urrea-Mejía," *Historia Mexicana* 2 (July, 1955–June, 1956): 212. Between 1837 and 1841, Mexico recorded some eighty-four pronouncements by proponents of federalism or advocates for the restoration of the Constitution of 1824.
20. *El Restaurador Mexicano,* January 2, 1839; *Memoria del Ministro de Guerra y Marina,* 1840, 47; Bustamante, *El gabinete mexicano,* 1:179–83; Robert Stevens, "Mexico's Forgotten Frontier: A History of Sonora, 1821–1846" (Ph.D. diss., University of California, Berkeley, 1963), 144–60; Frank D. Robertson, "The Military and Political Career of Mariano Paredes y Arrillaga, 1797–1849" (Ph.D. diss., University of Texas, 1955), 43–45, 62.
21. John Parrot to John Forsyth, Mazatlán, May 8 and July 1, 1838, in *Despatches from United States Ministers to Mexico, 1823–1906,* vii, NA, Record Group 59; *El*

Cosmopolita, November 14, 1838; *El Mosquito Mexicano,* October 26, 1838. The withdrawal of Paredes's forces from Michoacán set back government efforts to suppress the growing federalist rebellion led by Gordiano Guzmán. Once Paredes concluded the Sinaloa business, Bustamante reappointed him commandant-general of Jalisco and Michoacán with orders to bring the insurrection to an end. Despite the distraction of Urrea's abortive pronouncement of July 15, 1840, Paredes successfully pacified Michoacán by employing locally formed auxiliary companies to secure the countryside. Juan Ortíz Escamilla, "El pronunciamiento federalista de Gordiano Guzmán, 1837–1842," *Historia Mexicana* 38 (1988): 265–66 and 275–78.

22. *Diario del Gobierno,* January 21, 1839; *El Mexicano,* February 22, 1839; Vigness, "La expedición Urrea-Mejía," 212–13.

23. *Memoria del Ministro de Guerra y Marina,* 1840, 47; Vigness, "La expedición Urrea-Mejía," 215; Alfonso Trueba, *Santa Anna,* 3rd ed. (Mexico: Editorial Jus, 1958), 50; Fernando Díaz Díaz, *Caudillos and caciques: Antonio López de Santa Anna y Juan Álvarez* (Mexico: El Colegio de Mexico, 1972), 148. Essentially a fourth branch of government charged with maintaining constitutional equilibrium between the other three branches, the Supreme Conservative Power was specifically intended to moderate the ability of the chief executive to impose his will upon the Congress and Judiciary. In the long-term the concept failed utterly to deter presidents from illegal or unconstitutional acts. Frank N. Samponaro, "The Political Role of the Army in Mexico, 1821–1848" (Ph.D. diss., State University of New York at Stony Brook, 1971), 282.

24. *Memoria del Ministro de Guerra y Marina,* 1840, 48; *Diario del Gobierno,* May 4, 1839; Vigness, "La expedición Urrea-Mejía," 216; Díaz Díaz, *Caudillos y caciques,* 148; Niceto de Zamacois, *Historia de México desde sus tiempos más remotos hasta nuestros días* (Barcelona: J. F. Parres, y Cía., 1876–88), 12:178–87.

25. *Memoria del Ministro de Guerra y Marina,* 1840, 6–8, 48; Vigness, "La expedición Urrea-Mejía," 216; Sánchez Lamego, *The Second Mexican-Texas War,* 4–5.

26. *Diario del Gobierno,* May 8, 9, June 9, 1839; Decreto del Congreso, May 5, 1839, AGN, GM, unnumbered vol.; Bustamante, *El gabinete mexicano,* 1:185; José Ramón Malo, *Diario de sucesos notables, 1832–1853* (Mexico: Editorial Patria, 1948), 1:168.

27. *El Mexicano,* July 11, 1839; Callcott, *Santa Anna,* 164; José María Bocanegra, *Memorias para la historia de México independiente, 1821–1842* (Mexico: Imprenta del Gobierno Federal, 1892–97), 2:787–89; Dublán y Lozano, *Legislación mexicana,* 3:642.

28. Bustamante, *El gabinete mexicano,* 1:185; Callcott, *Santa Anna,* 164; Díaz Díaz, *Caudillos y caciques,* 148.

29. *Memoria del Ministro de Guerra y Marina,* 1840, 48. A natural son of insurgent hero Jóse María Morelos, The U.S. educated Almonte held various staff positions to include aide-de-camp to Santa Anna during the Texas campaign. Appointed minister of war in 1841, he subsequently served as Mexican minister to the United States, London, and France. Carreño, *Jefes del Ejército Mexicano,* 67–70.

30. Decreto . . . para organizar los cuerpos de infantería y caballería del Ejército

Nacional Mexicano, March 16, 1839, AGN, GM, vol. 8; Decreto . . . para organizar los cuerpos de infantería y caballería de Milicia Activo, June 12, 1840, AGN, GM, vol. 10; *Memoria de la Secretaría de Estado y del despacho de la guerra y marina,* 1839, 13; *Memoria del Ministro de Guerra y Marina,* 1840, estados 2, 3, 7–11. By regulation a permanent army battalion comprised eight companies of 80 men each for a total strength of 640 men. In reality most battalions operated at manning levels considerably lower than those prescribed.

31. Establicimiento de la plana mayor del ejército mexicano, October 30, 1838, AGN, GM, vol. 8; Estatuto para el Regimen interior de la plana mayor del ejército, October 30, 1838, AGN, GM, vol. 8; *Memoria del Secretario de Estado y del despacho de la guerra y marina,* 1835, 31; *Memoria del Ministro de Guerra y Marina,* 1840, 9–10; *Ministerio de Guerra y Marina Memoria del Ministerio de Guerra y Marina* (Mexico: Imprenta del Águila, 1841), 9–11; Decreto que se extingue el estado mayor general del ejército, April 22, 1828, AGN, GM, vol. 18.
32. *Memoria del Ministro de Guerra y Marina,* 1840, 8–9; Decreto arreglando el numero de generales, February 19, 1839, AGN, GM, vol. 8. Legislation promulgated on October 24, 1824, had limited the army to twelve division and eighteen brigade generals.
33. Juan Manuel Torrea, *La vida de una institución gloriosa. El Colegio Militar, 1821–1930* (Mexico: Talleres Tipografía Centenario, 1931), 34; *Memoria del Ministro de Guerra y Marina,* 1840, 14. The United States Military Academy, at West Point, had been providing just such professional socialization since 1821. William B. Skelton, *An American Profession of Arms: The Army Officer Corps, 1784–1861* (Lawrence: Univ. Press of Kansas, 1992), 179–80.
34. *Memoria de la Secretaría de Estado y del despacho de la guerra y marina,* 1939, 14–15; Decreto . . . establiciendo una escuela de aplicación para Capitanes y Tenientes de Artillería y Plana Mayor del Ejército, September 11, 1840, AGN, GM, vol. 27; Decreto separando el Colegio Militar y la Escuela de Aplicación, January 20, 1842, AGN, GM, vol. 27.
35. At about this same time the U.S. Army was experimenting with similar post-commissioning institutions. Companies of light infantry and artillery rotated through Jefferson Barracks (Missouri) and Fort Monroe (Virginia), respectively. The purpose of these "Schools of Practice" was to improve discipline, esprit, and uniformity. Nearly all the West Point graduates commissioned in these branches drew a School of Practice as their initial assignment. The skills acquired while in attendance stood these officers in good stead during the war with Mexico. Skelton, *An American Profession of Arms,* 249–53.
36. Decreto para reemplazar las bajas del ejército mexicano por Sorteo General, January 26, 1839, AGN, GM, vol. 8; *Diario del Gobierno,* May 6, 1839; *Memoria de la Secretaría de Estado y del despacho de la guerra y marina,* 1839, 14–15; Dublán y Lozano, *Legislación mexicana,* 3:558–61, 582–89, and 592–600; Serrano Ortega, *El contingente de sangre,* 82–84. The total number of citizens to be conscripted nationally was determined each September when the department governors announced their respective requirements for the upcoming year.

37. *Memoria de la Secretaría de Estado y del despacho de la guerra y marina,* 1839, 18–20.
38. Reglamento para la enseñanza primeria de los cuerpos del ejército, September 3, 1835, published in *Diario del Gobierno,* September 5, 1835; Decreto extingiendo la escuela normal del ejército, July 26, 1846, AGN, GM, vol. 27.
39. *Memoria del Ministerio de Guerra y Marina,* 1841, 35–36. During the colonial period the Spaniards had been remarkably successful in forming alliances that pitted traditional Indian enemies against one another.
40. *Memoria del Ministro de Guerra y Marina,* 1840, 45–46. The Reglamento of 1772, it will be recalled, governed Spanish-Indian policy for the balance of the colonial period.
41. *Memoria del Ministerio de Guerra y Marina,* 1841, 37. A resurgence of Yaqui hostilities in Sonora and Sinaloa imposed yet another burden on an army already stretched to the limit by multiple crises. For a detailed account of the Yaqui quest for sovereignty, see Evelyn Hu-DeHart, *Yaqui Resistance and Survival: The Struggle for Land and Autonomy, 1821–1910* (Madison: Univ. of Wisconsin Press, 1984).
42. *El Cosmopolita,* October 20, 1838; *Diario del Gobierno,* June 15, 1838; Pakenham to Palmerston, no. 86, October 22, 1839, Mexico, Foreign Office 50/126; Michael P. Costeloe, "The Triangular Revolt in Mexico and the Fall of Anastasio Bustamante, August-October 1841," *Journal of Latin American Studies* 20 (1988): 339–40; Josefina Zoraida Vázquez, "The Texas Question in Mexican Politics, 1836–1845," *Southwestern Historical Quarterly* 89 (January, 1986): 327.
43. *El Monitor Republicano,* April 6, 1840; *El Cosmopolita,* August 4, 1840; Pakenham to Palmerston, no. 5, January 3, 1840, Mexico, Foreign Office 50/134; Dublán y Lozano, *Legislación mexicana,* 3:512–13, 568–69; Margarita Urías Hermosillo, "Militares y comerciantes en México, 1828–1846: las mercancías de la nacionalidad," *Historias* 6 (April–June, 1984): 49–69.
44. *Memoria del Ministerio de Guerra y Marina,* 1841, 11–12, 15–18, 37–39; Serrano Ortega, *El contingente de sangre,* 84–86.
45. *El Mosquito Mexicano,* July 17, 1840; Pakenham to Palmerston, no. 10, February 9, 1840, Mexico, Foreign Office 50/134; Costeloe, "The Triangular Revolt," 342; Vázquez, "The Texas Question," 332.
46. Decreto para la formación del Regimiento Ligera Comercio de México, June 13, 1838, AGN, GM, vol. 38; *Boletín Oficial,* July 16, 1840; Urrea to Gómez Farías, April 6, 1840, UTLAC, Gómez Farías Papers; *Memoria del Ministerio de Guerra y Marina,* 1841, 39–40; Michael P. Costeloe, "A Pronunciamiento in Nineteenth Century Mexico: 15 de julio de 1840," *Mexican Studies/Estudios Mexicanos* 4 (Summer, 1988): 249; Noriega Elío, *El Constituyente de 1842,* 21. Bustamante was released the following day and promptly joined General Valencia's loyalists.
47. Leopoldo Martínez Caraza, *La intervención norteamericana en México, 1846–1848* (Mexico: Panorama Editorial, S.A., 1981), 231–32; Carreño, *Jefes del Ejército Mexicano,* 33–35. Valencia died in Mexico City in 1848.
48. Pakenham to Palmerston, July 29, 1840, Mexico, Foreign Office 50/136;

Hutchinson, Cecil. A. "Valentín Gómez Farías: A Biographical Study" (Ph.D. diss., University of Texas, 1948), 480–86; Malo, *Diario de sucesos notables,* 1:180–84; *Memoria del Ministerio de Guerra y Marina,* 1841, 40. The rebels were reported to have attracted in excess of 4,000 fighters, a figure Carlos Bustamante attributes to Gómez Farías paying each volunteer two pesos. El *gabinete mexicano,* 2:64.

49. Frances Calderón de la Barca, *Life in Mexico* (Berkeley: Univ. of California Press, 1982), 239.
50. Costeloe, "A Pronunciamiento," 246; Noriega Elío, *El Constituyente de 1842,* 22–23. Carlos Bustamante put total casualties at 886 killed and wounded. *El gabinete mexicano,* 2:79–80; Pakenham reported some 400 killed. Pakenham to Palmerston, July 29, 1840, Mexico, Foreign Office 50/136.
51. Calderón de la Barca, *Life in Mexico,* 263; *Memoria del Ministerio de Guerra y Marina,* 1841, 40; Costeloe, "A Pronunciamiento," 257–60.
52. Decreto del Congreso, August 19, 1840, AGN, GM, vol. 42; *Memoria del Ministerio de Guerra y Marina,* 1841, 12, 40.
53. "Manifiesto de la Guarnición de Jalisco," Guadalajara, August 8, 1841, BN, Colección Lafragua, tomo 305; Bustamante, *El gabinete mexicano,* 2:133; Noriega Elío, *El Constituyente de 1842,* 27; Bocanegra, *Memorias para la historia,* 2:836; Costeloe, "A Pronunciamiento," 263.
54. "Manifiesto del ciudadano Gabriel Valencia, general de división y jefe de la plana mayor del ejército sobre su conducta en la ultima revolución," Mexico, October 1, 1841, BN, Colección Lafragua, tomo 305; Dublán y Lozano, *Legislación mexicana,* 4:32; Bustamante, *El gabinete mexicano,* 2:141–42; Callcott, *Santa Anna,* 172–74; Calderón de la Barca, *Life in Mexico,* 419–21.
55. Calderón de la Barca, *Life in Mexico,* 426.
56. Álvarez to Ministro de Guerra y Marina, September 10, 1841, published in *El Cosmopolita,* October 20, 1841; "Exposición que el General D. Mariano Paredes hace a sus conciudadanos en manifestación de su conducta política, militar y económica en la presente revolución," Mexico, 1841, BN, Colección Lafragua, tomo 305; Noriega Elío, *El Constituyente de 1842,* 32–33.
57. *Boletín Oficial,* September 20, 1841; Bocanegra, *Memorias para la historia,* 2:837–38; Zamacois, *Historia de México,* 12:226.
58. Calderón de la Barca, *Life in Mexico,* 433–34.
59. *El Cosmopolita,* November 10, 1841; Noriega Elío, *El Constituyente de 1842,* 36; Costeloe, "The Triangular Revolt," 355. The "Bases de organización para el gobierno provisional de la república adoptada en Tacubaya" was the product of Santa Anna's meeting with Paredes and Valencia at the archbishop's residence on September 28 in anticipation of Bustamante's imminent capitulation. The plan called for the appointment of a council of representatives *(junta de representantes)* composed of two deputies from each department to choose an official to assume control of a provisional government. As commander-in-chief of the army, Santa Anna was empowered to select the deputies. Bustamante, *El gabinete mexicano,* 2:177; Dublán y Lozano, *Legislación mexicana,* 4:32–34; *El Cosmopolita,* October 23, 1841; *Boletín Oficial,* September 30, 1841.

60. Costeloe, "The Triangular Revolt," 357–58; Noriega Elío, *El Constituyente de 1842*, 27–28, 34.
61. Calderón de la Barca, *Life in Mexico*, 443–44; Dublán y Lozano, *Legislación mexicana*, 4:35; Pakenham to Palmerston, October 9, 1841, Mexico, Foreign Office 50/151; Zamacois, *Historia de México*, 12:237–38. On October 6, Santa Anna and Bustamante ratified the Convenios de la Estanzuela, which placed all belligerent forces under the former's control and brought an end to the civil war. Dublán y Lozano, Legislación mexicana, 4:34–35.
62. *Memoria del Ministerio de Guerra y Marina*, 1841, 9–10, and 72–77; *Diario del Gobierno*, October 11, 1841; Calderón de la Barca, *Life in Mexico*, 447; Noriega Elío, *El Constituyente de 1842*, 41, 49.
63. *El Siglo XIX*, October 31, 1841; Francisco R. Almada, *Diccionario de historia, geografía y biografía Sonorenses* (Hermosillo: Instituto Sonorense de Cultura, 1990), 654–55; Stevens, "Mexico's Forgotten Frontier," 155–59; Zamacois, *Historia de México*, 12:239–43; Díaz Díaz, *Caudillos y caciques*, 162–63; Parrish, "The Life of Nicolás Bravo," 249–51; Mariano Cuevas, *Historia de la Nación Mexicana*, 3rd ed. (Mexico: Editorial Porrúa, S.A., 1967), 624.
64. *El Cosmopolita*, January 29, 1842; Dublán y Lozano, *Legislación mexicana*, 4:301–302; Jan Bazant, *Historia de la deuda exterior de México* (Mexico: El Colegio de Mexico, 1968), 80–81. Santa Anna confiscated the Pious Fund for the California Missions, sold church land, confiscated silver plate, and extorted a forced loan of some 200,000 pesos. Callcott, *Santa Anna*, 176–78; Cuevas, *Historia de la nación mexicana*, 127; Noriega Elío, *El Constituyente de 1842*, 50–51.
65. *Memoria del Ministerio de Guerra y Marina*, 1841, 38–39. A detailed discussion of the interminable Yucatán conflict is beyond the scope of this study. Thorough accounts can be found in Nelson Reed, *The Caste War of Yucatán* (Stanford, Calif.: Stanford Univ. Press, 1964); and Leticia Reina, *Las rebeliones campesinas en México (1819–1906)* (Mexico: Siglo Veintiuno Editores, 1980), 363–416.
66. Ministerio de Guerra y Marina, *Memoria del Secretario de Estado y del despacho de guerra y marina* (Mexico: Impreso por Ignacio Cumplido, 1844), 19–21.
67. Dublán y Lozano, *Legislación mexicana*, 4:675–78.
68. Carreño, *Jefes del Ejército Mexicano*, 141–54; Fayette Robinson, *Mexico and Her Military Chieftains, From the Revolution of Hidalgo to the Present Time* (Hartford: Silas Andrus & Sons, 1848), 256–63.
69. Ministerio de Guerra y Marina, *Memoria de los ramos de guerra y marina* (Mexico: Impreso por Ignacio Cumplido, 1845), 5; Porter to Buchanan, July 20, 1844, *Despatches from United States Ministers to Mexico, 1823–1906*, vii, NA, Record Group 59; Carreño, *Jefes del Ejército Mexicano*, 141–54. Worth conferred this sobriquet during the United States' war with Mexico.
70. *El Cosmopolita*, April 9, November 26, 1842; *El Siglo XIX*, April 18, 1842; Carlos María Bustamante, *Apuntes para la historia del gobierno del General Antonio López de Santa Anna, desde principios de octubre de 1841 hasta 6 de diciembre de 1844, en que fué depuesto de mando por uniforme voluntad de la nación* (Mexico: Imprenta de J. Mariano Lara, 1845), 90–91; Noriega Elío, *El Constituyente de*

1842, 105–106. Elected by the *ayuntamientos* in April and convened in June, the Congress of 1842 consisted mostly of young (ages 21–40) liberal deputies who were committed to a federalist constitution and a civic militia capable of counterbalancing the permanent army.

71. Michael P. Costeloe, *The Central Republic in Mexico, 1835–1846: Hombres de Bien in the Age of Santa Anna* (New York: Cambridge Univ. Press, 1993), 210; Noriega Elío, *El Constituyente de 1842,* 109–11. Overt opposition to the constituent project first manifested on December 11, 1842, when military leaders in the city of Huetjotzingo publicly demanded a return to the Tacubaya principles.
72. Tornel to Comandante-general de México, May 3, 1843, AGN, AG, vol. 46, fojas 217–18; Dublán y Lozano, *Legislación mexicana,* 4:353–56; Noriega Elío, *El Constituyente de 1842,* 117–18, 123–31.
73. *El Siglo XIX,* June 16, 17, 1843; Callcott, *Santa Anna,* 183, 189; Thomas E. Cotner, *The Military and Political Career of José Joaquín de Herrera 1792–1854* (Austin: Institute of Latin American Studies, University of Texas at Austin, 1949), 101–102; Dublán y Lozano, *Legislación mexicana,* 4:428–60; Noriega Elío, *El Constituyente de 1842,* 131–73.
74. *El Siglo XIX,* November 2, 1843; Bustamante, *Apuntes,* 249–50; Costeloe, *The Central Republic,* 240–41; Díaz Díaz, *Caudillos y caciques,* 177–78; Dublán y Lozano, *Legislación mexicana,* 4:721.
75. Arista to Vázquez, Monterrey, January 8, 1842, ADN, expediente XI/481.3/1728, fojas 120–22.
76. Arista to Ministro de Guerra y Marina, Monterrey, March 12, 1842, ADN, expediente XI/481.3/1728, fojas 229–31.
77. Ministro de Guerra y Marina to Arista, Mexico City, March 21, 1842, ADN, expediente XI/481.3/1728, fojas 235–38.
78. Reyes to Woll, Rio Grande, August 27, 1842, ADN, expediente XI/481.3/1731, fojas 11–12.
79. Carreño, *Jefes del Ejército Mexicano,* 114–16. Thereafter, Woll occupied several key leadership positions but did not participate in the war with the United States. For reasons not entirely clear, he chose to reside in France until 1853, when he returned to Mexico and resumed his military duties. Woll died in France at age eighty-five.
80. Reyes to Ministro de Guerra y Marina, San Fernando de Rosas, September 20, 1842, ADN, expediente XI/481.3/1735, fojas 31–38.
81. Reyes to Ministro de Guerra y Marina, San Fernando, September 28, 1842, ADN, expediente XI/481.3/1735, fojas 40–42. Whether Woll was forced out of Texas or withdrew of his own volition is a matter of parochial interpretation. For the Texan viewpoint, see John Milton Nance, *Attack and Counterattack: The Texas-Mexican Frontier, 1842* (Austin: Univ. of Texas Press, 1964), 382–408; and Sam W. Haynes, *Soldiers of Misfortune: The Somervell and Mier Expeditions,* (Austin: University of Texas Press, 1990).
82. Ampudia to Ministro de Guerra y Marina, Mier, December 29, 1842, published in *El Siglo XIX,* March 1, 1843; *El Siglo XIX,* December 8, 1842. Victory was not

achieved without significant cost to Ampudia, whose forces sustained thirty killed and sixty-six wounded.

83. Santa Anna to Bocanegra, May 17, 1844, published in *Diario del Gobierno,* June 8, 1844; Bankhead to Aberdeen, March 31, 1844, Mexico, Foreign Office 50/173. Terms of this agreement are set forth in ADN, expediente XI/481.3/2018.
84. Ministro de Guerra y Marina to Canalizo, September 8, 1844, ADN, expediente XI/481.3/2024; *Memoria de los ramos de guerra y marina,* 1845, 2–3. Herrera substituted as president until September 21, when Canalizo reached the capital.
85. Arista to Ministro de Guerra y Marina (Conde), July 26, 1845, ADN, expediente XI/481.3/2068, foja 28; Arista to Ministro de Guerra y Marina (Anaya), September 4, 1845, ADN, expediente XI/481.3/2069, foja 41; *Memoria de los ramos de guerra y marina,* 1845, 4.
86. Bankhead to Aberdeen, May 30, 1844, Mexico, Foreign Office 50/174; *El Siglo XIX,* May 16, 1844; *Diario del Gobierno,* April 23, 1844. Estimates for the proposed Texas campaign ranged as high as 22 million pesos; but the 12 million peso deficit reported by the minister of finance (hacienda) for 1844 clearly disinclined the Congress from financing such an expensive and speculative venture. Ministro de Relaciones to Almonte, May 30, 1844, AGN, Gobernación, vol. 201; Memoria de Hacienda, July 1844, reported in *El Siglo XIX,* November 15, 1844; Presupuesto del gasto que debe erogarse al año en los ramos de guerra y marina . . . June 30, 1844, published in *El Siglo XIX,* July 5, 1844.
87. Bankhead to Aberdeen, September 24, 1844, Mexico, Foreign Office 50/175; *El Siglo XIX,* October 5, 1844; Dublán and Lozano, *Legislación mexicana,* 4:760–64; Costeloe, *The Central Republic,* 240.
88. *Memoria de los ramos de guerra y marina,* 1845, ii, 15; Callcott, *Santa Anna,* 208; Robertson, "The Career of Paredes," 136.
89. Bocanegra to Paredes, March 7, 1843, UTLAC, Paredes Papers, folder 140; José María Jarero to Paredes, March 18, 1843, Paredes Papers, folder 140; Michael P. Costeloe, "Los Generales Santa Anna y Paredes y Arrillaga en México, 1841–1843: Rivales por el poder o una copa más," *Historia Mexicana* 39 (1989): 417–40. Robertson contends that Paredes had been set up by Santa Anna and suggests that a compulsion to redress alleged grievances over Santa Anna's failure to offer sufficient recompense for his role in the ouster of Bustamante was the principal motivating factor. "The Career of Paredes," 156.
90. *Diario del Gobierno,* November 9, 1844; *Memoria de los ramos de guerra y marina,* 1845, 10–11; Pedro Barasorda to Paredes, October 25, 1844, in Genaro García, ed., *Documentos inéditos o muy raros para la historia de México* (Mexico: Editorial Porrúa, S.A., 1974), 32:184–93; Bustamante, *Apuntes,* 321–28; Robertson, "The Career of Paredes," 157–59. In a furtive effort to neutralize Urrea's growing mischief in Sonora and distance Paredes from the capital at the same time, Santa Anna appointed his chief rival governor and commandant-general of that northwestern department. Previously, Santa Anna had tried to rid himself of the troublesome general by offering him command of government forces in Yucatán, a proposition Paredes summarily declined citing ill health. Ministro de Guerra y Marina to Paredes, August 27, 1844, UTLAC, Paredes Papers,

folder 141; Santa Anna to Paredes, February 20, 1843, UTLAC, Paredes Papers, folder 140.

91. *Memoria de los ramos de guerra y marina,* 1845, 10–11; Bustamante, *Apuntes,* 340.
92. *Memoria de los ramos de guerra y marina,* 1845, 11–12; Bustamante, *Apuntes,* 355–56; Dublán y Lozano, *Legislación mexicana,* 4:769–70; Cotner, *Herrera,* 105–106; Costeloe, *The Central Republic,* 255–56.
93. *El Siglo XIX,* December 8, 18, 1844; *Memoria de los ramos de guerra y marina,* 1845, 11–12.
94. *Memoria de los ramos de guerra y marina,* 1845, 13–14.
95. *Memoria de los ramos de guerra y marina,* 1845, 15; Callcott, *Santa Anna,* 212–15; Zamacois, *Historia de México,* 12:375–77. The Congress actually had voted to expatriate him to Venezuela for life with half-pay, but Santa Anna managed to wind up in a more proximate country for a considerably shorter duration.
96. Dublán y Lozano, *Legislación mexicana,* 5:7–8; Carreño, *Jefes del Ejército Mexicano,* 22–27; Cotner, *Herrera,* 1–8, 55–57. The nation's fiscal prostration was not improved when Herrera repealed most of the taxes imposed by his predecessor, but the abolition of such odious levies as the *impuesto de capitación* alleviated public discontent and enhanced the new president's popularity.
97. *Memoria de los ramos de guerra y marina,* 1845, 17. Tornel shared the belief that stationing military units in the major cities prejudiced discipline and exposed military personnel to the seduction of political parties. José María Tornel y Mendívil, *Breve reseña histórica de los acontecimientos mas notables de la nación mexicana desde el año de 1821 hasta nuestros días* (Mexico: Imprenta de Cumplido, 1852), 21.
98. *Memoria de los ramos de guerra y marina,* 1845, 17; Fernando Escalante Gonzalbo, *Ciudadanos imaginarios: Memorial de los afanes y desventuras de la virtud y apología del vicio triunfante en la República Mexicana* (Mexico: El Colegio de Mexico, 1992), 178.
99. Dublán y Lozano, *Legislación mexicana,* 5:19–22; *Memoria de los ramos de guerra y marina,* 1845, 30–31. By consolidating military formations into large garrisons and reducing the number of commandancies, Herrera hoped to attenuate the ability of such caudillos as Santa Anna to create loyalist factions within the army.
100. Decreto establiciendo la plana mayor del ejército, October 30. 1838, AGN, GM, vol. 8; *Memoria de los ramos de guerra y marina,* 1845, 17, 20; Dublán y Lozano, *Legislación mexicana,* 3:592–600. In its July 11, 1845, issue, *El Siglo XIX* complained that there were eighteen officers for every five soldiers on active duty and that officers on indefinite leave were costing the treasury 820,830 pesos annually.
101. *Memoria de los ramos de guerra y marina,* 1845, 31–32; Decreto separando el Colegio Militar y la Escuela de Aplicación, January 20, 1842, AGN, GM, vol. 27. Successful completion of the Colegio Militar's three-year program was supposed to be a prerequisite for commissioning, but political influence still enabled unqualified persons to receive officer appointments, weakening both the institution and the prestige of the academy.

102. *Memoria de los ramos de guerra y marina,* 1845, 25; Andreas V. Reichstein, trans. Jeanne R. Wilson, *Rise of the Lone Star: The Making of Texas* (College Station: Texas A&M Univ. Press, 1989), 177–78; Serrano Ortega, *El contingent de sangre,* 117–20.
103. *Memoria de los ramos de guerra y marina,* 1845, 25; Pedro Santoni, "A Fear of the People: The Civic Militia of Mexico in 1845," *Hispanic American Historical Review* 68 (May, 1988): 279–81.

CHAPTER 5

1. Manuel Armijo to Ministro de Guerra y Marina, Cuartel general de operaciones contra los rebeldes Texanos, September 22, 1841, published in *Diario de Gobierno,* October 16, 1841; Thomas E. Cotner, *The Military and Political Career of José Joaquín de Herrera 1792–1854* (Austin: Institute of Latin American Studies, University of Texas at Austin, 1949), 121–22. Mexico's territorial difficulties at this time were not limited to Texas; by 1845, both California and New Mexico had become vulnerable to United States incursions. Purported Texan invasions of New Mexico in September and October 1841, Commodore Thomas ap Catesby Jones's seizure of Monterey in 1842, and the 1844 California revolt instigated by John C. Frémont merely amplified Mexican apprehensions.
2. Seymour V. Conner and Odie B. Faulk, *North America Divided: The Mexican War, 1846–1848* (New York: Oxford Univ. Press, 1971), 22; Glen W. Price, *Origins of the War with Mexico: The Polk-Stockton Intrigue* (Austin: Univ. of Texas Press, 1967), 103; Justin H. Smith, *The War with Mexico* (New York: Macmillan, 1919), 1:155.
3. Balanced analyses of the war's causes can be found in Norman A. Graebner, "The Mexican War: A Study in Causation," *Pacific Historical Review* 49 (August, 1980): 404–26; and David Pletcher, *The Diplomacy of Annexation: Texas, Oregon and the Mexican War* (Columbia: Univ. of Missouri Press, 1973), 273–311, 352–92.
4. *Diario del Gobierno,* July 17, 23, 1845; *El Siglo XIX,* August 1, 1845; Cotner, *Herrera,* 123–25; George L. Rives, *The United States and Mexico, 1821–1848: A History of the Relations Between the Two Countries from the Independence of Mexico to the Close of the War with the United States* (New York: Charles Scribner's Sons, 1913), 1:589; José Fernando Ramírez, *Mexico During the War with the United States,* ed. Walter V. Scholes, trans. Elliott B. Scherr (Columbia: Univ. of Missouri Press, 1950), 65; Gene M. Brack, *Mexico Views Manifest Destiny 1821–1846: An Essay on the Origins of the Mexican War* (Albuquerque: Univ. of New Mexico Press, 1975), 137–38. Herrera's *moderados* favored a negotiated a settlement of the Texas question; the radical federalists of Gómez Farías promoted armed conflict as a means of reducing the influence of the army and the Church, restoring the Constitution of 1824 and reestablishing the civic militias. Advocates of "pure" reform, the radical federalists were also known as *puros.*
5. Peña y Peña to Black, October 15, 1845, in William R. Manning, ed., *Diplomatic Correspondence of the United States: Inter-American Affairs, 1831–1860* (Washington, D.C.: Carnegie Endowment for International Peace, 1932–39), 8:761–65.

6. *Diario del Gobierno,* November 6, 1846; *La Voz del Pueblo,* December 3, 1845; Ministerio de Relaciones Interiores y Exteriores, *Memoria de la Secretaría de Estado y del despacho de relaciones interiores y exteriores* (Mexico: Imprenta de Torres, 1846), 3–6; Pletcher, *Diplomacy of Annexation,* 276–78. Slidell carried instructions to purchase California and New Mexico for a "pecuniary consideration" as high as $40 million and to convince the Mexican government to accept the Rio Bravo as the legitimate international boundary.
7. *El Siglo XIX,* March 26 and 27, 1845; *Diario del Gobierno,* April 3, 1845. Public opinion on the Texas issue is examined in Jesús Velasco Márquez, *La Guerra de 47 y la opinión pública (1845–1848)* (Mexico: Secretaría de Educación Pública, 1975); Homer Campbell Chaney, Jr., "The Mexican–United States War as Seen by Mexican Intellectuals, 1846–1956" (Ph.D. diss., Stanford University, 1959), 1–53; and Gene M. Brack, "Mexican Opinion, American Racism and the War of 1846," *Western Historical Quarterly* 1 (1970): 161–74.
8. Quoted in Enrique Olavarría y Ferrari, *México independiente, 1821–1855,* vol. 4 of *México a través de los siglos,* ed. Vicente Riva Palacios (Mexico: Editorial Cumbre, S.A., 1953), 546; Jóse Manuel Micheltorena to Paredes, April 2, 1845, UTLAC, Paredes Papers, García Collection; Tornel to Paredes, November 19, 1845, UTLAC, Paredes Papers, García Collection; *La Voz del Pueblo,* November 1, 15, 1845; Carlos María Bustamante, *El nuevo Bernal Díaz de Castillo o sea historia de la invasión de los Anglo-Americanos en México* (Mexico: Secretaría de Educación Pública, 1949), 1:6. Redeployment of Paredes' army carried the ancillary benefit of further distancing Herrera's chief political rival from the capital.
9. *El Siglo XIX,* December 17, 20, 1845; Cotner, *Herrera,* 146; Ramírez, *Mexico During the War,* 38; Niceto de Zamacois, *Historia de México desde sus tiempos más remotos hasta nuestros días* (Barcelona: J. F. Parres, y Cía., 1876–88), 12:399. Several generals, including Filisola, Arista, and Micheltorena (the commandant-general of Alta California), had expressed concerns similar to those raised by Paredes regarding the lack of food, clothing, and equipment for the army during 1845. Arista to Paredes, October, 24, 1845, UTLAC, Paredes Papers, García Collection.
10. Quoted in *El Siglo XIX,* December 31, 1845; Miguel E. Soto, *La conspiración monárquica en México, 1845–1846* (Mexico: Editorial Offset, S.A., 1988), 70–73, 80–83; Josefina Zoreida Vázquez, "The Texas Question in Mexican Politics, 1836–1845," *Southwestern Historical Quarterly* 89 (January, 1986), 344. Following Herrera's resignation, Valencia attempted to usurp the presidency, but Paredes's determination to have that prize and the general lack of enthusiasm for this ploy convinced Valencia not to pursue the matter. Valencia to Paredes, December 30, 1845, UTLAC, Paredes Papers, García Collection.
11. Alberto M. Carreño, ed., *Jefes del Ejército Mexicano en 1847: Biografías de generales de división y de brigada y de coroneles del ejército por fines del año 1847* (Mexico: Secretaría de Fomento, 1914), 35–38; Cotner, *Herrera,* 149–53; Manuel Dublán and José María Lozano, eds., *Legislación Mexicana; ó Colección completa de las disposiciones legislativas expedidas desde la independencia de la República* (Mexico: Imprenta del Comercio, 1876–93), 5:101–102, 133; Frank D. Robertson,

"The Military and Political Career of Mariano Paredes y Arrillaga, 1797–1849" (Ph.D. diss., University of Texas, 1955), 202–205; José C. Valadés, *Orígenes de la república mexicana* (Mexico: Editores Mexicanos Unidos, 1972), 445–46.

12. Marcy to Taylor, January 13, 1846, House Executive Document 60, 30th Cong., 1st sess., Ser. 520, 90–91, 107–109 (hereinafter cited as HED 60).
13. Bankhead to Aberdeen, November 29, 1845, Mexico, Foreign Office 50/178; Graebner, "The Mexican War," 420; Pletcher, *Diplomacy of Annexation,* 370; Smith, *War with Mexico,* 1:91. Mexico looked to Britain for territorial guarantees, but the British declined involvement, suggesting instead that the government negotiate a boundary settlement before the two countries drifted any closer to armed conflict.
14. *El Monitor Republicano,* February 20, 1846; Milo Milton Quaife, ed. *The Diary of James K. Polk During His Presidency, 1845–1849* (Chicago: A. C. McClurg & Co., 1910), 1:13, 228–29.
15. Quaife, *Diary of Polk,* 1:226–27; Pletcher, *Diplomacy of Annexation,* 366–67; Rives, *The United States and Mexico,* 2:119–22; Smith, *War with Mexico,* 1:201–203.
16. Quaife, *Diary of Polk,* 1:379–80; Graebner, "The Mexican War," 422.
17. "Manifesto del Excmo. Señor Presidente Interino de la republica á sus conciudadanos," México, March 21, 1846, in *Diario del Gobierno,* March 25, 1846, and *El Tiempo,* March 27, 1846.
18. Ultimas comunicaciones entre el Gobierno Mexicano y el enviado extraordinario y ministro plenipotenciario de los Estados Unidos, sobre la cuestión de Texas, México, March 21, 1846.
19. Brack, *Mexico Views Manifest Destiny,* 179.
20. *Memoria de los ramos de guerra y marina,* 1845, 30–31; Ministerio de Guerra y Marina, *Memoria del Ministerio de Estado y del despacho de guerra y marina* (Mexico: Imprenta de Torres, 1846), 6; Leopoldo Martínez Caraza, *La intervención norteamericana en México, 1846–1848* (Mexico: Panorama Editorial, S.A., 1981), 46.
21. Reestablicimiento de la Plana mayor de ejército, September 17, 1846, AGN (GM), vol. 145; Manuel Balbontín, *Estado militar de la República Mexicana en 1846* (Mexico: Tipografía Ignacio Pombo, 1890), 12–14; *El Siglo XIX,* August 19, 21, 1845.
22. Dublán y Lozano, *Legislación mexicana,* 5:122–23.
23. Arista to Paredes, July 13 and October 30, 1845, UTLAC, Paredes Papers, García Collection; Decreto que arregla los cuerpos de caballería, July 27, 1846, AGN, GM, vol. 27; Balbontín, *Estado militar,* 16–18 and 25; *El Monitor Republicano,* November 30, 1847; Ministerio de Guerra y Marina, *Reglamento para el corso de particulares contra los enemigos de la nación* (Mexico: Imprenta del Águila, 1846), 3–20; Martínez Caraza, *La intervención norteamericana,* 45–47; Major Frederick Myatt, *The Illustrated Encyclopedia of 19th Century Firearms* (New York: Crescent Books, 1979), 16.
24. K. Jack Bauer, *The Mexican War, 1846–1848* (New York: Macmillan Publishing Co., 1974), 33; James M. McCaffrey, *Army of Manifest Destiny: The American*

Soldier in the Mexican War, 1846–1848 (New York: New York Univ. Press, 1992), 6–7; William B. Skelton, *An American Profession of Arms: The Army Officer Corps, 1784–1861* (Lawrence: Univ. Press of Kansas, 1992), 134–35, 253. The 3rd and 4th Infantry Regiments, which recently had undergone extensive unit training at the Jefferson Barracks "School of Brigade Drill," formed the core of Taylor's army.

25. George Winston Smith and Charles Judah, eds., *Chronicle of the Gringos: The U.S. Army in the Mexican War, 1846–1848, Accounts of Eyewitnesses and Combatants* (Albuquerque: Univ. of New Mexico Press, 1968), 26; McCaffrey, *Army of Manifest Destiny,* 16–22; Skelton, *An American Profession of Arms,* 172. Since 1821, West Point had furnished the U.S. Army with a steady influx of technically skilled and institutionally socialized junior officers endowed with the ability to transform ordinary citizens into competent soldiers.
26. Allan R. Millet and Peter Maslowski, *For the Common Defense: A Military History of the United States of America* (New York: The Free Press, 1984), 123–24; Myatt, *19th Century Firearms,* 42–44; John S. D. Eisenhower, *So Far From God: The U.S. War with Mexico 1846–1848* (New York: Random House, 1989), 379–80; James A. Houston, *The Sinews of War: Army Logistics, 1775–1953* (Washington, D.C.: Government Printing Office, 1966), 129; McCaffrey, *Army of Manifest Destiny,* 38–42. Carried primarily by skirmishers operating in front of and on the flanks of the main body, rifles did not replace muskets in significant numbers until the 1850s, when French army captain Claude E. Minié perfected an elongated cylindo-conoidal bullet that could easily fit down a rifled barrel.
27. William C. Henry, *Campaign Sketches of the War with Mexico* (New York: Harper & Bros., 1847), 45–47; Houston, *The Sinews of War,* 128–32; Millet and Maslowski, *For the Common Defense,* 124–25.
28. Mejía to Paredes, March 26 and 27, 1845, Paredes Papers, UTLAC, García Collection; *Diario del Gobierno,* April 25, 1846; José María Roa Bárcena, *Recuerdos de la invasión norteamericana, 1846–1848* (Mexico: Editorial Porrúa, S.A., 1947), 1:61; Albert C. Ramsey, ed. and trans., *The Other Side, or Notes for the History of the War between Mexico and the United States* (New York: John Wiley, 1850), 36–37.
29. Mejía, "Proclamación," March 18, 1846, HED 60, 123–29; Henry, *Campaign Sketches,* 58–60.
30. "Manifiesto de Excmo. Señor presidente Interino de la república, a la nación, April 23, 1846," in *El Tiempo,* April 25, 1846; Bankhead to Aberdeen, March 30, 1846, Mexico, Foreign Office 50/96; Rives, *The United States and Mexico,* 2:141–42.
31. Arista to Paredes, December 15, 1845, UTLAC, Paredes Papers, García Collection; Ramsey, *The Other Side,* 39; Roa Bárcena, *Recuerdos,* 1:148; Smith, *War with Mexico,* 1:149. This was nearly two thousand more than were reported to be in Taylor's command at the time.
32. Tornel to Arista, April 4, 1846, UTLAC, Smith Papers, 11:224–25. Content to wait for the Mexicans to make the first move, Taylor used the mandated hiatus to improve his positions.

33. Carreño, *Jefes del Ejército Mexicano,* 44–57; Ramsey, *The Other Side,* 39–40; Fayette Robinson, *Mexico and Her Military Chieftains, From the Revolution of Hidalgo to the Present Time* (Hartford: Silas Andrus & Sons, 1848), 255.
34. Arista to Ministro de Guerra y Marina, February 25, 1845, ADN, expediente XI/481.3/2063, foja 1; Arista to Paredes, July 22, 1845, in Genero García, *Documentos inéditos o muy raros,* 56:557.
35. Arista to Torrejón, April 24, 1846, ADN, expediente xi/481.3/2152; Torrejón to Arista, April 26, 1846, ADN, expediente xi/481.3/2152; Arista to Paredes, April 25, 1846, ADN, expediente xi/481.3/2152; Henry, *Campaign Sketches,* 82–85; Ramsey, *The Other Side,* 42; Roa Bárcena, *Recuerdos,* 1:62; Smith, *War with Mexico,* 1:161–62.
36. Torrejón to Arista, April 27, 1846, ADN, expediente xi/481.3/2152; Emilio del Castillo Negrete, *Invasión de los Norte-Americanos en México* (Mexico: Imprenta del Editor, 1890) 1:167.
37. Oficial de infantería, *Campaña contra los Americanos del Norte, primera parte: relación histórica de los cuarenta días que mando en Gefe el ejército del norte el E. Sr. General de División Don Mariano Arista* (Mexico: Ignacio Cumplido, 1846), 5 (hereinafter cited as Oficial de infantería, *Campaña*); Henry, *Campaign Sketches,* 86; Roa Bárcena, *Recuerdos,* 1:63. Owing to a shortage of boats and poor planning, Arista needed twenty-four hours to cross the river, a delay that afforded Taylor ample warning to react appropriately.
38. Pedro de Ampudia, *El ciudadano General Pedro de Ampudia ante el tribunal respectable de opinión pública, por los primeros sucesos ocurridos en la guerra a que nos provoca, decreta y sostiene el gobierno de los Estados Unidos de America* (San Luís Potosí: Imprenta del Gobierno, 1846), 18; Arista to Mejía, May 1, 1846, ADN, expediente xi/481.3/2153; *El Monitor Republicano,* June 5, 1846; Oficial de infantería, *Campaña,* 7; Roa Bárcena, *Recuerdos,* 1:63–64, 79. The figure 3,270 includes Ampudia's brigade less 190 men left behind to besiege Fort Brown. Ampudia reached Palo Alto just as the battle was beginning but had no time to reconnoiter the battlefield or prepare fighting positions and thus had negligible impact on the outcome of the engagement.
39. Ampudia, *El ciudadano,* 17–23; Arista to Tornel, In Sight of the Enemy, May 8, 1846, Arista Papers, National Archives of the United States (NA), Records of the Office of the Adjutant General, Record Group 94 (hereinafter cited as RG 94); *Diario del Gobierno,* May 29, 1846; Oficial de infantería, *Campaña,* 8–14.
40. *Daily Picayune,* September 24, 1846; Taylor to Jones, May 16, 1846, House Executive Document 209, 29th Cong., 1st sess., ser. 486, 2–3 (hereinafter cited as HED 209); Twiggs to Taylor, May 11, 1846, HED 209, 13–14.
41. Ampudia, *El ciudadano,* 17–23; Arista to Tornel, In Sight of the Enemy, May 8, 1846, Arista Papers, NA, RG 94; *El Monitor Republicano,* June 2, 1846; Ramsey, *The Other Side,* 48–49; Roa Bárcena, *Recuerdos,* 1:66–67.
42. Nathan Covington Brooks, *A Complete History of the Mexican War: Its Causes, Conduct, and Consequences: Comprising an Account of the Various Military and Naval Operations, from its Commencement to the Treaty of Peace* (Chicago: Rio Grande Press, 1965), 131–32; Donald E. Houston, "The Role of Artillery in the Mexican War," *Journal of the West* 11 (April, 1972): 276; Smith, *War*

with Mexico, 1:166. While Mexican artillery was limited to solid shot, American guns fired both canister (a tin cylinder of small shot fused with a powder charge) and grape (a cluster of balls between two wooden sabots). Lester R. Dillon, Jr., *American Artillery in the Mexican War 1846–1847* (Austin: Presidial Press, 1975), 14.

43. Arista to Tornel, In Sight of the Enemy, May 8, 1846, Arista Papers, NA, RG 94; Arista to Paredes, Matamoros, May 14, 1846, UTLAC, Paredes Papers, García Collection; Balbontín, *Estado militar,* 33–39.
44. Arista to Tornel, In Sight of the Enemy, May 8, 1846, Arista Papers, NA, RG 94; Taylor to Adjutant General, May 16 and 17, 1846, with enclosed subordinate reports, Senate Executive Document 388, 29th Cong., 1st sess., 6–30 (hereinafter cited as SED 388). Casualty figures appearing in the various accounts of this war are difficult to reconcile. Mexican versions, especially commanders' official reports, almost invariably understate friendly losses while exaggerating those of the enemy. American battle casualty reports tend to be more accurate for both sides and are the figures cited most often in this study.
45. Ramsey, *The Other Side,* 49–50; Smith, *War with Mexico,* 1:172.
46. Thomas R. Irey, "Soldiering, Suffering and Dying in the Mexican War," *Journal of the West* 11 (April, 1972): 285–98; McCaffrey, *Army of Manifest Destiny,* 52–65.
47. John B. Porter, "Medical and Surgical Notes of Campaigns in the War with Mexico, during the Years 1845, 1846, 1847, and 1848," *American Journal of Medical Sciences,* 23 (January, 1852): 31–33; Irey, "Soldiering, Suffering and Dying," 285–86. In an era with poor sanitation, contaminated food, and polluted water but lacking antibiotics, the absence of personal hygiene created an ideal environment for the spread of diarrhea, malaria, dysentery, yellow fever, and cholera. Of the 12,338 Americans who died in the war with Mexico, 10,790 perished from disease.
48. Oficial de infantería, *Campaña,* 15–20; Roa Bárcena, *Recuerdos,* 1:68–69; Arista to Lieutenant Colonel Mariano Moret, May 8, 1846, Arista Papers, NA, RG 94. Americans referred to this battle as Resaca de la Palma.
49. Arista to Paredes, Matamoros, May 14, 1846, UTLAC, Paredes Papers, García Collection; Olavarría y Ferrari, *México independiente,* 564–66; Ramsey, *The Other Side,* 52.
50. Ampudia, *El ciudadano,* 18–23; Arista to Paredes, Matamoros, May 14, 1846, UTLAC, Paredes Papers, García Collection; *Daily Picayune,* May 19, 1846; Roa Bárcena, *Recuerdos,* 1:82–84; Smith, *War with Mexico,* 1:173–75; Taylor to Adjutant General, May 9, 1846, HED 60, 295–96. Fortunately for the Mexican army, the consecutive battles had so battered and disorganized Taylor's forces that the Americans were unable to mount an effective pursuit.
51. Arista to Paredes, Matamoros, May 14, 1846, UTLAC, Paredes Papers, García Collection; Guillermo Vigil y Robles, *La invasión de México por los Estados Unidos en los años 1846, 1847 y 1848, Apuntes históricos, anecdoticos y descriptivos* (Mexico: Correccional, 1923), 18–19; Smith, *War with Mexico,* 1:176, 467. Mexican casualties amounted to 160 killed, 228 wounded, and 159 missing, many of

the latter attributable to drowning while attempting to cross the Rio Bravo. American losses were reported as 33 killed and 89 wounded of the 1,700 troops engaged. Among those taken prisoner was Rómulo Díaz de la Vega, the general to whom Arista had entrusted tactical command of the battlefield.

52. Ampudia, *El ciudadano,* 20–23; Arista to Paredes, Matamoros, May 14, 1846, UTLAC, Paredes Papers, García Collection; Oficial de infantería, *Campaña,* 12–14; Ramsey, *The Other Side,* 54–56; Roa Bárcena, *Recuerdos,* 1:83–84.
53. Oficial de infantería, *Campaña,* 29–36; Roa Bárcena, *Recuerdos,* 1:72–73, 89–90; Taylor to Adjutant General, Matamoros, May 18, 1846, HED 60, 297–98. The flies, mosquitos, ticks, chiggers, fleas, and sundry other pests abounding in Matamoros soon convinced Taylor to relocate his army to the slightly more hospitable area around Camargo.
54. Tornel to Arista, May 27, 1846, ADN, expediente XI/481.3/2153. Shortly after assuming command, Mejía redeployed the Army of the North to Monterrey.
55. Quoted in Brooks, *Complete History,* 158; and Smith, *War with Mexico,* 1:181–82; Pletcher, *Diplomacy of Annexation,* 385–86.
56. *The Statutes at Large of the United States of America,* vols. 1–9 (Boston: C.C. Little and J. Brown, 1845–65), 9:9–10. The first two battles of the war were fought exclusively by regulars, reproving the vociferous American faction that advocated militia-based armed forces.
57. Bustamante, *El nuevo Bernal Díaz,* 2:48–49; Dublán y Lozano, *Legislación mexicana,* 5:136.
58. George Bancroft to Connor, May 18, 1847, HED 60, 744; Wilfred Hardy Callcott, *Santa Anna: The Story of an Enigma Who Once Was Mexico* (Norman: Univ. of Oklahoma Press, 1936), 236; Pletcher, *Diplomacy of Annexation,* 445–46.
59. *El Monitor Republicano,* February 16, 1847; Mackenzie to Buchanan, July 7, 11, 1846, Nicholas P. Trist Papers, Library of Congress (LC); Quaife, *Diary of Polk,* 3:290; Rives, *The United States and Mexico,* 2:228–36; Smith, *War with Mexico,* 1:201–203, 478–79.
60. Conner to Bancroft, August 16, 1846, HED 60, 776; Quaife, *Diary of Polk,* 3:289–92; Robertson, "Career of Paredes," 257–60.
61. Bustamante, *El nuevo Bernal Díaz,* 2:195–98; *Diario del Gobierno,* July 28, 30, 1846; Dublán y Lozano, *Legislación mexicana,* 5:134–36; *Memoria del Ministerio de Estado y del despacho de guerra y marina,* 1846, 3–6; Zamacois, *Historia de México,* 12:490–504.
62. *Diario del Gobierno,* July 31, 1846; Dublán y Lozano, *Legislación mexicana,* 5:144–46; *El Monitor Republicano,* August 4, 1846; Bankhead to Aberdeen, August 4, 1846, Mexico, Foreign Office 50/198. In a futile attempt to salvage his regime, Paredes rushed back to the capital only to be arrested and incarcerated until October, when he was allowed by Santa Anna to expatriate.
63. Bustamante, *El nuevo Bernal Díaz,* 2:101; UTLAC, Gómez Farías Papers, 1406, 1412; José Mariano Salas to Paredes, August 4, 1846, AGN, GM, unnumbered vol.
64. Dublán y Lozano, *Legislación mexicana,* 5:155–61; *El Monitor Republicano,* September 15, 29, 1846; Bankhead to Aberdeen, August 29, 1846, Mexico, Foreign Office 50/198; Callcott, *Santa Anna,* 241–48.

65. Dublán y Lozano, *Legislación mexicana,* 5:238–39; *El Monitor Republicano,* September 15, 25, 1846; Pakenham to Palmerston, September 28, 1846, Mexico, Foreign Office 50/190; Smith, *War with Mexico,* 1:220–23.
66. Ministro de Guerra y Marina to Ampudia, August 17, 1846, ADN, expediente XI/481.3/2175.
67. Manuel Balbontín, *La invasión americana 1846 á 1848: Apuntes del subteniente de artillería Manuel Balbontín* (Mexico: Tipografía de Gonzalo A. Esteva, 1883), 26; *Memoria del Ministerio de Estado y del despacho de guerra y marina,* 1846, 5–8; Mejía to Ampudia, August 31, 1846, ADN, expediente XI/481.3/2175; Ramsey, *The Other Side,* 67–68. The United States too was without a grand strategy in this war, an omission that accorded Taylor significant latitude in determining follow-on operations. Quaife, *Diary of Polk,* 3:16–17; Taylor to Adjutant General, July 2, 1846, HED 60, 155–58; Marcy to Taylor, July 9, 1846, HED 60, 329–32.
68. Santa Anna to Ministro de Guerra y Marina, September 25, 1846, Tacubaya, in Justin H. Smith, ed., "Letters of General Antonio López de Santa Anna Relating to the War Between the United States and Mexico, 1846–1848," *Annual Report of the American Historical Association for the Year 1917* (Washington: Government Printing Office, 1920), 364; Roa Bárcena, *Recuerdos,* 1:91–92.
69. Balbontín, *Invasión,* 26; *El Monitor Republicano,* September 18, 1846; Ramsey, *The Other Side,* 69.
70. *Daily Picayune,* October 6, 1846; Smith, *War with Mexico,* 1:496; Taylor to Adjutant General, September 25, 1846, HED 60, 345–50.
71. Ampudia to Ministro de Guerra y Marina, September 25, 1846, Monterrey, in *Niles Register,* November 7, 1846, 166; Ampudia, *Manifiesto,* 1–10; Balbontín, *Invasión,* 35–36; *Daily Picayune,* November 13, 1846; *El Monitor Republicano,* October 20, 31, 1846; Smith, *War with Mexico,* 1:243–48; Taylor to Adjutant General, September 25, 1846, HED 60, 345–50.
72. Ampudia to Ministro de Guerra y Marina, September 25, 1846, Monterrey, in *Niles Register,* November 7, 1846, 166; Ampudia, *Manifiesto,* 11–15; Balbontín, *Invasión,* 33–35; *Daily Picayune,* October 23, 1846; *El Monitor Republicano,* November 15, 1846; Ramsey, *The Other Side,* 73–74.
73. Ampudia to Ministro de Guerra y Marina, September 25, 1846, Monterrey, in *Niles Register,* November 7, 1846, 166; Worth to Taylor, September 22, 1846, House Executive Document 4, 29th Cong., 2nd sess., ser. 497, 103–105 (hereinafter cited as HED 4); Ramsey, *The Other Side,* 75–76; Vigil y Robles, *Invasión de México,* 21–22; José C. Valadés, *Breve Historia de la guerra con los Estados Unidos* (Mexico: Editorial Patria, 1947), 131–35.
74. Taylor to Adjutant General, October 9, 1846, Senate Executive Document 1, 29th Cong., 2nd sess., 83–86 (hereinafter cited as SED 1–29); Henry, *Campaign Sketches,* 204–207. During the height of this battle, *soldadera* María Josefa carried water and food to the wounded of both sides until she too was felled by a musket ball. Elizabeth Salas, *Soldaderas in the Mexican Military: Myths and History* (Austin: Univ. of Texas Press, 1990), 31.
75. Quoted in Brooks, *Complete History,* 188–89; *Diario del Gobierno,* October 2,

1846; Rives, *United States and Mexico,* 2:272–75; Roa Bárcena, *Recuerdos,* 1:100–101.

76. Balbontín, *Invasión,* 44–45; Ramsey, *The Other Side,* 79–80; Roa Bárcena, *Recuerdos,* 1:122; Smith, *War with Mexico,* 1:260–61.

77. Bankhead to Aberdeen, no. 122, October 16, 1846, Mexico, Foreign Office 50/190; McCaffrey, *Army of Manifest Destiny,* 132–35; Marcy to Taylor, October 13, 22, 1846, HED 60, 355–57, 363–67; Smith, *War with Mexico,* 1:503–506. This was the first battle in which American volunteers participated. By most accounts they acquitted themselves reasonably well.

78. Balbontín, *Invasión,* 50–51; Martínez Caraza, *La intervención norteamericana,* 113–14; Negrete, *Invasión de los norteamericanos,* 2:354–56; Roa Bárcena, *Recuerdos,* 1:98–102, 122–23.

79. Dwight L. Clarke, *Stephen Watts Kearny Soldier of the West* (Norman: Univ. of Oklahoma Press, 1961), 108–109; John T. Hughes, *Doniphan's Expedition; Containing an Account of the Conquest of New Mexico: General Kearny's Overland Expedition to California; Doniphan's Campaign Against the Navajos; His Unparalled March Upon Chihuahua and Durango; and the Operations of General Price at Santa Fe* (Cincinnati: J. A. and U. P. James, 1848), 24–27, 30–59; Quaife, *Diary of Polk,* 1:396; Marcy to Stephen W. Kearny, June 3, 1846, HED 60, 153–55; Smith, *War with Mexico,* 1:286–90.

80. Armijo to Kearny, Santa Fe, August 12, 1846, AGN, GM, unnumbered vol.; Clarke, *Kearny,* 151–54; *Diario del Gobierno,* September 9, 10, 1846; *Memoria del Ministerio de Estado y del despacho de guerra y marina,* 1846, 8–10; Kearny to Wool, August 22, 1846, HED 60, 171; Donald Tyler, "Governor Armijo's Moment of Truth," *Journal of the West* 11 (April, 1972): 307–16.

81. Price to Adjutant General, February 15, 1847, Senate Executive Document 1, 30th Cong., 1st sess., 520–26 (hereinafter cited as SED 1); Rodolfo Acuña, *Occupied America: The Chicano Struggle Toward Liberation* (New York: Canfield Press, 1972), 58–59; Conner and Faulk, *North America Divided,* 66–74. One hundred and fifty rebels died defending the Taos Pueblo; fifteen of those captured were subsequently tried and executed.

82. Clarke, *Kearny,* 163–90; Philip St. George Cooke, *The Conquest of New Mexico and California: An Historical and Personal Narrative* (New York: G. P. Putnam's Sons, 1878), 71; James Madison Cutts, *The Conquest of California and New Mexico by the Forces of the United States in the Years 1846 and 1847* (Philadelphia: Clay & Hart, 1847), 44; *Niles Register,* October 10, 1846; Pletcher, *The Diplomacy of Annexation,* 433–35.

83. José Castro to Comandante-general de Sonora, Monterey, July 25, 1846, ADN, expediente XI/483.1/2155; Cutts, *Conquest of California,* 118–19; *Diario del Gobierno,* October 16, December 1, 1846; *Niles Register,* October 10, 1846; Smith, *War with Mexico,* 1:333–39.

84. José María Flóres to Stockton, Los Angeles, January 1, 1847, AGN, GM, unnumbered vol.; Clarke, *Kearny,* 249–53; Cutts, *Conquest of California,* 203, 207; *Diario del Gobierno,* January 24, 1847; Roa Bárcena, *Recuerdos,* 1:231; Smith, *War with Mexico* 1:340–44. The California guerrillas, led by Lieutenant Colonel

José María Flóres, were dispersed following consecutive defeats in small but decisive engagements at La Mesa and San Gabriel.

85. Balbontín, *Invasión,* 53–54; Dublán y Lozano, *Legislación mexicana,* 5:238–39; *El Monitor Republicano,* October 18 and 31, 1846; Santa Anna to Ministro de Guerra y Marina, October 10, 1846, San Luís Potosí, in Smith, "Letters," 369; Smith, *War with Mexico,* 1:374–75.
86. Balbontín, *Invasión,* 55–56; Bankhead to Aberdeen, no. 126, September 7, 1846, Mexico, Foreign Office 50/189; *Memoria del Ministerio de Estado y del despacho de guerra y marina,* 1846, 9–11; Ramsey, *The Other Side,* 83–85; Santa Anna to Ministro de Guerra y Marina, October 14, 1846, San Luís Potosí, in Smith, "Letters," 372.
87. Taylor to Santa Anna, November 5, 1846, HED 60, 437–38; *Diario del Gobierno,* November 14, 29, 1846; Ramsey, *The Other Side,* 92–93; Roa Bárcena, *Recuerdos,* 1:126–27; Smith, *War with Mexico,* 1:264–66.
88. Chaney, "The Mexican-United States War," 24; Santa Anna to Ministro de Guerra y Marina, January 19, 1847, San Luís Potosí, in Smith "Letters," 407–408; Balbontín, *Invasión,* 58–59.
89. Army of Operations Order No. 139, November 27, 1846, HED 60, 377–78; McCaffrey, *Army of Manifest Destiny,* 139–41.
90. *Diario del Gobierno,* September 11, 1846; Gefe Político, Parras, to Santa Anna, December 17, 1846, AGN, GM, unnumbered vol.; Roa Bárcena, *Recuerdos,* 1:133, 153; Smith, *War with Mexico,* 1:270–75; Scott to Taylor, June 12, 1846, HED 60, 323–26; Taylor to Adjutant General, December 8, 1846, HED 60, 379–81.
91. Bustamante, *El nuevo Bernal Díaz,* 2:90; *Diario del Gobierno,* December 6, 8, 1846; Santa Anna to Ministro de Guerra y Marina, January 6, 1847, San Luís Potosí, in Smith, "Letters," 405–406; Smith, *War with Mexico,* 1:379–80. The letter in question, dated December 12, 1846, was from Brigadier General Robert Patterson to the assistant adjutant general in Monterrey.
92. Army of the North General Order, January 26, 1847, SED 1, 153–56; *El Monitor Republicano,* January 22, 1847; Santa Anna to Ministro de Guerra y Marina, December 4, 1846, San Luís Potosí, in Smith, "Letters," 385–86; Bankhead to Palmerston, no. 173, November 29, 1846, Mexico, Foreign Office 50/201. Throughout most of the war the ubiquitous Sonoran led a guerrilla force that infested the Monterrey-Camargo road, causing significant damage to American supply lines. Henry, *Campaign Sketches,* 254; Roa Bárcena, *Recuerdos,* 1:199–201.
93. Balbontín, *Invasión* 60–62, 78; *El Monitor Republicano,* January 14, 1847; Ramsey, *The Other Side,* 98; Roa Bárcena, *Recuerdos,* 1:140.
94. Salas, *Soldaderas,* 33–35. Mexican women of all ages followed the American army as well. Besides doing laundry and selling food to American solders, they also provided female companionship to officers and enlisted men.
95. *El Monitor Republicano,* February 19, 1847, 4; Ramón Alcaraz et al., *Apuntes para la historia de la guerra entre México y los Estados Unidos* (Mexico: Tipografía de Manuel Payno, 1848), 97; Roa Bárcena, *Recuerdos,* 1:143; Santa Anna to Ministro de Guerra y Marina, February 17, 1847, San Salvador, in Smith, "Letters," 412–13.

96. [John A. Scott], *Encarnación Prisoners, Comprising an Account of the March of the Kentucky Cavalry . . .* (Louisville: Prentice and Weissanger, 1848), 44–45. The capture of Major Borland's Arkansas Cavalry along with some Kentucky horse soldiers on February 20, prompted Taylor, whose entire force did not exceed 6,500 men, to withdraw his forward outposts to the more secure Angostura Pass.
97. Balbontín, *Invasión,* 56.
98. Balbontín, *Invasión,* 68–70; *El Monitor Republicano,* March 24, 1847; Smith, *War with Mexico,* 1:381; Taylor to Adjutant General, February 24, 1847, SED 1, 132–40. Americans refer to this battle as Buena Vista because Taylor was headquartered at a hacienda bearing that name.
99. Santa Anna, General Order, Encarnación, February 20–21, 1847, SED 1, 156–58.
100. Quoted in Roa Bárcena, *Recuerdos,* 1:161–62, and in Brooks, *Complete History,* 208–209; SED 1, 98.
101. Alcaraz, *Apuntes,* 99; Balbontín, *Invasión,* 72–74; *Diario del Gobierno,* April 17, 1847; Santa Anna to Ministro de Guerra, February 22, 1847, Angostura, SED 1, 98.
102. Balbontín, *Invasión,* 80–81; *El Monitor Republicano,* March 24, 1847; Santa Anna to Ministro de Guerra y Marina, February 23, 1847, Campo en la Angostura sobre Buenavista, in Smith "Letters," 413–14; Roa Bárcena, *Recuerdos,* 1:166–67.
103. Alcaraz, *Apuntes,* 100–102; Balbontín, *Invasión,* 85–88; Brooks, *Complete History,* 210–23; Negrete, *Invasión de los norteamericanos,* 3:33–35; Santa Anna to Ministro de Guerra y Marina, February 27, 1847, *Niles Register* (April 3, 1847), 80; Smith, *War with Mexico,* 1:384–94; Taylor to Marcy, March 3, 1847, SED 1, 97–98; Lt. Col. William B. Warren to Wool, March 1, 1847, SED 1, 205–206. Brigade General Francisco Pérez took command of Lombardini's division when the latter sustained an incapacitating wound.
104. Alcaraz, *Apuntes,* 102–104; Balbontín, *Invasión,* 85–88; *Daily Picayune,* March 27, April 14, 1847; Roa Bárcena, *Recuerdos,* 1:166–74; Santa Anna to Ministro de Guerra, February 23, 1847, Campo en la Angostura, in Smith, "Letters," 414.
105. Alcaraz, *Apuntes,* 100, 105; Roa Bárcena, *Recuerdos,* 1:186–87; Santa Anna to Ministro de Guerra y Marina, February 23, 1847, Campo en la Angostura, in Smith, "Letters," 414; Wool to Taylor, February 26, 1847, House Executive Document 8, 30th Cong., 1st sess., ser. 515, 147 (hereinafter cited as HED 8). The battle was rekindled in such haste that soldiers had no time to prepare breakfast and fought the entire day on empty stomachs.
106. Alcaraz, *Apuntes,* 105–106; Balbontín, *Invasión,* 89–91, 93–95; *El Monitor Republicano,* May 6, 1847; Martínez Caraza, *La intervención norteamericana,* 128–29; Roa Bárcena, *Recuerdos,* 1:185–88.
107. Balbontín, *Invasión,* 91–92; Martínez Caraza, *La intervención norteamericana,* 129; Roa Bárcena, *Recuerdos,* 1:185; Smith, *War with Mexico,* 1:398. Except for Santa Anna, whose report greatly exaggerated American losses (he claimed more than 2,000), casualty figures from the various accounts of this battle are reasonably consistent.
108. Houston, "The Role of Artillery," 280–81.
109. *El Monitor Republicano,* March 10, 31, 1847.

110. Quoted in Roa Bárcena, *Recuerdos,* 1:187n; Santa Anna to Ministro de Guerra y Marina, February 26, 1847, in Antonio de la Peña y Reyes, ed., *Algunos documentos sobre el tratado de Guadalupe y la situación de México durante la invasión americana* (Mexico: Editorial Porrúa, 1930), 46–48. In his February 23, 1847, after-action report to the minister of war and marine, Santa Anna wrote, "[T]hese soldiers merit every consideration, and it gives me great pride to say that I am at the head of an Army of heroes." Smith, "Letters," 414.

111. *El Monitor Republicano,* March 7, 11, 1847.

112. Balbontín, *Invasión,* 98–100; Ramsey, *The Other Side,* 137–41. Balbontín estimates the army's loss at more than three thousand men, the majority to desertion.

113. Balbontín, *Invasión,* 104–105; Dublán y Lozano, *Legislación mexicana,* 5:246, 252–55; *El Monitor Republicano,* February 13, March 23, 1847; Bankhead to Palmerston, no. 7, January 29, 1847, Mexico, Foreign Office 50/208; Michael P. Costeloe, "The Church and the Rebellion of the Polkos," *Hispanic American Historical Review* 46 (May, 1966): 170–73; Pletcher, Diplomacy of Annexation, 484–87; Ramírez, *Mexico During the War,* 91, 107; Roa Bárcena, *Recuerdos,* 1:245–48; Carreño, ed. *Jefes del Ejército Mexicano*, cclxix–ccl. Gómez Farías nationalized ecclesiastical properties to the amount of 15 million pesos, approximately one-tenth of the Church's entire wealth.

114. Bankhead to Aberdeen, no. 34, March 23, 1847, Mexico, Foreign Office 50/196; Bustamante, *El nuevo Bernal Díaz,* 2:146–47; *Diario del Gobierno,* March 27, 1847; Dublán y Lozano, *Legislación mexicana,* 5:263, 268; Costeloe, "Rebellion of the Polkos," 173–78; Cecil. A. Hutchinson, "Valentín Gómez Farías: A Biographical Study" (Ph.D. diss., University of Texas, 1948), 739–40; Ramsey, *The Other Side,* 150–64. Because the Church lacked ready cash, these funds were raised by selling discounted, short-term government bonds to the *agiotistas,* with a guarantee of eventual church redemption. Santa Anna acquired additional funds by appropriating ninety-eight bars of silver from the San Luís Potosí mint and offering merchants of that city mortgages on his own estates. Jan Bazant, "Mexico," in Leslie Bethell, ed., *Spanish America after Independence, c.1820–c.1870* (New York: Cambridge University Press, 1987), 143; Rives, *The United States and Mexico,* 1:391–94.

CHAPTER 6

1. Heredia to Santa Anna, February 13, 20, 1847, AGN, GM, unnumbered vol.; Ramón Alcaraz, et al., *Apuntes para la historia de la guerra entre México y los Estados Unidos* (Mexico: Tipografía de Manuel Payno, 1848), 139–50; *Daily Picayune,* March 6, 1847; *El Monitor Republicano,* January 26, 1847; John T. Hughes, *Doniphan's Expedition: Containing an Account of the Conquest of New Mexico; General Kearny's Overland Expedition to California; Doniphan's Campaign Against The Navajos; His Unparalled March upon Chihuahua and Durango; and the Operations of General Price at Santa Fe* (Cincinnati: J. A. and U. P. James, 1848), 256–67; Santa Anna to Ministro de Guerra y Marina, January 4, 1847, San Luís Potosí, in Justin H. Smith, "Letters of General Antonio López

de Santa Anna Relating to the War Between the United States and Mexico, 1846–1848," *Annual Report of the American Historical Association for the Year 1917* (Washington: Government Printing Office, 1920), 403–405. For an account of the action at Temascalitos, see Andrew Armstrong, "The Brazito Battlefield," *New Mexico Historical Review* 35 (January, 1960): 63–74, and F. M. Gallagher, ed., "Parte oficial de la acción de armas de Temascalitos," *New Mexico Historical Review* 3 (October, 1928): 381–89.

2. *Daily Picayune,* March 18, 1847; *Diario del Gobierno,* March 17, 1847; Carlos María Bustamante, *El nuevo Bernal Díaz del Castillo o sea historia de la invasión de los anglo-americanos en México* (Mexico: Secretaría de Educación Pública, 1949), 2:105–106; Doniphan to Jones, March 4, 1847, SED 1, 497–508; Justin H. Smith, *The War with Mexico* (New York: Macmillan, 1919), 1:312–13; James M. McCaffrey, *Army of Manifest Destiny: The American Soldier in the Mexican War, 1846–1848* (New York: New York Univ. Press, 1992), 257–62. In this one-sided battle, Doniphan's command sustained one killed and five wounded while reportedly inflicting upon the defenders some six hundred casualties.
3. Marcy to Taylor, May 6, 1847, HED 56, 360–61; K. Jack Bauer, *The Mexican War, 1846–1848* (New York: Macmillan Publishing Co., 1974), 220–22. Because the Veracruz invasion had become the ascendant war-winning strategy, Taylor's prospects for acquiring substantial reinforcements were virtually nonexistent.
4. *Daily Picayune,* March 13, 28, 1847; Taylor to Adjutant General, November 2, 1847, HED 56, 397; Leopoldo Martínez Caraza, *La intervención norteamericana en México, 1846–1848* (Mexico: Panorama Editorial, S.A., 1981), 130; José María Roa Bárcena, *Recuerdos de la invasión norteamericana, 1846–1848* (Mexico: Editorial Porrúa, S.A., 1947), 1:199–202; Smith, *War with Mexico,* 1:400, 552.
5. Albert C. Ramsey, ed. and trans. *The Other Side, or Notes for the History of the War between Mexico and the United States* (New York: John Wiley, 1850), 179; James W. Pohl, "The Influence of Antoine Henri Jomini on Winfield Scott's Campaign in the Mexican War," *Southwestern Historical Quarterly* 78 (July, 1973): 91–92. In addition to the Veracruz undertaking, Polk decided to seize Tampico and instructed Marcy to assign that mission to Brigadier General Robert Patterson, a political appointee with almost no military experience. Milo Milton Quaife, ed., *The Diary of James K. Polk During His Presidency, 1845–1849* (Chicago: A. C. McClurg & Co., 1910), 2:156–58, 181; Marcy to Patterson, September 22, 1846, HED 60, 373.
6. Marcy to Scott, November 23, 1846, HED 60, 372.
7. *El Monitor Republicano,* March 16, 1847; Ramsey, *The Other Side,* 181–82; Roa Bárcena, *Recuerdos* 1:259–61. Both Twiggs's and Patterson's commands were extracted from Taylor's Army of Occupation, a decision that relegated the northern campaign to a supporting role and elicited vehement protest from the theater commander. Taylor to Adjutant General, January 26, 1847, HED 60, 1100–102.
8. Manuel Balbontín, *Estado militar de la república mexicana en 1846* (Mexico: Tipografía de Ignacio Pombo, 1890), 52; Bauer, *The Mexican War,* 244; Alberto

M. Carreño, ed., *Jefes del Ejército Mexicano en 1847: Biografías de generales de división y de brigada y de coroneles del ejército por fines del año 1847* (Mexico: Secretaría de Fomento, 1914), 132; Ramsey, *The Other Side,* 182; Roa Bárcena, *Recuerdos,* 1:260–62; Scott to Marcy, March 12, 1847, SED 1, 216–17; Smith, *War with Mexico,* 2:23–26, 334. On the one occasion Morales's Veracruz defenders challenged the invaders outside the fortifications, they were driven back after a sharp engagement.

9. Scott to Marcy, March 27, 1847, SED 1, 229–30; Scott, General Orders 80, March 27, 1847, SED 1, 239–40; *Memoria del Ministerio de Estado y del despacho de guerra y marina,* 1846, 22, estado 11; Roa Bárcena, *Recuerdos,* 1:268–70; Smith, *War with Mexico,* 2:26.
10. Scott to Marcy, March 27, 1847, SED 1, 229–30; Bustamante, *El nuevo Bernal Díaz,* 2:265; *Daily Picayune,* March 26, 30, 1847; *El Monitor Republicano,* March 16, 1847; Winfield Scott, *Memoirs of Lieut.-General Scott, LL.D., Written by Himself* (New York: Sheldon & Co., 1864), 2:423–24. His humanitarian rhetoric notwithstanding, Scott showed little compunction about pummeling the city indiscriminately with naval and artillery gunfire.
11. *Diario del Gobierno,* March 27, 29, 1847; Alcaraz, *Apuntes,* 161; Roa Bárcena, *Recuerdos,* 1:284–86; Scott, *Memoirs,* 2:426–27.
12. Landero to Ministro de Guerra y Marina, April 3, 1847, AGN, GM, unnumbered vol.; Alcaraz, *Apuntes,* 164–65; *El Monitor Republicano,* April 4, 1847; Scott, *Memoirs,* 2:427–29; Smith, *War with Mexico,* 2:340.
13. Scott to Marcy, March 29, 1847, SED 1, 235–36; Francis Gifford to Palmerston, no. 9, March 29, 1847, Mexico, Foreign Office 50/214; Nathan Covington Brooks, *A Complete History of the Mexican War: Its Causes, Conduct, and Consequences: Comprising an Account of the Various Military and Naval Operations, from its Commencement to the Treaty of Peace* (Chicago: Rio Grande Press, 1965), 311–12; *Diario del Gobierno,* April 4, 1847; Miguel M. Lerdo de Tejada, *Apuntes de la heróica ciudad de Veracruz,* (Mexico: Imprenta de ignacio Cumplido, 1850–58), 2:552–53; Roa Bárcena, *Recuerdos,* 1:312–18.
14. Santa Anna to Ministro de Guerra y Marina, January 14, 1847, in Smith, "Letters," 407.
15. Bustamante, *El nuevo Bernal Díaz,* 2:160; *Daily Picayune,* April 9, 1847; Santa Anna to Ministro de Guerra y Marina, April 4, 1847, ADN, expediente XI/481.3/2493; Smith, *War with Mexico,* 2:340–41.
16. Donald E. Houston, "The Role of Artillery in the Mexican War," *Journal of the West* 11 (April, 1972), 281; Martínez Caraza, *La intervención norteamericana,* 152; Scott to Marcy, March 23, 1847, HED 8, 224–25. The Americans also experimented with some Cosgreve and Hale rockets, but they caused more panic than damage and were not pivotal to the outcome.
17. *Daily Picayune,* April 9, 1847; *El Monitor Republicano,* April 4, 1847; Landero to Ministro de Guerra y Marina, April 3, 1847, ADN, expediente XI/481.3/2493; Lerdo de Tejada, *Apuntes de la heróica ciudad,* 2:558–64. The most widely accepted estimate of Mexican casualties in this battle is 350 military and 400 civilians killed and wounded. Scott reported his losses as 13 killed and 55 wounded.

Martínez Caraza, *La intervención norteamericana,* 154; Bauer, *The Mexican War,* 252.

18. Balbontín, *Estado militar,* 50–51; *El Monitor, Republicano,* March 29, 1847, 4; Ramsey, *The Other Side,* 179.
19. *Diario del Gobierno,* March 27, 1847; Lerdo de Tejada, *Apuntes de la heróica ciudad,* 2:574; *Memoria del Ministerio de Estado y del despacho de guerra y marina,* 1846, 20; Santa Anna to Canalizo, March 21, 1847, in Smith, "Letters," 415; Ramsey, *The Other Side,* 198.
20. Landero, General Orders of March 29, 30, 1847, AGN, GM, unnumbered vol.; Roa Bárcena, *Recuerdos,* 1:318–19.
21. Bankhead to Aberdeen, no. 34, April 1, 1847, Mexico, Foreign Office 50/199; Manuel Dublán and José María Lozano, eds., *Legislación Mexicana; ó Colección completa de las disposiciones legislativas expedidas desde la independencia de la República* (Mexico: Imprenta del Comercio, 1876–93), 5:264–65; *El Monitor Republicano,* March 31, 1847; José Fernando Ramírez, *Mexico During the War with the United States,* edited by Walter V. Scholes and translated by Elliott B. Scherr (Columbia: Univ. of Missouri Press, 1950), 112; Roa Bárcena, *Recuerdos,* 2:10–12.
22. Bustamante, *El nuevo Bernal Díaz,* 2:157, 189; *El Monitor Republicano,* April 27, 28, 1847; Ramsey, *The Other Side,* 200; Roa Bárcena, *Recuerdos,* 2:11; Santa Anna to Ministro de Guerra y Marina, April 13, 1847, Cerro Gordo, in Smith, "Letters," 418; Smith, *War with Mexico,* 2:42.
23. Sumario averiguación contra el Sr. General graduado de Brigada José María Jarero . . . December 5, 1833, AGN, AG, vol. 86, expediente 914, fojas 220–400; Carreño, *Jefes del Ejército Mexicano,* 126–27. Jarero ended his military career as commandant-general of Puebla in 1857.
24. *Diario del Gobierno,* April 30, 1847; Roa Bárcena, *Recuerdos,* 2:16–17; Antonio López de Santa Anna, *Apelación al buen criterio de los nacionales y estrangeros* (Mexico: Ignacio Cumplido, 1849), 33–37; Santa Anna to Ministro de Guerra y Marina, April 13, 1847, ADN, expediente XI/481.3/2494; Smith, *War with Mexico,* 2:347.
25. *El Monitor Republicano,* April 24, 27, 1847; Ramsey, *The Other Side,* 201–202; Roa Bárcena, *Recuerdos,* 2:18–19; Smith, *War with Mexico,* 2:45. What supplies the sutlers brought in fell woefully short of the army's needs.
26. Pohl, "Influence of Jomini," 94–94; Santa Anna to Ministro de Guerra y Marina, April 17, 1847, Cerro Gordo, in Smith, "Letters," 419; Scott to Marcy, April 8, 1847, HED 56, 126. American losses were reported at ninety men killed and wounded. Smith, *War with Mexico,* 2:52.
27. HQ Army GO no. 111, April 17, 1847, quoted in Brooks, *Complete History,* 325, and Roa Bárcena, *Recuerdos,* 2:23–24.
28. *Daily Picayune,* May 1, 2, 1847; HQ Army GO no. 111, April 17, 1847, in Brooks, *Complete History,* 325–27; Ramsey, *The Other Side,* 208; Scott to Marcy, April 19, 23, 1847, SED 1, 255–60; Scott, *Memoirs,* 2:432. One of five civilians politically appointed to flag rank during the war, Pillow was President Polk's former law partner.
29. *El Monitor Republicano,* May 3, 6, 1847; Martínez Caraza, *La intervención*

norteamericana, 156–58; Roa Bárcena, *Recuerdos,* 2:42–48; Santa Anna to Ministro de Guerra y Marina, Cerro Gordo, April 21, 1847, ADN, expediente XI/481.3/2494; Scott to Marcy, April 19, 23, 1847, SED 1, 258, 261.

30. Quoted in Alcaraz, *Apuntes,* 183; *El Monitor Republicano,* June 24, 1847.

31. *Daily Picayune,* May 9, 1847; Jarero to Ministro de Guerra y Marina, April 22, 1847, *Niles Register,* June 5, 1847, 219; Pillow to Scott, April 19, 1847, SED 1, 296; Pohl, "Influence of Jomini," 95–96; Scott to Marcy, April 19, 1847, SED 1, 257. American casualties were reported as 64 killed and 353 wounded out of the 8,500 troops engaged. Mexican losses have been estimated at between 500 and 1,200 killed and wounded and 3,000 prisoners. Roa Bárcena, *Recuerdos,* 2:63; Smith, *War with Mexico,* 2:58–59.

32. Houston, "The Role of Artillery," 281–82; Twiggs to Scott, April 19, 1847, HED 8, 275.

33. Bustamante, *El nuevo Bernal Díaz,* 2:190; *El Monitor Republicano,* April 24, 27, 1847; Ramsey, *The Other Side,* 218–19; Santa Anna to Ministro de Guerra y Marina, April 27, 1847, Orizaba, in Smith, "Letters," 420.

34. Santa Anna to Ministro de Guerra y Marina, April 22, 1847, Orizaba, quoted in Roa Bárcena, *Recuerdos,* 2:80n.

35. Worth to Scott, April 22, 1847, SED 1, 300–301; Brooks, *Complete History,* 339.

36. *El Monitor Republicano,* May 13, 23, 1847; Santa Anna to Ministro de Guerra y Marina, May 11, 1847, ADN, expediente XI/481.3/2495; Santa Anna, *Apelación,* 41–43.

37. Santa Anna to Ministro de Guerra y Marina, May 13, 1847, Puebla, in Smith, "Letters," 425; *Diario del Gobierno,* May 16, 1847; Ramsey, *The Other Side,* 224–25; Roa Bárcena, *Recuerdos,* 2:129–32; Antonio López de Santa Anna, *Detall de las operaciones ocurridas en la defensa de la capital de la república, atacada por el ejército de los Estados Unidos del Norte, año de 1847* (Mexico: Imprenta de Ignacio Cumplido, 1848), 8; Vargas Rea, ed., *Apuntes históricos sobre los acontecimientos notables de la guerra entre México y los Estados Unidos del Norte* (Mexico: Bibliotéca Aportación Histórica, 1945), 25.

38. Ramsey, *The Other Side,* 222–23; Gifford to Palmerston, no. 23, July 2, 1847, Mexico, Foreign Office 50/214; Roa Bárcena, *Recuerdos,* 2:78–82; Scott to Marcy, May 10, 1847, HED 60, 944–48; Smith, *War with Mexico,* 2:69–71.

39. Roa Bárcena, *Recuerdos,* 2:114–16, 133–136; Santa Anna to Ministro de Guerra y Marina, May 15, 1847, San Martín Tesmelucan, in Smith, "Letters," 426–28; Santa Anna to Ministro de Guerra y Marina, May 16, 1847, Cuartel Gral en San Martín, in Smith "Letters," 428. Before leaving, Santa Anna took steps to activate a guerrilla force to prey upon the extended and exposed logistical tail of Scott's army. The American commander reciprocated by severing his supply line to the coast and living off the land.

40. *El Monitor Republicano,* April 25, 1847; Homer Campbell Chaney, Jr. "The Mexican-United States War as Seen by Mexican Intellectuals, 1846–1959" (Ph.D. diss., Stanford University, 1959), 36–37; Ramsey, *The Other Side,* 231. Similar, though less vitriolic, tirades were aimed at military personnel as a whole.

41. Pedro María Anaya, Decreto, May 6, 1847, UTLAC, Smith Papers; Bustamante,

El nuevo Bernal Díaz, 2:196–98; *El Monitor Republicano,* May, 2, 1847; Santa Anna, *Apelación,* 44–45. Apparently dissatisfied with the support it was receiving from the Mexico City *ayuntamiento,* the government placed the entire federal district under military authority on June 28. Proclamación de José Ignacio Gutierrez, México, June 29, 1847, AHA, Historia en General, legajo 2265, expediente 24.

42. Dublán y Lozano, *Legislación mexicana,* 5:264; Ramírez, *Mexico During the War,* 144–46; Santa Anna to Ministro de Guerra y Marina, May 18, 1847, ADN, expediente XI/481.3/2496; Ministro de Guerra y Marina to Santa Anna, May 21, 1847, ADN, expediente XI/481.3/2496.
43. *El Monitor Republicano,* May 20, 1847.
44. *El Monitor Republicano,* May 31, June 13, 1847; Santa Anna to Alcorta, June 12, 1847, ADN, expediente XI/481.3/2505; Santa Anna, *Detall,* 10–11. Convinced that Taylor could penetrate no farther into Mexico, the war ministry ordered the Army of the North to the capital. Departing San Luís Potosí between July 9 and 11, the four thousand destitute remnants of this once formidable force closed on Guadalupe Hidalgo two weeks later after an uneventful march. Ramsey, *The Other Side,* 259; Smith, *War with Mexico,* 2:87–88.
45. Quoted in Alcaraz, *Apuntes,* 216; *Diario del Gobierno,* July 15, 1847; Roa Bárcena, *Recuerdos,* 2:183–84; Santa Anna, *Detall,* 10–11. This exhibition was not unlike the phenomenon that preceded First Manassas in 1861.
46. *Diario del Gobierno,* August 10, 13, 1847; Ramírez, *Mexico During the War,* 150; Ramsey, *The Other Side,* 241–42; Roa Bárcena, *Recuerdos,* 2:169–70; Santa Anna, *Detall,* 10; Smith, *War with Mexico,* 2:89–91. *Garitas* were entrances to the city, usually located at the end of each causeway, where duties were collected and passports examined.
47. Ramsey, *The Other Side,* 261; Roa Bárcena, *Recuerdos,* 2:181–83; Santa Anna to Alcorta, August 3, 1847, ADN, expediente XI/481.3/2601. Valencia strongly opposed Santa Anna's static defense, preferring to engage Scott during his approach from Puebla. This disagreement between these two adversaries was merely the first of several whose ramifications were detrimental to the synchronized defense of the capital.
48. Roa Bárcena, *Recuerdos,* 2:175; Santa Anna, *Detall,* 10–11; Smith, *War with Mexico,* 2:87–88. In regard to artillery, the Mexicans defenders had just 104 cannon of varying caliber some of which had only recently been manufactured by the local foundries.
49. Chaney, "The Mexican-United States War," 38–39. Ramsey, *The Other Side,* 242–43; George L. Rives, *The United States and Mexico, 1821–1848: A History of the Relations Between the Two Countries from the Independence of Mexico to the Close of the War with the United States* (New York: Charles Scribner's Sons, 1913), 2:493; Santa Anna, *Detall,* 9.
50. Buchanan to Secretaría de Relaciones Exteriores, April 15, 1847, LC, Trist Papers, xxiii; Marcy to Scott, April 14, 1847, HED 60, 940; Richard Griswold del Castillo, *The Treaty of Guadalupe Hidalgo: A Legacy of Conflict* (Norman: University of Oklahoma Press, 1990), 23–26.

51. Buchanan to Trist, July 13, 1847, LC, Trist Papers, xxiv; Trist to Bankhead, June 6, 1847, in William R. Manning, ed., *Diplomatic Correspondence of the United States: Inter-American Affairs, 1831–1860* (Washington, D.C.: Carnegie Endowment for International Peace, 1932–39), 8:908–14; Marcy to Scott, July 12, 1847, Senate Executive Document 52, 30th Cong., 1st sess., ser. 509, 133 (hereinafter cited as SED 52); Roa Bárcena, *Recuerdos,* 2:156–62; Bankhead to Palmerston, no. 75, July 29, 1847, Mexico, Foreign Office 50/210. It has been asserted that Scott advanced Santa Anna the sum of $10 thousand to help sway the Mexican Congress toward negotiation. However, even such monetary incentives foundered in the prevailing environment of political divisiveness. See Carlos E. Castañeda, "Relations of General Scott with Santa Anna," *Hispanic American Historical Review* 39 (November, 1949), 467–73; and Scott to Trist, July 17, 1847, LC, Trist Papers, xxiv.
52. *Diario del Gobierno,* August 18, 1847; Pohl, "Influence of Jomini," 100; Ramsey, *The Other Side,* 256; Santa Anna to Valencia, San Antonio, August 14, 1847, ADN, expediente XI/481.3/2601; Santa Anna, *Detall,* 11–12; Scott to Marcy, August 19, 1847, SED 1, 303–15; Scott, *Memoirs,* 2:467–68; Smith, *War with Mexico,* 2:93–98, 372–73. Between mid-May and August 5, when Scott set his army in motion toward the capital, incremental reinforcements raised American army strength to 10,738 men.
53. Santa Anna to Herrera, San Antonio, August 15, 1847, ADN, expediente XI/481.3/2601; Pohl, "Influence of Jomini," 102.
54. Quoted in Alcaraz, *Apuntes,* 221.
55. Ramsey, *The Other Side,* 270; Scott to Marcy, August 19, 1847, HED 8, 304–305.
56. Santa Anna to Valencia, San Antonio, August 18, 1847, ADN, expediente XI/481.3/2602; Manuel Balbontín, *La invasión americana 1846 á 1848: Apuntes del subteniente de artillería Manuel Balbontín* (Mexico: Tipografía de Gonzalo A. Esteva, 1883), 110–11; Smith, *War with Mexico,* 2:102.
57. Valencia to Alcorta, Padierna, August 18, 1847, ADN, expediente XI/481.3/2602; Santa Anna to Valencia, San Antonio, August 19, 1847, ADN, expediente XI/481.3/2602; Roa Bárcena, *Recuerdos,* 2:198–201; Santa Anna, *Detall,* 12. Santa Anna was dissuaded from taking vituperative action against Valencia when he was shown that such chastisement might be perceived as treasonous and spark a mutiny.
58. *Daily Picayune,* September 8, 1847; HQ Army GO no. 258, August 19, 1847, NA, Records of the Office of the Adjutant General, RG 94, 476–77; Scott to Marcy, August 19, 1847, HED 8, 304–308; Worth to Scott, August 18, 1847, SED 1, 325.
59. Balbontín, *Invasión,* 112–14; Ramsey, *The Other Side,* 274–75; Roa Bárcena, *Recuerdos,* 2:218–20; Santa Anna, *Detall,* 12–13; Smith to Scott, August 23, 1847, HED 8, 326; Smith, *War with Mexico,* 2:102–106. The subject of an official inquiry into his performance at Padierna, Torrejón ultimately was absolved of any culpability. Antonio Bonilla to Lino José Alcorta, August 25, 1847, AGN, AG, vol. 65, expediente 722, fojas 405–406.
60. Santa Anna to Valencia, San Antonio, August 19, 1847, ADN, expediente XI/481.3/2602; Balbontín, *Invasión,* 115–16; Santa Anna, *Detall* 13–14; Smith, *War with Mexico,* 2:106–110.

61. Salas to Ministro de Guerra y Marina, Tlálpam, August 23, 1847, ADN, expediente XI/481.3/2604; Ramsey, *The Other Side,* 279–81; Roa Bárcena, *Recuerdos,* 2:220–28, 242; George Winston Smith and Charles Judah, eds., *Chronicle of the Gringos: The U.S. Army in the Mexican War, 1846–1848, Accounts of Eyewitnesses and Combatants* (Albuquerque: Univ. of New Mexico Press, 1968), 239–44; Smith, *War with Mexico,* 2:378–80. Upon learning that Santa Anna intended to have him shot, Valencia prudently retreated along a road where he was unlikely to encounter the irate general-in-chief.
62. Rincón to Santa Anna, August 26, 1847, ADN, expediente XI/481.3/2604; Balbontín, *Invasión,* 117–20; *El Monitor Republicano,* October 24, 1847; Ramírez, *Mexico During the War,* 151–52; Roa Bárcena, *Recuerdos,* 2:241–42; Santa Anna, *Detall,* 14–15.
63. *Daily Picayune,* September 8, 1847; Pillow to Scott, August 24, 1847, SED 1, 338; Shields to Scott, August 21, 1847, SED 1, 344; Scott to Marcy, August 21, SED 1, 306–309; Smith, *War with Mexico,* 2:112–18.
64. Balbontín, *Invasión,* 121–22; Ramsey, *The Other Side,* 294–99; Roa Bárcena, *Recuerdos,* 2:257–61, 275–76; Santa Anna, *Detall,* 15. A request for ammunition resupply produced cartridges without ball and of a caliber too large for the defenders' muskets. This incident has been cited as evidence of Santa Anna's complicity with Scott to bring the war to a conclusion. The discrepancy, however, was more likely attributable to the precarious condition of the military's logistical system than to any connivance between the two antagonists.
65. *El Monitor Republicano,* September 30, 1847; Rincón to Santa Anna, August 26, 1847, ADN, expediente XI/481.3/2604; Scott to Marcy, August 21, 1847, SED 1, 306–309; Worth to Scott, August 23, 1847, HED 8, 317–18.
66. HQ Army GO Nos. 281, 283, September 8, 11, 1847, NA, Office of the Adjutant General, RG 94; *The American Star,* September 20, November 12, 1847. For further elaboration on the *Legión de Estrangeros,* or San Patricio Battalion, as the Americans called it, see Richard Blaine McCornack, "The San Patricio Deserters in the Mexican War," *The Americas* 8 (October, 1951): 131–42; Edward S. Wallace, "Deserters in the Mexican War," *Hispanic American Historical Review* 15 (August, 1935): 374–82; and Robert Ryal Miller, *Shamrock and Sword: The Saint Patrick's Battalion in the U.S.–Mexican War* (Norman: University of Oklahoma Press, 1989).
67. *Diario del Gobierno,* September 2, 1847; Rincón to Santa Anna, August 26, 1847, ADN, expediente XI/481.3/2604; Santa Anna to Alcorta, August 30, 1847, ADN expediente XI/481.3/2607; Roa Bárcena, *Recuerdos,* 2:303–306; Smith, *War with Mexico,* 2:382–85.
68. Scott to Marcy, August 21, 1847, SED 1, 309–15. The combined total of American losses for both battles was reported as 133 killed, 865 wounded, and 40 missing. Mexican losses including captured and missing may have approached ten thousand. Roa Bárcena, *Recuerdos,* 2:301; Smith, *War with Mexico,* 2:118, 120–21.
69. Chaney, "The Mexican-United States War," 40–41; Ramírez, *Mexico During the War,* 298–99.

70. Scott to Santa Anna, August 21, 1847, Coyoacán, in Manning, *Diplomatic Correspondence,* 8:922–23; Alcorta to Scott, Palacio Nacional de México, August 21, 1847, SED 52, 308; Bankhead to Aberdeen, no. 76, August 21, 1847, Mexico, Foreign Office 50/210; *Diario del Gobierno,* August 31, 1847; Balbontín, *Invasión,* 123; Santa Anna, *Detall,* 17–18.

71. HQ Army General Order no. 262, August 24, 1847, SED 52, 350, 356–58; Alcorta to Scott, August 23, 1847, Palacio Nacional de Mexico, SED 52, 310–12; Alcaraz, *Apuntes,* 262; Brooks, *Complete History,* 388–89. The Mexican government was able to convene only twenty-six deputies of the National Congress to ratify the proposal. A. M. Salonio to Jóse Ramón Pacheco, August 21, 1847, SED 52, 309–10.

72. Bankhead to Palmerston, no. 77, August 27, 1847, Mexico, Foreign Office 50/211, 6–9; Trist to Buchanan, August 29, 1847, no. 16, in Manning, *Diplomatic Correspondence,* 8:931–32; Ramsey, *The Other Side,* 315; Santa Anna, *Detall,* 16; Griswold del Castillo, *The Treaty of Guadalupe Hidalgo,* 30–31.

73. *Daily Picayune,* October 16, 1847; Scott to Santa Anna, September 6, 1847, SED 52, 346; Trist to Buchanan, no. 16, September 27, 1847, in Manning, *Diplomatic Correspondence,* 8:953–54; Herrera to Trist, September 5, 1847, in Manning, *Diplomatic Correspondence,* 8:946–52; Griswold del Castillo, *The Treaty of Guadalupe Hidalgo,* 33–35. Scott also was provoked by what he perceived to be a Mexican violation of the terms of the armistice, when a wagon train that had entered the city to procure supplies for the American army was attacked by angry residents who killed two teamsters. The incident revitalized, at least for the moment, Mexican desire to resist the invaders and undermined ongoing peace initiatives. Guillermo Prieto, *Memorias de mis tiempos, 1840 á 1853* (Mexico: Librería de la Vda de Ch. Bouret, 1906), 2:58; *The North American,* October 8, 1847; Santa Anna, *Detall,* 18–19.

74. Santa Anna to Scott, September 7, 1847, SED 52, 346–48; Santa Anna, *Detall,* 19–20.

75. Balbontín, *Invasión,* 125–26; Ministerio de Guerra y Marina, *Memoria presentada por el Ministerio de la Guerra* (Mexico: Imprenta del Torres, 1847), 6–7; Pohl, "Influence of Jomini," 104; Ramsey, *The Other Side,* 333–34; Santa Anna, *Detall,* 23; Scott to Marcy, September 11, 1847, SED 1, 354–56; Smith, *War with Mexico,* 2:140–42.

76. Álvarez to Santa Anna, September 25, 1847, AGN, GM, unnumbered vol.; Ramírez, *Mexico During the War,* 155–56; Santa Anna, *Detall,* 23; Guillermo Vigil y Robles, *La invasión de México por los Estados Unidos en los años 1846, 1847 y 1848, Apuntes históricos anecdoticos y descriptivos* (Mexico: Correccional, 1923), 53–55.

77. *Daily Picayune,* October 14, 1847; HQ Army General Order no. 279, September 7, 1847, NA, Office of the Adjutant General, RG 94; *Memoria presentada por el Ministerio de la Guerra,* 1847, 7–8; Ministerio de Guerra y Marina, *Reglamento sobre la organización del cuerpo de artillería* (Mexico: Imprenta del Aguila, 1846), 2–5; Scott to Marcy, September 11, 1847, SED 1, 355–65; Smith, *War with Mexico,* 2:142–43.

78. Balbontín, *Invasión,* 127–28; *Diario del Gobierno,* September 8, 1847; Ramsey, *The Other Side,* 339–40; Santa Anna, *Detall,* 23–24. Ramírez not only failed to support the counterattack; he left the field of battle entirely and was not seen again until after the fight.

79. Álvarez to Santa Anna, September 25, 1847, AGN, GM, unnumbered vol.; Santa Anna, *Detall,* 23–24.

80. Worth to Scott, September 10, 1847, HED 8, 363–64; *Daily Picayune,* October 14, 1847; Martínez Caraza, *La intervención norteamericana,* 178–79; Prieto, *Memorias de mis tiempos,* 2:238–39; Ramsey, *The Other Side,* 342. Balbontín raises the argument that, as a guerrilla fighter, Álvarez was unschooled in the tactics and techniques of maneuvering a large mass of cavalry on a linear battlefield. This may be a legitimate point, but it neither explains nor excuses the cacique's passive behavior at a critical juncture in the battle. *Invasión,* 128. Subsequently, Álvarez attempted unsuccessfully to shift the blame to Generals Manuel Andrade and Antonio María Jáuregui, his principal subordinates. Sumario en averiguación . . . October 18, 1847, AGN, AG, vol. 274, expediente 2687, fojas 69–167.

81. Balbontín, *Invasión,* 128–29; Brooks, *Complete History,* 405–10; Emilio del Castillo Negrete, *Invasión de los Norte-Americanos en México* (Mexico: Imprenta del Editor, 1890), 3:20–27; Robert Ryal Miller, ed., *The Mexican War Journal and Letters of Ralph W. Kirkham* (College Station: Texas A&M University Press, 1991), 56–58; *Daily Picayune,* October 14, November 3, 1847; *Diario del Gobierno,* September 8, 1847; Smith, *War with Mexico,* 2:143–46, 401–404; Santa Anna, *Detall,* 24; Scott to Marcy, September 11, 1847, SED 1, 370–77; Worth to Scott, September 10, 1847, HED 8, 361. Scott reported American casualties as 116 killed, 665 wounded, and 18 missing. Estimates of Mexican losses range as high as 2,000, with 685 recorded as having been taken prisoner, most of the latter unable to escape from the *azoteas* on which they had been posted. Ramsey, *The Other Side,* 343; Scott to Marcy, September 10, 1847, HED 8, 384. Among those killed were Brigade General Antonio León and Colonel Lucas Balderas.

82. *Diario del Gobierno,* September 11, 1847; Ramsey, *The Other Side,* 346–47; Santa Anna, *Detall,* 25. Balbontín contends that, had these additional forces been present "during the moment the first American attacks were repulsed, their defeat could have been assured." *Invasión,* 127.

83. Scott to Marcy, September 18, 1847, SED 1, 375–77; Scott, *Memoirs,* 2:509–10; Smith, *War with Mexico,* 2:148–49, 153. The marshy southern approach culminated in an unappealing confrontation with the *ciudadela,* and bypassing Chapultepec left Scott's line of retreat uncovered in the event that contingency materialized.

84. Scott to Marcy, September 18, 1847, SED 1, 375–76; Ramsey, *The Other Side,* 356–57; Smith, *War with Mexico,* 2:152–53.

85. Bravo to Santa Anna, September 14, 1847, ADN, expediente XI/481.3/2612; *El Monitor Republicano,* April 27, 1848; Carlos Alvear Acevedo, *La Guerra del 47* (Mexico: Editorial Jus, 1957), 59–62; Santa Anna, *Detall,* 26; Santa Anna to

Bravo, September 10, 1847, ADN, expediente XI/481.3/2612; Miguel A. Sánchez Lamego, *El Colegio Militar y la defensa de Chapultepec en septiembre de 1847* (Mexico: n.p., 1947), 10–16; Martinez Caraza, *La intervención norteamericana,* 183–84.

86. Scott to Marcy, September 18, 1847, SED 1, 377.
87. Bravo to Santa Anna, September 14, 1847, ADN, expediente XI/481.3/2612; *El Monitor Republicano,* April 27, 1848; Balbontín, *Invasión,* 130; Prieto, *Memorias de mis tiempos,* 2:241–43; Quitman to Scott, September 29, 1847, HED 8, 410–11; Ramsey, *The Other Side,* 358–59; Santa Anna, *Detall,* 27; Scott to Marcy, September 18, 1847, SED 1, 375–81; Smith, War with Mexico, 2:154–57, 408–11.
88. Bravo to Santa Anna, September 14, 1847, ADN, expediente XI/481.3/2612; Balbontín, *Invasión,* 131; *El Monitor Republicano,* October 24, 1847; Pillow to Scott, September 16, 1847, HED 8, 363–64; Ramsey, *The Other Side,* 362–63; Sánchez Lamego, *El Colegio Militar,* 23–34; Santa Anna, *Detall,* 28–29; Scott to Marcy, September 18, 1847, SED 1, 377–78. Today the heroism of the six cadets (*los niños héroes*) is celebrated by the Colegio Militar in a moving retreat ceremony conducted each day at sundown.
89. Arista to Comandante-general de México, July 27, 1848, AGN, AG, vol. 273.
90. Parte oficial del General Terrés sobre la defensa de la Garita de Belén, September 16, 1847, AGN, AG, vol. 155, exp. 1639; Terrés to Bonilla, March 16, 1848, AGN, AG, vol. 155, exp. 1639; Alcaraz, *Apuntes,* 320; Balbontín, *Invasión,* 132; Santa Anna, *Detall,* 30–31; Carreño, *Jefes del Ejército Mexicano,* 166.
91. *Daily Picayune,* November 20, 1847; *El Monitor Republicano,* November 3, 1847; Ramsey, *The Other Side,* 366–68; Santa Anna, *Detall,* 29–30; Scott to Marcy, September 18, 1847, SED 1, 381–83; Quitman to Scott, September 29, 1847, HED 8, 410–11; Smith and Judah, *Chronicle of the Gringos,* 262.
92. *El Monitor Republicano,* December 16, 1847; Ramsey, *The Other Side,* 370–71; Rea, *Apuntes históricos,* 46–47; Santa Anna, *Detall,* 31–32; Scott to Marcy, September 18, 1847, SED 1, 381–83; Smith and Judah, *Chronicles of the Gringos,* 264–66; Worth to Scott, September 16, 1847, SED 1, 391–93.
93. Santa Anna to Manuel Reyes Veramendi, Guadalupe, September 15, 1847, AHA, Historia en General, legajo 2268, hojas 145–46; Alcaraz, *Apuntes,* 324; Balbontín, *Invasión,* 133; Santa Anna, *Detall,* 32–33.
94. *El Monitor Republicano,* October 2, 1847; Scott to Marcy, September 18, 1847, SED 1, 383–85; Scott, *Memoirs,* 2:535; Smith, *War with Mexico,* 2:162–63, 415–16; Worth to Scott, September 16, 1847, SED 1, 391–93.
95. Anonymous, *Consideraciones sobre la situación política y social de la república mexicana en el año 1847* in *El Monitor Republicano,* 13–24 June, 1848.
96. Ramírez, *Mexico During the War,* 152. Ramírez exempted from his vitriolic castigation of senior military leadership General Valencia and "some of those with him," who, he believed, were less infected by the predatory militarism that characterized the subjects of his excoriation.
97. Anonymous, *Consideraciones sobre la situación political y social,* in *El Monitor Republicano*, June 13–24, 1848. For a more detailed analysis of the liberal and conservative perceptions of the war and its outcome, see Charles A. Hale, "The

War with the United States and the Crisis in Mexican Thought," *The Americas* 14 (October, 1957): 153–73.

98. *Ibid.*

CHAPTER 7

1. Manuel Reyes Veramendi to E. S. Gral. en Gefe del Ejército Norte Americano, México, D.F. September 13, 1847, AHA, Historia en General, legajo 2265, expediente 17.
2. Santa Anna to Veramendi, Guadalupe, September 15, 1847, AHA, Historia en General, legajo 2268, fojas 145–46; Veramendi to Santa Anna, México, September 16, 1847, AHA, Historia en General, legajo 2268, fojas 147–48; Antonio López de Santa Anna, *Detall de las operaciones ocurridas en la defensa de la capital de la república, atacada por el ejército de los Estados Unidos del Norte, año de 1847* (Mexico: Imprenta de Ignacio Cumplido, 1848), 44–45.
3. Manuel de la Peña y Peña, *Colección de los documentos mas importantes relativas á la instalación y reconocimiento del gobierno provisional del Ecsmo. Sr. Presidente de la Suprema Corte de Justica* (Mexico: Ignacio Cumplido, 1847), 4–5, 10–12; Wilfred Hardy Callcott, *Santa Anna: The Story of an Enigma Who Once Was Mexico* (Norman: Univ. of Oklahoma Press, 1936), 270; José María Roa Bárcena, *Recuerdos de la invasión norteamericana, 1846–1848* (Mexico: Editorial Porrúa, S.A., 1947), 3:119; Santa Anna, *Detall,* 44–45. For a cogent analysis of municipal government relations with the American Army of Occupation, see Dennis E. Berge, "A Mexican Dilemma: The Mexico City Ayuntamiento and the Question of Loyalty, 1846–1848," *Hispanic American Historical Review* 50 (May, 1970): 229–56.
4. Antonio de la Peña y Reyes, ed., *Algunos documentos sobre el tratado de Guadalupe y la situación de México durante la invasión americana* (Mexico: Editorial Porrúa, 1930), 174; Edward Thornton to Palmerston, no. 6, October 29, 1847, Mexico, Foreign Office 50/212; Guillermo Prieto, *Memorias de mis tiempos, 1840 á 1853* (Mexico: Librería de la Vda de Ch. Bouret, 1906), 260–68.
5. Santa Anna to Ministro de Guerra y Marina, September 23, 1847, ADN, expediente XI/481.3/2830; Albert C. Ramsey, ed. and trans., *The Other Side, or Notes for the History of the War between Mexico and the United States* (New York: John Wiley, 1850), 383–87; Roa Bárcena, *Recuerdos,* 3:155–56; Santa Anna, *Detall,* 35–36.
6. Quoted in Ramón Alcaraz et al., *Apuntes para la historia de la guerra entre México y los Estados Unidos* (Mexico: Tipografía de Manuel Payno, 1848), 341.
7. Joseph Lane to Scott, October 18, 1847, HED 60, 1030–31; Ramsey, *The Other Side,* 393–97; Thomas Childs to Santa Anna, September 25, 1847, in *Detall,* 46; Santa Anna to Ministro de Guerra y Marina, September 23, 1847, ADN, expediente, XI/481.3/2830; Justin H. Smith, *The War with Mexico* (New York: Macmillan, 1919), 2:174–75. Lane's passage from Veracruz to Puebla encountered less resistance than usual because Juan Aburto, one of the two principal guerrilla chieftains in that region, had died of fever in mid-August, significantly reducing insurgent activity along the road.

8. Lombardini to Ministro de Guerra y Marina, October 20, 1847, AGN, AG, vol. 272, expediente 2671, fojas 228–29; Lane to Scott, October 18, 1847, HED 60, 1030–31; Lane to Adjutant General, October 18, 1847, SED 1, 477–79; Lane to Marcy, October 22, 1847, SED 1, 479–82; Ramsey, *The Other Side,* 399–401; Roa Bárcena, *Recuerdos,* 3:157–62; Santa Anna, *Detall,* 37; George Winston Smith and Charles Judah, eds., *Chronicle of the Gringos: The U.S. Army in the Mexican War, 1846–1848, Accounts of Eyewitnesses and Combatants* (Albuquerque: Univ. of New Mexico Press, 1968), 270–71; Smith, *War with Mexico,* 2:176–77. Preoccupied with looting Huamantla, Lane's troops were surprised by Captain Eulalio Villaseñor's counterattack that inflicted upon the Americans 13 killed and 11 wounded before being driven off.
9. Luís de la Rosa to Santa Anna, October 7, 1847, *Niles Register,* December 12, 1847, 216; Thomas E. Cotner, *The Military and Political Career of José Joaquín de Herrera 1792–1854* (Austin: Institute of Latin American Studies, University of Texas at Austin, 1949), 163–64; Ramsey, *The Other Side,* 403–404; Roa Bárcena, *Recuerdos,* 3:163. On February 29, 1848, General Butler signed an order authorizing the expatriation of Santa Anna; two months later the caudillo departed for Jamaica, where he remained until 1853. Army of Mexico, Orders no. 18, March 6, 1848, NA, Office of the Adjutant General, RG 94.
10. Marcy to Scott, October 6, 1847, HED 60, 1027–28; Brigadier General Roger Jones to Scott, October 6, 1847, NA, Office of the Adjutant General, RG 94.
11. HQ Army GO no. 287, September 17, 1847, SED 1, 386–87.
12. Persifor Smith to Ayuntamiento, México, D.F., 1847, in Francisco Suárez Iriarte, *Defensa pronunciada ante el gran jurado el 21 de marzo de 1850, por Francisco Suárez Iriarte, acusado en 8 de agosto de 1848 por el Secretaría de Relaciones en aquella fecha, de los crimenes de sedición contra el Gobierno de Querétaro é infidencia contra la patria en sus actos como presidente de la asamblea municipal de la Ciudad y Distrito de México* (Mexico: Editorial Porrúa, 1850), 65; *The North American,* December 28, 29, 1847; Smith, *War with Mexico,* 2:226–27.
13. Suárez Iriarte, *Defensa,* 24; Berge, "A Mexican Dilemma," 250.
14. Trist to de la Rosa, October 20, 1847, SED 52, 214–15; de la Rosa to Trist, October 31, 1847, in William R. Manning, ed., *Diplomatic Correspondence of the United States: Inter-American Affairs, 1831–1860* (Washington, D.C.: Carnegie Endowment for International Peace, 1932–1939), 8:971; Peña y Peña to Trist, November 22, 1847, in Manning, *Diplomatic Correspondence,* 8:973–74; Bankhead to Palmerston, no. 88, September 28, 1847, Mexico, Foreign Office 50/211, 246–49; *Daily Picayune,* November 14, 1847; Manuel Dublán and José María Lozano, eds., *Legislación Mexicana; ó Colección completa de las disposiciones legislativas expedidas desde la independencia de la República* (Mexico: Imprenta del Comercio, 1876–93), 5:305; David Pletcher, *The Diplomacy of Annexation: Texas, Oregon and the Mexican War* (Columbia: Univ. of Missouri Press, 1973), 536–38.
15. Buchanan to Trist, October 6, 1847, SED 52, 214–16; Buchanan to Trist, October 25, 1847, SED 52, 217–18; Thornton to Palmerston, nos. 1, 7, October 29, 1847, Mexico, Foreign Office 50/212; Trist to Buchanan, November 27, 1847, in

Manning, *Diplomatic Correspondence,* 8:980–84; Griswold del Castillo, *The Treaty of Guadalupe Hidalgo*, 36-38. Among those influencing Trist's decision to stay on was James L. Freaner, a reliable, level-headed correspondent for the *New Orleans Delta* with whom Trist had become close friends. Thomas J. Farnham, "Nicholas Trist & James Freaner and the Mission to Mexico," *Arizona and the West* 2 (Autumn, 1969): 247–60.

16. Trist to Edward Thornton, December 4, 1847, in Manning, *Diplomatic Correspondence,* 8:984–85n; Trist to Buchanan, December 6, 1847, in Manning, *Diplomatic Correspondence,* 8:984–1020; Roa Bárcena, *Recuerdos,* 3:270–73; Griswold del Castillo, *The Treaty of Guadalupe Hidalgo*, 40-42.

17. *Daily American Star,* December 2, 1847; *El Monitor Republicano,* December 20, 1847; *The North American,* December 29, 1847; Trist to Buchanan, January 12, 25, 1848, in Manning, *Diplomatic Correspondence,* 8:1032–34; Trist to Buchanan, February 2, 1848, in Manning, *Diplomatic Correspondence,* 8:1059–60; Percy C. Doyle to Palmerston, no. 14, February 2, 1848, Mexico, Foreign Office 50/219.

18. The text of the treaty as signed appears in SED 52, February 2, 1848, 38–66; and Griswold del Castillo, *The Treaty of Guadalupe Hidalgo*, 183–99; Trist to Buchanan, no. 14, February 2, 1848, Mexico, Foreign Office 50/219; Homer Campbell Chaney, Jr., "The Mexican-United States War as Seen by Mexican Intellectuals, 1846–1959" (Ph.D. diss., Stanford University, 1959), 51–52; Ramsey, *The Other Side,* 446–47; Roa Bárcena, *Recuerdos,* 3:307–10. A complete elaboration of the treaty's antecedents and provisions can be found in Pletcher, *Diplomacy of Annexation,* 522–50; Roa Bárcena, *Recuerdos,* 3:293–334; Griswold del Castillo, *The Treaty of Guadalupe Hidalgo*, 3–42; George L. Rives, *The United States and Mexico, 1821–1848: A History of the Relations Between the Two Countries from the Independence of Mexico to the Close of the War with the United States* (New York: Charles Scribner's Sons, 1913), 2:584–613; and Smith, *War with Mexico,* 2:240–52, 468–72.

19. Doyle to Palmerston, March 14, 1848, Mexico, Foreign Office 50/219; Marcy to Scott, January 13, 1848, HED 56, 230–35; HQ, Army of Occupation Orders no. 59, February 18, 1848, NA, Office of the Adjutant General, RG 94; Dublán y Lozano, *Legislación mexicana,* 5:345–48. Polk, who had become increasingly suspicious of Scott's political motives, availed himself of the July, 1847, alleged bribery scheme with Santa Anna to remove his potential rival from command. Scott remained in Mexico City until April 23 to testify before a court of inquiry convened to consider, among other things, the matter of the bribe. When the court concluded that military operations had not been influenced by any such action, Polk allowed the matter to drop. Milo Milton Quaife, ed., *The Diary of James K. Polk During His Presidency, 1845–1849* (Chicago: A. C. McClurg & Co., 1910), 3:245–46, 262–63; Court of Inquiry Transcript, Senate Executive Document 65, 30th Cong., 1st sess.

20. *Daily American Star,* February 25, March 9, 1848; Berge, "A Mexican Dilemma," 251–52; Roa Bárcena, *Recuerdos,* 3:334–35. Even before ratification, Butler withdrew his garrisons from Toluca, Orizaba, and Cuernavaca, and on May 27 the

main body of the American army began evacuating Mexico City. At the end of July the American rear detachment restored Ulúa to Mexican control and set sail from Veracruz.

21. Ambrose H. Sevier and Nathan Clifford to Buchanan, May 25, 1848, in Manning, *Diplomatic Correspondence,* 8:1086–87; Peña y Reyes, ed., *Algunos documentos sobre el tratado de Guadalupe,* 51–65, 168–72, 279–92; Carlos María Bustamante, *El nuevo Bernal Díaz del Castillo o sea historia de la invasión de los anglo-americanos en México* (Mexico: Secretaría de Educación Pública, 1949), 2:78; Rives, *The United States and Mexico,* 2:651–54; Roa Bárcena, *Recuerdos,* 3:327–34. On March 10 the United States Senate had ratified the treaty by the slim margin of three votes. SED 52, March 10, 1848, 4–36; Pletcher, *Diplomacy of Annexation,* 562–68.
22. *El Siglo XIX,* June 3, 13, 1848; *Leyes y decretos mejicanos de enero a diciembre 1848* (Mexico: Bibliotéca de Ministerio de Hacienda—Imprenta en el Palacio, 1852), 159–60; Niceto de Zamacois, *Historia de México desde sus tiempos más remotos hasta nuestros días* (Barcelona: J. F. Parres, y Cía., 1876–88), 13:157–60; Cotner, *Herrera,* 169–71. Sworn into office in Querétaro on June 2, Herrera returned the seat of government to Mexico City ten days later.
23. *El Siglo XIX,* July 11, 1848; Frank D. Robertson, "The Military and Political Career of Mariano Paredes y Arrillaga, 1797–1849" (Ph.D. diss., University of Texas, 1955), 298–99. Allowed to return to Mexico during Winfield Scott's invasion, Paredes took no part in hostilities, mainly because the government, suspecting his motives, offered him no position of authority.
24. *El Siglo XIX,* July 19, 1848; Agustín R. Gonzalez, *Historia del estado de Aguascalientes* (Mexico: V. Villada, 1881), 169–70; Zamacois, *Historia de México,* 13:162–63.
25. Nathan Clifford to James Buchanan, June 26, 1848, UTLAC, Smith Papers, vol. 6, 304–306.
26. *El Siglo XIX,* June 17, 19, 1848; Robertson, "Mariano Paredes," 304–308; Zamacois, *Historia de México,* 13:181–84.
27. *El Siglo XIX,* June 13, 29, 1848; Cotner, *Herrera,* 178–83; Robertson, "Mariano Paredes," 309–10; Zamacois, *Historia de México,* 13:198–203, 262. A summary court-martial conducted at nearby Valenciana found Padre Jarauta guilty of treason; shortly thereafter, on orders from Mariano Arista, he was executed.
28. Ministerio de Guerra y Marina, *Memoria del Secretario de Estado y del despacho de guerra y marina* (Mexico: Imprenta de Torres, 1848), 9; Roa Bárcena, *Recuerdos,* 3:248.
29. *Memoria del Secretario de Estado y del despacho de guerra y marina,* 1848, 8; Roa Bárcena, *Recuerdos,* 3:249. The attrition process was accelerated by the lack of money to pay both permanent army and national guard soldiers, causing commanders to dissolve their units.
30. *Memoria del Secretario de Estado y del despacho de guerra y marina,* 1848, 10; Roa Bárcena, *Recuerdos,* 3:244.
31. *Memoria del Secretario de Estado y del despacho de guerra y marina,* 11; Roa Bárcena, *Recuerdos,* 3:250.

32. *Alcance al Republicano Jalícience* numero 23, November 23, 1847, AGN, AG, vol. 275, expediente 2700, foja 94.
33. *El Siglo XIX,* June 11, 1848; *Leyes y decretos mejicanos, 1848,* 161.
34. "Dictamen de la junta de señores generales nombrada por el supremo gobierno para informar el arreglo del ejército," in *Ejército de México,* vol. 2, *1848–1882* (Mexico: Imprenta del Gobierno, n.d.), 115; *Memoria de la Secretaría de Estado y del despacho de guerra y marina,* 1839, 13–16.
35. Ley de 4 de noviembre de 1848 sobre arreglo del ejército, AGN, GM, vol. 15; Ministerio de Guerra y Marina, *Memoria del Secretario de Estado y del despacho de guerra y marina* (Mexico: Tipografía de Vicente Torres, 1850), 20. The 10,000-man force was to comprise 6,000 infantrymen, 1,800 cavalrymen, 1,800 artillerymen and 400 sappers.
36. Decreto para el contingente de hombres que deben proporcionar los estados . . . , May 3, 1848, AGN, GM, vol. 38; Ley de 4 de noviembre de 1848 sobre el arreglo del ejército, AGN, GM, vol. 15.
37. *Memoria del Secretario de Estado y del despacho de guerra y marina,* 1850, 20–21, estado 4.
38. *Memoria del Secretario de Estado y del despacho de guerra y marina,* 1850, 26–27; Gloria Fuentes, *El ejército mexicano* (Mexico: Grijalbo, 1983), 145–46. When the repairs were complete, the Colegio Militar reoccupied Chapultepec on August 1, 1849.
39. Ley de 22 de abril de 1851 sobre arreglo del Ejército, AGN, GM, vol. 16; *Memoria del Secretario de Estado y del despacho de guerra y marina,* 1850, 27, estado 16; Ministerio de Guerra y Marina, *Memoria del Secretario de Estado y del despacho de guerra y marina* (Mexico: Tipografía de Vicente G. Torres, 1851), 32; *Leyes y decretos mejicanos,* 1850, 184–89. Since its inception in 1823, the Colegio Militar had been unable to furnish enough graduates to officer the army's standing formations. Jorge Alberto Lozoya, *El ejército mexicano,* 3rd ed. (Mexico: El Colegio de México, 1984), 29–30.
40. *Memoria del Secretario de Estado y del despacho de guerra y marina,* 1850, estado 11.
41. The U.S. Army, it should be noted, did not establish a war college as a capstone for its military educational system until after the Spanish-American War. William B. Skelton, *An American Profession of Arms: The Army Officer Corps, 1784–1861* (Lawrence: Univ. Press of Kansas, 1992), 179–80.
42. Autorización al gobierno para comprar fusiles, rifles y carabinas de largo alcance, April 21, 1849, AGN, GM, vol, 27; *Memoria del Secretario de Estado y del despacho de guerra y marina,* 1850, 21–22, 24; *Memoria del Secretario de Estado y del despacho de guerra y marina,* 1851, 29–30. Despite its reliance upon French military theory and technology, Mexico disdained sending its officers to France or any other European country for advanced education and training.
43. *Memoria del Secretario de Estado y del despacho de guerra y marina,* 1850, 23–24, estados 13–15. To keep pace with their highly mobile guns, the French system required that all artillery officers be mounted.
44. Ley orgánica de la guardia nacional (Mexico: Imprenta Ignacio Cumplido, 1848), AGN, GM, vol. 27, 4; *Leyes y decretos mejicanos,* 1848, 242–61.

45. Ley orgánica de la guardia nacional, AGN, GM, vol. 27, 1–17; *Leyes y decretos mejicanos,* 1849, 74; Reglamento de la guardia de policía del distrito, in *Ejército de México,* vol. 2, document 4. Coincident with these latest augmentations, the mobile militia was redesignated the Ejército Federal de la Reserva.

46. *Memoria del Secretario de Estado y del despacho de guerra y marina,* 1850, 28, estado 17. The active militia, it will be recalled, was originally conceived to reinforce permanent army formations in the event of national emergency. *Memoria del Secretario de Estado y del despacho de la guerra,* 1826, 10–11.

47. *Memoria del Secretario de Estado y del despacho de la guerra,* 1850, estado 18.

48. *Memoria del Secretario de Estado y del despacho de la guerra,* 1850, 30, 34, estados 22, 25. Officers for whom there existed no valid positions were held as officers with limited leave (*oficiales con licencia limitada*), drawing two-thirds pay until authorized slots to which they could be assigned opened up.

49. *Memoria de los ramos de guerra y marina,* 1845, 17–18.

50. Leticia Reina, *Las rebeliones campesinas en México (1819–1906)* (Mexico: Siglo Veintiuno Editores, 1980), 291–92, 299. Economic distress brought on by the war with the United States exacerbated the already dismal living standards of Sierra Gorda peasants, engendering conditions conducive to rebellion.

51. Manuel María Lombardini to Ministro de Guerra y Marina, January 20, 1847, ADN, expediente XI/481.3/2337.

52. Bases para la pacificación de la Sierra Gorda elaborados por el Supremo Gobierno de la unión, April 11, 1849, ADN, expediente XI/481.3/3092; Sumamente reservado: Estipulaciones secretas para la pacificación de la Sierra Gorda, April 11, 1849, ADN, expediente XI/481.3/3092; *El Siglo XIX,* May 12, 1849.

53. *El Monitor Republicano,* January 5, 1849; *El Siglo XIX,* February 26, 1849.

54. Sumaria averiguación contra Gen. Vicente Rosas Landa, November 1857, AGN, AG, vol. 31, expediente 31, fojas 1–227. On June 19, 1867, Republicans executed Mejía, with Archduke Maximilian and General Miramón, for their respective roles during the French intervention.

55. *El Siglo XIX,* February 11, 1849. Few military leaders of significance rallied to Márquez's standard, and his uprising quickly collapsed when the Querétaro garrison refused to join in. Márquez, however, went on to become a general in the imperialist army of Archduke Maximilian and commanded one of the divisions defending Querétaro against the republicans in May, 1867.

56. *El Siglo XIX,* February 26, March 19, 1849; *Memoria del Secretario de Estado y del despacho de guerra y marina,* 1850, 6–7; Zamacois, *Historia de México,* 13:265. Rebel knowledge of the terrain and skillful use of guerrilla tactics limited government gains while exacting a heavy toll in casualties.

57. *El Monitor Republicano,* February 24, 1849; *El Siglo XIX,* February 19, 20, 1849; Zamacois, *Historia de México,* 13:270–71. Convinced that Márquez' desertion would deal the insurgents a mortal blow, Colonel Rafael Vázquez allowed him to escape. Vázquez was excoriated both by the press and by his military superiors, but his indiscretion seems to have imposed no lasting professional harm: later he was appointed commandant-general of Jalisco. Alberto M. Carreño, ed., *Jefes del Ejército Mexicano en 1847: Biografías de generales de división y de*

brigada y de coroneles del ejército por fines del año 1847 (Mexico: Secretaría de Fomento, 1914), 219–20.

58. *El Siglo XIX,* April 14, 15, 1849; *Memoria del Secretario de Estado y del despacho de guerra y marina,* 1850, 7; Partes militares sobre deportados, December 1849, ADN, expediente XI/481.3/3092; Dublán y Lozano, *Legislación mexicana,* 5:275–79, 292–93; Zamacois, *Historia de México,* 13:300–301.
59. Decreto para establicer las colonias militares, December 1849, ADN, expediente XI/481.3/4780; Reglamento para el establicimiento de las colonias militares en la Sierra Gorda, October 26, 1849, AGN, GM, vol. 15; *El Monitor Republicano,* April 28, 1849; *Memoria del Secretario de Estado y del despacho de guerra y marina,* 1850, estados 1, 5–7.
60. Reina, *Las rebeliones campesinas,* 363–64; Cotner, *Herrera,* 223–24. The intractable inhabitants of Yucatán, it will be recalled, inconvenienced the government during an earlier rebellion that ended only when Santa Anna conceded the territory's de facto autonomy.
61. *El Siglo XIX,* June 30, 1848; Reina, *Las rebeliones campesinas,* 365; Zamacois, *Historia de México,* 13:155. Alarmed by the rebellion's gains, and no longer pestered by a centralistic constitution, in July, 1848, Yucatán's federalist leaders elected to rejoin the Mexican Federation.
62. Micheltorena to Ministro de Guerra y Marina, May 25, 1850, ADN, expediente XI/481.3/2914; *El Fénix de la Libertad,* February 10, 1850; Carreño, *Jefes del Ejército Mexicano,* 205–206.
63. Ministro de Guerra to Díaz de la Vega, April 16, 1851, ADN, expediente XI/481.3/3255. Díaz de la Vega, it will be recalled, commanded a brigade with distinction while defending the town of Mier against Texan invaders in December, 1842. Four years later he was captured at Resaca del Guerrero and subsequently paroled, only to be apprehended again at Cerro Gordo and incarcerated for the duration of hostilities with the United States. From September 12 to October 3, 1855, he served as interim president.
64. Díaz de la Vega to Ministro de Guerra y Marina, May 6, 1851, ADN, expediente XI/481.3/3258.
65. Nelson Reed, *The Caste War of Yucatán* (Stanford: Stanford Univ. Press, 1964), 153–57; Reina, *Las rebeliones campesinas,* 378–79; Zamacois, *Historia de México,* 13:365–70.
66. *Memoria del Secretario de Estado y del despacho de guerra y marina,* 1850, 12. Arista hoped that the Indian threat could be contained through cooperation with the United States, which was experiencing similar onslaughts, but such collaboration never materialized.
67. *Memoria del Secretario de Estado y del despacho de guerra y marina,* 1850, 13; Hubert H. Bancroft, *History of Mexico* (San Francisco: A. L. Bancroft and Co., 1883–88), 5:579–80. In desperation the state of Chihuahua entered into "blood contracts" with American adventurers who agreed to kill hostile Indians for a per-head price on a graduated scale based on age and sex. Needless to say, these outlaws exercised few scruples in discriminating between hostile and friendly Indians.

68. *Memoria del Secretario de Estado y del despacho de guerra y marina*, 1850, 14–16, estados 2, 3; Zamacois, *Historia de México*, 13:284–85. As previously noted, the government also relocated groups of Sierra Gorda rebels to military colonies on the northern frontier in an effort both to remove the troublemakers and to exploit their guerrilla-warfare expertise.

69. Jóse Joaquín de Herrera, *Discurso pronunciado por el presidente de la república mexicana, General de división, José Joaquín de Herrera, el día 1 de enero de 1851, en la aperatura de las sesiones del congreso* (Mexico: Vicente Torres, 1851), AGN, GM, vol. 30, 8; *Memoria del Secretario de Estado y del despacho de guerra y marina*, 1850, 14–15.

70. Reglamento para el establicimiento de las colonias militares en la Sierra Gorda, October 26, 1849, AGN, GM, vol. 15; Dublán y Lozano, *Legislación mexicana*, 5:422–26; *Leyes y decretos mejicanos*, 1848, 264–65; *Memoria del Secretario de Estado y del despacho de guerra y marina*, 1850, 17–18.

71. Croix to Gálvez, no. 595, Arispe, January 23, 1781, AGI, Guadalajara, 281–A, para. 76–130, carpetas 7–9.

72. *Memoria del Secretario de Estado y del despacho de guerra y marina*, 1850, 16. The three new military jurisdictions, Oriente (Tamaulipas and Coahuila), Chihuahua, and Occidente (Sonora and Baja California), were essentially a rehash of one of the organizational formats with which the former Commandancy-General of New Spain's interior provinces experimented.

CONCLUSION

1. Jan Bazant, "Mexico," in Leslie Bethell, ed., *Spanish America after Independence, c.1820–c.1870* (New York: Cambridge University Press, 1987), 157–58.

2. Richard Sinkin, *The Mexican Reform 1855–1876: A Study in Liberal Nation Building* (Austin: Institute of Latin American Studies, University of Texas at Austin, 1979), 49-56. Bazant, "Mexico," 164–65.

3. Gloria Fuentes, *El ejército mexicano* (México: Grijalbo, 1983), 48–57; Jorge Alberto Lozoya, *El ejército mexicano*, 3rd ed., (Mexico: El Colegio de México, 1984), 31–32; Jack Autrey Dabbs, *The French Army in Mexico 1861–1867: A study in Military Government*, (The Hague: Mouton & Co., 1963), 16–31. The units retained on active duty were reorganized into five divisions of 4,000 men each, one of which was commanded by General Porfirio Díaz.

4. Edwin Lieuwen, *Arms and Politics in Latin America*, rev. ed. (New York: Frederick A. Praeger, 1961), 29; Alan Rouquié, *L'Etat militaire en Amerique Latine* (Paris: Editions du Seuil, 1982), 51; Decreto de la Secretaría de Guerra y Marina, Organización Definitiva del Ejército, June 28, 1881, AGN, GM, unnumbered vol. For the first time, army officers were sent to Europe for advanced military schooling.

5. John J. Johnson, *The Military and Society in Latin America* (Stanford: Stanford Univ. Press, 1964), 245; Fuentes, *El ejército mexicano*, 64–66. Officer corp intellectualism was given a public forum with the inauguration of the *Revista del Ejército y la Marina*.

6. Alan Knight, *The Mexican Revolution*, vol. 1, *Porfirians, Liberals and Peasants*

(Lincoln: Univ. of Nebraska Press, 1986), 18, 178–82. A comprehensive rendering of federal army forces at the onset of the Revolution is given in Fuentes, *El ejército mexicano,* 72–74.

7. Alicia Hernández Chávez, "Militares y negocios en la revolución mexicana," *Historia Mexicana* 34 (October–December, 1984): 182–84; Knight, *The Mexican Revolution,* vol. 2, *Counter-revolution and Reconstruction,* 209.
8. Edwin Lieuwen, *Mexican Militarism: The Political Rise and Fall of the Revolutionary Army, 1910–1940* (Albuquerque: Univ. of New Mexico Press, 1968), 143.

GLOSSARY

Activo. Member of active militia.

Agiotista. Financial speculator who made high interest loans to the government.

Alcalde. Magistrate and member of an *ayuntamiento*.

Alférez. Rank equivalent to second lieutenant.

Albóndiga. Public granary.

Arbitrios. Excise tax levied on selected goods.

Artillería de campaña. Mobile field artillery.

Artillería de plaza. Stationary artillery, usually confined to fortresses and other permanent installations.

Audiencia. Royal court of justice with administrative functions.

Ayuntamiento. Elective municipal council (*see also* cabildo).

Azotea. Flat roof of house.

Bagages. Privilege empowering army officers in transit to appropriate horses or mules from any citizen.

Bando. Proclamation.

Bases orgánicas. Centralistic constitution enacted in 1843 by Santa Anna's Council of Representatives.

Benemérito de la patria. "Well-deserving of the country." Title bestowed upon Santa Anna in recognition of his role in defeating Spanish invasion of 1829.

Borbónico. Advocate of return to Bourbon monarchical rule.

Bosque. Forest or woods.

Cabildo. Municipal council (*see also* ayuntamiento).

Cacique. Dominant regional military leader who derived influence from landownership and patronage.

Caciquismo. Political dominance of regional military chieftains.

Capellanías. Benefice for chaplain to say masses for soul of benefactor.

Carbonero. Charcoal maker.

Caudillaje. Political dominance of national military warlords.

Caudillo. Dominant military leader who exercised political influence and power at the national level.

Casta. Caste; person of mixed blood.

Cazador. Light infantryman, usually armed with rifle.

Ciudadela. Citadel; the fortress in Mexico City that served as headquarters for the capital military command.

Cívico. Member of the state-affiliated civic militia.

Comandante general. Commandant-general; leader of military territorial jurisdiction *(comandancia general)*.

Comisionado. Commissioner representing foreign government.

Compañía de preferencia. Elite company with specialized missions.
Compañía fija de pie. Foot artillery company usually confined to a fixed installation.
Compañía suelta. Mobile company.
Consulado. Merchant guild and commercial court.
Contabilidad. Army administrative unit that processed salaries for military personnel.
Cortes. Representative assembly in Spain, in which provincial delegates from New Spain participated.
Criollo. Creole. Spaniard born in New Spain.
Cuartel. Semipermanent site where military forces were garrisoned.
Cuartelazo. Revolt of military garrison against incumbent government.
Cuerpo ligero. Light corps prominent in war with United States.
Cura. Curate; local parish priest or rector.
Curanderos. Healers practically skilled in the use of herbal medicines who accompanied the army on campaign to provide medical treatment to soldiers.
Degüello. Bugle call signifying "no quarter" (literally "destruction or beheading")
Derecho de consumo. Special levy on imports, imposed to increase government revenues.
Destacamento volante. Highly mobile royalist counterinsurgency detachment.
Discurso. Speech or discourse.
Donativo. Contribution solicited from prosperous landowners.
Duranguеño. Resident of Durango.
Dzule. Member of white landed elite in Yucatán.
Ejército Restaurador. Army of Restoration that drove the French from Mexico in 1867.
Entrada. Entrance, usually forced penetration, into hostile territory.
Escopeta. Light musket or fowling piece.
Escoses. Member of conservative Scottish Rite masonic order.
Escuela de aplicación. Military school intended to impart skills necessary for branch-related proficiency.
Escuela normal. Normal school designed to inculcate soldiers with their responsibilities as Mexican citizens.
Estado mayor del Ejército. Army general staff.
Expediente. File of papers on specific subject.
Exposición. Explanation or interpretation of topic.
Fanega de Tierra. Unit of arable land, approximately one-third acre.
Fijo. Battalion or regiment raised and stationed permanently in colonies.
Foja. Double leaves of paper.
Fortaleza. Fortress or stronghold.
Fortín. Small fort or expedient fortification.
Frontón. Defensible position reinforced with rudimentary breastworks.
Fuero Militar. Corporate privileges and right of soldiers to trial by military jurisdiction.
Fusil (nickname: "Brown Bess"): .753 caliber flintlock-operated, smoothbore musket of British manufacture; saw widespread use during Napoleonic Wars (*see also* morena licha).

Gachupín. Spaniard born in Europe, residing in New Spain.

Garita. Entrance to Mexico City, usually situated at end of causeway, where duties were collected and passports examined.

General graduado. General by rank, but without concomitant pay or effective command.

Generalisimo. Supreme general.

Golpe. Coup d'etat; coercive removal of incumbent political regime.

Golpista. Perpetrator or participant in a coup d'etat.

Granadero. Grenadier; elite soldier with special physical attributes.

Guanajuatense. Resident of Guanajuato.

Guardia de policía. Police guard; a provincial law-enforcement organization intended to protect travelers from bandits, and to administer prisons in the Federal District.

Guardia nacional. National guard; successor to active and civic militias.

Hacendado. Owner of large landed estate.

Hacienda. Large landed estate with a mixed economic base of ranching and agriculture.

Hombre de bien. Mexican of high station; gentleman.

Húsar. Hussar; lightly armed cavalryman.

Impuesto de capitación. Head tax imposed upon all Mexican citizens regardless of income.

Jalapista. Native of Jalapa.

Jalícience. Resident of Jalisco.

Jefe político. Political chief; position created by Cortes to replace viceroy.

Junta. Council or gathering of officials.

Junta de gobierno. Governing council.

Junta de guerra. Council of war.

Junta de Notabales. Council of Notables. The assemblage of conservative elites that produced the *Bases orgánicas* in 1843.

Junta Instituyente. Hand-picked legislature used by Iturbide to supplant legitimate congress.

Lancero. Lancer; cavalryman armed with long lance.

Legajo. Bundle of loose papers tied together.

Legión de estrangeros. Unit of mostly American deserters who opted to fight for Mexico (known also as San Patricios).

Leñador. Woodcutter.

Leva. Levy; coercive means of military conscription.

Ley del caso. Law permitting government to exile anyone considered a threat to public safety or welfare.

Licenciado. Spanish legal official.

Magueyal. Thick wall of maguey (agave) plants.

Manga. Poncho used as covering while traveling on horseback.

Manifiesto. Public declaration.

Marqués. Marquis.

Memoria. Memorial or record of events.

Mestizo. Person of mixed Spanish and Indian ancestry.
Moderados. Moderate faction of Mexican national politics.
Morena Licha. "Brown Bess" (*see* Fusil).
Oaxaqueño. Resident of Oaxaca.
Obras Pías. Charitable contributions to Church, usually land or voluntary lien rendering annuity.
Oficial con licencia limitada. Officer drawing two-thirds pay but for whom no valid position existed.
Pardo. Mexican with some African blood.
Patria. Fatherland.
Peninsular. Spaniard born in Europe, resident in New Spain.
Peón. Resident hacienda laborer.
Permanente. Member of permanent army.
Peso. Monetary unit comprising eight *reales*.
Plana Mayor. Army staff.
Polkos. Socially well-to-do members of the capital's national guard battalions, so named for their fondness of the polka.
Preeminencias. Special immunities and exemptions awarded to deserving soldiers.
Presidial. Soldier assigned to presidio.
Presidio. Frontier military fortress.
Pronunciado. Perpetrator of pronouncement.
Pronunciamiento. Pronouncement; act of declaring against incumbent political regime.
Puros. Radical anticlerical element of Mexican national politics.
Quintal. One hundred pounds.
Ranchería. Collection of huts or cottages.
Rancho. Small farm or ranch.
Real Cédula. Royal order or decree.
Real de minas. Mining town founded with royal government assistance and subject to special regulations.
Regimiento expedicionario. Spanish expeditionary regiment.
Reglamento. Regulation.
Resaca. Long, erratic depression cutting otherwise flat terrain.
Santanista. Supporter of Antonio López de Santa Anna.
Serape. Narrow cloak or blanket worn or carried over saddle (also *sarape*).
Siete Leyes. Seven Laws. Centralistic constitution promulgated in 1836.
Solare. Plot of land awarded to soldier who fulfilled arduous military obligations.
Soldadera. Woman, generally soldier's wife or girlfriend, accompanying military campaigns.
Soldado razo. Low-ranking enlisted soldier.
Sorteo. Lottery to select recruits for permanent army and active militia.
Tamaulipeco. Resident of Tamaulipas.
Tercerola. Carbine with which Mexican cavalrymen generally were armed during war with United States.

Tesorería de ejército. Privilege by which army officers were authorized to collect certain revenues.

Tierra baldía. Unoccupied communal land eligible for sale to private interests.

Tierra caliente. Warm tropical lowlands.

Vale real. Bond issued by Crown to finance war against Napoleon.

Vecino. Free citizen who generally owns property.

Veracruzano. Native of Veracruz.

Villa. Municipality one level below city *(ciudad).*

Visita. Official tour or inspection.

Visitador general. Royal official charged with inspecting King's possessions.

Vómito negro. Euphemism for yellow fever, derived from tendency of disease to cause bloody vomiting.

Yorkino. Member of liberal York Rite masonic order.

Zacatecano. Resident of Zacatecas.

SELECTED BIBLIOGRAPHY

1. ARCHIVAL MATERIALS

A. MANUSCRIPTS

Archivo General de Indias (AGI)
  Audiencia de Guadalajara
  Audiencia de México
Archivo General de la Nación (AGN)
  Archivo de Guerra (AG)
  Bienes Nacionales (BN)
  Civil
  Correspondencia de los Virreyes (CV)
  Gobernación
  Guerra y Marina (GM)
  Historia
  Impresos Oficiales (IO)
  Indiferente de Guerra (IG)
  Operaciones de Guerra (OG)
  Provincias Internas (PI)
  Reales Cédulas (RC)
Archivo Histórico de la Secretaría de la Defensa Nacional (ADN)
Archivo Histórico del Ayuntamiento de la Ciudad de México (AHA)
  Actas de Cabildo
  Historia en General
Bibliotéca Nacional (BN)
  Colección Lafragua
  División de Manuscritos (MS)
Bibliotéca Eusebio Dávalos del Instituto Nacional de Antropología e História (BINAH)
  Colección Antigua
Library of Congress (LC)
  William L. Marcy Papers
  Nicholas P. Trist Papers
National Archives of the United States (NA)

Records of the Department of State, Foreign Affairs Section-Record Group 59
Records of the Office of the Adjutant General—Record Group 4
Records of the Office of the Secretary of War—Record Group 107
Records of the Judge Advocate General Office—Record Group 153
Public Record Office (London), Foreign Office Papers, Series 50, Mexico
University of Texas, Nettie Lee Benson Latin American Collection (UTLAC)
Genaro García Manuscript Collection
Justin Smith Papers
Lucas Alamán Papers
Mariano Paredes y Arrillaga Archive
Valentín Gómez Farías Archive
Mariano Riva Palacio Archive

B. NEWSPAPERS

Alcance al Republicano Jalícience (1847)
American Star, The (Mexico City) (1847–48)
Anteojo, El (1835–36)
Boletín Oficial (1841)
Cosmopolita, El (1837–43)
Daily Picayune (New Orleans) (1839–48)
Diario del Gobierno de la República Mexicana (1824–46)
Fénix de la Libertad, El (1831–34)
Gaceta de México (1810–21)
Gaceta Extraordinaria del Gobierno Imperial de México (1822)
Gazeta del Gobierno Supremo de México (1824)
Mexicano, El (1839)
Monitor Republicano, El (1846–47)
Mosquito Mexicano, El (1834–43)
Niles National Register (Baltimore) (1845–48)
North American, The (Mexico City) (1847–48)
Restaurador Mexicano, El (1838–39)
Siglo XIX, El (1842–45, 1848–52)
Sol, El (1821–30)
Telégrafo, El (1833–34)
Tiempo, El (1846)
Universal, El (1830)

Voz de la Patria (1830–32)
Voz del Pueblo, La (1845)

2. PUBLISHED MATERIALS

Acuña, Rodolfo. *Occupied America: The Chicano Struggle Toward Liberation.* New York: Canfield Press, 1972.

Alamán, Lucas. *Historia de Méjico desde los primeros movimientos que preparon su independencia en el año de 1808 hasta la época presente.* 5 vols. Mexico: J. Marino Lara, 1850.

Alcaraz, Ramón, et al. *Apuntes para la historia de la guerra entre México y los Estados Unidos.* Mexico: Tipografía de Manuel Payno, 1848.

Alessio Robles, Vito. *Coahuila y Téjas, desde la consumación de la Independencia hasta el Tratado de paz de Guadalupe Hidalgo.* 2 vols. Mexico: Imprenta Universaria Talleres Gráficas de la Nación, 1945–46.

Almada, Francisco R. *Diccionario de historia, geografía y biografía Sonorenses.* Hermosillo: Instituto de Cultura Sonorense, 1990.

Almonte, Juan N. "The Private Journal of Juan Nepomuceno Almonte, February 1–April 16, 1836." *Southwestern Historical Quarterly* 48 (July, 1944): 10–32.

Alvear Acevedo, Carlos. *La Guerra de 47.* Mexico: Editorial Jus, 1957.

Amador, Elías. *Bosquejo histórico de Zacatecas.* Zacatecas: Talleres Tipográficos "Pedroza" Ags., 1943.

Ampudia, Pedro de. *El ciudadano General Pedro de Ampudia ante el tribunal respectable de opinión pública, por los primeros sucesos ocurridos en la guerra a que nos provoca, decreta y sostiene el gobierno de los Estados Unidos de America.* San Luís Potosí: Imprenta de Gobierno, 1846.

———. *Manifiesto del General Ampudia a sus conciudadanos.* Mexico: Ignacio Cumplido, 1847.

Anna, Timothy E. "Francisco Novella and the Last Stand of the Royal Army in New Spain." *Hispanic American Historical Review* 51 (February, 1971): 92–111.

———. *The Fall of Royal Government in Mexico City.* Lincoln: Univ. of Nebraska Press, 1978.

———. *The Mexican Empire of Iturbide.* Lincoln: Univ. of Nebraska Press, 1990.

Apodoca, Fernando de Gabriel y Ruíz de. *Apuntes biográficos de exmo. señor D. Juan Ruíz de Apodoca y Eliza, Conde de Venadito.* Burgos, n.p., 1849.

Archer, Christon I. *The Bourbon Army in Mexico, 1760–1810.* Albuquerque: Univ. of New Mexico Press, 1977.

———. "Pardos, Indians and the Army of New Spain: Interrelationships and Conflicts, 1780–1810." *Journal of Latin American Studies* 6 (November, 1974): 231–55.

———. "The Army of New Spain and the Wars of Independence." *Hispanic American Historical Review* 61 (November, 1981): 705–20.

———. "The Royalist Army in New Spain: Civil-Military Relationships." *Journal of Latin American Studies* 13 (May, 1981): 57–83.

Arista, Mariano. *Reseña histórica de la revolución que desde 6 junio hasta 8 octubre tuvo lugar en la República en el año 1833 a favor del sistema central.* Mexico: Mariano Arévalo, 1835.

Armstrong, Andrew. "The Brazito Battlefield." *New Mexico Historical Review* 35 (January, 1960): 63–74.
Arrangoiz y Berzábel, Francisco de Paula de. *México desde 1808 hasta 1867*. 2nd ed. Mexico: Editorial Porrúa, S.A., 1968.
Arrom, Silvia M. "Popular Politics in Mexico City: The Parián Riot, 1828." *Hispanic American Historical Review* 68 (May, 1988): 245–68.
Balbontín, Manuel. *La invasión americana 1846 á 1848: Apuntes del subteniente de artillería Manuel Balbontín*. Mexico: Tipografía de Gonzalo A. Esteva, 1883.
———. *Estado militar de la república mexicana en 1846*. Mexico: Tipografía de Ignacio Pombo, 1890.
Bancroft, Hubert H. *History of Mexico*. 6 vols. San Francisco: A. L. Bancroft and Co., 1883–88.
Barker, Nancy Nichols. *The French Experience in Mexico, 1821–1861*. Chapel Hill: Univ. of North Carolina Press, 1979.
Barker, Eugene C. *Mexico and Texas, 1821–1835: "The Development of the Revolution."* New York: Russell and Russell, 1965.
———. "President Jackson and the Texas Revolution." *American Historical Review* 12 (July, 1907): 788–809.
———. "The Texan Revolutionary Army." *Southwestern Historical Quarterly* 9 (1906): 227–61.
Bauer, K. Jack. *The Mexican War, 1846–1848*. New York: Macmillan Publishing Co., 1974.
Bazant, Jan. *Alienation of Church Wealth in Mexico: Social and Economic Aspects of the Liberal Revolution, 1856–1875*. London: Cambridge Univ. Press, 1971.
———. *A Concise History of Mexico from Hidalgo to Cárdenas, 1805–1940*. Cambridge: Cambridge Univ. Press, 1977.
———. *Historia de la deuda exterior de México, 1823–1946*. Foreword by Antonio Ortíz Mena. Mexico: El Colegio de Mexico, 1968.
———. "Mexico." In Leslie Bethell, ed. *Spanish America after Independence, c.1820–c.1870*. New York: Cambridge University Press, 1987, 123–70.
Beezley, William H. "Caudillismo: An Interpretive Note." *Journal of Inter-American Studies* 11 (July, 1969): 345–52.
Benson, Nettie Lee, ed. *Mexico and the Spanish Cortes, 1810–1822*. Austin: Univ. of Texas Press, 1968.
———. *La diputación provincial y el federalismo mexicano*. Mexico City: El Colegio de México, 1955.
———. "The Plan of Casa Mata." *Hispanic American Historical Review* 25 (February, 1945): 45–56.
Berge, Dennis E. "A Mexican Dilemma: The Mexico City Ayuntamiento and the Question of Loyalty, 1846–1848." *Hispanic American Historical Review* 50 (May, 1970): 229–56.
Bermúdez, José María. *Verdadera causa de la revolución del Sur, justificándose el que la suscribe con documentos que existen en la Secretaría del Supremo Gobierno del estado de México que los certifica*. Toluca: Imprenta del Gobierno del Estado, 1831.

Bethell, Leslie, ed. *Spanish America after Independence, c.1820–c.1870*. Cambridge: Cambridge Univ. Press, 1987.

Bidwell, Robert L. "The First Mexican Navy, 1821–1830." Ph.D., diss., University of Virginia, 1960.

Blanchard, P., and A. Dauzats. *San Juan de Ulùa [sic], ou rélation de l'expédition Française au Mexique sous les ordres de M. le contre-amiral Baudin*. Paris: Gide, 1859.

Bobb, Bernard E. *The Viceregency of Antonio María Bucareli in New Spain 1771–1779*. Austin: Univ. of Texas Press, 1962.

Bocanegra, José María. *Memorias para la historia de México independiente, 1821–1841*. 2 vols. Mexico: Imprenta del Gobierno Federal, 1892–97.

Brack, Gene M. "Mexican Opinion, American Racism and the War of 1846." *Western Historical Quarterly* 1 (April, 1970): 161–74.

———. *Mexico Views Manifest Destiny 1821–1846: An Essay on the Origins of the Mexican War*. Albuquerque: Univ. of New Mexico Press, 1975.

Brading, David A. "Government and Elite in Late Colonial Mexico." *Hispanic American Historical Review* 53 (August, 1973): 389–414.

———. *Haciendas and Ranchos in the Mexican Bajío: León, 1700–1860*. Cambridge: Cambridge Univ. Press, 1978.

Bravo Ugarte, José, ed. *Instrucción reservada al Marqués de Branciforte*. Mexico: Editorial Jus, 1966.

Bravo Ugarte, José. *Historia de México: Independencia, caracterización politica e integración social*. 2nd ed., rev. México: Editorial Jus, 1953.

———. *Historia sucinta de Michoacán*. 3 vols. Mexico: Editorial Jus, 1962–64.

———. "La Guerra a México de Estados Unidos 1846–1848." *Historia Mexicana* 2 (October–December, 1951): 185–226.

Brinckerhoff, Sidney B., and Odie B. Faulk. *Lancers for the King: A Study of the Frontier Military System of Northern New Spain, with a Translation of the Royal Regulations of 1772*. Phoenix: Arizona Historical Foundation, 1965.

Brooks, Nathan Covington. *A Complete History of the Mexican War: Its Causes, Conduct, and Consequences: Comprising an Account of the Various Military and Naval Operations, from its Commencement to the Treaty of Peace*. Chicago: Rio Grande Press, 1965.

Buisson, Inge, et al., eds. *Problemas de la formación del Estado de la Nación en Hispanoamérica*. Cologne: Bohlau Verlang, 1984.

Bulnes, Francisco. *Las grandes mentiras de nuestra historia: la nación y el ejército en las guerras extranjeras*. Mexico: Editora Nacional, S.A., 1969.

Bushnell, Clyde Gilbert. *La carrera política y militar de Juan Álvarez*. Mexico: Miguel Angel Porrúa, 1988.

Bustamante, Carlos María. *Apuntes para la historia del gobierno del General Antonio López de Santa Anna, desde principios de octubre de 1841 hasta 6 de diciembre de 1844, en que fué depuesto de mando por uniforme voluntad de la nación*. Mexico: Imprenta de J. Mariano Lara, 1845.

———. *Campañas del general D. Félix María Calleja, comandante en gefe del ejército real de operaciones, llamado del centro*. Mexico: Imprenta del Águila, 1828.

———. *Cuadro Histórico de la revolución mexicana.* 3 vols. Mexico: Ediciones de la Comisión Nacional, 1961.

———. *Diario histórico de México* [for 1823]. Edited by Elías Amador. 2 vols. Zacatecas: J. Ortega, 1896.

———. *El gabinete mexicano durante el segundo período de la administración del exmo. señor presidente d. Anastasio Bustamante.* 2 vols. Mexico: J. Mariano Lara, 1842.

———. *El nuevo Bernal Díaz del Castillo o sea historia de la invasión de los anglo-americanos en México.* 2 vols. Mexico: Secretaría de Educación Pública. 1949.

———. *Memorias para la historia de la invasión española sobre la costa de Tampico de Tamaulipas hecha en el año de 1829.* Mexico: Valdés, 1831.

Calderón de la Barca, Frances. *Life in Mexico.* Berkeley: Univ. of California Press, 1982.

Calderón Quijano, José Antonio, ed. *Los virreyes de Nueva España en el reinado de Carlos III (1779–1787).* Sevilla: Publicaciones de la Escuela de Estudios Hispano-Americanos de Sevilla, 1968.

———, ed. *Los virreyes de Nueva España en el reinado de Carlos IV (1787–1798).* Sevilla: Publicaciones de la Escuela de Estudios Hispano-Americanos, 1972.

Callcott, Wilfred Hardy. *Santa Anna: The Story of an Enigma Who Once Was Mexico.* Norman: Univ. of Oklahoma Press, 1936.

Cámara de Diputados. *Dictamen de las comisiones de guerra de la Cámara de Diputados sobre reorganización del ejército permanente.* Mexico: Ignacio Cumplido, 1833.

Carreño, Alberto M., ed. *Jefes del Ejército Mexicano en 1847: Biografías de generales de división y de brigada y de coroneles del ejército mexicano por fines del año de 1847.* Mexico: Imprenta de la Secretaría de Fomento, 1914.

Castañeda, Carlos E. "Relations of General Scott with Santa Anna." *Hispanic American Historical Review* 39 (November, 1949): 455–73.

———, trans. and ed. *The Mexican Side of the Texas Revolution [1836]: By the Chief Mexican Participants, General Antonio López de Santa Anna, D. Ramón Martínez Caro (Secretary to Santa Anna), General Vicente Filisola, General José Urrea, General José María Tornel (Secretary of War).* Dallas: P. L. Turner Co., 1928.

Chaney, Homer Campbell, Jr. "The Mexican-United States War as Seen by Mexican Intellectuals, 1846–1959." Ph.D. diss., Stanford University, 1959.

Chevalier, François. "Conservateurs et libéraux aux Mexique. Essai de sociologie et géographie politiques de l'independance a l'intervention française." *Cahiers d'histoire mondiale* 8 (1964): 457–74.

Clarke, Dwight L. *Stephen Watts Kearny: Soldier of the West.* Norman: Univ. of Oklahoma Press, 1961.

Connor, Seymour V., and Odie B. Faulk. *North America Divided: The Mexican War, 1846–1848.* New York: Oxford Univ. Press, 1971.

"Controversia entre el obispo de Puebla y el virrey Calleja." *Boletín del Archivo General de la Nación* 4 (1937): 650–59.

Cooke, Philip St. George. *The Conquest of New Mexico and California: An Historical and Personal Narrative.* New York: G. P. Putnam's Sons, 1878.

Costeloe, Michael P. *Church and State in Independent Mexico: A Study of the Patronage Debate, 1821–1857*. London: Royal Historical Society, 1978.
———. "A Pronunciamiento in Nineteenth Century Mexico: 15 de julio de 1840." *Mexican Studies/Estudios Mexicanos* 4 (Summer, 1988): 245–64.
———. *La primera república federal en México (1824–1835): (un estudio de los partidos políticos en el México independiente)*. Mexico: Fondo de Cultura Económica, 1975.
———. "Los generales Santa Anna y Paredes y Arrillaga en México, 1841–1843: Rivales por el poder o una copa más." *Historia Mexicana* 39 (1989): 417–40.
———. "Santa Anna and the Gómez Farías Administration in Mexico, 1833–1834." *The Americas* 31 (July, 1974): 18–50.
———. *The Central Republic in Mexico, 1835–1846: Hombres de Bien in the Age of Santa Anna*. New York: Cambridge Univ. Press, 1993.
———. "The Church and the Rebellion of the Polkos." *Hispanic American Historical Review* 46 (May, 1966): 170–78.
———. "The Mexican Press of 1836 and the Battle of the Alamo." *Southwestern Historical Quarterly* 91 (April, 1988): 533–43.
———. "The Triangular Revolt in Mexico and the Fall of Anastasio Bustamante, August-October 1841." *Journal of Latin American Studies* 20 (1988): 337–60.
Cotner, Thomas E. *The Military and Political Career of José Joaquín de Herrera 1792–1854*. Austin: Institute of Latin American Studies, University of Texas at Austin, 1949.
Cuevas, Luís Gonzaga. *Exposición del Ex-Ministro que la suscribe sobre las diferencias con Francia*. Mexico: Ignacio Cumplido, 1839.
Cuevas, Mariano, ed. *El Libertador: Documentos selectos de Don Agustín de Iturbide*. Mexico: Editorial Patria, 1947.
——. *Historia de la Nación Mexicana*. 3rd ed. Mexico: Editorial Porrúa, S.A., 1967.
Cutts, James Madison. *The Conquest of California and New Mexico by the Forces of the United States in the Years 1846 and 1847*. Philadelphia: Carey & Hart, 1847.
Dobbs, Jack Autrey. *The French Army in Mexico, 1861–1867: A Study in Military Government*. The Hague: Mouton & Co., 1963
Delgado, Jaime. "El conde del Venadito ante el Plan de Iguala." *Revista de Indias* 33–34 (1948): 957–66.
———. "La misión a Méjico de Don Juan de O'Donojú." *Revista de Indias* 35 (1949): 25–87.
Di Tella, Torcuato S. "The Dangerous Classes in Early Nineteenth Century Mexico." *Journal of Latin American Studies* 5 (May, 1973): 79–105.
Díaz Díaz, Fernando. *Caudillos y caciques: Antonio López de Santa Anna y Juan Álvarez*. Mexico: El Colegio de Mexico, 1972.
Diccionario Porrúa de historia, biografía, y geografía de México. 4 vols. 6th ed. Mexico: Editorial Porrúa, 1995.
Dillon, Lester R. *American Artillery in the Mexican War 1846–1848*. Austin: Presidial Press, 1975.
Dublán, Manuel, and José María Lozano, eds. *Legislación Mexicana; ó Colección completa de las disposiciones legislativas expedidas desde la independencia de la República*. 22 vols. Mexico: Imprenta del Comercio, 1876–93.

Eisenhower, John S. D. *So Far From God: The United States War with Mexico 1846–1848*. New York: Random House, 1989.

Ejército de México. Vol. 2, *1848–1882*. Mexico: Imprenta del Gobierno, n.d.

Escalante Gonzalbo, Fernando. *Ciudadanos imaginarios: Memorial de los afanes y desventuras de la virtud y apología del vicio triunfante en la República Mexicana*. Mexico: El Colegio de México, 1992.

Farnham, Thomas J. "Nicholas Trist & James Freaner and the Mission to Mexico." *Arizona and the West* 2 (Autumn, 1969): 247–60.

Farriss, Nancy M. *Crown and Clergy in Colonial Mexico 1750–1821, The Crisis of Ecclesiastical Privilege*. London: Athlone Press, 1968.

Ferguson, Carol. "The Spanish Tamerlaine? Félix María Calleja, Viceroy of New Spain, 1813–1816." Ph.D. diss., Texas Christian University, 1973.

Filisola, Vicente. *Memorias para la historia de la guerra de Téjas, por el Sr. General de división y actual presidente del Supremo Tribunal de guerra y marina de la República*. 2 vols. Mexico: Tipografía de R. Rafael, 1849.

———. *Representación dirigida al Supremo Gobierno por gral . . . , en defensa de su honor y aclaración de sus operaciones como general en jefe del ejército sobre Téjas*. México: Ignacio Cumplido, 1836.

Flaccus, Elmer William. "Guadalupe Victoria: Mexican Revolutionary, Patriot and First President, 1786–1843." Ph.D. diss., University of Texas, 1951.

Flóres Caballero, Romeo. *La contrarevolución en la independencia: los españoles en la vida política, social y económica de México, 1804–1838*. Mexico: El Colegio de México, 1969.

Foote, Henry Stuart. *Texas and The Texans; or, Advance of the Anglo-Americans to the Southwest Including a History of Leading Events in Mexico, From the Conquest of Fernando Cortes to the Termination of the Texas Revolution*. 2 vols. Austin: Univ. of Texas Press, 1935.

Frías, Heriberto. *Episodios militares mexicanos: principales campañas, jornados, batallas, combates y actos heróicos que ilustran la historia del ejército nacional desde la independencia hasta el triunfo definitivo de la república*. 2 vols. Mexico: Librería de la Vda. de Ch. Bouret, 1901.

Fuentes Díaz, Vicente. *La Intervención Norteamericana en México, 1847*. Mexico: Nuevo Mundo, 1947.

Fuentes, Gloria. *El ejército mexicano*. Mexico: Grijalbo, 1983.

Fuentes Mares, José. *Santa Anna: Aurora y ocaso de un comediante*. 3rd ed. Mexico: Editorial Jus, 1967.

Gaddy, Jerry. J., comp. and ed. *Texas in Revolt: Contemporary Newspaper Accounts of the Texas Revolution*. Fort Collins, Colo.: Old Army Press, 1973.

Gallagher, F. M. "Parte oficial de la acción de armas de Temascalitos." *New Mexico Historical Review* 3 (October, 1928): 381–89.

García, Genaro, ed. *Documentos inéditos o muy raros para la historia de México*. 59 vols. Mexico: Editorial Porrúa, S.A., 1974.

Gómez Pedraza, Manuel. *Manifiesto que Manuel Gómez Pedraza, Ciudadano de la República de Méjico, dedica á sus compatriotas ó sea una reseña de su vida pública*. Guadalajara: La Oficina de Brambila, 1831.

Gonzalez, Agustín R. *Historia del estado de Aguascalientes.* Mexico: V. Villada, 1881.

Gonzáles Flóres, Enrique, and Francisco R. Almada, eds. *Informe de Don Hugo O'Conor sobre el estado de las Provincias Internas del Norte 1771–1776.* Mexico: Editorial Cultura, 1952.

Graebner, Norman A. "The Mexican War: A Study in Causation." *Pacific Historical Review* 49 (August, 1980): 404–26.

Green, Michael Robert. "El Soldado Mexicano, 1835–1836." *Military History of Texas and the Southwest* 13 (1975): 5–10.

Green, Stanley C. "Lucas Alamán: Domestic Activities, 1823–1835." Ph.D. diss., Texas Christian University, 1970.

———. *The Mexican Republic: The First Decade, 1823–1832.* Pittsburgh: Univ. of Pittsburgh Press, 1987.

Greenleaf, Richard E. "The Nueva Vizcaya Frontier, 1787–1789." *Journal of the West* 8 (January, 1969): 56–66.

Griswold del Castillo, Richard. *The Treaty of Guadalupe Hidalgo: A Legacy of Conflict.* Norman: University of Oklahoma Press, 1991.

Hale, Charles A. *Mexican Liberalism in the Age of Mora, 1821–1853.* New Haven: Yale Univ. Press, 1968.

———. "The War with the United States and the Crisis in Mexican Thought." *The Americas* 14 (October, 1957): 153–73.

Hamill, Hugh M. "Royalist Counterinsurgency in the Mexican War for Independence: The Lessons of 1811." *Hispanic American Historical Review* 55 (August, 1973): 470–89.

———. *The Hidalgo Revolt: Prelude to Mexican Independence.* Gainesville: Univ. of Florida Press, 1966.

Hamnett, Brian R. "Anastasio Bustamante y la Guerra de Independencia, 1810–1821." *Historia Mexicana* 112 (April-June, 1979): 527–31.

———. "Mexico's Royalist Coalition: The Response to Revolution, 1808–1821." *Journal of Latin American Studies* 12 (May, 1980): 55–86.

———. "Royalist Counterinsurgency and the Continuity of Rebellion: Guanajuato and Michoacán, 1813–20." *Hispanic American Historical Review* 62 (February, 1982): 19–48.

———. "The Appropriation of Mexican Church Wealth by the Spanish Bourbon Government—The 'Consolidación de Vales Reales,' 1805–1809." *Journal of Latin American Studies* 1 (November, 1969): 85–113.

Hanighen, Frank C. *Santa Anna, the Napoleon of the West.* New York: Coward-McCann, 1934.

Hardin, Steven L. *Texian Iliad: A Military History of the Texas Revolution, 1835–1836.* Austin: Univ. of Texas Press, 1994.

Harrell, Eugene Wilson, "Vicente Guerrero and the Birth of Modern Mexico, 1821–1831." Ph.D. diss., Tulane University, 1976.

Haynes, Sam W. *Soldiers of Misfortune: The Somervell and Mier Expeditions.* Austin: University of Texas Press, 1990.

Henry, William C. *Campaign Sketches of the War with Mexico.* New York: Harper & Bros., 1847.

Hernández y Dávalos, Juan E., ed. *Colección de documentos para la historia del la guerra de independencia de México de 1808 a 1821.* 6 vols. México: J.M. Sandoval, 1877–1882.

Hernández Chávez, Alicia. "Militares y negocios en la revolución mexicana." *Historia Mexicana* 34 (October–December, 1984): 181–212.

Herrera, Jóse Joaquín de. *Discurso pronunciado por el presidente de la república mexicana, General de división, José Joaquín de Herrera, el día 1 de enero de 1851, en la apertura de las sesiones del congreso.* Mexico: Vicente Torres, 1851.

House Executive Document 209, 29th Cong., 1st sess., ser. 486. *Reports from General Taylor.*

House Executive Document 4, 29th Cong., 2nd sess., ser. 497. *Message From the President . . . at the Commencement of the Second Session of the Twenty-Ninth Congress.*

House Executive Document 8, 30th Cong., 1st sess., ser. 515. *Message from The President . . . at the Commencement of the Second Session of the Twenty-Ninth Congress.*

House Executive Document 56, 30th Cong., 1st sess. *Correspondence Between the Secretary of War and Generals Scott and Taylor and Between General Scott and Mr. Trist.*

House Executive Document 60, 30th Cong., 1st sess., ser. 520. *Mexican War Correspondence.*

Houston, Donald E. "The Role of Artillery in the Mexican War." *Journal of the West* 11 (April, 1972): 273–84.

Houston, James A. *The Sinews of War: Army Logistics, 1775–1953.* Washington, D.C.: Government Printing Office, 1966.

Hu-DeHart, Evelyn. *Yaqui Resistance and Survival: The Struggle for Land and Autonomy, 1821–1910.* Madison: Univ. of Wisconsin Press, 1984.

Hughes, John T. *Doniphan's Expedition: Containing an Account of the Conquest of New Mexico; General Kearny's Overland Expedition to California; Doniphan's Campaign Against The Navajos; His Unparalled March upon Chihuahua and Durango; and the Operations of General Price at Santa Fe.* Cincinnati: J. A. and U. P. James, 1848.

Humphreys, R. A., and John Lynch, eds. *The Origins of the Latin American Revolutions, 1808–1826.* New York: Alfred A. Knopf, 1965.

Hutchinson, Cecil Alan. "Valentín Gómez Farías: A Biographical Study." Ph.D. diss., University of Texas, 1948.

Instrucción reservadada que el conde de Revilla Gigedo dió a su sucesor en el mando, marqués de Branciforte. Mexico: Imprenta a Cargo de C.A. Guio, 1831.

Irey, Thomas R. "Soldiering, Suffering and Dying in the Mexican War." *Journal of the West* 11 (April, 1972): 285–98.

Jenkins, E. H. A. *A History of the French Navy from Its Beginnings to the Present Day.* London: MacDonald and Jane's, 1973.

Jenkins, John H., ed. *The Papers of the Texas Revolution, 1835–1836.* 10 vols. Austin: Presidial Press, 1973.

Johnson, John J. *The Military and Society in Latin America.* Stanford: Stanford Univ. Press, 1964.

Jones, Oakah L., Jr. *Santa Anna.* New York: Twayne Publishers, 1968.
Katz, Friedrich, ed. *Riot, Rebellion, and Revolution: Rural Social Conflict in Mexico.* Princeton: Princeton Univ. Press, 1968.
Kearny, Thomas. "The Mexican War and the Conquest of California." *California Historical Society Quarterly* 8 (September, 1929): 251–61.
Kinnaird, Lawrence, ed. *The Frontiers of New Spain: Nicolás de Lafora's Description 1766–1768.* Quivira Society Publications, Berkeley: The Quivira Society, 1958.
Knight, Alan. *The Mexican Revolution.* Vol. 1, *Porfirians, Liberals and Peasants.* Lincoln: Univ. of Nebraska Press, 1986.
———. *The Mexican Revolution.* Vol. 2, *Counter-revolution and Reconstruction.* Lincoln: Univ. of Nebraska Press, 1986.
Ladd, Doris M. *The Mexican Nobility at Independence 1780–1826.* Austin: Univ. of Texas Press, 1976.
Lafuente Ferrari, Enrique. *El Virrey Iturrigaray y los orígenes de la independencia de México.* Madrid: Instituto Gonzalo Fernández de Oviedo, 1941.
Lavrin, Asunción. "The Execution of the Law of *Consolidación* in New Spain: Economic Aims and Results." *Hispanic American Historical Review* 53 (February, 1973): 27–49.
Lerdo de Tejada, Miguel M. *Apuntes de la heróica ciudad de Veracruz.* 3 vols. Mexico: Imprenta de Ignacio Cumplido, 1850–58.
Ley orgánica de la guardia nacional. Mexico: Imprenta de Ignacio Cumplido, 1848.
Leyes y decretos mejicanos de enero á diciembre 1848. Mexico: Bibliotéca del Ministerio de Hacienda—Imprenta en el Palacio, 1852.
Lieuwen, Edwin. *Arms and Politics in Latin America.* Revised Edition. New York: Frederick A. Praeger, 1961.
———. *Mexican Militarism: The Political Rise and Fall of the Revolutionary Army, 1910–1940.* Albuquerque: Univ. of New Mexico Press, 1968.
Long, Jeff. *Duel of Eagles: The Mexican and U.S. Fight for the Alamo.* New York: William Morrow and Co., 1990.
Lozoya, Jorge Alberto. *El ejército mexicano.* 3rd ed. Mexico: El Colegio de México, 1984.
———. "Un guión para el estudio de los ejércitos mexicanos del siglo diecinueve." *Historia Mexicana* 17 (April–June, 1968): 553–68.
Lynch, John. *The Spanish American Revolutions, 1808–1826.* New York: Norton, 1973.
MacLachlan, Colin M., and Jaime E. Rodriguez O. *The Forging of the Cosmic Race: A Reinterpretation of Colonial Mexico.* Expanded Edition. Berkeley: Univ. of California Press, 1990.
Maissen, Eugène. *The French in Mexico and Texas (1838–1839).* Translated and with an introduction and notes by James L. Shepherd III. Salado: Anson Jones Press, 1961.
Manning, William R., ed. *Diplomatic Correspondence of the United States: Inter-American Affairs, 1831–1860.* 12 vols. Washington, D.C.: Carnegie Endowment for International Peace, 1932–39.
Marchena Fernández, Juan. *Oficiales y soldados en el ejército de América.* Sevilla: Publicaciones de la Escuela de Estudios Hispano-Americanos de Sevilla, 1983.

Márquez, Jesús Velasco. *La Guerra del 47 y la opinión pública (1845–1848)*. Mexico: Secretaría de Educación Pública, 1975.
Martínez Caraza, Leopoldo. *La intervención norteamericana en México, 1846–1848*. Mexico: Panorama Editorial, S.A., 1981.
Martínez Caro, Ramón. "A True Account of the First Texas Campaign and the Events Subsequent to the Battle of San Jacinto." In *The Mexican Side of the Texas Revolution*. Translated and edited by Carlos E. Castañeda, 88. Dallas: P. L. Turner Co., 1928.
McAlister, Lyle N. "Reorganization of the Army in New Spain, 1763–1766." *Hispanic American Historical Review* 33 (February, 1953): 1–32.
———. *The "Fuero Militar" in New Spain, 1764–1800*. Gainesville: Univ. of Florida Press, 1957.
———. "Social Structure and Social Change in New Spain." *Hispanic American Historical Review* 43 (August, 1963): 349–70.
McCaffrey, James M. *Army of Manifest Destiny: The American Soldier in the Mexican War, 1846–1848*. New York: New York Univ. Press, 1992.
McCornack, Robert Blaine. "The San Patricio Deserters in the Mexican War." *The Americas* 8 (October, 1951): 131–42.
Meade, Mercedes. "Don Félix María Calleja del Rey. Actividades anteriores a la Guerra de Independencia." *Boletín del Archivo General de la Nación* 1 (1960): 59–86.
Mejía, Francisco. *Sumaria mandada formar a pedimento . . . en los puntos del Palo Alto y Resaca de Guerrero*. Mexico: Navarro, 1846.
Miller, Robert Ryal. *Shamrock and Sword: The Saint Patrick's Battalion in the U.S.-Mexican War*. Norman: Univ. of Oklahoma Press, 1989.
———. *The Mexican War Journal and Letters of Ralph W. Kirkham*. College Station: Texas A&M University Press, 1991
Millet, Allan R., and Peter Maslowski. *For the Common Defense: A Military History of the United States of America*. New York: The Free Press, 1984.
Ministerio de Guerra y Marina, *Memoria del Secretario de Estado y del despacho de la guerra*. Mexico: Imprenta a Cargo de Martín Rivera, 1822.
———. *Memoria del Secretario de Estado y del despacho de la guerra*. Mexico: Imprenta a Cargo de Martín Rivera, 1823.
———. *Memoria del Secretario de Estado y del despacho de la guerra*. Mexico: Imprenta a Cargo de Martín Rivera, 1825.
———. *Memoria del Secretario de Estado y del despacho de la guerra*. Mexico: Imprenta del Supremo Gobierno, 1826.
———. *Memoria del Secretario de Estado y del despacho de la guerra*. Mexico: Imprenta del Supremo Gobierno, 1827.
———. *Memoria del Secretario de Estado y del despacho de la guerra*. Mexico: Imprenta del Supremo Gobierno, 1828.
———. *Memoria del Secretario de Estado y del despacho de la guerra*. Mexico: Imprenta del Supremo Gobierno, 1829.
———. *Memoria del Secretario de Estado y del despacho de la guerra*. Mexico: Imprenta del Supremo Gobierno, 1830.

———. *Memoria del Secretario de Estado y del despacho de la guerra.* Mexico: Imprenta del Supremo Gobierno, 1831.

———. *Memoria de la Secretaría de Guerra y Marina.* Mexico: Imprenta del Supremo Gobierno, 1833.

———. *Memoria del Secretario de Estado y del despacho de la guerra.* Mexico: Imprenta del Águila, 1834.

———. *Memoria del Secretario de Estado y del despacho de guerra y marina.* Mexico: Impreso por Ignacio Cumplido, 1835.

———. *Memoria de la Secretaría de Estado y del despacho de la guerra y marina.* Mexico: Imprenta del Águila, 1839.

———. *Memoria del Ministro de Guerra y Marina.* Mexico: Imprenta del Águila, 1840.

———. *Memoria del Ministerio de Guerra y Marina.* Mexico: Imprenta del Águila, 1841.

———. *Memoria del Secretario de Estado y del despacho de Guerra y Marina.* Mexico: Impreso por Ignacio Cumplido, 1844.

———. *Memoria de los ramos de guerra y marina.* Mexico: Impreso por Ignacio Cumplido, 1845.

———. *Memoria del Ministerio de Estado y del despacho de guerra y marina.* Mexico: Imprenta de Torres, 1846.

———. *Memoria presentada por el Ministerio de la Guerra.* Mexico: Imprenta de Torres, 1847.

———. *Memoria del Secretario de Estado y del despacho de guerra y marina.* Mexico: Imprenta de Torres, 1848.

———. *Memoria del Secretario de Estado y del despacho de guerra y marina.* Mexico: Imprenta de Vicente García Torres, 1849.

———. *Memoria del Secretario de Estado y del despacho de guerra y marina.* Mexico: Tipografía de Vicente G. Torres, 1850.

———. *Memoria del Secretario de Estado y del despacho de guerra y marina*, Mexico: Tipografía de Vicente G. Torres, 1951.

———. *Reglamento del estado mayor del ejército que debe operar sobre Téjas.* Mexico: J. Mariano Lara, 1844.

———. *Reglamento de la milicia activa, y general de la cívica de la República Mejicana, con el particular de la segunda en el Distrito Federal.* Mexico: Imprenta de Galván, 1833.

———. *Reglamento para el corso de particulares contra los enemigos de la nación.* Mexico: Imprenta del Águila, 1846.

———. *Reglamento sobre la organización del cuerpo de artillería.* Mexico:Imprenta del Águila, 1846.

Ministerio de Relaciones Interiores y Exteriores. *Memoria de la Secretaría de Estado y del despacho de relaciones interiores y exteriores.* México: Imprenta de Torres, 1846.

Molina, Ignacio. "El Asalto al Castillo de Chapultepec el Día 13 de Septiembre de 1847." *Revista Positiva* 2 (October 1, 1902): 444–64.

Moorhead, Max L. *The Apache Frontier: Jacobo Ugarte and Spanish-Indian Relations in Northern New Spain 1769–1791.* Norman: Univ. of Oklahoma Press, 1968.

Mora, José María Luís. *México y sus revoluciones.* 3 vols. Mexico: Editorial Porrúa, S.A., 1950.

Mora y Villamil, Ignacio. *Las Defensas de México en 1824.* Edited by W. Michael Mathes. Monterrey: Capilla Alfonsina/Bibliotéca Universitaria, 1983.

Myatt, Major Frederick. *The Illustrated Encyclopedia of 19th Century Firearms.* New York: Crescent Books, 1979.

Nance, John Milton. *After San Jacinto: The Mexican-Texas Frontier, 1836–1841.* Austin: Univ. of Texas Press, 1963.

———. *Attack and Counterattack: The Texas-Mexican Frontier, 1842.* Austin: Univ. of Texas Press, 1964.

Navarro y Rodrigo, Carlos. *Vida de Agustín de Iturbide.* Madrid: Editorial América, 1919

Navarro García, Luís. *Don José de Gálvez y la Comandancia General de las Provincias Internas del Norte de Nueva España.* Sevilla: Publicaciones de la Escuela de Estudios Hispano-Americanos de Sevilla, 1964.

Negrete, Emilio del Castillo. *Invasión de los Norte-Americanos en México.* 4 vols. Mexico: Imprenta del Editor, 1890.

Nieto, Angelina, Joseph Hefter and Mrs. John Nicholas Brown. *El soldado mexicano, 1837–1847: Organización, vestuario, equipo y reglamentos militares.* Mexico: Ediciones Nieto-Brown-Hefter, 1958.

Noriega Elío, Cecilia. *El Constituyente de 1842.* Mexico: Universidad Nacional Autónoma de México, 1986.

Oficial de Infantería. *Campaña Contra los Americanos del Norte. Primera parte: Relación histórica de las Cuarenta Días que mandó en Gefe el Ejército del Norte el E. Sr. General de División Don Mariano Arista.* Mexico: Ignacio Cumplido, 1846.

Olavarría y Ferrari, Enrique. *México independiente, 1821–1855.* Vol. 4 of *México a través de los siglos.* Edited by Vicente Riva Palacios. Mexico: Editorial Cumbre, S.A., 1953.

Orozco Linares, Fernando. *Gobernates de México: Desde la época Prehispánica hasta nuestros días.* México: Panorama Editorial, 1985.

Ortíz Escamilla, Juan. "El pronunciamiento federalista de Gordiano Guzmán, 1837–1842." *Historia Mexicana* 38 (1988): 241–82.

Paredes y Arrillaga, Mariano. *Ultimas comunicaciones entre el gobierno mexicano y el enviado extraordinario y ministro plenipotenciario de los Estados Unidos, sobre la cuestión de Téjas.* Mexico: Ignacio Cumplido, 1846.

Parrish, Leonard D. "The Life of Nicolás Bravo, Mexican Patriot (1786–1854)." Ph.D. diss., University of Texas, 1951.

Parrodi, Anastasio. *Memoria sobre la evacuación militar de Puerto de Tampico de Tamaulipas.* San Luís Potosí, n.p., 1848.

Paz, Eduardo. *Reseña histórica del estado mayor mexicano, 1821–1860.* 2 vols. Mexico: Talleres del Estado Mayor, 1907.

Peña y Peña, Manuel de la. *Colección de los documentos mas importantes relativas á la instalación y reconocimiento del gobierno provisional del Ecsmo. Sr. Presidente de la Suprema Corte de Justica.* México: Ignacio Cumplido, 1847.

Peña y Reyes, Antonio de la, ed. *Algunos documentos sobre el tratado de Guadalupe y la situación de México durante la invasión americana*. Mexico: Editorial Porrúa, 1930.

———. *La Primera guerra entre México y Francia*. Mexico: Publicaciones de la Secretaría de Relaciones Exteriores, 1927.

Pereyra, Carlos de. *De Barradas a Baudin. Un libro de polémica historial*. Mexico: Tipografía Económica, 1904.

Plana Mayor del Ejército. *Noticia histórica de los cuerpos de caballería permanente y activa que actualmente existen en la república*. Mexico: Imprenta del Águila, 1840.

———. *Noticia histórica de los cuerpos de infantería permanente y activa que actualmente existen en la república*. Mexico: Imprenta del Águila, 1840.

———. *Noticia histórica de todos los cuerpos del Ejército Nacional, que desde 1821 han existido y existen actualmente*. Mexico: Imprenta del Águila, 1845.

Pletcher, David. *The Diplomacy of Annexation: Texas, Oregon and the Mexican War*. Columbia: Univ. of Missouri Press, 1973.

Pohl, James W. "The Influence of Antoine Henri Jomini on Winfield Scott's Campaign in the Mexican War." *Southwestern Historical Quarterly* 78 (July, 1973): 85–110.

Pohl, James W., and Stephen L. Hardin. "The Military History of the Texas Revolution: An Overview." *Southwestern Historical Quarterly* 89 (January, 1986): 269–308.

Porter, John B. "Medical and Surgical Notes of Campaigns in the War with Mexico, during the Years 1845, 1846, 1847, and 1848." *American Journal of Medical Science* 23 (January, 1852): 13–37.

Potash, Robert A. *Mexican Government and Industrial Development in the Early Republic: The Banco de Avío*. Amherst: Univ. of Massachusetts Press, 1983.

Presley, James. "Santa Anna in Texas: A Mexican Viewpoint." *Southwestern Historical Quarterly* 62 (April, 1959): 489–512.

Price, Glen W. *Origins of the War with Mexico: The Polk-Stockton Intrigue*. Austin: Univ. of Texas Press, 1967.

Priestley, Herbert I. *José de Gálvez: Visitador General of New Spain, 1765–1771*. Berkeley: Univ. of California Press, 1916.

Prieto, Guillermo. *Memorias de mis tiempos, 1840 á 1853*. 2 vols. Mexico: Librería de la Vda de Ch. Bouret, 1906.

Quaife, Milo Milton, ed. *The Diary of James K. Polk During His Presidency, 1845–1849*. 4 vols. Chicago: A. C. McClurg & Co., 1910.

Ramírez y Sesma, Joaquín, ed. *Colección de decretos, ordenes y circulares espedidas por los gobiernos nacionales de la federación mexicana desde el año de 1821 hasta el de 1826 para el arreglo del ejército de los Estados Unidos Mexicanos y ordenados por el teniente coronel de caballería J. R. S.* Mexico: Martín Rivera, 1827.

Ramírez, José Fernando. *Mexico During the War with the United States*. Edited by Walter V. Scholes and translated by Elliott B. Scherr. Columbia: Univ. of Missouri Press, 1950.

Ramón Malo, José. *Diario de sucesos notables, 1832–1853*. 2 vols. Mexico: Editorial Patria, 1948.

Ramsey, Albert C., ed. and trans. *The Other Side, or Notes for the History of the War between Mexico and the United States*. New York: John Wiley, 1850.

Rea, Vargas, ed. *Apuntes históricos sobre los acontecimientos notables de la guerra entre México y los Estados Unidos del Norte.* Mexico: Bibliotéca Aportación Histórica, 1945.

Reed, Nelson. *The Caste War of Yucatán.* Stanford: Stanford Univ. Press, 1964.

Rees Jones, Ricardo. *Real ordenanza para el establicimiento é instrucción de Intendentes de Exército y Provincia en el reino de Nueva España.* Mexico: UNAM, 1984.

"Referentes a la Campaña Sobre las Colonias Sublevadas de Téjas, Verificada el año de 1836." In Richard G. Santos, *Santa Anna's Campaign Against Texas, 1835–1836.* 2nd ed., rev. Salisbury N.C.: Documentary Publications, 1968.

Reichstein, Andreas V. Translated by Jeanne R. Wilson. *Rise of the Lone Star: The Making of Texas.* College Station: Texas A&M Univ. Press, 1989.

Reina, Leticia. *Las rebeliones campesinas en México (1819–1906).* Mexico: Siglo Veintiuno Editores, 1980.

Richmond, Douglas, ed. *Essays on the Mexican War.* College Station: Texas A&M Univ. Press, 1986.

Rivera Cambras, Manuel. *Historia antigua y moderna de Jalapa y de las revoluciones del estado de Veracruz.* Vols. 2, 3. Mexico: Imprenta de Ignacio Cumplido, 1869–70.

Rives, George L. *The United States and Mexico, 1821–1848: A History of the Relations Between the Two Countries from the Independence of Mexico to the Close of the War with the United States.* 2 vols. New York: Charles Scribner's Sons, 1913.

Roa Bárcena, José María. *Recuerdos de la invasión norteamericana, 1846–1848.* 3 vols. Mexico: Editorial Porrúa, S.A., 1947.

Robertson, Frank D. "The Military and Political Career of Mariano Paredes y Arrillaga, 1797–1849." Ph.D. diss., University of Texas, 1955.

Robertson, William S. *Iturbide of Mexico.* Durham: Duke Univ. Press, 1952.

———. "The French Intervention in Mexico in 1838." *Hispanic American Historical Review* 24 (May, 1944): 222–52.

Robinson, Fayette. *Mexico and Her Military Chieftains, From the Revolution of Hidalgo to the Present Time.* Hartford: Silas Andrus & Sons, 1848.

Rodriguez O., Jaime E., ed. *The Independence of Mexico and the Creation of the New Nation.* Los Angeles: Univ. of California Press, 1989.

———. *The Mexican and the Mexican American Experience in the Nineteenth Century.* Tempe: Arizona State Univ. Press, 1989.

Rouquié, Alain. *L'Etat Militaire en Amerique Latine.* Paris: Editions du Seuil, 1982.

Rubio Mañé, Jorge Ignacio. "Síntesis histórica de la vida del II Conde de Revillagigedo, Virrey de Nueva España." *Anuario de Estudios Americanos* 6 (1949): 451–96.

———. "Antecedentes del Virrey de Nueva España, Félix María Calleja." *Boletín del Archivo General de la Nación* 19 (1948): 323–30.

———. "Don Félix María Calleja del Rey: Actividades anteriores a la guerra de independencia." *Boletín del Archivo General de la Nación,* 2nd ser., no. 1 (1960): 57–86, 253–97.

———. "Política de Virrey Flórez en la Comandancia General de Provincias Internas." *Boletín del Archivo General de la Nación* 24 (1953): 213–57.

Salas, Elizabeth. *Soldaderas in the Mexican Military: Myths and History.* Austin: Univ. of Texas Press, 1990.

Samponaro, Frank N. "La alianza de Santa Anna y los federalistas, 1832–1834: Su formación y desintegración." *Historia Mexicana* 30 (January–March, 1981): 358–90.

———. "The Political Role of the Army in Mexico, 1821–1848." Ph.D. diss., State University of New York at Stony Brook, 1971.

———. "Santa Anna and the Abortive Anti-federalist Revolt of 1833 in Mexico." *The Americas* 40 (July, 1983): 95–107.

Sánchez Garza, Jesus. ed. *La Rebelión de Téxas—Reseña y Diario de la Campaña de Téxas por José Enrique de la Peña.* Mexico: Impresora Mexicana, 1955.

Sánchez Lamego, Miguel A. *El Colegio Militar y la defensa de Chapultepec en septiembre de 1847.* Mexico: n.p., 1947.

———. *La invasión española de 1829.* Mexico: Editorial Jus, 1971.

———. *The Second Mexican-Texas War, 1841–1843.* Translated by Joseph Hefter. Hill Junior College Monograph no. 7. Hillsboro, Tex.: Hill Junior College, 1972.

Sánchez Navarro, Carlos. *La guerra de Téjas: Memorias de un Soldado.* 2nd ed. Mexico: Editorial Jus, S.A., 1960.

Santa Anna, Antonio López de. *Apelación al buen criterio de los nacionales y estangeros.* Mexico: Ignacio Cumplido, 1849.

———. *Detall de las operaciones ocurridas en la defensa de la capital de la república, atacada por el ejército de los Estados Unidos del Norte, año de 1847.* Mexico: Imprenta de Ignacio Cumplido, 1848.

———. "Las Guerras de México con Téjas y los Estados Unidos." vol. 32 of Genero García, *Documentos inéditos ó muy raros para la Historia de México,* 59 vols. Mexico: Librería de la Vda. de Ch. Bouret, 1910.

———. *Manifiesto que de sus operaciones en la campaña de Téxas y en su Cautiverio dirige a sus conciudadanos el general Antonio López de Santa Anna.* Veracruz: Imprenta Liberal á cargo de Antonio María Valdés, 1837.

Santoni, Pedro. "A Fear of the People: The Civic Militia of Mexico in 1845." *Hispanic American Historical Review* 68 (May, 1988): 268–88.

Santos, Richard G. *Santa Anna's Campaign Against Texas, 1835–1836, Featuring the Field Commands Issued to Major General Vicente Filisola.* 2nd ed., rev. Salisbury, NC: Documentary Publications, 1968.

Schmitt, Karl M. "The Clergy and the Independence of New Spain." *Hispanic American Historical Review* 34 (August, 1954): 289–312.

[Scott, John A.] *Encarnación Prisoners: Comprising an Account of the March of the Kentucky Cavalry. . . .* Louisville: Prentice and Weissanger, 1848.

Scott, Winfield. *Memoirs of Lieut.-General Scott, LL.D., Written by Himself.* New York: Sheldon & Co., 1864.

Secretaría de la Defensa Nacional. Dirección de Archivo Militar. *Guía del Archivo Histórico Militar de México.* Mexico: Taller Autográfico, 1949.

Senate Executive Document 388, 29th Cong., 1st sess., Ser. 515. *Message from The President . . . Relative to the Recent Engagements on the Mexican Frontier.*

Senate Executive Document 1, 29th Cong., 2nd sess. *Message from The President . . . at the Commencement of the Second Session of the Twenty-Ninth Congress.*

Senate Executive Document 1, 30th Cong., 1st sess., ser. 503. *Message from The President . . . at the Commencement of the First Session of the Thirtieth Congress.*
Senate Executive Document 52, 30th Cong., 1st sess., ser. 509. *The Treaty Between the United States and Mexico. . . .*
Senate Executive Document 65, 30th Cong., 1st sess. . . . *Proceedings of the Two Courts of Inquiry in the Case of Major General Pillow.*
Serrano Ortega, Jóse Antonio. *El contingente de sangre: Los gobiernos estatales y departmentales y los métodos de reclutamiento del ejército permanente mexicano, 1824–1844.* México: Instituto Nacional de Antropología e Historia, 1993.
Sierra, Justo. *Evolución política del pueblo mexicano.* 2nd ed. Mexico: Fondo de Cultura Económica, 1950. Translated by Charles Ramsdell as *The Political Evolution of the Mexican People.* Austin: Univ. of Texas Press, 1970.
Sims, Harold D. *Descolonización en México; el conflicto entre mexicanos y españoles (1821–1831).* Mexico: Fondo de Cultura Económica, 1982.
Sinkin, Richard. *The Mexican Reform 1855–1876: A Study in Liberal Nation Building.* Austin: Institute of Latin American Studies, University of Texas at Austin, 1979.
Skelton, William B. *An American Profession of Arms: The Army Officer Corps, 1784–1861.* Lawrence: Univ. Press of Kansas, 1992.
Smith, George Winston, and Charles Judah, eds. *Chronicle of the Gringos: The U.S. Army in the Mexican War, 1846–1848, Accounts of Eyewitnesses and Combatants.* Albuquerque: Univ. of New Mexico Press, 1968.
Smith, Justin H. *The War with Mexico.* 2 vols. New York: Macmillan, 1919.
———. "Letters of General Antonio López de Santa Anna Relating to the War Between the United States and Mexico, 1846–1848." *Annual Report of the American Historical Association or the Year 1917.* Washington: Government Printing Office, 1920.
Sordo Cedeño, Reynaldo. "El general Tornel y la guerra de Téxas." *Historia Mexicana* 62 (1993): 919–51.
Soto, Miguel Estrada. *La conspiración monárquica en México, 1845–1846.* Mexico: Editorial Offset S.A., 1988.
Sprague, William F. *Vicente Guerrero, Mexican Liberator: A Study in Patriotism.* Chicago: R. R. Donnelley and Sons, 1939.
Stevens, Donald Fithian. *Origins of Instability in Early Republican Mexico.* Durham, N.C.: Duke Univ. Press, 1991.
Stevens, Robert. "Mexico's Forgotten Frontier: A History of Sonora, 1821–1846." Ph.D. diss., University of California, Berkeley, 1963.
Suárez Iriarte, Francisco. *Defensa pronunciada ante el gran jurado el 21 de marzo de 1850, por Francisco Suárez Iriarte, acusado en 8 de agosto de 1848 por el Secretaría de Relaciones en aquella fecha, de los crimenes de sedición contra el Gobierno de Querétaro é infidencia contra la patria en sus actos como presidente de la asamblea municipal de la Ciudad y Distrito de México* (México: Editorial Porrúa, 1850).
Taylor, William B. "Landed Society in New Spain: A View from the South." *Hispanic American Historical Review* 54 (August, 1974): 387–413.
Tena Ramírez, Felipe, ed. *Leyes fundamentales de México, 1808–1971.* Mexico: Porrúa, 1971.

Tenenbaum, Barbara A. *The Politics of Penury: Debts and Taxes in Mexico, 1821–1856.* Albuquerque: Univ. of New Mexico Press, 1986.
Thomas, Alfred B. *Teodoro de Croix and the Northern Frontier of New Spain, 1776–1783.* Norman: Univ. of Oklahoma Press, 1941.
Timmons, Wilbert H. "Los Guadalupes: A Secret Society in the Mexican Revolution for Independence." *Hispanic American Historical Review* 30 (November, 1950): 453–79.
———. *Morales of Mexico: Priest, Soldier, Statesman.* El Paso: Texas Western Press, 1963.
Tornel y Mendívil, José María. *Breve reseña histórica de los acontecimientos mas notables de la nación mexicana desde el año de 1821 hasta nuestros días.* Mexico: Imprenta de Cumplido, 1852.
———. *Manifestación del C. José María Tornel.* Mexico: Impreso por Ignacio Cumplido, 1833.
———. *Téjas y los Estados Unidos de América en sus relaciones con la república mexicana.* Mexico: Impresaro por Ignacio Cumplido, 1837.
Torrea, Juan Manuel. *La vida de una institución gloriosa. El Colegio Militar, 1821–1930.* Mexico: Talleres Tipografía Centenario, 1931.
Tratados y convenciones celebrados y ratificados por la República Mexicana desde su independencia hasta el año actual, acompañados varios documentos que les son referentes. Edición oficial. Mexico: Gonzalo A. Esteva, 1878.
Trueba, Alfonso. *Santa Anna.* 3rd ed. Mexico: Editorial Jus, 1958.
Tutino, John. *From Insurrection to Revolution in Mexico: Social Bases of Agrarian Violence, 1750–1940.* Princeton: Princeton Univ. Press, 1986.
Tyler, Daniel. "Governor Armijo's Moment of Truth." *Journal of the West* 11 (April, 1972): 307–16.
Urías Hermosillo, Margarita. "Militares y comerciantes en México: 1828–1846. Las mercancías de la nacionalidad." *Historias* 6 (April–June, 1984): 49–69.
Urrea, Jóse. "Diario de las operaciones militares de la división que al mando del General José Urrea hizo la campaña de Téjas, Victoria de Durango, 1838." In *Documentos Para la Historia de la guerra de Téjas.* Mexico: Editorial Nacional, S.A., 1952.
Valadés, José C. *Breve Historia de la guerra con los Estados Unidos.* Mexico: Editorial Patria, 1947.
———. *Orígenes de la república mexicana.* Mexico: Editores Mexicanos Unidos, 1972.
———. *Santa Anna y la guerra de Téjas.* Mexico: Editores Mexicanos Unidos, 1965.
Valencia, Gabriel. *Detalle de las acciones de los días 19 y 20 en los campos de Padierna y otros pormenores recientemente comunicados por personas fidedignas.* Morelia: Ignacio Arango, 1847.
Vázquez, Josefina Zoraida. "El ejército: un dilema del gobierno mexicano, 1841–1846," in Inge Buisson, et al., eds., *Problemas de la formación del Estado de la Nación en Hispanoamérica.* Cologne: Bohlau Verlang, 1984.
———. "Iglesia, ejército y centralismo." *Historia Mexicana* 39 (July–September, 1989): 205–34.

———. "The Texas Question in Mexican Politics, 1836–1845." *Southwestern Historical Quarterly* 89 (January, 1986): 309–44.

Velázquez, María del Carmen. *El estado de guerra en Nueva España, 1760–1803.* Mexico: El Colegio de México, 1950.

Vigil y Robles, Guillermo. *La invasión de México por los Estados Unidos en los años 1846, 1847 y 1848, Apuntes históricos anecdoticos y descriptivos.* Mexico: Correccional, 1923.

Vigness, David M. "Don Hugo O'Conor and New Spain's Northeastern Frontier." *Journal of the West* 6 (January, 1967): 27–40.

———. "La expedición Urrea-Mejía." *Historia Mexicana* 2 (July, 1955–June, 1956): 211–19.

Villaseñor y Villaseñor, Alejandro. *Biografías de los héroes y caudillos de la independencia.* 2nd ed. 2 vols. Mexico: Editorial Jus, 1962.

Wallace, Edward S. "Deserters in the Mexican War." *Hispanic American Historical Review* 15 (August, 1935): 374–82.

Ward, Henry George. *Mexico in 1827.* 2 vols. London: H. Colburn, 1828.

Weber, David J. *The Mexican Frontier, 1821–1846: The American Southwest under Mexico.* Albuquerque: Univ. of New Mexico Press, 1982.

Wolf, Eric R., and Edward C. Hansen. "*Caudillo* Politics: A Structural Analysis." *Comparative Studies in Society and History* 9 (January, 1967): 168–79.

———. "The Mexican Bajío in the Eighteenth Century." In *Synoptic Studies of Mexican Culture,* 192. New Orleans: Tulane University, Middle America Research Institute, 1957.

Woodward, Margaret L. "The Spanish Army and the Loss of America, 1810–1824." *Hispanic American Historical Review* 48 (November, 1968): 586–607.

Worcester, Donald E., trans. and ed. *Instructions for Governing the Interior Provinces of New Spain, 1786, by Bernardo de Gálvez.* Quivira Society Publications. Berkeley: The Quivira Society, 1951.

Yoakum, Henderson K., Esq. *History of Texas, from its first Settlements in 1685 to its Annexation by the United States in 1846.* 2 vols. New York: Redfield, 1855.

Young, Eric Van. *Hacienda and Market in Eighteenth Century Mexico: The Rural Economy of the Guadalajara Region, 1625–1820.* Berkeley: Univ. of California Press, 1981.

Zamacois, Niceto de. *Historia de México desde sus tiempos más remotos hasta nuestros días.* 22 vols. Barcelona: J. F. Parres, y Cía., 1876–88.

Zárate, Julio. *La Guerra de independencia.* Vol. 3 of *México a través de los siglos.* Edited by Vicente Riva Palacio. Mexico: Editorial Cumbre, 1953.

Závala, Lorenzo de. *Ensayo histórico de las revoluciones de México desde 1808 hasta 1830.* 2 vols. Mexico: Manuel N. de la Vega, 1845.

———. *Umbral de la Independencia.* Mexico: Empresas Editoriales, S.A., 1949.

Zorilla, Luís G. *Historia de las relaciones entre México y los Estados Unidos de América, 1800–1958.* 2 vols. Mexico: Editorial Porrúa, 1965–66.

INDEX

The Mexican National Army,
1822–1852

TEXAS A&M UNIVERSITY
52
MILITARY HISTORY SERIES